D0142959

Politics and Culture
in Renaissance
Naples

\ Politics and Culture in ͨRenaissance Naples /

Jerry H. ˈBentley

*Princeton University
Press*

Randall Library UNC-W

Copyright © 1987 by Princeton University Press

Published by Princeton University Press, 41 William Street,
Princeton, New Jersey 08540
In the United Kingdom: Princeton University Press, Guildford, Surrey

All Rights Reserved

Library of Congress Cataloging in Publication Data will be found
on the last printed page of this book

ISBN 0-691-05498-3

Publication of this book has been aided by a grant from
The Andrew W. Mellon Foundation

This book has been composed in Linotron Garamond

Clothbound editions of Princeton University Press books are printed
on acid-free paper, and binding materials are chosen for
strength and durability. Paperbacks, although satisfactory
for personal collections, are not usually suitable
for library rebinding

Printed in the United States of America by Princeton
University Press, Princeton, New Jersey

DG
847.17
.B46
1987

For my brothers,
Murry and Larry
Bentley

Contents

Preface, *ix*   Abbreviations, *xi*   Maps, *xii*

1. Naples and Renaissance Italy, *3*

2. Patterns of Patronage, *47*

3. Clientage and Career, *84*

4. The Foundations of a Realistic Political Ethic, *138*

5. The Implications of Humanism for Renaissance
Political Thought, *195*

6. The Domestication of Humanism in the Mezzogiorno, *253*

7. Neapolitan Humanism and Renaissance Europe, *288*

Bibliography, *301*   Index, *321*

Preface

RENAISSANCE humanism developed in response to two kinds
of influence. In the first place, humanists in general concerned themselves with a well-defined group of cultural interests,
including most notably the study and appreciation of classical literature and the cultivation of their own rhetorical and literary
skills. In the second place, however, humanists also responded to
the particular problems and pressures of the various localities in
which they themselves lived and worked. In examining the humanist movement in the kingdom of Naples, the following book
takes account of both the cosmopolitan and the local influences
that operated in fifteenth-century Italy. It acknowledges the point
that Neapolitan humanists derived much of their inspiration from
the work of their predecessors in central and northern Italy. Yet it
argues also that in several important ways the Neapolitan humanists drew creatively upon their particular experiences and helped
to shape the larger, cosmopolitan culture of Renaissance humanism. More specifically, the Neapolitan humanists advanced the
development of philological scholarship, reflected provocatively
on the role of fortune in human affairs, and reconsidered traditional western political ethics. In all these efforts, the Neapolitan
humanists contributed distinctive elements to the culture of Italian humanism and of Renaissance Europe in general.

Without large doses of material and moral aid, this book could
hardly have come to publication. It is a pleasure for me to acknowledge the institutions and individuals who made it possible
for the study to appear. At the University of Hawaii, both the College of Arts and Sciences and the Office of Research Administration underwrote research travel. The American Council of Learned
Societies provided a research fellowship that supported extensive

study during my sabbatical leave from the University of Hawaii. Meanwhile, individuals generously supplied advice, encouragement, and other support that has improved my work. I appreciate especially deeply the efforts of Eric Cochrane, Germano Gualdo, Lucia Gualdo Rosa, John O'Malley, James D. Tracy, and Charles Trinkaus, all of whom took an interest in this research and provided unstinting aid over a long term in order to advance it. Thanks go also to Elton Daniel, Michele Gattini, Felix Gilbert, Paul O. Kristeller, Daniel W. Y. Kwok, Francesca Petrucci, Donald J. Raleigh, Mario Santoro, Francesco Tateo, and Richard R. Vuylsteke, who all went beyond the bounds of friendship and duty in supporting my efforts. Sae Kusaka prepared the maps, under the direction of Everett Wingert. Finally, with customary good humor and cheer, my wife Jeani helped to prevent me from becoming too serious.

Abbreviations

AAP	*Atti della Accademia Pontaniana*
ACA	Archivo de la Corona de Aragón
ASPN	*Archivio storico per le provincie napoletane*
ASV	Archivio Segreto Vaticano
BAV	Biblioteca Apostolica Vaticana
BNN	Biblioteca Nazionale di Napoli
BU	Biblioteca Universitaria
DBI	*Dizionario biografico degli italiani* (Rome, 1960–)
de Marinis, *La biblioteca*	Tammaro de Marinis, *La biblioteca napoletana dei re d'Aragona*, 4 vols. (Milan, 1947–52)
de Marinis, *Supplemento*	Tammaro de Marinis, *La biblioteca napoletana dei re d'Aragona: supplemento*, 2 vols. (Verona, 1969)
Gravier, ed., *Raccolta*	Giovanni Gravier, ed., *Raccolta di tutti i più rinomati scrittori dell'istoria generale del regno di Napoli*, 25 vols. (Naples, 1769–77)
Trinchera, ed., *Codice aragonese*	Francesco Trinchera, ed., *Codice aragonese*, 3 vols. (Naples, 1866–74)
Volpicella, ed., *Instructionum liber*	Luigi Volpicella, ed., *Regis Ferdinandi primi instructionum liber* (Naples, 1916)

Italy in the Mid-Fifteenth Century

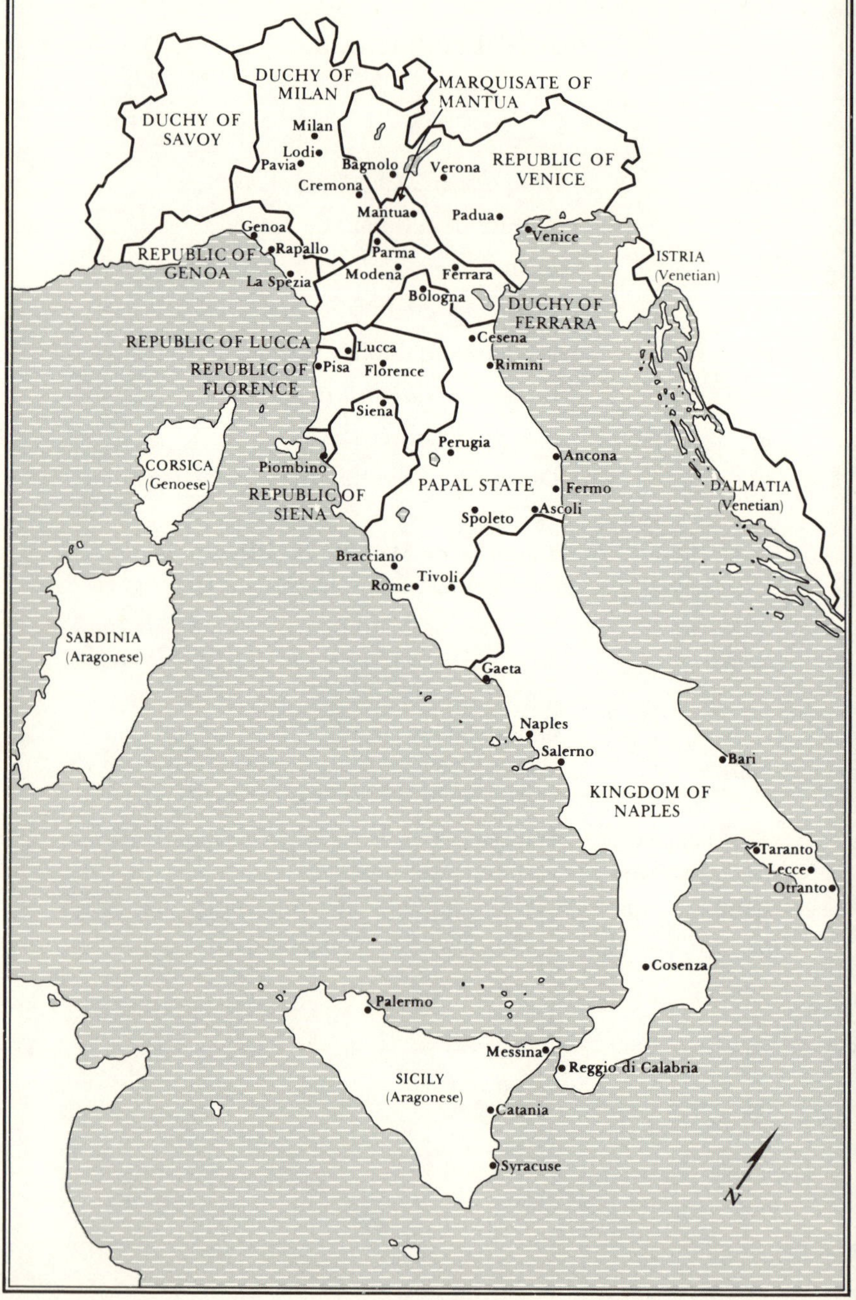

Kingdom of Naples

Politics and Culture
in Renaissance
Naples

1

Naples and Renaissance Italy

I, Loise de Rosa, wish to announce some good news to our Neapolitans. The news is this: Neapolitans are by nature the best men in the world. You ask me to prove it? Listen to my explanation."

With these words, a garrulous octogenarian opened a short treatise that amounts to an encomium of the city and kingdom of Naples. The author, Loise de Rosa, does not figure prominently in studies of Italian, or even of Neapolitan history. Yet his praise of Naples suggests something important about Neapolitan culture in the Renaissance, so that his life and work repay a bit of study.

Born in 1385 at Pozzuoli, near Naples, Loise served as a courtier (a rather important one, by his testimony) to several kings and queens of Naples (six of each, by his count). He credited himself with a staggering array of offices during the course of his career: he claimed to have served as viceroy of Bisceglie and the Val di Gaudo, governor of several districts and towns, vice-admiral of the royal fleet, and majordomo of numerous important households, including those of the cardinal of Naples, prince of Salerno, duke of Sora, count of Troia, and King Ferrante of Naples, among other illustrious princes and prelates. Although Loise exaggerated the importance and variety of his political services, it seems well established that he served as a sort of master of the household to several Neapolitan monarchs. In that capacity he became acquainted with various fables, stories, and miscellaneous lore concerning the kingdom of Naples. In 1452 he composed a set of memoirs discussing his career and notable events that took place during his lifetime. In 1471 he produced a chronicle of Neapolitan history

3

from the time of Conrad IV through that of King Ferrante in Loise's own day. Modern historians consider both works defective and highly inaccurate, though valuable for their rather pure Neapolitan dialect and for the light they throw on the culture of the barely literate in Renaissance Naples.[1]

Loise's encomium of Naples, also composed in 1471, holds special interest for present purposes because it takes up a theme—praise of a city—commonly developed in Renaissance Italy: thus his argument that Neapolitans ranked as the best men of the world. At creation, Loise explained, God divided the world into Asia, Africa, and Europe. In fifteenth-century Italy, it went without saying that Europe was the best part of the three. Neapolitans enjoyed the benefits not only of Europe, however, but also of Italy, the best part of Europe; of Campania, the best part of Italy; and of Naples itself, the best part of Campania. That settled it—at least to Loise's satisfaction.

After his rather deductive introduction, Loise enumerated in inductive fashion and in great detail the advantages of Naples and environs. He took a surprisingly analytical approach—even if he did not develop it in a very systematic way—that enabled him to compare Naples to other cities and to judge it superior to them all. He recognized thirteen categories as important in the evaluation of cities: the four elements as found in a particular city (earth, air, fire, and water), the four environments expected in the ideal city or its surrounding countryside (mountains, plains, sea, and waters), and the five accouterments of the city itself (walls, streets, houses, churches, and fountains). Naples merited Loise's praise on almost every one of these counts, plus a few additional ones as well. It boasted pure spring water; fine air, neither dry, hot, oppressive, nor thin; perfect fire, fueled by plentiful oak wood; and bountiful earth that provided an abundance of game, fruit, and

[1] The best discussion of Loise de Rosa is that of Benedetto Croce, "Sentendo parlare un vecchio napoletano del Quattrocento," in his *Storie e leggende napoletane*, 4th ed. (Bari, 1948), pp. 121–39. See also Antonio Altamura's edition of Loise's works, *Napoli aragonese nei ricordi di Loise de Rosa* (Naples, 1971).

4

vegetables. Loise described the environs as no less marvelous: within a day's journey from Naples, one finds mountains, plains, sea, forests, all the four seasons, hot baths, and sixty other cities. Most impressive, however, was Naples itself. No other city of the world numbered so many nobles—counts, marquises, dukes, princes, and kings—among its inhabitants. Loise praised Neapolitan hospitals, physicians, and schools, but devoted special attention to churches and relics. Chief of them, of course, was the cathedral of Naples, which possessed "the most beautiful relic in all the world"—the head of San Gennaro, fourth-century bishop of Benevento and patron saint of Naples, along with a vial of his dried blood, which miraculously liquefied when publicly displayed several times each year.

Loise did not wish to overstate his case. He admitted that Naples did not possess beautiful city walls. Yet even with this defect, Naples overshadowed all rivals when evaluated against the thirteen categories. Rome, for example, counted not a single perfect element in Loise's opinion, only one ideal environment (presumably either the mountains or the sea), and but four of the five accouterments. (The lack of fountains that Loise noted has been abundantly remedied in the intervening centuries.) Loise considered Venice even more miserable than Rome: though founded in the sea, so that it at least possessed one of the four environments, the Venetians enjoyed none of the other twelve advantages that Loise considered essential for civilized life. They had no fresh water, no springs, no mountains, no plains, nor a single perfect one of the four elements. Other world-renowned cities—Loise mentioned Milan, Florence, Paris, Genoa, Constantinople, and even Cairo!—likewise failed to measure up to the magnificence of Naples, which earned perfect marks in twelve of Loise's thirteen categories.[2]

---

[2] Loise's works have been edited twice, first by G. de Blasiis as "Tre scritture napoletane del secolo XV," *ASPN*, 4 (1879), 411–67; more recently by Antonio Altamura in the edition cited in note 1. I mention both editions because that of de Blasiis provides annotation, lacking in Altamura's, while that of Altamura

Historians have long recognized civic pride as a distinctive element in the thought of those Renaissance political thinkers, humanist and nonhumanist alike, who contributed to the development of a lay-oriented political ethic. Indeed, Leonardo Bruni's encomium of the city of Florence (composed ca. 1403 to 1404) served as the centerpiece of Hans Baron's influential analysis of early Florentine humanism and political thought.[3] So far, however, the civic pride of Loise de Rosa and other Neapolitans of the Quattrocento—quite similar to the sentiments of their contemporaries in other parts of Italy—has gone almost unnoticed by historians of the Italian Renaissance.

In fact, the city and kingdom of Naples in general have not attracted their fair share of attention from Renaissance scholars. The republics, the despotic city-states, and even the minor tyrannies of central and northern Italy have succeeded in capturing historians' interest at the expense of Naples and southern Italy, the *Mezzogiorno*. This point holds especially true for non-Italian studies, but even in Italy scholars have directed their attention to the center and north rather than the south. It is not difficult to understand the fascination exercised by central and northern Italy over Renaissance historians. The creative approaches taken by Florentines in particular to political, moral, and philosophical problems—not to mention their extraordinary artistic and cultural production—ensure them an enduring and prominent position in Renaissance studies. Yet historians ignore the experience of Renaissance Naples only at great cost. The kingdom of Naples was at least potentially the most powerful of all the various states of fifteenth-century Italy. The *Regno* (as the kingdom of Naples is often called in Italy) influenced peninsular and Mediterranean politics

---

provides a glossary of Neapolitan dialect as represented in Loise's work, missing from the earlier edition. The encomium appears on pp. 428–40 of de Blasiis' edition, pp. 183–94 of Altamura's edition.

[3] Hans Baron, *The Crisis of the Early Italian Renaissance*, 2d ed. (Princeton, 1966), pp. 189–211. See also J. K. Hyde's important article: "Medieval Descriptions of Cities," *Bulletin of the John Rylands Library*, 48 (1966), 308–40.

throughout the century, and Neapolitan cultural figures commanded respect on both the Italian and the European scale.

These considerations I hope will help to justify the following effort to analyze the political and cultural experience of Renaissance Naples and to interpret Neapolitan humanism in the light of the broader cultural history of Renaissance Italy.

Establishment of the Aragonese Dynasty of Naples

The following study concentrates on the Aragonese period of Neapolitan history, from the conquest of the kingdom (1435 to 1442) by Alfonso V of Aragon (Alfonso I of Naples), until the imposition of direct Spanish rule through the viceroys (1504). The Regno of the fifteenth century presents historians with a fascinating combination of problems and possibilities, the study of which can throw new light on both the history of Naples and the character of the Renaissance as a historical period. The policy and diplomacy of the Aragonese kings of Naples played a role in almost every political issue of fifteenth-century Italy—including, to cite only a few examples, struggles for the kingdom itself, the emergence of a state system after the Peace of Lodi in 1454, and the French invasion of 1494 that led to the calamity of Italy and the establishment of Spanish hegemony in the peninsula. Meanwhile, the works of cultural figures in Naples reflected both the broader concerns of Renaissance Italy and the more local interests of the city and kingdom of Naples. Many of their works dealt with political issues—often with narrow and specific questions of policy and diplomacy, though sometimes also with more general ethical or theoretical problems. Hence the approach of the following study is to analyze the interaction between men of power and men of culture in fifteenth-century Naples.

The analysis presumes a basic understanding of Neapolitan and Italian politics in the Quattrocento. Thus I begin with a review of the major issues in both the domestic and the external politics of the Aragonese monarchy of Naples. Specialists in the history of the

Italian Renaissance will perhaps find much of this chapter reasonably familiar, but the plan of the study as a whole mandates this sort of introduction. Specific historical events, including almost every element of the following account, figure prominently in the works of cultural figures discussed in later chapters. An analysis of Neapolitan politics that synthesizes the results of modern scholarship will thus serve as a useful foundation for the ensuing study of Renaissance men of culture, whose works faithfully reflected the political society they inhabited.

The background to this period consists of the expansive, imperialist efforts of the rulers of Aragon and Catalonia during the Middle Ages.[4] Two forces helped drive these efforts: the territorial ambitions of the Aragonese nobility in the Iberian peninsula and, more important for present purposes, the commercial ambitions of the Catalan merchants in the Mediterranean basin. The interests of the Aragonese nobles contributed to the *Reconquista* in eastern Iberia, most notably to the absorption in 1244 of the kingdom of Valencia into the Aragonese-Catalan empire. Meanwhile, the maritime expansion favored by the merchants of Barcelona set the stage for the Aragonese presence in Naples. Jaime I the Conqueror, king of Aragon (1213–1276), engineered a successful invasion of the Balearic Islands in 1299 as the first episode of a relentless drive to establish a Catalan naval and mercantile presence in all parts of the Mediterranean. In following years, Jaime and his successors captured Genoese markets in North Africa, established commercial relations in Constantinople and Egypt, and even attempted an ill-fated crusade to Palestine. The sea-based empire of Aragon and Catalonia grew by the addition of Sicily (1283-1284), the duchy of Athens (1311), and Sardinia (1323–1324), to name only the most important conquests. Thus by the early fourteenth century, the kings of Aragon and the merchants of Catalonia became the dominant power in the western Mediterranean, and a force to be reckoned with in the entire Mediterranean basin.

[4] For a detailed account, see J. Lee Shneidman, *The Rise of the Aragonese-Catalan Empire, 1200–1350*, 2 vols. (New York, 1970), esp. vol. 2.

During the conquest of Sicily, Aragonese forces crossed the Strait of Messina and established a toehold on the Italian peninsula around Reggio di Calabria, but they did not command the resources to subjugate the Angevin kingdom of Naples. After about a century and a half, however, Aragonese ambition exploited new opportunities that presented themselves in the Mezzogiorno.[5]

The Angevin kings of Naples (1268–1435) had never succeeded in controlling their barons; indeed, in efforts to win support and curb domestic violence, they increased both the numbers and the powers of the Neapolitan nobility. By the end of the Angevin period, for example, nobles routinely gained powers of full criminal jurisdiction—the famous *merum mixtumque imperium*—along with their fiefs. During the last century of the Angevin monarchy, the barons intrigued, struggled for power, and forged alliances with parties both inside and outside the kingdom—all to such a point that chaos reigned throughout the Mezzogiorno.[6]

The personal and political instability of the last Angevin monarch, Queen Giovanna II (1414–1435), compounded this problem by delivering the kingdom of Naples into a state of anarchic civil war. For the first six years of her reign, Giovanna sought to bolster her position against the barons by intriguing with Aragonese royalty, French nobility, and Italian condottieri. In 1420 she turned to Alfonso V (1396–1458), king of Aragon and Sicily since 1416, whom she legally adopted as her heir in July 1421. By this ploy she hoped to gain Alfonso's support, without encumbering her own freedom to maneuver and establish policy.

Alfonso ranks easily as one of the most fascinating and complicated characters of the Quattrocento. Born in Castile, he exercised

---

[5] The best short account of Neapolitan history is Benedetto Croce's *History of the Kingdom of Naples*, trans. F. Frenaye (Chicago, 1970). For more recent and detailed accounts, see the contributions by various authors to the *Storia di Napoli*, 10 vols. (Naples, 1975–81).

[6] See the withering indictment returned against the barons by Croce, *History of the Kingdom of Naples*, pp. 58–75. Though overstated at points, Croce's argument illustrates well the excessively selfish and individualist temperament of the Neapolitan barons.

his talents to the fullest in Italy. By nature a restless adventurer, ambitious to expand his influence to every corner of the western Mediterranean, he devoted most of his adult energies to the kingdom of Naples, with the intention of founding a stable dynasty in the Mezzogiorno. Bred in the culture of medieval Spain, with emphasis on piety and militarism, he valued and encouraged the civilization of Renaissance Italy, with emphasis on lay values and devotion to literature.[7] In the half-millennium since his time, no account of Alfonso's life has captured his personality quite as well as that of his contemporary, Vespasiano da Bisticci, the Florentine bookseller and biographer, who devoted one of his best crafted sketches to Alfonso.[8] Vespasiano's friend, Giannozzo Manetti, who knew Alfonso well, provided the biographer with anecdotes and personal information that enabled him to characterize the king in concrete detail. Vespasiano portrayed Alfonso in a flattering light: he was king to the common man, forgiving of those who offended him, moderate to the point of abstemiousness at the table, simple in his dress, just and honest in his judgment. Three qualities emerge with exceptional clarity from Vespasiano's account: Alfonso's piety, which prompted him to devote himself to the Mass and other religious ceremonies, also to read many times the scriptures and the commentaries of Nicholas of Lyra; his love of literature, which he cultivated even on the battlefield, where humanists read and discussed portions of Livy before Alfonso and his soldiers; and his generosity, so lavish that Vespasiano described Alfonso and Pope Nicholas V as "the two singular lights who brightened the world of letters" through their patronage and promotion of learned and literary men. No wonder, then, that King

---

[7] I obviously cannot accept Benedetto Croce's grossly exaggerated caricature of Alfonso as an uncouth, barbarian, provincial Spaniard stuck incongruously in the sophisticated milieu of Renaissance Italy: *La Spagna nella vita italiana durante la Rinascenza*, 2d ed. (Bari, 1922), pp. 33–54.

[8] Vespasiano da Bisticci, *Le vite*, ed. A. Greco, 2 vols. (Florence, 1970–76), 1.83–117. Vespasiano's lives have been translated into English as *Renaissance Princes, Popes, and Prelates*, trans. W. George and E. Waters (New York, 1963). See pp. 59–83 for the biography of Alfonso.

Alfonso of Aragon and Naples is known more generally as Alfonso the Magnanimous.

When Giovanna II approached him in 1420, of course, Alfonso possessed none of this reputation. Yet even at that early point of his career, Alfonso's ambition and energy had begun to manifest themselves. Born the eldest son of Ferdinand of Antequera, crusading hero and infante of Castile, Alfonso followed his father and his fortune to Aragon. In 1412 Ferdinand won the crown of Aragon under the terms of the Compromise of Caspe. Heir apparent to the throne, Alfonso quickly became infected by the expansionist zeal of the Catalan merchants. In fact, he had just begun an expedition to conquer the island of Corsica from Genoa when Giovanna sought his aid in 1420. When approached, Alfonso readily shifted his sights to Naples, far richer than Corsica, especially since the Genoese offered more effective defense than he had anticipated. Soon after the adoption, however, Alfonso and Giovanna began to quarrel, and even to make war on each other. In 1423 Giovanna disinherited Alfonso, naming her French cousin, Louis d'Anjou, and later his brother, René d'Anjou, as her new heirs. Giovanna and her allies drove the Aragonese out of Italy in 1423, and Alfonso devoted his attention in the following years mostly to affairs in Spain, Sicily, and the island of Jerba, which he conquered from the Tunisians in 1432.

Thus Alfonso had to fight his way to the Neapolitan throne.[9] When Giovanna died in 1435, both René d'Anjou and Alfonso laid claim to the kingdom. René had the support of many barons, the pope, and the other Italian states; but he could not effectively organize his forces, since the duke of Burgundy held him prisoner until 1438. Alfonso had the support only of a small party of barons, but he stood poised in Messina at the head of a powerful fleet, ready to enforce his claim. His first attempt to do so, however, ended in near disaster. As Alfonso and his ground forces laid siege

[9] Nunzio F. Faraglia tells the story of Alfonso's war for Naples in exhaustive detail: *Storia della lotta tra Alfonso V d'Aragona e Renato d'Angiò* (Lanciano, 1908).

to Gaeta, the Genoese—traditional and bitter enemies of Catalan expansion—sent a fleet to relieve the city. Alfonso put out to sea with his own fleet and engaged the Genoese near the island of Ponza. There the Aragonese suffered a shattering defeat: Alfonso and his two brothers fell prisoner to the Genoese; the Aragonese fleet was almost annihilated; and Alfonso's claim to the throne of Naples seemed worthless.

Succeeding weeks, however, brought an about-face so astonishing that almost every figure discussed in later chapters commented on it at least once. The Genoese delivered Alfonso to their overlord and protector, Duke Filippo Maria Visconti of Milan. Alfonso had earlier sought an alliance with the duke, but Filippo Maria had hesitated to encourage Aragonese adventures in Italy. In their negotiations following Ponza, Alfonso convinced Filippo Maria that a French dynasty in Naples posed a far greater threat to Milanese independence than an Aragonese presence. A revived Angevin monarchy of Naples would lead inevitably to pressure on Milan, as the French sought to increase their influence by working south from France and north from Naples. These considerations—aided by Alfonso's agreement to abandon his designs on Corsica and to pay thirty thousand ducats to the duke[10]—induced Filippo Maria not only to free Alfonso, but to enter into an alliance with him. In effect, the two men divided Italy into two spheres of influence— the north and center, where Alfonso agreed to recognize the primacy of Visconti interests; and the south, where Filippo Maria offered diplomatic support for the Aragonese campaign to conquer and stabilize the Regno.

Once freed, Alfonso devoted himself again to the task of making good his claim to Naples. Seven years of almost constant war followed, complicated by shifting alliances, diplomatic maneuvering, and the presence of René d'Anjou, who after 1438 went to Naples and personally managed the Angevin defensive effort. By

[10] Tammaro de Marinis, "La liberazione di Alfonso V d'Aragona prigioniero dei genovesi," *ASPN*, n.s. 34 (1953–54), 101–6.

the spring of 1442, Alfonso had subdued resistance in all parts of the kingdom and stood before the city of Naples itself. He avoided a protracted siege when a Neapolitan laborer revealed the existence of an aqueduct that led into the city. During the night of 1 to 2 June 1442, Alfonso sent a force of two hundred men, including his most loyal and effective supporters, through the drain into Naples, where they captured a tower and opened a gate to the main body of Aragonese forces outside the walls. This development appealed particularly to humanists, who in recounting the episode delighted to point out that the Byzantine general Belisarius had employed the same method some nine centuries earlier when he took Naples from the Ostrogoths. A sharp battle followed the penetration and brought the city of Naples securely into Alfonso's hands.

Thus Alfonso won the kingdom of Naples by military conquest, but he took great care to capture popular and diplomatic support for his rule. He earned a measure of immediate gratitude from the people of Naples when he limited the sack of the city to a period of only four hours and hanged a number of undisciplined troops who committed excesses while looting and plundering. A few months later, 26 February 1443, Alfonso made his triumphal entry into Naples. The pageantry, ceremony, and lavish expenditures promoted the image of Alfonso as victor in the classical style and as worthy monarch of a deserving realm. In following years, Alfonso showered money on Naples, repaired streets and walls, refurbished houses and buildings, and constructed new piazzas and fountains. Most notably, he had the old Angevin fortress rebuilt along new lines; then he had the new stronghold, the Castelnuovo, outfitted with a magnificent marble arch celebrating his victory and reign in Naples.

More significantly, Alfonso moved to consolidate his position by organizing political and diplomatic support.[11] Within the

[11] There is no modern biography of Alfonso, though Alan Ryder expects to publish one soon. The following discussion of Alfonso's politics and diplomacy relies most heavily on Ernesto Pontieri, *Alfonso il Magnanimo re di Napoli (1435–*

kingdom he worked to accomplish two major objectives: he sought an agreement with the barons that would enable him to institute stable rule, and he sought to have his bastard son Ferrante recognized as his legal heir and successor. Alfonso addressed both these issues shortly after the conquest at the parliament held in February and March 1443 in the convent of San Lorenzo in Naples. In exchange for recognition of Ferrante (legitimized since 1440) as his heir, Alfonso confirmed the barons in their holding of *merum mixtumque imperium*—thus acknowledging them as ultimate judicial and political authorities in their own lands. The same parliament restructured the kingdom's finances, replacing the cumbersome system of aids with a single direct tax levied on hearths, but not on the barons. The new tax, modified in succeeding parliaments, served as the foundation of Neapolitan finances throughout the Aragonese period, and it enabled the monarchs to employ a standing royal army for use both in the Regno and elsewhere in Italy. Thus within a few months of his victory over the Angevins and their supporters, Alfonso and the barons arrived at a compromise on the distribution of power that provided the Mezzogiorno with reasonably stable government all through Alfonso's reign.

Relations with other Italian powers proved a great deal more difficult to conduct. Alfonso began his conquest of Naples with only a few barons as allies. In 1435 he won the support of Filippo Maria Visconti, but many barons and all the other Italian states took positions ranging from unfriendly neutrality to active hostility toward the Aragonese. By the time of his victory over Naples in 1442, Alfonso had brought most of the barons onto his side by confirming them in their rights and holdings, but he had gained

---

1458) (Naples, 1975). See also Alan Ryder, *The Kingdom of Naples Under Alfonso the Magnanimous* (Oxford, 1976). Ryder perhaps exaggerates the modernity of Alfonso's kingdom, but his work remains extremely valuable because he grounds it on documents surviving in the Archivo de la Corona de Aragón in Barcelona, which few historians of Naples have examined. A review article by A. M. Compagna-Perrone Capano discusses the merits of both these books: "A proposito di *Alfonso il Magnanimo re di Napoli* e di *The Kingdom of Naples Under Alfonso the Magnanimous*," ASPN, 4th ser. 15 (1977), 375–82.

the friendship of not a single new Italian power. Long-term success for a new dynasty—not to mention the ability to influence Italian affairs—would obviously depend upon peninsular allies. Thus Alfonso moved soon after his victory to improve his diplomatic position among the Italian states.

He began this diplomatic campaign with the papacy—for good reason, since papal intervention had the potential to create havoc in Neapolitan affairs.[12] Ever since Pope Nicholas II recognized Robert Guiscard as duke of Apulia and Calabria in 1059, the popes regarded southern Italy and Sicily as their own possession to be granted as a fief first to the dukes and later, after the coronation of Roger II in 1130, to the kings of Naples. This political and legal relationship between popes and rulers was complicated by the proximity of the kingdom of Naples to the papal state, which itself guaranteed tense relations over the long term. Ambitious thirteenth-century popes like Innocent III and Innocent IV waged an almost constant battle against the Ghibelline Hohenstaufen, though the Angevin kings of Naples, holding rather pronounced Guelf sympathies, enjoyed much more cordial relations with the papacy. The aftermath of the Great Schism, the conciliar movement, and the conflict between Angevin and Aragonese all complicated an already confusing ecclesiastical and political situation, since rival parties jockeyed to control the papal tiara even as rival contenders fought for the Neapolitan throne.

Though personally a man of deep zeal and piety, Alfonso intended chiefly to advance his own political designs when conducting relations with the papacy. Since Pope Eugenius IV (1431–1447) supported the Angevins in Naples, he and Alfonso experienced numerous difficulties before the consolidation of the Aragonese hold on the Regno. Upon the death of the childless Giovanna II and the expiration of her line, Eugenius claimed the right

---

[12] Besides the works mentioned above, see also Ludwig von Pastor, *History of the Popes*, trans. F. I. Antrobus, 2d ed., 40 vols. (St. Louis, 1913–53), esp. vols. 1 and 2 on Alfonso's time, vols. 3 through 6 on the period of Ferrante and the later Aragonese kings of Naples.

to grant the kingdom of Naples to a new vassal of his own choice, and he recognized René d'Anjou as the most suitable claimant. His support naturally encouraged René's faction and the barons allied with the Angevins. But Alfonso also had cards to play, thanks to the Council of Basel (1431–1449) and its effort to institute effective conciliar supervision over the papacy. In June 1439 the council proclaimed the deposition of Eugenius, and in November of the same year it selected Felix V as antipope. Alfonso maintained close relations with the council and listened with interest to Felix V, who offered to recognize Alfonso instead of René as king of Naples. With these maneuvers Alfonso maintained pressure on Eugenius, but he never allied himself irrevocably with either the council or the antipope.

Alfonso's adroit diplomacy served him well. It prevented Eugenius from excessive interference in Neapolitan affairs, lest Alfonso side wholeheartedly with the council and Felix. Yet it did not commit him deeply to a council and antipope with dubious political prospects. Finally, it did not rule out an eventual reconciliation with Eugenius. Alfonso's military successes in 1441 and 1442 prepared the way for this development. With the Aragonese victory and the departure of René from Naples, Eugenius' Angevin policy offered few attractive possibilities, if any. Negotiations thus led rather easily to the Treaty of Terracina (signed 14 June 1443), which normalized relations between the king and the pope. Eugenius agreed to recognize and invest Alfonso as king of Naples, further to legitimize Ferrante and recognize him as Alfonso's legal heir and successor. For his part, Alfonso recognized Eugenius as pope and withdrew his representatives from the Council of Basel. He promised further to drive the condottiere Francesco Sforza out of the March of Ancona, which he held in defiance of Eugenius, in a campaign that increased Alfonso's influence in the peninsula as well as restoring Eugenius' authority in the marches.

Thus by late 1443 Alfonso had gained two powerful Italian allies—Filippo Maria Visconti and Eugenius IV—and he began to think about extending his influence in the peninsula.[13] Alfonso complied happily with the terms of his agreement with Eugenius: he dislodged Francesco Sforza from the March of Ancona and helped to stabilize the papal state. But the year 1447 brought changed circumstances—both Eugenius and Filippo Maria died that year—and new opportunities for Alfonso. The papacy of Nicholas V (1447–1455) posed no threat, since the new pope devoted his efforts to the pacification of Italy and the encouragement of scholarship rather than to political ambition. Meanwhile, the disappearance of Filippo Maria left a gaping power vacuum in Lombardy, and Alfonso promptly moved to fill it. His chief rival, Francesco Sforza, enjoyed several advantages: he had supporters in Milan, since he had previously served as chief condottiere for the Visconti, and he had married the late duke's only child, his illegitimate daughter Bianca Maria. Alfonso by contrast had the support of a will, possibly spurious, in which he was named Filippo Maria's political heir. The citizens of Milan developed their own policy, however, and declared a revival of the Ambrosian Republic the day after Filippo Maria's death. Alfonso's army spent almost two years in central and northern Italy pursuing his claim to the duchy of Milan, but military reverses forced him to withdraw from the field late in 1448. Sforza went on to crush the republic and establish himself as the new lord of Milan, thus annulling Alfonso's best opportunity to extend his sway over the Italian peninsula.

But it was not his last such opportunity. The aftermath of Sforza's victory brought a minor diplomatic revolution: Cosimo de' Medici led the Florentines into an alliance with their former archenemy, Milan, while Venice and Alfonso forged an alliance in anticipation of a campaign to increase their holdings in central and northern Italy. Thus in 1452 and 1453 Alfonso's forces—under the command of Ferrante—again threatened to extend Aragonese

---

[13] Besides the works cited above, see also the following studies of fifteenth-century Italian politics: Luigi Simeoni, *Le signorie*, 2 vols. (Milan, 1950); Nino Valeri, *L'Italia nell'età dei principati* (Verona, 1949); and Garrett Mattingly, *Renaissance Diplomacy* (Baltimore, 1964).

influence in Italy. The conflict might easily have developed, like many others, into a long, slow, dull, and costly war, except that external events brought it to an early end. The fall of Constantinople (29 May 1453) encouraged Pope Nicholas V to pacify Italy and join the various peninsular states in a common effort against the Turks. The Peace of Lodi (1454) and the League of Italy (1455) thus brought an end to the war, if not genuine peace to Italy. In at least one respect Alfonso made good use of the opportunities presented by the occasion. He settled his differences with Francesco Sforza, enabling Naples and Milan eventually to resume their bilateral relationship as an especially strong alliance within the Italian League. Yet Alfonso refused to agree to any settlement that included Genoa, and indeed within a year he had again taken up arms against the Genoese.

His aggressive policy in fact helps to account for the last and perhaps the most bitter of all Alfonso's conflicts—that with Alonso de Borja, Pope Calixtus III (1455–1458).[14] Alfonso had brought Borja into his service in 1417, summoned him to Italy in 1432, charged him with important political responsibilities in the Regno, and zealously promoted his ecclesiastical career, so that in 1444 Eugenius IV elevated him into the college of cardinals. Called to the papacy at age seventy-six, Calixtus devoted himself with incredible energy and an almost maniacal zeal to one task— the organization of a land and sea crusade to recapture Constantinople, expel the Turks from other Christian lands, and even to liberate the Holy Land. Early in his pontificate, he persuaded Alfonso to contribute a fleet and serve as admiral of the crusade's naval prong. But Alfonso had no intention of undertaking such a risky enterprise, especially in the absence of meaningful support from other western kings and princes. Instead, he pursued an Italian policy designed to hamper Calixtus' crusading effort: he encouraged the condottiere Jacopo Piccinino, recently released from the

---

[14] Besides Pastor, *History of the Popes*, vol. 2, see also Michael Mallett, *The Borgias* (New York, 1969), esp. pp. 67–89.

Venetians' service, to make war in Tuscany; and Alfonso himself cynically diverted a papal fleet, sent by Calixtus to strengthen the crusaders' forces, to the task of ravaging the Genoese coast and battling other Christian ships.

No wonder, then, that relations between Alfonso and Calixtus rapidly deteriorated. By June 1457 the two men came to the point of threatening to depose each other.[15] In fact, however, Calixtus had little effective recourse except to menace the succession of Ferrante to the Neapolitan throne. This he did with zeal. He declined to recognize either the legitimization of Ferrante or his status as Alfonso's political heir. When Alfonso died on 27 June 1458, Calixtus refused to invest Ferrante and actively encouraged pretenders to the throne. His policy would probably have caused Ferrante considerable grief, had he not followed Alfonso to the grave within six weeks (6 August 1458).

Alfonso's political achievement won praise from contemporary historians and humanists at court, and certainly not without reason. His conquest and consolidation of the kingdom of Naples ranks as perhaps the single most outstanding political accomplishment of fifteenth-century Italy, especially considering the setbacks Alfonso suffered in the early stages of his campaign. Modern historians have devoted more attention to the institutions of Aragonese Naples, and they have found that Alfonso took thoughtful, useful and often creative approaches to the solution of administrative and financial problems. He encouraged the development of a class of educated, talented, bourgeois bureaucrats to help counterbalance the barons. He thought of Naples as a capital city in a modern sense, intending it to play a preeminent role in the administration and glorification of all his territories. He fostered the development throughout his various realms of interregional commerce, which then served him as a source of credit and played an important role in his war finance. He even supervised the creation

---

[15] See the document reported and published in Pastor, *History of the Popes*, 2.425–26, 552–53.

of a fledgling imperial government to serve as central administration, albeit in a limited way, for his far-flung realms.[16] If one can avoid hyperbole, then, it seems reasonable to characterize Alfonso as an incipient modern state-builder of the sort that later constructed the absolute national monarchies of western Europe.[17]

A balanced evaluation of Alfonso's political achievement, however, must take account also of several serious, long-term problems that his policies created or exacerbated. Alfonso lacked a clear set of goals to guide his policy in the years following the conquest. As a result, compromise solutions to domestic problems and unstable relations with foreign powers left the kingdom in a precarious position at Alfonso's death. At home, for example, Alfonso came to terms with the barons, so that they had little cause to challenge his reign. But he did so by confirming and even strengthening them in their powers, privileges, and entrenched positions. The fruit of this policy came ripe only in the reign of Ferrante, who had to suppress two dangerous barons' revolts in order to retain his

[16] See Pontieri, *Alfonso il Magnanimo*, esp. pp. 11–14, 384–88; two articles by Alan Ryder, "The Evolution of Imperial Government in Naples under Alfonso V of Aragon," in J. R. Hale et al., eds., *Europe in the Late Middle Ages* (London, 1965), 332–57; and "Cloth and Credit: Aragonese War Finance in the Mid Fifteenth Century," *War and Society*, 2 (1984), 1–21; and two articles by Ruggero Moscati, "Nella burocrazia centrale di Alfonso d'Aragona: le cariche generali," in *Miscellanea in onore di Roberto Cessi*, 3 vols. (Rome, 1958), 1.365–77; and "Lo stato 'napoletano' di Alfonso d'Aragona," *Clio*, 9 (1973), 165–82.

[17] I cannot entirely agree, however, with the theses of two recent historians. Eugenio Dupré Theseider offers no solid evidence for his contention that Alfonso based his policy on imitation of the ancients and sought for himself the crown of a unified Italian monarchy: *La politica italiana di Alfonso d'Aragona* (Bologna, 1956). Alan Ryder presents a more sophisticated thesis in his *Kingdom of Naples Under Alfonso the Magnanimous*, where he argues that Alfonso introduced all the salient apparatus of the early modern absolute state: a dependent nobility and clergy, direct taxation of the entire realm, a professional bureaucratic administration, and a standing royal army. But Ryder exaggerates the degree of Alfonso's accomplishments. This is especially true in the case of the barons, who simply did not depend upon the crown for their power and authority. Otherwise they could not have threatened Ferrante's position with two serious rebellions (discussed below). Cf. also the review article of A. M. Campagna-Perrone Capano cited above, note 11.

crown. Meanwhile, Alfonso's adventures in the Italian peninsula did not improve the kingdom's security. His two land campaigns left the Tuscans suspicious of his intentions. His intermittent alliances with the papacy, Milan, and Venice failed to provide a reliable Neapolitan ally for the long term. And Alfonso's visceral hostility to Genoa helped set the stage for the calamities of 1494 and following years—the French invasion, the collapse of the Aragonese dynasty in Naples, and the Italian wars—by driving the Genoese into an inevitable and irrevocable alliance with France.[18]

Alfonso does not merit blame for all of Italy's problems, and I have no wish to impose upon him responsibility for decisions implemented by policy makers in the decades after his death, much less for the hardships that plagued Italy in the centuries after his death. This critical review of Alfonso's politics, however, will prove useful to the following study in two ways. In the first place, it provides a solid political foundation for the analysis and interpretation of works produced by Neapolitan cultural figures of Alfonso's time. Furthermore, it helps to explain some of the difficulties faced by Ferrante during his long reign as king of Naples (1458–1494).

The Reign of Ferrante

Ferrante never enjoyed a reputation for magnanimity, generosity, and learning like that of Alfonso. A combination of unusual personality traits and unfavorable publicity resulted in a negative image of Ferrante that has persisted even into the twentieth century. Many contemporaries bore witness to his taciturnity, and Ferrante's own actions prove his capacity for cold political calculation. Giovanni Pontano, Ferrante's secretary for almost nine years

---

[18] Pontieri's rather harsh evaluation of Alfonso's achievement thus strikes me as largely justified. Besides *Alfonso il Magnanimo*, pp. 341–45, 367–88, see also Pontieri's "Alfonso V d'Aragona nel quadro della politica italiana del suo tempo," in his *Divagazioni storiche e storiografiche* (Naples, 1960), esp. pp. 296–306.

and one of his most faithful servants, himself made mention once of a certain sadistic satisfaction that Ferrante took from the imprisonment of his enemies. He kept them well nourished, Pontano said, so as to prolong the experience, and derived from their condition the same pleasure that boys took from their caged birds.[19] Pontano and many other contemporaries praised Ferrante's more attractive qualities and talents, but the more positive image of Ferrante did not long survive the collapse of the Aragonese dynasty of Naples in 1501. Ferrante did not benefit from the sort of continuing public-relations campaign that carefully shaped the image of his contemporary, Lorenzo the Magnificent, both in his own day and in later periods of Medici rule in Florence. Meanwhile, a malevolent effort at negative propaganda actively sought to damage Ferrante's reputation. Thus Philippe de Commynes, fifteenth-century French historian and the chief agent of this enterprise, portrayed Ferrante in colors favored by the Angevin pretenders to the Neapolitan throne. His characterization, which gained wide currency in the sixteenth and later centuries, depended largely on gossip in accusing Ferrante of cruelty, avarice, vindictiveness, violence, vice, and impiety.[20] Granted that Ferrante did not possess the genial personal qualities of his father, the following pages will present a Ferrante endowed with considerable administrative skills and a remarkable sense of political reality.

Born at Valencia 2 June 1431, Ferrante went to Italy at Alfonso's call in 1438.[21] Alfonso had his son legitimized in 1440 and

[19] Giovanni Pontano, *De immanitate liber*, ed. L. Monti Sabia (Naples, 1970), pp. 21–22.

[20] Philippe de Commynes, *Mémoires*, ed. J. Calmette (Paris, 1924–25), esp. 3.78–81.

[21] There is no modern biography of Ferrante, nor even a complete study of his reign. The most useful scholarship is that of Ernesto Pontieri, *Per la storia del regno di Ferrante I d'Aragona re di Napoli*, 2d ed. (Naples, 1969), which serves as the main foundation for the following account, along with Pontieri's article, "La Puglia nel quadro della monarchia degli aragonesi di Napoli," in *Atti del congresso internazionale di studi sull'età aragonese* (Bari, 1972), pp. 19–52; and Guido d'Agostino, *La capitale ambigua: Napoli dal 1458 al 1580* (Naples, 1979), esp. pp.

recognized as his political heir by the parliament of San Lorenzo in 1443. Alfonso took care also to have both Eugenius IV and Nicholas V certify Ferrante's right to succeed to the throne, though he could not move the hostile Calixtus III to follow suit. Alfonso entertained the possibility of marrying Ferrante to Bianca Maria Visconti in the interests of his Milanese alliance, or even to a daughter of King Charles VII in the hope of improving his relations with France. Eventually, however, he selected Isabella di Chiaromonte—beloved niece of the most powerful of all the Neapolitan barons, Giovanni Antonio del Balzo Orsini, prince of Taranto— in the interests of domestic political stability. The wedding took place in May 1445, and by 1461 it had resulted in four sons and two daughters. Meanwhile, Alfonso took care also to provide Ferrante with administrative experience. Besides holding the duchy of Calabria—the benefice traditionally bestowed upon the heir apparent to the Neapolitan throne—Ferrante also served (from an uncertain date after 1438) as lieutenant-general in Naples, in other words, as de facto governor of the Regno. And in 1452 Alfonso sent Ferrante into Tuscany at the head of the army that sought to extend Neapolitan influence during the War of the Milanese Succession.

Alfonso's death in 1458 quickly led to circumstances that required Ferrante to call upon all the skills—administrative, military, and diplomatic—that he had developed during the previous twenty years. Alfonso's political testament provided for his brother to succeed him as King Juan II of Aragon, Sardinia, and Sicily, and for Ferrante to inherit only the kingdom of Naples. Yet the Regno by itself presented enormous difficulties to Ferrante, who battled five years to retain his crown.

He quickly overcame the first problem—Calixtus III's attempt to prevent his succession. Immediately after Alfonso's death, the pope proclaimed the kingdom of Naples a lapsed fief and declared

---

7–107. On Ferrante's birthdate see the editor's note in Panormita, *Liber rerum gestarum Ferdinandi regis*, ed. G. Resta (Palermo, 1968), p. 72 n. 1.

Ferrante ineligible to inherit it. Ferrante responded in the very month of his father's death (July 1458) by convoking a parliament at Capua, where the assembled barons recognized Ferrante as heir and called on the pope to do so. Calixtus, however, favored the claims of the now aged René d'Anjou, whom Alfonso had driven out of the kingdom in 1442, and his son and heir Jean d'Anjou. Only the early death of Calixtus removed this diplomatic hurdle, which otherwise, combined with other obstacles, might well have prevented Ferrante from gaining a secure hold on his kingdom. Enea Silvio Piccolomini, in times past a reasonably close acquaintance of Alfonso, succeeded Calixtus as Pope Pius II (1458–1464). He immediately recognized Ferrante (August), concluded a treaty with him (October), and published a bull investing him with the kingdom (November). By 1 December 1458 Ferrante wore his crown.

His troubles, however, had just begun. Always eager to diminish or destroy royal power, the Neapolitan barons recognized opportunity in the ambitions of two pretenders to the throne. The first was the adventurous Don Carlos, prince of Viana, eldest son of Alfonso's brother Juan of Aragon. Driven out of the kingdom of Navarre, which he claimed through his mother, Carlos went to Naples in 1456 as a guest of his uncle Alfonso. During the uncertain days after Alfonso's death, he intrigued with the barons, but by 1460 he had opted to return to Spain and fish in the troubled waters of Aragon. He quarreled with his father, and his arrest (1460) and death (1462) helped ignite a decade-long revolt of nobility, clergy, and peasantry against the Aragonese monarchy.

Even before Don Carlos' departure, the barons had allied with René and Jean d'Anjou, who posed a far greater threat to Ferrante. In October 1459 Jean arrived in Naples with twenty-four galleys and sparked a rebellion by some of the most powerful Neapolitan barons, including the prince of Taranto. Ferrante's principal support came from Pius II and Francesco Sforza, who both recognized that a revived Angevin monarchy in Naples would inevitably limit the independence of Italian states. Thus in the spring of 1460, papal, Milanese, and Neapolitan forces moved to expel the Angevin invaders and put down the barons' rebellion. Almost on the point of success, Ferrante ordered a surprise attack (7 July 1460) against his enemies encamped at Sarno (near Naples) in the hope of winning a quick and decisive victory. Instead, his army suffered a complete rout, and most of his troops fell prisoner. Ferrante himself escaped to Naples along with twenty cavalry. Had Jean d'Anjou and the barons quickly followed up their victory at Sarno, they could very likely have ended the Aragonese monarchy in Naples. Instead they delayed, enabling Ferrante to organize his resources. Most significant of these were his friendships with Pius II and Francesco Sforza, who showered Ferrante with military, financial, and diplomatic support. Sforza even instigated a rebellion against the French garrison in Genoa, resulting in disruption of the Angevins' line of supplies. The turning point of the war came on 29 August 1462 at the battle of Troia (near Foggia), where Neapolitan and Milanese forces decisively defeated Jean d'Anjou. As a result the prince of Taranto made his peace with Ferrante. In succeeding months, other barons followed suit. In November 1463 the prince of Taranto died, and internal, Neapolitan opposition to Ferrante quickly disappeared. Jean d'Anjou continued to press his cause, however, until the summer of 1465: he abandoned it only after the naval battle of Ischia (7 July 1465), where his fleet suffered a crushing defeat inflicted by a squadron of Neapolitan ships and a flotilla sent by Ferrante's uncle, King Juan II of Aragon.

Ferrante's battle for his kingdom provided humanists and other cultural figures with abundant raw material in the years that followed. Their reflections on fortune, fortitude, and the unpredictable nature of military affairs make frequent reference to the events of the period 1458 to 1463. Ferrante himself provided one especially striking example of courage discussed by several commentators. Shortly before the battle of Sarno, on 30 May 1460, he met with one of the most powerful of the barons—Marino Marzano, duke of Sessa, prince of Rossano, and husband of Ferrante's sister Eleonora—in an effort to come to terms. At the meeting's end,

Marzano and his two companions attacked Ferrante and attempted an assassination. Ferrante defended himself with a sword until supporters came to his rescue and put the assailants to flight.[22]

Ferrante's early response to the barons' threat helped to fix upon him the reputation for treachery and vindictiveness that has long marred his memory. Under pretext of reconciliation, he entrapped and imprisoned several barons, including Marino Marzano and his five-year-old son, both of whom spent the next thirty years in the dungeon of the Castelnuovo. Furthermore, after coming to terms with Jacopo Piccinino, the Angevin condottiere, Ferrante lured him to Naples and executed him. The antifeudal cast of Ferrante's domestic policy thus manifested itself almost at the beginning of his reign. Ferrante confronted the most powerful of the barons, even if not by his own choosing, and repressed them in a more thoroughgoing way than Alfonso would ever have done.

The antifeudal policy, however, also had its more positive aspect. Ferrante sought to undermine the barons' position by encouraging economic and social development in the Mezzogiorno.[23] The major towns of the Regno enjoyed a shower of royal grants, exemptions, and privileges during Ferrante's reign. He never surrendered ultimate royal control, especially over finances, but he allowed the towns a large measure of autonomy in matters of local importance, and even in the mechanics of tax collection. Ferrante also sought to remove baronial obstacles to the development of Neapolitan commerce. In 1466 he issued two proclamations that provided for the free circulation of goods in the Regno and ended the monopolies and tolls previously enjoyed by the barons. In later years he removed the barons' monopoly on inns and taverns, forced barons to reopen pasture lands that they had en-

---

[22] For early accounts of this episode, see Ferrante's own description of the attack in a letter to his wife, published in Pontieri, *Per la storia del regno di Ferrante I*, pp. 158–59; and Giuniano Maio, *De maiestate*, ed. F. Gaeta (Bologna, 1956), pp. 31–34.

[23] For the economic history of Aragonese Naples, see Ludovico Bianchini, *Storia delle finanze del Regno delle due Sicilie*, ed. L. de Rosa (Naples, 1971), pp. 155–214.

closed in recent times, and provided that any subject could freely produce and trade goods without hindrance from the barons and without need of any special privilege. Finally, Ferrante positively encouraged the development of certain industries. He introduced the manufacture of silk into the Mezzogiorno, granted privileges that enabled entrepreneurs to mine and produce iron in Calabria, and generously supported printers who opened shops in Naples. Although agricultural and industrial production increased during Ferrante's reign, his efforts did not entirely succeed: the barons did not always cooperate well, and the merchant and industrial classes failed to develop into social groups powerful enough to counterbalance the entrenched baronage. Yet Ferrante's policy remains impressive as a creative and realistic approach to the chief domestic problem of fifteenth-century Naples—the excessive power wielded by the barons in their own narrow and largely selfish interests.

If Ferrante displayed more imagination than Alfonso in the development of domestic policy, he exhibited more caution in the management of foreign relations. Throughout his reign Ferrante schemed, maneuvered, and manipulated issues in the interests of his own realm—as did political leaders in all parts of Italy without exception, even in the years after the Peace of Lodi and formation of the Italian League. Yet he did not inherit Alfonso's expansionist ambitions, and he never attempted to extend Neapolitan influence over the entire Italian peninsula, as his father had done. He resorted often to bluff, bullying, or browbeating, but rarely to outright hostilities. Indeed, between the conclusion of his battle for the throne and the end of his thirty-six-year reign, Ferrante engaged Naples in open warfare for a period just short of a decade (1478–1487), and much of that time he fought only because others had foisted war on his realm.

Unstable relations between Naples and the papacy help to explain a great deal of Ferrante's foreign policy. His close alliance with Pius II helped him first to gain, then to retain his crown, but the death of Pius (1464) brought the election of a more prickly character, Paul II (1464–1471), with whom Ferrante always had tense relations. Almost immediately, a dispute arose over the annual tribute paid by the kings of Naples to their feudal overlords, the popes. Since the earliest days of the Angevin monarchy, the kings had presented a white riding horse and a large sum of money (of variable amounts) to the popes on the feast of St. Peter and St. Paul. Alfonso had gained a lifetime exemption from payment of the tribute in his settlement with Eugenius IV, and Pius II had voluntarily released Ferrante from his obligation, in view of the Angevin invasion and the barons' revolt. When Paul II demanded payment of the tribute, Ferrante sent no money, but only the white palfrey, which Paul angrily returned. Though ostensibly a small matter, the question of tribute clouded papal relations during the whole of Ferrante's reign. During the papacy of Paul II alone, it complicated other disputes over territory in the papal state, and it helped to create such a tense political environment that Ferrante and Paul stood on the brink of war during much of Paul's reign.

The long papacy of Sixtus IV (1471–1484) brought relief on the issue of the tribute—Sixtus remitted it entirely, though Ferrante pledged to send the white horse anyway—but it entangled Naples in an alliance with a determined and martial pope. In his effort to impose firm control over the papal state, Sixtus inspired deep suspicion on the part of Lorenzo de' Medici and the Florentines. The Pazzi conspiracy, the assassination of Giuliano de' Medici, and the attack on Lorenzo himself led to outright war between Florence and Sixtus in 1478. Almost two years of fighting ensued. Ferrante's eldest son, Alfonso, duke of Calabria and later King Alfonso II, led the Neapolitan army in Tuscany; in the autumn of 1479 he might even have seriously menaced Florence itself, except that he did not follow up a surprise victory over Florentine forces. The war came to an end only after Lorenzo de' Medici traveled personally to Naples and spent almost four months in negotiations with Ferrante (December 1479 to March 1480). Their conversations resulted in more than peace, however, since they identified common interests and agreed to cooperate in an effort to limit the expansion of Venice and the papacy. The new alliance represented a victory for both parties: Florence extricated herself from an increasingly difficult military and diplomatic position, while Ferrante gained the most useful and reliable of all his allies in the years that followed.

The war ended at a convenient time for Naples as well as for Florence: barely two months after peace was made, the Turkish admiral Ahmed Pasha appeared off the Italian coast with a fleet of some 140 ships carrying 18,000 soldiers and 700 horses. Acting with the benevolent neutrality, or possibly even with the malevolent encouragement of Venice, on 28 July 1480 Ahmed landed his forces near Otranto in Apulia.[24] By 11 August he had captured the city and begun to secure it for use as a point from which to extend Turkish power in Italy. The bloody fate of the city's inhabitants has inspired numerous accounts of the episode over the centuries. The invaders murdered Archbishop Stefano Pendinelli at the high altar of the cathedral. On 14 August they marched eight hundred inhabitants of Otranto to a hill near the city and executed them all for refusing to convert to Islam. Of the city's twenty thousand inhabitants, twelve thousand died at Turkish hands, including the entire male population. Yet the invasion produced no long-term benefit for the Turks. A large Neapolitan army led by Duke Alfonso of Calabria, freshly returned from Tuscany, succeeded in confining the Turks to the city and placing them under siege. On 10 September 1481, after eleven months of siege, Otranto fell back into Aragonese hands.

Though angry at Ferrante for making a separate peace with Lorenzo de' Medici, Pope Sixtus energetically contributed to the ef-

---

[24] See Franz Babinger, *Mehmed the Conqueror and His Time*, trans. R. Manheim (Princeton, 1978), pp. 389–96; Kenneth M. Setton, *The Papacy and the Levant (1204–1571)*, 4 vols. (Philadelphia, 1976–84), 2.339-45, 364–80; and Robert Schwoebel, *The Shadow of the Crescent: The Renaissance Image of the Turk (1493–1517)* (Nieuwkoop, 1967), pp. 131–39. A large literature has appeared, much of it in recent years, on the episode at Otranto. See the four bibliographical notes in Lucia Gualdo Rosa et al., eds., *Gli umanisti e la guerra otrantina* (Bari, 1982).

fort to expel the Turks. Within a year's time, however, he concluded an alliance with Venice and prepared for war against Naples and Ferrara, whose duke, Ercole d'Este, had married Ferrante's daughter Eleonora in 1474. The resulting War of Ferrara (1482–1484) revealed perhaps more clearly than anything else the shortsightedness of Sixtus' martial policy. In its first phase (April to December 1482), the war pitted Sixtus and Venice against Ferrara, Naples, Florence, and Milan. At the head of the Neapolitan army, Duke Alfonso ravaged the papal state, while Venetian pressure brought Ferrara to the brink of collapse. Meanwhile, however, Sixtus grew increasingly fearful of Venetian power; thus during the war's second phase (April 1483 to August 1484), he abandoned Venice and allied with his former enemies. The locus of fighting shifted: Duke Alfonso cooperated with Milanese forces combating the Venetian condottiere Roberto Sanseverino in Lombardy and the Veneto, while in May 1484 Venetian naval forces captured Gallipoli and other ports in Apulia. Only the withdrawal of Milan from the alliance forced the parties to come to terms. The Peace of Bagnolo (7 August 1484) returned affairs to an approximation of the status quo ante; the martial Sixtus IV survived the settlement by only a few days.

Sixtus' death, however, did not bring an end to Ferrante's problems. The new pope, Innocent VIII (1484–1492), came from a Genoese family with strong Angevin sympathies; indeed, Innocent's father had fought with René d'Anjou against Alfonso in the years after 1438. Disputes over territorial rights and the annual tribute caused relations between Rome and Naples to degenerate immediately after Innocent assumed the papacy. The development that led to the rupture of relations and eventually to war was the second barons' revolt against Ferrante, in which Innocent supported the rebels.

The barons feared royal plans to diminish their powers.[25] Long

[25] A modern study of the barons' revolt remains a great desideratum, since it could throw light on the political, constitutional, and social history of Aragonese Naples. For the present, besides the more general works cited above, there is the

known for his antifeudal sentiments, Duke Alfonso saw an opportunity after the Otranto and Ferrara wars to increase the authority of the monarchy. He spoke openly of his plan to establish around the city of Naples an immense royal demesne in which no feudal holdings or armies would be allowed, and he persuaded Ferrante to support the project. During the early months of 1485, the barons responded by organizing among themselves and seeking an alliance with Pope Innocent. By the summer of 1485, Duke Alfonso's readiness to implement his plans prompted the barons to take more definitive action. They encouraged the city of Aquila to rebel and expel the royal garrison in September 1485, and they offered to support Ferrante's second son, Federico, in a bid for the throne. Federico scornfully rejected the barons' offer of his father's throne, but the combined efforts of Innocent and the barons caused serious difficulties for Ferrante and Duke Alfonso. Innocent obtained the services of the Venetians' chief condottiere, Roberto Sanseverino. In perhaps his most threatening move, he even invited Duke René of Lorraine—who claimed the inheritance of his now-dead cousins, René and Jean d'Anjou—to enter the fray and make good his claim to rule Naples. Finally, Ferrante suffered the betrayal of two especially powerful ministers, Francesco Coppola and Antonello Petrucci. Coppola's father had risen from poverty to wealth as a merchant, gaining a title of nobility along the way. Francesco followed in his father's steps: through skillful business practices and royal favors he became fabulously wealthy and powerful. On several occasions he came to the aid of Ferrante with money and galleys from his own fleet; in return he gained the county of Sarno, the office of admiral of the realm, and a post as royal counsellor, as well as numerous other rewards. Petrucci had risen even more dramatically. Born into a peasant family, he entered the service of a Neapolitan notary, then came to the attention of King Alfonso's royal secretary, Juan Olzina, who appreciated Antonello's talents.

---

classic sixteenth-century account of Camillo Porzio, *La congiura de' baroni del regno di Napoli contra il re Ferdinando il primo*, ed. E. Pontieri (Naples, 1964); also Enrico Perito, *La congiura dei baroni e il conte di Policastro* (Bari, 1926).

Alfonso and Ferrante protected and promoted him, and Petrucci eventually became royal secretary to Ferrante, as well as holder of other offices, a knighthood, and many fiefs.

Despite insurrection, betrayal, and the threat of foreign intervention, Ferrante prevailed handily over his enemies. He had the diplomatic support of Milan, Florence, and his son-in-law, King Mathias Corvinus of Hungary. More important, he had an effective army led by Duke Alfonso, who ravaged the papal state, routed the forces of Roberto Sanseverino, and repressed individual rebel barons. Thus by 11 August 1486 Innocent came to terms with Ferrante. The king made large concessions on paper: he agreed to honor the papacy, to pay the annual tribute faithfully, to pardon the rebel barons, and to restore them in their holdings.[26]

In fact, however, Ferrante never intended to observe the treaty's provisions, all of which he instantly violated. He honored the papacy only with scorn, and he never sent tribute money, but only the white horse to the pope in following years. Furthermore, even as Duke Alfonso ratified the pact on 13 August 1486, two days after its completion, Ferrante began to take his revenge on the barons. He struck at a banquet held at the Castelnuovo to celebrate the marriage of Francesco Coppola's son. His forces arrested at least ten of the celebrants, including Coppola, his two sons, Antonello Petrucci, his wife, and his two sons. Three months later a tribunal read sentences of death in the cases of Francesco, Antonello, and Petrucci's two sons. Executions of the two younger Petrucci took place on 11 December 1486. Francesco Petrucci, a surly man and one of the most determined leaders of the conspiracy, was drawn in disgrace through all sections of the city of Naples, then quartered; his brother Gianantonio, a lover of letters and a poet who joined the rebellion through family connections rather than political ambition, was paraded through the city, then beheaded. Five months later, 11 May 1487, similar public cere-

[26] On the making and breaking of this peace of 1486, see P. Fedele, "La pace del 1486 tra Ferdinando d'Aragona ed Innocenzo VIII," *ASPN*, 30 (1905), 481–503.

monies preceded the beheading of Antonello Petrucci and Francesco Coppola. But Ferrante had not completed his revenge. New rounds of suppression in June and July 1487 resulted in the arrest and interrogation of numerous other barons, including several of the most powerful ones of the realm. Though not formally tried for their activities, they languished for years in the dungeon of the Castelnuovo, where presumably they made up the contingent of political prisoners that Pontano said provided amusement for Ferrante.

Though difficult to justify morally, Ferrante's policy certainly proved effective, at least in the short run. Innocent VIII never again exhibited much determination to move against Ferrante. Despite the constant pressure of Giuliano della Rovere—nephew of Pope Sixtus IV, later Pope Julius II himself, and one of Ferrante's most outspoken enemies in the college of cardinals—Innocent took no decisive action, even in the face of Ferrante's constant taunts and threats. Meanwhile, the barons had no desire to confront Duke Alfonso's army, now for the first time in almost ten years unencumbered by the need to fight foreign forces. Nor did Ferrante's foreign enemies take advantage of the natural opportunity to intervene in Neapolitan affairs—thanks partly to an energetic diplomatic effort discussed in later chapters.

Thus Ferrante's last years brought no major threat to his rule, not even after the death of Innocent VIII and election of Rodrigo de Borja as Pope Alexander VI (1492–1503). Alexander inherited the antipathy of his uncle, Calixtus III, toward the Aragonese dynasty in Naples. Though always uneasy, relations between Alexander and Ferrante never degenerated to the point of serious tension. Ferrante behaved with unusual caution when involved in territorial disputes with the second Borgia pope. For his part, Alexander recognized the legitimacy of Ferrante's rule and Duke Alfonso's right to succeed him as king of Naples.

Yet in these same years political developments and changes in leadership set the stage for the tragedies suffered by Naples and Italy after 1494. In 1490 the death of King Mathias Corvinus of

Hungary deprived Ferrante not only of a loyal son-in-law, but also of a staunch source of diplomatic and political support. In 1492 the death of Lorenzo de' Medici deprived him of his most reliable ally in Italy and placed the leadership of Florence in the hands of the undependable Piero de' Medici. Meanwhile, Milan moved increasingly into the French orbit. As early as the mid-1460s, Francesco Sforza had begun to seek improved relations with France, and in 1468 his son and successor, Galeazzo Maria (1466–1476), married Bona of Savoy, cousin of King Louis XI of France. The establishment of truly close ties, however, came only after Ludovico il Moro gained influence in the making of Milanese foreign policy. Ludovico served as power behind the throne for his nephew, Duke Giangaleazzo II (1476–1494), then usurped the duchy in 1494 and ruled in his own name until deposed by the same French whom he had cultivated (1500). Nervous about the illegitimacy of his position and unable to find reliable peninsular allies, Ludovico looked beyond the Alps for the diplomatic and military muscle that would enable him to retain his hold on Milan. His interests coincided neatly with the juvenile dreams of young King Charles VIII of France (1483–1498), who planned to conquer the kingdom of Naples, which he claimed by virtue of his Angevin inheritance, then to lead a crusade to the Holy Land, win himself an imperial crown, cleanse the papacy, reform the church, and establish his reputation as a courageous and chivalric hero.

The kingdom of Naples and the Aragonese dynasty thus stood at a perilous pass on 25 January 1494, when death put an end to Ferrante's long reign. That event encouraged a rapidly increased tempo in Neapolitan affairs.[27]

[27] On the period from the French invasion of 1494 through the imposition of the Spanish viceroys, see d'Agostino, *La capitale ambigua*, pp. 56–174; Mallett, *The Borgias*, esp. pp. 117–265; and Luigi Volpicella, *Federico d'Aragona e la fine del regno di Napoli nel MDI* (Naples, 1908). On the military history of the period, see Piero Pieri, *Il Rinascimento e la crisi militare italiana* (Turin, 1952), esp. pp. 320–535.

The Invasions of Italy and the Collapse
of the Aragonese Dynasty of Naples

The duke of Calabria succeeded Ferrante as Alfonso II. Although many barons continued to hold grudges against Alfonso, the urban nobility and the inhabitants of the city of Naples cordially received the new king as one born among themselves. Alexander VI rebuffed the French claim to the Neapolitan throne and dispatched a cardinal to crown Alfonso on 8 May 1494.

Alfonso's early diplomatic triumphs did nothing, however, to diminish Charles VIII's enthusiasm for his visionary projects. Reports arrived regularly in Naples with news of Charles's plans to invade Italy and conquer the Regno. Against this possibility Alfonso undertook both diplomatic and political initiatives. He sought to strengthen or repair relations with Florence, Milan, Venice, and other powers. But only with Alexander VI did Alfonso succeed in establishing a reasonably close rapport. He eagerly submitted to Alexander both the white horse and the tribute money that had so often served as bone of contention between Ferrante and various popes. Alfonso also gave his illegitimate daughter Sancia in marriage to Alexander's illegitimate son Jofrè. And he showered all three of Alexander's sons with benefits: Jofrè became prince of Squillace, Juan became prince of Tricaria, and Cesare received numerous valuable benefices in the Regno. Alexander of course never desired a fresh and vigorous French monarchy in Naples. But the prospect of bringing considerable advantage to his own house certainly contributed to his policy of supporting the Aragonese monarchy in Naples, at least during the early days of the conflicts that began in 1494.

Alfonso's military preparations seemed likely to thwart Charles VIII's plan to conquer the kingdom of Naples. Alfonso strengthened defenses, rebuilt walls, and provisioned fortresses, both in the city of Naples and in other parts of the realm. He sent his brother Federico at the head of a fleet to aid Genoese exiles in their effort to expel the dominant Adorno faction—allies of Milan and France—and thus to remove Genoa as a source of supply and support for French invaders. Finally, Alfonso sent his son Ferrante (generally called Ferrandino so as to distinguish him from the elder Ferrante) at the head of Neapolitan and papal ground forces into the Romagna, where he could threaten Lombardy and any French invaders who appeared there.

The defensive measures, however, all went for naught. In September 1494, Charles VIII crossed the Alps with a force of some forty thousand men. Federico suffered naval defeat at Rapallo, so that Charles gained the use of Genoa. Charles's main force then evaded Ferrandino's army in Lombardy and progressed unmolested down the peninsula on a leisurely march to Naples. Charles entered Florence on 17 November, as the Medici regime crumbled; and on the advice of his astrologers, he entered Rome itself on 31 December. Several weeks of negotiations with the wily Alexander VI brought him much courtesy but no substantial aid. Thus when Charles left Rome (27 January 1495), he departed without Alexander's blessing and without the investiture of the Regno.

Meanwhile, after it had become plain that the road to Naples stood open to Charles, Alfonso II fell into a panic. Despairing of his chances to save his crown, he decided to entrust it to his son, in the hope that the more popular Ferrandino could rally the kingdom to repel the French.[28] Thus about 23 January 1495, after less than one year of rule, Alfonso II abdicated the monarchy and retired to Sicily, where he died of an infection the following November.

Despite heroic political and military efforts during the next month, Ferrandino also failed to halt the French advance. Cities opened their gates to Charles, barons deserted the Aragonese monarchy, and the city of Naples itself fell into chaos. Finally, Charles

[28] On Ferrandino see Benedetto Croce, "Re Ferrandino," in his *Storie e leggende napoletane*, pp. 157–79.

victoriously entered Naples, on 22 February 1495, the same day that Ferrandino escaped to Ischia.

Though warmly greeted at first, the French soon encountered difficulties in Naples. The army made itself unpopular through its brutality, while Charles himself caused dissatisfaction in his distribution of lands and offices. Meanwhile, Ferrandino and Federico sparked insurrections, and King Ferdinand the Catholic of Spain prepared an army in Sicily to aid his Aragonese cousins in Naples. Finally, the League of Venice (concluded 31 March 1495) joined a group of formidable powers—Pope Alexander VI, King Ferdinand of Spain, Emperor Maximilian I, Venice, and Milan—in a coalition determined not to allow the consolidation of a French monarchy in Naples.

Charles gradually realized the perils he faced, with few provisions, long supply lines, and numerous enemies blocking his path to safety. So he departed from Naples with about half of his army 24 May 1495. Ferrandino reentered Naples to great rejoicing on 7 July, but he did not succeed in expelling the remaining French troops from the city until almost the end of the year. Liberation of the entire kingdom required almost another whole year: only after the French capitulation at Atella (23 June 1496) could Ferrandino turn his attention to the business of governance. In fact, however, he had no opportunity to rule in a more or less normal way, for Ferrandino's own time had almost expired. Barely three months after his expulsion of the French, a virulent illness struck him. He was carried into Naples in grave condition 5 October 1496, and two days later the popular young king lay dead.

Thus came to the throne Federico, second son of the elder Ferrante, younger brother of Alfonso II, and uncle of Ferrandino. Under normal circumstances, Federico might have built a reputation as the most successful and accomplished of all the Aragonese kings of Naples. He possessed military skills, attractive personal qualities, and the ability to inspire confidence and loyalty. His humanist tutors had instilled in him an appreciation for high culture, but he also enjoyed great popularity among the common people of the

Regno. He based his rule on the sensible principles of forgetting old hostilities and addressing instead the current difficulties that plagued the kingdom. Thus he concentrated his efforts on solving economic problems, aggravated by several years of dubious financial management, and on eliminating hunger and famine, caused by several years of warfare in the kingdom.

Despite his good intentions and undeniable talents, Federico did not succeed in mending the social and political fabric of the Regno. As the fourth Aragonese king of Naples in less than three years' time, he sat upon an unstable throne. Ever eager to diminish royal power and authority, many barons deserted the Aragonese cause and intrigued with the French. More significantly, in 1498 Alexander VI also abandoned Federico, who had recoiled violently at the proposal to marry his daughter Carlotta to the pope's illegitimate son Cesare. In the aftermath, Alexander concluded an alliance with King Louis XII of France (1498–1515) and married Cesare to a French princess (1499). Meanwhile, in an even more ominous development, King Ferdinand the Catholic began to develop his own Neapolitan ambitions. Ferdinand had long played a role in Italian affairs: he had aided Ferrante during the second barons' revolt; he had supported Alfonso II and Ferrandino against Charles VIII; and at century's end his army enabled Federico to retain his hold on the monarchy. About that same time, however, the combination of instability and opportunity in Naples tempted Ferdinand to undertake action there on his own behalf.

The year 1500 marked the beginning of the end for the Aragonese monarchy of Naples. In November, Louis XII and Ferdinand the Catholic secretly concluded the Treaty of Granada, by which they agreed to conquer and partition the kingdom of Naples. Unaware of the pact, Federico called for Spanish aid when Louis's army invaded Naples in 1501. He soon discovered that Ferdinand's general, Gonsalvo de Córdoba—*el gran capitán*, who had conquered the Moors in Granada in 1492—no longer sought to bolster the shaky monarchy, but rather to establish Spanish hegemony over the provinces of Apulia and Calabria, leaving the remainder of the kingdom, including the city of Naples, to the French. The Spanish and French armies quickly subdued the Regno, but the new lords almost immediately quarreled over their spoils. Already by 1502 they were to fight over disputed territories. In 1503 Gonsalvo took the field against the French, and by 1 January 1504 he had evicted them from all their Neapolitan holdings. He then became the first in a long series of viceroys, who for the next 210 years ruled Naples in the name of the kings of Spain.

Federico surrendered to the French in 1501. Louis XII granted him the duchy of Anjou as his reward, and the former king lived in France until his death at Tours in 1504. His son Ferrante, the last of the Aragonese dukes of Calabria, fell prisoner to Spanish troops when Gonsalvo de Córdoba captured the city of Taranto in 1502. Packed off immediately to Spain, the young duke lived more or less quietly under the close watch of King Ferdinand and later of Charles V—despite one attempt at escape, which led to ten years of imprisonment (1513–1523), and despite intermittent hopes on the part of disenchanted Neapolitans that he would return to the kingdom and reestablish the Aragonese dynasty there. He eventually became a grandee and died, childless, as viceroy of Valencia in 1550. The Aragonese monarchy of Naples had come to an end.

Renaissance Naples

The kingdom of Naples thus played an important role during the Quattrocento in the political affairs both of Italy and of states beyond the Alps. In fact, its political significance alone would seem to warrant for the Regno far more attention than historians have devoted to it. But fifteenth-century Naples figured also as one of the most outstanding and influential cultural centers of Renaissance Italy. Some of the most illustrious and creative of all the Italian humanists lived and worked at the court of Naples, and they contributed to humanism, the single most important cultural movement of the Renaissance, several of its distinctive elements.

Meanwhile, other men—not humanists, but lawyers, theologians, philosophers, political thinkers, educators, and moralists—helped to define the characteristics of Renaissance culture in a more general way. The analysis of Neapolitan culture in the Quattrocento can thus lead to an improved understanding of cultural life in Renaissance Italy as a whole.

Naples and southern Italy figured more or less prominently in the development of humanism from the earliest days of its history. Petrarch chose King Robert the Wise (1309–1343) as his sponsor when seeking coronation with the poet's laurel; he traveled to Naples to submit to examination by Robert in 1341, and returned there on a papal mission two years later. Boccaccio spent many of his most productive years at the Angevin court of Naples, which he preferred to his native Florence because of its peace and stability. Both men developed circles of friends, admirers, and imitators in the kingdom. Meanwhile, an old tradition of Greek learning flourished in the Mezzogiorno during the Hohenstaufen and Angevin monarchies. Both Petrarch and Boccaccio sought Greek instruction in the kingdom, for lack of any other available source.[29]

After the death of King Robert the Wise, however, Naples suffered factional struggles, disputed successions, and eventually the turmoil that ended with the establishment of the Aragonese dynasty there. For almost a century, then, the kingdom could not offer the security and patronage required by the fledgling humanist movement. The cultural initiative passed to the cities of central and northern Italy, where followers of Petrarch and Boccaccio imparted to humanism a thoroughly urban spirit. Developed under the tutelage of educators like Vittorino da Feltre and Guarino da Verona, of professional administrators like Coluccio Salutati and Leonardo Bruni, and of moralists like Francesco Barbaro and Pog-

---

[29] On the cultural history of Angevin Naples, see Francesco Sabatini, *Napoli angioina: cultura e società* (Naples, 1975). See also two articles by Roberto Weiss: "The Translators from the Greek of the Angevin Court of Naples," *Rinascimento*, 1 (1950), 195–226; and "The Greek Culture of South Italy in the Later Middle Ages," *Proceedings of the British Academy*, 37 (1951), 23–50.

gio Bracciolini, humanism in its formative years acquired a vocabulary and a set of concerns that reflected the interests of the early humanists' urban environments. Except for the century of disorder in the Regno, early humanists attracted to Naples and nurtured in southern courts might well have contributed an alternate set of feudal or monarchical values to the intellectual interests of humanism.

In the event, however, humanism returned to the Mezzogiorno at a time in which many of its characteristic traits had taken on recognizable shape. Humanism did not reappear as a natural expression of Neapolitan society and culture, but instead reentered the kingdom through the court of Alfonso the Magnanimous—a point of fundamental importance for the following study. Humanism in fifteenth-century Naples began by reflecting the taste, the interests, and the needs of King Alfonso. In later years humanism spread its roots throughout Neapolitan society, finding fertile ground for growth in the universities, the printing industry, and even the aristocracy of the kingdom. Yet throughout the dynasty, the Aragonese kings of Naples employed humanists in political capacities, as secretaries, diplomats, advisers, and spokesmen. Furthermore, political questions dominated as the most important of all the issues treated by humanists and other cultural figures in fifteenth-century Naples. The following study therefore concentrates on politics—rather than economic or social structure, for example—as the most important influence on Neapolitan culture during the Quattrocento.

This is not the place to undertake a thorough review of the scholarly literature on Renaissance humanism, but I wish to draw attention to two especially prominent interpretations that have deeply influenced the following analysis. The first is that of Paul O. Kristeller, who almost single-handedly made it possible to speak meaningfully of humanism as a cultural movement.[30] Kris-

[30] For samplers of his voluminous work, see Kristeller's *Renaissance Thought: The Classic, Scholastic, and Humanist Strains* (New York, 1961); and *Renaissance Thought and Its Sources*, ed. M. Mooney (New York, 1979).

teller rejected earlier scholars' efforts to associate humanism with some specific philosophical doctrine, religious belief, or ideological stance. Instead he relied on numerous empirical studies to characterize humanism as an educational, literary, and cultural movement of the period roughly 1300 to 1600. Humanists in general studied and appreciated classical literature, according to Kristeller, while cultivating the rhetorical and literary skills that helped to define the classical cultural tradition. Renaissance humanism developed as the peculiar idiom of a sophisticated, cosmopolitan cultural elite. Yet the literary, rhetorical, and philological interests cultivated by humanists had quite broad implications: humanists restored currency to long-forgotten works of classical thought and literature; they reoriented philosophical, moral, and religious thought by establishing the nature and behavior of humanity as their central concerns; and they instituted the critical, philological, historical study of literature. Thus humanism figured as an especially powerful cultural force in the transition from medieval to modern times.

While Kristeller focused his attention on the cosmopolitan interests shared by all Renaissance humanists, Hans Baron concerned himself with the local pressures that led to the development in Florence of a peculiar strain of civic humanism.[31] By Baron's account, civic humanism emerged in the period around the turn of the fifteenth century, as the Florentine republic defended herself from the military and political threats posed by expansionist regimes in Milan, Naples, and Venice. The pressures of those years encouraged humanists—who had previously devoted their efforts largely to cultural pursuits without grounding themselves solidly in the broader society—to ally with civic patriots in defense of the republic. As a result of the alliance, humanists like Leonardo Bruni focused their talents not only on literature and scholarship, but also on issues of immediate political and social relevance. The civic commitments made by Bruni and others thus helped to bring

[31] See especially Baron's *Crisis of the Early Italian Renaissance.*

about several cultural developments that Baron presented as the hallmarks of civic humanism: a new historiography, which brought humanist critical analysis to bear on the examination of coherent, well-integrated topics; a new social ethic, which emphasized the value and virtue of the active over the contemplative life; a new appreciation of vernacular literature, which possessed a beauty and dignity equal to those of the classical languages; and most importantly, a new commitment to republican political values, which served Florentines as a powerful ideological weapon in their conflicts with other states. Once again, then, humanism figures as a potent force in western civilization, but this time as one that reflected local pressures more faithfully than cosmopolitan interests.

The views of Kristeller and Baron do not cancel each other out, in my opinion, but rather complement each other as interpretations of Renaissance humanism. Taken together, they suggest the value of studies that acknowledge the influence both of cosmopolitan interests common to all the humanists and of local circumstances that shaped the work and thought of individual humanists.[32] Humanism always reflected to a large extent the interests of intellectuals in all parts of Italy and Europe, after all, but it inevitably acquired distinctive characteristics as individual humanists encountered the problems and pressures of a particular society. The following analysis thus draws considerable inspiration from both Kristeller and Baron in its effort to understand Renaissance humanism in its Neapolitan manifestation.

Previous scholarship has resulted in several works of high interest for the understanding of Neapolitan culture, especially humanism, in the fifteenth century. Eberhard Gothein produced a portrait of Quattrocento Naples, for example, that strikes readers

---

[32] See two especially wise articles that point in this direction: George M. Logan, "Substance and Form in Renaissance Humanism," *Journal of Medieval and Renaissance Studies*, 7 (1977), 1–34; and Charles G. Nauert, Jr., "Renaissance Humanism: An Emergent Consensus and Its Critics," *Indiana Social Studies Quarterly*, 33 (1980), 5–20.

today—a full century after its original publication—as remarkable for its attention to the nuances of Neapolitan society.[33] Antonio Altamura, Andres Soria, and Francesco Tateo have thrown useful light on the individual humanists and literary figures active in Renaissance Naples.[34] Most sensitive and thoughtful of all, Mario Santoro has offered a survey of Neapolitan humanism that links cultural life more directly to the general experience of fifteenth-century Naples. Santoro recognizes that in its early stages, humanism depended on the talents of foreigners attracted to the Regno by King Alfonso, but he argues that during the course of the Aragonese dynasty, humanism established itself as a genuine Neapolitan cultural movement. By the end of the fifteenth century, natives of the city or kingdom of Naples had taken the place of foreign humanists; their works reflected not only the interests of the monarchs, but also the problems of the entire realm.[35]

The following book does not pretend to supersede or displace the works mentioned here, but seeks instead to complement them and perhaps to augment them in a useful way. It pays more attention than previous studies to developments in humanism and Renaissance culture in central and northern Italy. At the same time, it concentrates more rigorously than any previous study on the interrelations between politics and culture in Quattrocento Naples. This approach will make it possible to take into account both cosmopolitan influences and local pressures at work in fifteenth-century Naples. More particularly, the study seeks to contribute to the understanding of the Renaissance on several different levels. In the first place, most obviously, it seeks to throw light on the his-

[33] Eberhard Gothein, *Die Culturentwicklung Süd-Italiens* (Breslau, 1886), better known in the Italian translation, *Il Rinascimento nell'Italia meridionale*, ed. and trans. T. Persico (Florence, 1915).

[34] Antonio Altamura, *L'umanesimo del Mezzogiorno d'Italia* (Florence, 1941); Andres Soria, *Los humanistas de la corte de Alfonso el Magnanimo* (Granada, 1956); and Francesco Tateo, *L'umanesimo meridionale* (Bari, 1976). See also Tateo's *Tradizione e realtà nell'umanesimo italiano* (Bari, 1967).

[35] See Santoro's book-length contribution, "La cultura umanistica," in the *Storia di Napoli*, 7.115–291.

tory of Naples, long and unduly neglected as a subject of research by Renaissance scholars. In the second place, it also seeks to add texture to the understanding of Italian humanism by examining the work and thought of humanists operating in a specific political context. Finally, the effort to interpret the political and cultural history of Naples in the light of the more general experience of fifteenth-century Italy will lead to an improved understanding of Renaissance civilization in general.

The study proceeds by investigation of several themes that permit direct examination of the connecting points between the realm of ideas and the world of politics. The first theme, royal patronage of cultural figures, examines the financial and professional relationships between the Aragonese kings of Naples and their protégés. Issues addressed here include royal tastes and cultural preferences, but also, more importantly, royal investment in culture and the returns that the kings of Naples received from their investments. The second theme, clientage and career prospects for humanists in Renaissance Naples, deals with similar issues, but from the viewpoint of men of culture rather than their royal patrons. Considerable documentation survives to illuminate the careers of five Neapolitan humanists, the tasks they undertook, the fortunes they amassed, the powers they accumulated, the influence they wielded, and the legacies they left. Analysis of their experiences will lead to an understanding of the benefits derived by humanists themselves from their relationships with the Aragonese kings of Naples. The third theme, the development of a realistic approach to politics and statecraft, deals not so much with the history of ideas as with the influence exercised by events and experience on thought and culture. The readiness of the Neapolitan humanists to reconsider western political ethics becomes comprehensible only in the light of their practical experience as secretaries, advisers, and diplomats for the Aragonese kings. The fourth theme, the implications of humanism for Renaissance politics, expands somewhat the scope of the study. This theme brings into focus the contributions of the Neapolitan humanists to the development of a distinctive Renaissance culture and to the emergence of a secular political consciousness in early modern Europe. The book continues with an investigation of the extent to which humanist values and insights penetrated the Mezzogiorno. In studying the thought of five natives of the city or kingdom of Naples, it seeks to understand how humanism helped men of learning to interpret the turbulent political experience of Italy during the late fifteenth and early sixteenth centuries. A final, brief chapter assesses the contributions made by Neapolitan humanists to humanism as a cultural movement and to the broader cultural history of early modern Europe.

The study begins on a more modest level, however, with an analysis of the material and monetary relationships between the Aragonese kings and their cultured clients.

2

Patterns of Patronage

O NLY THOSE adorned by letters deserve to be called true kings and princes"—or so the humanist historian Flavio Biondo informed King Alfonso in an elegant epistle of 1443. Biondo wrote Alfonso in order to request the loan of chronicles and documents bearing on the history of Spain. Alongside praise of Alfonso's military accomplishments, he argued the importance of history and letters for men of action who want the memory of their deeds to survive. Think of all the Roman emperors who dominated Europe, Africa, and Asia, Biondo said, but whose names have fallen into oblivion because they neglected arts and letters. Consider by contrast the legacy of emperors like Augustus, Trajan, and Hadrian, who cultivated men of letters and thereby ensured themselves a favorable reputation.[1] Biondo's encouragement happened to coincide with Alfonso's personal interests and tastes: indeed, Alfonso rewarded men of culture so lavishly that even in his own day he had earned his cognomen, the Magnanimous. Meanwhile, the duty of princes to nurture literature and scholarship became something of a commonplace theme of humanists based in Naples as well as in other parts of Italy.

The study of patron-client relationships in early modern Europe developed impressively in the 1970s and 1980s. Most analyses have concentrated on the fine arts, but historians today seem increasingly interested in studying the role of patronage in politics,

[1] *Scritti inediti e rari di Biondo Flavio*, ed. B. Nogara (Rome, 1927), pp. 147–53, esp. pp. 150–53.

religion, and literary culture, as well as in the arts.[2] Recent scholarship has shown that the analysis of patron-client relationships can enrich historical understanding in several ways. In the first place, most obviously, it becomes possible to gauge the influence of patrons on the activity or production of their protégés. This information not only helps to explain the form or content of specific works, but also can illuminate the general theme of tradition and innovation. In the second place, less obviously but equally importantly, this sort of analysis enables the historian to clarify the social history, as it were, of clients. It throws light on the status of clients, for example, on the degree to which they influenced their patrons, and on their efforts to lead satisfying and purposeful careers. Finally, the study of patronage and clientage can contribute to the understanding of social and cultural history construed in a broader sense by helping to account for changes in tastes and values. If Gothic art and feudal chivalry yielded their places to Renaissance art and a bourgeois ethic, patrons certainly helped to bring about the transformations.

This threefold set of concerns helps to structure much of the following study. For the moment, however, analysis concentrates on the cultural tastes, interests, and needs of the Aragonese monarchs of Naples. Emphasis falls on the kings because the monarchy figured as the only significant source of patronage in Aragonese Naples. The barons of the Mezzogiorno evinced little interest in high culture. Only rarely did private individuals, like Antonello Petrucci, support literature or scholarship, and even then their patronage paled when compared to that of the Aragonese kings of Naples. Neapolitan patronage thus developed along much simpler lines than that in most of the other Italian states. In Venice, for example, aristocrats offered multiple opportunities to men of culture, both through private initiative and through state institutions; in Rome, numerous households of popes, cardinals, and in-

---

[2] For a sampler of recent studies see Guy Fitch Lytle and Stephen Orgel, eds., *Patronage in the Renaissance* (Princeton, 1982).

dependently wealthy men served as sources of patronage; in Florence, an extraordinarily heterogeneous group of merchants, bankers, aristocrats, and others supported humanists, artists, and musicians. Cultural patronage in Naples most closely resembled that in despotic states like Ferrara and Milan, where there arose little competition for the princely regimes as arbiters of taste and patrons of art and learning.[3] In the case of Naples, then, as in those of the despotic states, cultural patronage depended heavily on the private interests and public needs of the ruling prince.

Before exploring these points, however, the problem of source material deserves some comment. The Neapolitan archives have sustained heavy losses over the centuries, and materials from the Aragonese period have suffered much more severely than those from other ages. Insurrections in 1647 and 1701 resulted in the loss of most of the Aragonese chancellery registers—perhaps as much as 90 percent of those stored in Naples. An especially pointless act of wartime vandalism led to the destruction by fire of almost all the remaining registers in 1943.[4] A rich lode of sources

[3] On the general question of cultural patronage in Renaissance Italy, see Peter Burke, *Culture and Society in Renaissance Italy, 1420–1540* (New York, 1972), pp. 75–111; and the provocative, but somewhat overstated interpretation of Lauro Martines, *Power and Imagination: City-States in Renaissance Italy* (New York, 1979), pp. 218–40. On patronage in individual cities, see Margaret L. King, *Venetian Humanism in an Age of Patrician Dominance* (Princeton, 1986), pp. 49–76; John F. D'Amico, *Renaissance Humanism in Papal Rome: Humanists and Churchmen on the Eve of the Reformation* (Baltimore, 1983), pp. 3–88; Gene A. Brucker, *Renaissance Florence* (New York, 1969), pp. 213–30; Werner L. Gundersheimer, *Ferrara: The Style of a Renaissance Despotism* (Princeton, 1973), passim; and two articles by Eugenio Garin: "La cultura milanese nella prima metà del XV secolo," in *Storia di Milano*, 16 vols. (Milan, 1953–66), 6.545–608; and "La cultura milanese nella seconda metà del XV secolo," in *Storia di Milano*, 7.539–97. For a survey of Aragonese cultural policy, see Santoro, "La cultura umanistica," pp. 128–44.

[4] Jole Mazzoleni, *Le fonti documentarie e bibliografiche dal sec. X al sec. XX conservate presso l'Archivio di Stato di Napoli*, 2 vols. (Naples, 1974–78), 1.ix–x, 59–60; also the same author's introduction to his edition of the *Regesto della cancelleria aragonese di Napoli* (Naples, 1951), pp. ix–xiii. On the wartime loss, see also Riccardo Filangieri, "Report on the Destruction by the Germans, September 30, 1943, of the Depository of Priceless Historical Records of the Naples State Ar-

bearing on patron-client relationships in Aragonese Naples has thus vanished forever.

Yet by a variety of routes, other materials have come down to the present that make it possible to embark upon an analysis of these relationships. Although most documents preserved in Naples have perished, including almost all the materials produced after 1458, most of the registers produced by the chancellery of Alfonso the Magnanimous survive in the Archivo de la Corona de Aragón in Barcelona.[5] Furthermore, archivists published notices and brief descriptions of many documents before their destruction. While not as valuable as the original documents, the resulting information provides a considerable amount of raw information that illuminates patron-client relationships.[6] Meanwhile, other scholars have published the complete texts of several registers, almost all of which later perished. While most useful for issues discussed in later chapters, these sources occasionally throw light on the theme of this chapter as well.[7] Finally, a wealth of information survives in various writings of the humanists and other cultural figures—in their letters, treatises, histories, and perhaps most importantly in their prefaces and dedications to manuscripts and early printed works that they prepared for their patrons. All these categories of sources together make it possible

---

chives," *American Archivist*, 7 (1944), 252–55. I derive the 90 percent figure from A. Messer, ed., *Le codice aragonese* (Paris, 1912), pp. lxxxiv–xc. Writing before the incident of 1943, Messer reported 50 surviving volumes of registers out of more than 497 produced in Ferrante's chancellery.

[5] Ruggero Moscati, "Ricerche su gli atti superstiti della cancelleria napoletana di Alfonso d'Aragona," *Rivista storica italiana*, 65 (1953), 540–52. Alan Ryder's study of Neapolitan institutions under Alfonso depends heavily on these materials: *The Kingdom of Naples Under Alfonso the Magnanimous* (Oxford, 1976).

[6] I have in mind such publications as C. Minieri Riccio, "Alcuni fatti di Alfonso I. d'Aragona," *ASPN*, 6 (1881), 1–36, 231–58, 411–61; and Erasmo Percopo, "Nuovi documenti su gli scrittori e gli artisti dei tempi aragonesi," *ASPN*, 18 (1893), 527–37, 784–812; 19 (1894), 376–409, 561–91, 740–79; 20 (1895), 283–335.

[7] Mazzoleni, ed., *Regesto della cancelleria aragonese di Napoli*; Messer, ed., *Le codice aragonese*; Trinchera, ed., *Codice aragonese*; Volpicella, ed., *Instructionum liber*.

to perceive with reasonable clarity the patterns of patronage and clientage that took shape in Renaissance Naples.

Alfonso the Magnanimous and Renaissance Culture

Many sources testify to the deep, traditional piety of Alfonso the Magnanimous. According to Panormita, one of the most prominent humanists at his court, Alfonso washed and kissed the feet of sixty paupers on Holy Thursday of each year, then fed and clothed each one before sending him away with money. The record of a financial document lends at least partial credence to this story: on 20 April 1443, Alfonso ordered ten sets of clothes, including shirts, coats, and shoes, intended for ten paupers scheduled to have their feet washed on Holy Thursday.[8] Both Panormita and Vespasiano da Bisticci recorded the further fact that Alfonso had memorized the Bible and often read Nicholas of Lyra's commentaries.[9]

The undeniable fact of Alfonso's traditional piety, however, must not obscure the equally clear truth that Alfonso ranked as one of the most knowledgeable and important connoisseurs of humanism and Renaissance culture. Benedetto Croce somehow managed to lose sight of this point in portraying Alfonso as an uncouth provincial, a semibarbarian rustic who never adjusted to the sophistication of fifteenth-century Italy.[10] But from his own time until the present day, other commentators have spoken with a near-unanimous voice on Alfonso's appreciation for Italian as well as Spanish culture and on his importance as a patron of humanism in particular. Alfonso certainly hoped to gain political and diplo-

[8] Panormita, *De dictis et factis Alphonsi regis* (Basel, 1538), p. 107; Minieri Riccio, "Alcuni fatti di Alfonso," pp. 236–37.

[9] Panormita, *De dictis et factis*, p. 41; Vespasiano da Bisticci, *Le vite*, ed. A. Greco, 2 vols. (Florence, 1970–76), 1.84–86.

[10] *La Spagna nella vita italiana durante la Rinascenza*, 2d ed. (Bari, 1922), pp. 33–54.

matic advantages through his humanists, but personal taste also goes a long way toward explaining Alfonso's cultural patronage.

In his collection of anecdotes on Alfonso's character and career, Panormita speaks of numerous incidents that demonstrate Alfonso's appreciation of letters and learning. When told of an unnamed Spanish king's opinion that noblemen ought to avoid letters, for example, Alfonso replied passionately that he considered such teaching worthy of a cow, not a king. Alfonso adopted an open book as his personal emblem, and he paraphrased Plato in holding that "kings ought to be learned men themselves, or at least lovers of learned men." Alfonso did not even allow the inconveniences of war to interfere with his literary interests: he set aside time each day, even while encamped on the battlefield, for Panormita or another humanist to read to him from Livy or Caesar. At one point during the siege of Caiazzo in 1441, Alfonso and Panormita became deeply engaged in a discussion of the ancient Portuguese hero, Viriatus, who for almost a decade employed guerilla tactics to prevent the Roman conquest of Farther Spain. When the prefect of the camp approached on his horse and interrupted the conversation, Alfonso sternly rebuked him. "When dealing with matters of literature or ancient history," Alfonso said, "there is no place for men of arms, but rather for men of togas." When the prefect had excused himself, Alfonso and Panormita continued their discussion of Viriatus, whom Alfonso called an Iberian Romulus.[11] It is certainly possible that Panormita exaggerated the truth in telling such stories as these about his patron. Yet the basic point of the stories—Alfonso's deep, sincere interest in literature and learning—seems well established by the large number of the stories and by their widespread occurrence in works of Vespasiano and others as well as Panormita.

In any case, the proof of Alfonso's importance as a patron of humanism does not depend solely upon literary evidence. A variety

[11] Among many other passages of Panormita's *De dictis et factis*, see pp. 2, 3–4, 6, 13–14, 40, and 111 for the anecdotes referred to here.

of documentary and other sources throw considerable light on two significant, quasi-institutional frameworks of support—the court and the library—that humanists depended upon during Alfonso's reign.

The importance of the court as a source of patronage will become most clear in the next chapter, which examines in detail the careers of five humanists as secretaries, historians, and ambassadors. For the moment I wish to make some more general points about the court and cultural figures employed there. Vespasiano says that in the last year of his life, Alfonso spent twenty thousand ducats on men of learning.[12] Vespasiano no doubt obtained this figure, like most of his other information on Alfonso, from his close friend Giannozzo Manetti. It most likely did not include wages paid to marginal literary figures like Gaspare Pellegrino, Alfonso's physician since at least 1437, who in 1443 received a monthly salary of ninety ducats, and who about the same time wrote a history of Alfonso's deeds through the conquest of Naples.[13] It certainly did not include wages paid to craftsmen like Costantino de Tanti, an organ builder who in 1451 received an annual salary of three hundred ducats.[14] Even if Vespasiano exaggerated the amount of Alfonso's cultural expenditures, the king clearly took seriously the obligation urged on him by humanists to support literature and scholarship. Even documents bear witness to this point: the privilege appointing Geronimo Guarino (son of the educator Guarino da Verona) to a position as royal secretary emphasizes the point that princes must encourage men of talent to develop their skills in hopes that they will receive honor, praise, glory, and reward.[15]

Numerous such men of talent sought Alfonso's encouragement.

---

[12] *Le vite*, 1.91, 101.

[13] See Minieri Riccio, "Alcuni fatti di Alfonso," pp. 8, 242 on Pellegrino's service as physician. His account of Alfonso's deeds remains in manuscript in the BNN, MS IX. C. 22.

[14] Minieri Riccio, "Alcuni fatti di Alfonso," p. 412.

[15] Ryder, *Kingdom of Naples Under Alfonso the Magnanimous*, pp. 222–23, citing ACA, Reg. 2912, fol. 143r.

Besides the humanists discussed in the next chapter, who spent many years in Naples—Panormita, Valla, Facio, Manetti, and Pontano—a large number of prominent literary men enjoyed short-term support at Alfonso's court. Author of a poetic work glorifying Alfonso's victory and triumphal entry into Naples, Porcellio Pandoni obtained an appointment in 1450 as royal secretary and poet at an annual salary of three hundred ducats. He left Naples soon thereafter, possibly because of tensions with Panormita, but returned briefly during the reign of Ferrante. The Milanese humanist Pier Candido Decembrio lived intermittently in Naples between 1443 and 1458. In 1456 he bragged to Francesco Filelfo that he received an annual salary of six hundred ducats, but there exists no confirmation of his claim. Filelfo himself thought seriously about seeking a Neapolitan post in the late 1440s and early 1450s. He discussed the possibility several times in correspondence with Iñigo de Avalos, Alfonso's chamberlain and an influential courtier. Indeed, Filelfo traveled to Naples in the summer of 1453 and met several times with Alfonso, who crowned him with the poet's laurel just before Filelfo returned to his post in Milan. The humanist historian Flavio Biondo spent several months in Naples in 1451 and 1452; he certainly enjoyed Alfonso's hospitality, though I know of no evidence that he received financial support.[16]

Not only Italians, but also Greeks sought to benefit from Alfonso's patronage. The Greek humanist George of Trebizond received from Alfonso six hundred ducats annually from 1452 until 1455. He dedicated many translations to Alfonso during that period, though he had produced most of them before going to Naples, and in some cases had previously dedicated them to other patrons! His

---

[16] The strong point of Andres Soria, *Los humanistas de la corte de Alfonso el Magnanimo* (Granada, 1956) is clarification of Alfonso's relations with these and other humanists. See also de Marinis, *La biblioteca*, 1.1–11, and Ennio I. Rao, "Alfonso of Aragon and the Italian Humanists," *Esperienze letterarie*, 4 (1979), 43–57. On Porcellio see especially Percopo, "Nuovi documenti," 20 (1895), 317–26; and Ugo Frittelli, *Gianantonio de' Pandoni, detto il "Porcellio"* (Florence, 1900). For Filelfo's correspondence with Iñigo de Avalos, see his *Epistolarum familiarium libri* XXXVII (Venice, 1502), esp. fols. 42v, 48v, 64rv.

compatriot, Theodore Gaza, also found support at Naples: he lived there on an annual pension from 1455 until Alfonso's death in 1458, during which time he dedicated to the king his Latin translation of Chrysostom's *De incomprehensibili Dei natura* and to Panormita his version of Aelian's tactical work, *De instruendis aciebus*. Other humanists with independent means of support did not seek Alfonso's patronage, but paid goodwill visits to Naples—Cardinal Enea Silvio Piccolomini in 1456, for example, and the Greek Cardinal Bessarion in 1457.[17]

In one case, that of Leonardo Bruni, Alfonso did not succeed in his efforts to attract a famous humanist to his court. Alfonso had admired Bruni's work from the time preceding his victory over Naples. In August 1440 he learned that Bruni had recently completed his translation of Aristotle's *Politics*, and he wrote from Gaeta urgently requesting a copy of the work and promising to base his rule on its precepts. Bruni delayed sending the work until he could have it corrected and recopied, but in March 1441 Alfonso sent a special emissary to Florence to collect it, along with a highly laudatory letter that Bruni sent with the translation. In October 1442 Bruni addressed Alfonso again, this time to congratulate him on the successful conclusion of his siege of Naples. As an especially fitting token of his congratulations, he sent Alfonso also an excerpt from his recently completed history of the Goths. He chose the section discussing Belisarius' method of entering Naples—through an aqueduct—employed also by Alfonso almost a millennium later. Though they never met, Alfonso and Bruni enjoyed a cordial epistolary relationship; and since Bruni died in 1444, the friendship did not suffer from the tensions and outright

[17] In general, see again the works of Soria and de Marinis cited in the previous note. On George of Trebizond, see especially John Monfasani, *George of Trebizond: A Biography and a Study of His Rhetoric and Logic* (Leiden, 1976), pp. 114–36. For George's dedications to Alfonso, see John Monfasani, ed., *Collecteana Trapezuntiana: Texts, Documents, and Bibliographies of George of Trebizond* (Binghamton, N.Y. 1984), pp. 89–100. On Theodore Gaza, see Deno J. Geanakoplos, "Theodore Gaza, a Byzantine Scholar of the Palaeologan 'Renaissance' in the Italian Renaissance," *Medievalia et Humanistica*, n.s. 12 (1984), 61–81.

war that divided Naples and Florence over the Milanese succession (1447–1453). Yet Bruni did not accept Alfonso's offers, however generous, to take a position at the court in Naples—ostensibly because of his age and health, though as a staunch and active republican, Bruni might also have worried about difficulties in adjusting to the leisurely and scholarly life of a courtier.[18] In any case, despite the failure to attract Bruni to Naples, Alfonso's court hosted at least for a short term several of the most prominent humanists of mid-fifteenth-century Italy.

Though technically a part of the court, the royal library operated in such a special manner and filled such distinctive functions that it deserves particularly close attention. Alfonso had acquired a large and impressive collection of books even before leaving Spain, as numerous documents bear witness.[19] Only upon completing his victory over Naples, however, did he introduce a high degree of organization into the library. Housed in the early days in the Castel Capuano, the library moved after its restoration into the Castelnuovo, where it occupied a large room on an upper floor overlooking the Bay of Naples. Employees of the library included not only librarians, but also copyists, illuminators, and bookbinders. Perhaps most famous of them was Giacomo Curlo, a Genoese copyist who also had literary ambitions. He completed the translation of Arrian begun by his close friend Bartolomeo Facio, and he produced on his own account an epitome of Donatus' commentary on Terence and a Latin poem on the victory enjoyed by his Genoese friend Paolo Campofregoso over the French. Alfonso lavished money on the library, which has acquired a reputation not

[18] On the general relationship between Alfonso and Bruni, see Vespasiano, *Le vite*, 1.478; and Panormita, *De dictis et factis*, p. 58. See also their letters published in A. Gimenez Soler, ed., *Itinerario del Rey Don Alonso de Aragón y de Nápoles* (Saragossa, 1909), pp. 179–80, 185; Bruni's *Humanistisch-philosophische Schriften*, ed. H. Baron (Leipzig, 1928), pp. 144, 176, 214, 216; and Bruni's *Epistolarum libri VIII*, ed. L. Mehus, 2 vols. (Florence, 1741), 2.130–34, 165–66.

[19] Ramon d'Alos-Moner, "Documenti per la storia della biblioteca di Alfonso il Magnanimo," in *Miscellanea Francesco Ehrle*, 5 vols. (Rome, 1924), 5.390–422.

only for its cultural content, but also for the artistic quality of the works copied, illuminated, and bound there.[20]

The library served as the site of two special activities during Alfonso's reign: the literary seance and the education of promising Neapolitan youngsters. Adamo di Montaldo described the literary sessions in an oration praising Alfonso to Pope Calixtus III.[21] After eating dinner, Adamo said, Alfonso customarily retired to the library, where he took great delight in listening to learned men discuss literary and historical issues. Following the discussion, Alfonso served fruit and wine, and he himself enjoyed entertainment provided by actors or fools. The discussions themselves could become quite spirited, and on more than one occasion they were the forum for bitter disputes between humanists who sought to display their learning and gain credit with Alfonso. One of these disagreements, discussed in the next chapter, helped to fuel a controversy that raged between the major humanists at Alfonso's court: Lorenzo Valla battled Bartolomeo Facio and Panormita on literary, historical, and stylistic questions, several of which emerged as controversial points during debates in the library.

The library played a more important social role during Alfonso's reign as a school. Alfonso recognized the need for advanced education—in 1434 he founded the University of Catania—but he did not promote actively the *Studio* (University) of Naples. The Studio had closed probably at the death of Queen Giovanna II in 1435. Alfonso reopened it without much fanfare in 1451, but allowed it to close again in 1456 or 1457. Only in the reign of Ferrante did the Studio develop into an integral part of Neapolitan society.[22] Meanwhile, however, Alfonso had provided for deserv-

---

[20] For the best information on the Aragonese library at Naples, see the six volumes of de Marinis, *La biblioteca* (4 vols.) and *Supplemento* (2 vols.).

[21] The oration is edited in de Marinis, *La biblioteca*, 1.225–27.

[22] Remigio Sabbadini, *Storia documentata dell'Università di Catania* (Catania, 1898); Michele Catalano, *Storia documentata della R. Università di Catania* (Catania, 1913); Ercole Cannavale, ed., *Lo Studio di Napoli nel Rinascimento* (Naples, 1895); Riccardo Filangieri, "L'età aragonese," in *Storia dell'Università di Napoli* (Naples, 1924), pp. 151–99.

ing students to develop their intellectual talents in a rather special way. In August 1453 Alfonso paid fifty ducats to one of his librarians, Juan Torres, for the maintenance of several unnamed students in his care. In December of that year he hired Melchiore Miralles, master of theology, to teach the boys grammar in the library. In October 1455 he sent Miralles and three students to study theology at Paris.[23]

Alfonso's investment in the education of deserving students returned dividends in at least two ways. In the first place, his reputation benefited handsomely. Panormita praised Alfonso for his liberality in enabling poor youths to study rhetoric and philosophy, also for his piety in encouraging the study of theology. Similarly, Pontano recalled Alfonso's generosity from the distance of many years and mentioned it as an example of his admirable liberality.[24]

But Alfonso's investment in education also returned more concrete dividends to the Aragonese dynasty of Naples. Several sources make it possible to identify Francesco del Tuppo as one of the students who attended lessons in the library during the mid-1450s. His name occurs in several documents that provided for students' clothing and expenses during the period from 1443 to 1456.[25] Furthermore, Francesco himself referred to his education some twenty years after leaving the school in the library. He formed a partnership about 1473 with Sisto Riessinger, the Mezzogiorno's first printer, who had arrived in Naples about 1470. In May 1477 the partners published an edition of Giovanni da Imola's *Repetitio de iure iurando*, and Francesco supplied a preface dedicating the work to King Ferrante. Praise of Alfonso made up a large part of this preface and provided Francesco with the opportunity to recall his education in the magnificently appointed royal

---

[23] Minieri Riccio, "Alcuni fatti di Alfonso," pp. 423, 428, 437.

[24] Panormita, *De dictis et factis*, pp. 55–56; Giovanni Pontano, *I trattati delle virtù sociali*, ed. F. Tateo (Rome, 1965), pp. 37–38, 191.

[25] See the appendix of documents published in Alfredo Mauro, *Francesco del Tuppo e il suo "Esopo"* (Città di Castello, 1926), esp. nos. 1–12, pp. 227–30.

library. Alfonso promised great things to the young scholar: "Study, Francesco, study," Alfonso told him, "for the position I have arranged for you requires a man of learning."[26] In fact Alfonso did not live long enough to benefit by Francesco's services, but later pages will demonstrate his loyalty to the Aragonese dynasty and his particular value to Ferrante during the aftermath of the second barons' revolt.

Besides the two more or less institutionalized sources of support for cultural figures, Alfonso also rewarded humanists and others handsomely on an ad hoc basis when they presented him with some especially impressive work. No doubt the most famous such case concerned Poggio Bracciolini's Latin translation of Xenophon's *Cyropaedia*. Poggio completed his work about 1446 and composed a letter dedicating it to Alfonso in 1447. The translation immediately came under attack by critics in Florence, Venice, and Naples. Meanwhile, the death of Francesco Sforza led to war between Alfonso and Florence by the autumn of 1447. As a result of these circumstances, Poggio the Florentine received no immediate reward for his labor. There ensued a long exchange of correspondence between Poggio and Bartolomeo Facio, his closest supporter in Naples. Poggio felt himself so shabbily treated that he scratched Alfonso's name out of his own manuscript copy of the translation. Only after the conclusion of peace between Naples and Florence (June 1450) did the situation improve. Alfonso provided a lavish reward for Poggio—four hundred *alfonsini* (gold coins), worth six hundred ducats—and Poggio restored Alfonso's name in his personal copy of the translation.[27] Many other literary and scholarly figures also dedicated works to Alfonso in hopes of receiving favors of some sort: in an incomplete list concentrating on

[26] Francesco's preface is edited in Mariano Fava and Giovanni Bresciano, *La stampa a Napoli nel XV secolo*, 3 vols. (Leipzig, 1911–13), 2.30–32.

[27] See the correspondence published in Facio's *De viris illustribus liber*, ed. L. Mehus (Florence, 1745), pp. 98–101; and in Poggio's *Opera omnia*, ed. R. Fubini, 4 vols. (Turin, 1963–69), 4.671–77. Vespasiano mentions the amount of Poggio's reward in *Le vite*, 1.546–47.

particularly important items that still survive, Tammaro de Marinis mentioned fifty manuscripts prepared especially for Alfonso.[28]

Patronage of humanists and other cultural figures by various means—at court, through the library, or on an ad hoc basis—cost Alfonso a great deal of money, perhaps even the twenty thousand ducats that Vespasiano said he spent during his last year of life. Surviving sources unfortunately do not permit documentation of this figure, but it bears pointing out that for the most part, salaries of Neapolitan cultural figures compared favorably with those drawn in other Italian states during the mid-fifteenth century. Humanist teachers in Venetian schools earned between 100 and 200 ducats annually from the mid-fifteenth century to the early sixteenth century, while salaries of official secretaries might run between 50 and 200 ducats. During the same period, papal secretaries drew between 300 and 500 ducats per year, while professors at the University of Rome earned about 250 ducats.[29] The salaries that Alfonso paid to Porcellio Pandoni (300 ducats) and George of Trebizond (600 ducats) seem quite generous by this standard, not to mention the 400 *alfonsini* that the king bestowed as an extraordinary reward upon Poggio Bracciolini. The next chapter will show, furthermore, that the major humanists at Alfonso's court drew especially handsome salaries—as much as 900 ducats for Panormita in 1454, 900 for Giannozzo Manetti in 1455, and 500 for Bartolomeo Facio in 1457—besides benefiting from occasional extraordinary grants of money or property. Little wonder that Alfonso came to be known as the Magnanimous.

Whatever the precise figure of his cultural expenditures, the question naturally arises: what did Alfonso hope to gain from his investment? Surviving sources do not throw as much direct light on this as on other issues. To some extent detailed discussions in later chapters will make it possible to infer Alfonso's motives from

[28] De Marinis, *La biblioteca*, 1.8–9.
[29] King, *Venetian Humanism*, pp. 73, 88, 294–95; D'Amico, *Renaissance Humanism in Papal Rome*, pp. 27–28, 44, 59.

the work he expected his protégés to undertake. For the moment, it seems worthwhile at least to mention the two general categories of motives—the personal and the political—that help to explain Alfonso's lavish cultural expenditures. Many of the details on which this view of things rests, however, will emerge only in following chapters.

In the first place, Alfonso clearly enjoyed and respected humanist culture, so that the expectation of personal satisfaction encouraged him to patronize men of learning as lavishly as he did. Several humanists at his court, most notably Lorenzo Valla and Giannozzo Manetti, held positions as secretaries with few if any specific duties to perform. Alfonso commissioned both Valla and Bartolomeo Facio to produce historical works, but the humanists seem to have chosen for themselves most of their literary and scholarly projects. Panormita, Manetti, George of Trebizond, Theodore Gaza, and others do not appear to have received any specific commissions, but rather dedicated to Alfonso original works and translations as they became available. Alfonso's love of literature, interest in scholarship, pride in his library, and unconditional support for men of learning all point to personal interest as a powerful motive for his patronage of humanists and other cultural figures.

Political considerations, however, also exercised a large influence on Alfonso's patronage. As a foreigner, Alfonso no doubt hoped to gain some diplomatic advantage by employing Italian humanists in highly visible positions. The next two chapters will show that he relied especially on the talents of Panormita, who represented Alfonso's interests on several sensitive embassies, and who drafted a large amount of diplomatic correspondence for both Alfonso and Ferrante. Alfonso even had humanist script adopted for the first time in the Neapolitan chancellery, lest fifteenth-century Italian statesmen look with horror or condescension on documents composed in a gothic script long discarded by other chancelleries.[30] Furthermore, as a new monarch who had acquired his

[30] Nicola Barone, "Notizia della scrittura umanistica nei manoscritti e nei do-

throne by force of arms, Alfonso no doubt hoped also that humanists at his court would confer upon his house a sense of legitimacy that Queen Giovanna II, René d'Anjou, and Eugenius IV had all called into question. The several histories that Alfonso commissioned humanists to write on his family and deeds sought to portray his policy in the most favorable light, and in some cases their fame and popularity led to rather broad circulation, if not necessarily to widespread acceptance of the humanists' appreciative views of Alfonso. In any case, quite apart from his personal interest in humanist culture, Alfonso clearly patronized humanists in order to mobilize intellectual resources that could serve the political cause of his new dynasty.

Alfonso's spokesmen and glorifiers certainly succeeded in spreading his fame. Not only did Greek and Italian humanists seek positions at his court and echo his praise throughout the peninsula, but word of his character and qualities penetrated even to far distant lands. In July 1445, Duke Humphrey of Gloucester, England's most enthusiastic student of Italian humanism in the mid-fifteenth century, addressed Alfonso from Greenwich, seeking to win the king's goodwill. Duke Humphrey praised Alfonso's glory and military skills, but especially his virtues, his education in arts and letters, and his magnanimity. As a token of his admiration, he presented Alfonso with a gift copy of Livy, the king's favorite classical author, in French translation.[31] Alfonso's expenditures clearly bought him an impressive reputation.

Patronage and Policy Under Ferrante

In October 1471, the humanist Francesco Filelfo addressed an epistle to Iñigo de Avalos, a well-known and influential figure at the Neapolitan court. By 1471 Filelfo had lived in Milan for many

cumenti napoletani del XV secolo," *Atti della Reale Accademia di archeologia, lettere e belle arte*, 20 (1899), pt. 2, no. 2, pp. 1–14. See also Mazzoleni, ed., *Regesto della cancelleria aragonese di Napoli*, p. xvi.

[31] Mandell Creighton, "Some Literary Correspondence of Humphrey, Duke of Gloucester," *English Historical Review*, 10 (1895), 103–4.

years, and he had not visited the Mezzogiorno since his coronation as poet laureate in 1453. Yet Filelfo considered himself sufficiently informed on Neapolitan affairs to offer advice on Ferrante's cultural policy, or lack of it. He reminded Iñigo of Alfonso's interest in literary and scholarly matters, and he recalled a sophisticated discussion at Alfonso's court on the theme of human happiness. Filelfo himself had attended this session, where Panormita eloquently compared the views of various Greek and Latin philosophers, refuting some and approving others. At Ferrante's court, however, such literary refinement had disappeared: hunting had taken the place of scholarship. How could Ferrante develop into a man so different from Alfonso? How could Iñigo himself abandon his dedication to letters? Filelfo did not absolutely condemn recreational hunting, as long as it did not result in injury to serious literary and scholarly pursuits. But he registered clearly his disappointment that Iñigo had neglected civic affairs and letters while indulging himself in adolescent sports.[32]

Filelfo was one of the first men to suggest that Ferrante neglected cultural pursuits, but he was by no means the last. In a recent and very interesting study, Peter Burke asserts that with the death of Alfonso, cultural patronage in Naples stopped.[33] This view unfortunately represents a serious misunderstanding of cultural policy during Ferrante's reign. Ferrante did not support men of learning and culture on as grand a scale as did Alfonso. He did not attract famous humanists to Naples—though he did attempt to lure other cultural figures—and he did not inherit his father's reputation for magnanimity. The following pages will demonstrate, however, that royal patronage of culture continued on a generous, if not lavish scale during the reign of Ferrante.

More importantly, the following section will argue that the

---

[32] Filelfo, *Epistolarum familiarium libri XXXVII*, fols. 238v–239v.

[33] Burke, *Culture and Society in Renaissance Italy*, pp. 110–111. For a more accurate assessment of Ferrante's cultural policy, see Ernesto Pontieri, *Per la storia del regno di Ferrante I d'Aragona re di Napoli*, 2d ed. (Naples, 1969), pp. 128–33; and Jerry H. Bentley, "Il mecenatismo culturale di Ferrante I d'Aragona," *Esperienze letterarie*, 12 (1987).

patterns of patronage changed under Ferrante. Far from disappearing, royal support for cultural figures during Ferrante's reign assumed new as well as traditional forms and served new as well as old functions. To some extent Ferrante followed Alfonso's lead: he enriched the library, and he patronized humanists who engaged in both scholarly and political pursuits. Personal interest, however, moved him to support different kinds of cultural enterprise: he commissioned Italian rather than Latin writings, and he exhibited an even stronger interest in music than in literary culture. Furthermore, political considerations encouraged Ferrante to invest resources in altogether different cultural activities: his interest in law helps to explain his reopening of the Studio, and his need to disseminate laws and propaganda led him to support the work of early printers in Naples.

It is difficult to see how anyone could ever have doubted Ferrante's basic interest in cultural activities. Ferrante received his education from Panormita and Facio, among others, and he participated in the literary seances held in the library. A very interesting document of 1459 illustrates the expectations of Neapolitan cultural figures in the early days after Alfonso's death, showing that humanists and others at court had high hopes that Ferrante would continue his father's generous cultural policy. The author, Giacomo Curlo, had served as chief copyist in the library since 1445, and in later years had also developed literary ambitions. At a literary seance attended by Ferrante and Panormita among others, Alfonso had encouraged Curlo to prepare an epitome of Donatus' commentary on Terence. In his preface dedicating the finished work to Ferrante, Curlo lamented the recent death of Alfonso, who died just as his patronage began to bear fruit. Curlo consoled himself first with the thought that Alfonso continued to live through all the literary works he had sponsored, and then through the hope that Ferrante would equal and surpass Alfonso as a patron of letters and learning.[34] The preface betrays a bit of anxiety concerning Fer-

[34] This preface was originally published in C. Minieri Riccio, *Biografie degli*

rante's cultural plans, but Curlo clearly thought it reasonable to hope that Ferrante would follow Alfonso's example.

Curlo need not have worried, for Ferrante recognized a basic commitment both to men of culture and to the institutions that supported them. The library, where Curlo himself worked, benefited handsomely from Ferrante's patronage. Tammaro de Marinis compiled a partial list of 142 manuscripts prepared especially for Ferrante, who in the course of his reign employed more than thirty scribes to copy yet other volumes.[35] A document from the hand of the humanist Giovanni Brancati, the chief librarian, suggests that Ferrante himself paid close attention to the library. The document, a memorandum composed about 1480 or 1481, possibly at Ferrante's request, offers advice as to procedures the library ought to follow with respect to acquisition of materials and employment of staff. Brancati kept Ferrante's financial interests in mind: he noted that Neapolitan copyists received higher salaries than those at Florence or Venice, and he advised that they produce more finished copy in compensation. But Brancati also cared about quality. He argued that the library should purchase only the best grades of Tuscan parchment and should employ only the most accurate copyists and most talented miniaturists. He advised specifically against the use of mediocre artists or inconsistent scribes, no matter what the savings, in his effort to maintain a library both well decorated and well stocked.[36]

The library to some extent reflected the fortunes of Ferrante's reign: it faced a serious threat in 1481 after the Turkish invasion of Otranto, but by the end of the decade enrichment of the library reflected the restored stability of the Regno. Ferrante desperately needed funds to finance the campaign to recover Otranto, since he

---

accademici alfonsini, detto poi pontaniani, dal 1442 al 1543 (Naples, 1881), pp. 375–88. De Marinis reprinted Minieri Riccio's transcription in La biblioteca, 2.57–60. He later presented a new edition, based on the recently rediscovered manuscript of Curlo's work, in Supplemento, 1.34–37.

[35] De Marinis, La biblioteca, 1.41–70, 74–75 n. 29.

[36] Ibid., 1.185, 191 n. 31, 251–53.

had just emptied his treasury while fighting in Tuscany after the Pazzi conspiracy. Thus on 19 January 1481 he pawned 199 manuscripts, 46 printed books, and a large quantity of jewels to a Florentine banker, Battista Pandolfini. Ferrante obtained 38,000 ducats for the deal and agreed that Pandolfini could dispose of the goods as he wished if Ferrante failed to repay the loan within one year. Duke Alfonso's operations against the Turks succeeded the following September. By 10 January 1482 Ferrante had redeemed his books and jewels, and all items pawned had returned safely to Naples.[37] The restored library prospered especially in the months following Ferrante's victory over the rebel barons in 1486. At least 260 manuscripts and printed books—and probably a great many more as well—found their way from the barons' confiscated estates into the royal library.[38]

Ferrante did not envision library expenses as a purely scholarly investment. Besides administering the library, Giovanni Brancati also provided Ferrante with various political services. A manuscript of his works in fact illustrates well the range of duties a talented humanist might assume at Ferrante's court. Apart from the memorandum on the library discussed above, the manuscript preserves ten other epistles and orations composed in the period from about 1468 to 1481. The works include, among other things, an oration praising Ferrante's virtues, another celebrating the marriage of his daughter Eleonora, a third congratulating Ferrante himself on the occasion of his second marriage, and two pieces of diplomatic correspondence justifying Ferrante's policies to the duke of Milan and the king of France.[39] Brancati's works will make further appearances in this and following chapters, where

---

[37] Tammaro de Marinis edited two documents that throw light on this episode, along with an introduction, in a pamphlet, *Per la storia della biblioteca dei re d'Aragona in Napoli* (Florence, 1909). The documents are reprinted, but without the introduction, in idem, *La biblioteca*, 2.187–92.

[38] De Marinis, *Supplemento*, 1.143–259.

[39] Valencia, BU, MS 774. On Brancati's life see the article in the *DBI*, 13.824–27.

they help to throw important light on the relation between politics and culture during Ferrante's reign.

Brancati's experience was not unusual: a similar pattern emerges from the activities undertaken by other humanists at Ferrante's court. Ferrante did not invest resources in humanists who engaged in pure scholarship, as Alfonso had done; but he provided posts for numerous humanists who could perform some more or less useful service. Transition from the lavish patronage of Alfonso to the more frugal and utilitarian policy of Ferrante caused some problems in the case of Panormita (as the next chapter will demonstrate), but the deaths of some humanists and the voluntary departures of others enabled Ferrante to alter the conditions of patronage with a minimum of difficulty. Lorenzo Valla had already left Naples for Rome in 1448, and in any case he predeceased Alfonso in 1457. George of Trebizond left Naples for Rome in order to resume his position as apostolic secretary in 1455. Bartolomeo Facio died in November 1457, some seven months before Alfonso. Theodore Gaza departed upon Alfonso's death. Giannozzo Manetti obtained continuation of support from Ferrante, but he survived Alfonso by only sixteen months, dying in October 1459. Of the major humanists at court, only Panormita and Giovanni Pontano survived Alfonso for a long term. Both men contributed a large amount of administrative, political, and diplomatic service for Ferrante, as Panormita had long done for Alfonso the Magnanimous, and both of them retained the posts originally awarded to them by Alfonso.

Humanists who arrived at court during Ferrante's reign enjoyed opportunities to pursue their scholarly interests, but they always performed some kind of useful service for the monarchy in exchange for their salaries. Porcellio Pandoni, who had earlier served Alfonso as secretary and poet, taught in the Studio when it reopened in 1465, but only for one year at a salary of 240 ducats. Constantine Lascaris joined him for a few months at an annual rate of 120 ducats. Giuniano Maio taught rhetoric and poetry at the Studio for twenty-three years (1465–1488) at a modest stipend of

30 to 40 ducats per year. In December 1490 his loyalty and lengthy service to the Aragonese won him a post as tutor to Don Pietro, second son of Duke Alfonso of Calabria, at an annual salary of 100 ducats. When Pietro unexpectedly died the following year, Ferrante named Maio a courtier at the same salary. Francesco Pucci, a Florentine student of Poliziano, taught rhetoric in the Studio from about 1485 at a salary of 40 ducats per year; in 1490 he received 100 ducats per year as librarian, a post he held until the Aragonese dynasty of Naples fell in 1501; even then he continued in Aragonese service as a secretary to Cardinal Ludovico d'Aragona (legitimate son of King Ferrante's bastard son Enrico). Giovanni Albino appeared in the household of Duke Alfonso in 1478 and served the duke as librarian and courtier from 1481. Meanwhile, he represented Ferrante's interests as a political secretary and diplomat charged with several sensitive missions.[40]

Thus Ferrante continued Alfonso's policies of enriching the royal library and patronizing humanists at the Neapolitan court. He made no provisions for sinecures, however, but expected humanists to perform some useful service. Nor did he reward humanists on as lavish a scale as his father had done. Only Panormita and Pontano earned large salaries—and even they did not always receive regular payments until Ferrante had stabilized the Regno in 1462. Meanwhile, humanist professors in the Studio earned considerably less than their counterparts in Venice and Rome, though they could hope to receive relatively generous rewards after a period of loyal service.

This does not mean, however, that Ferrante dismantled his father's program of patronage for humanists and men of culture. More important than his frugality and economy was the fact that

[40] For documents on these five humanists, see Percopo, "Nuovi documenti," 19 (1894), 390–409, 740–56; 20 (1895), 283–97, 317–26, 329–35. On Porcellio see also Frittelli, *Gianantonio de' Pandoni*; on Pucci, Mario Santoro, *Uno scolaro del Poliziano a Napoli: Francesco Pucci* (Naples, 1948); on Albino, the DBI, 2.12–13.

Ferrante encouraged humanists to undertake projects that appealed to his own tastes, which differed from those of his father.

Thus, much to the chagrin of learned men at the Neapolitan court, Ferrante encouraged humanists to produce vernacular translations rather than Latin compositions. Already in 1444 or 1445, Bartolomeo Facio prepared at Ferrante's request an Italian version of Isocrates' oration *Ad Nicoclem*—the first translation of Isocrates into Italian. Facio equipped the work with two Latin epistles addressed to Ferrante—one dedicating and the other concluding the work—and with two laudatory Latin orations—one in praise of Alfonso and the other celebrating Ferrante's virtues. In the letter of dedication, Facio fretted lest learned men consider it ridiculous to translate an eloquent orator like Isocrates into the vulgar tongue. He admitted seeing Italian translations of Latin prose and poetry in Florence, but conveyed clearly enough the point that these enterprises did not impress him. In his concluding epistle Facio pointed out that he produced the version as quickly as possible, suggesting once again that he did not consider translation into the vernacular a task befitting a humanist.[41] As a recent student of Facio's work has pointed out, this emphasis on Latin and disparagement of the vernacular was by no means disinterested advice. Facio and others hoped to ensure humanists a position of honor by emphasizing the importance of their special skills, most notably their control of Latin.[42]

Several pieces of surviving information throw interesting light on another project, an Italian translation of the elder Pliny's *Natural History*. The Florentine Neoplatonist Cristoforo Landino dedicated an Italian version of the work to Ferrante in the 1460s or early 1470s.[43] Sometime before 1473, Ferrante asked Giovanni

[41] Valencia, BU, MS 443 (formerly 727), fols. 2r–3r for the letter of dedication, fols. 17v–23r for the two orations, and fols. 23rv for the concluding epistle. Lucia Gualdo Rosa has edited the letter of dedication: see her *La fede nella "paideia": aspetti della fortuna europea di Isocrate nei secoli XV e XVI* (Rome, 1984), pp. 190–91.

[42] Gualdo Rosa, *La fede nella "paideia,"* pp. 35–38.

[43] It survives in the Escorial, MSS h. I. 2 and h. I. 3; also in published form as

Brancati to vet the translation and correct it if necessary. Soon thereafter Brancati addressed to Ferrante a long epistle containing a preliminary report on his work. He did not mention Landino by name, but referred to the translator as an eminent philosopher and author of a work *De anima*, who writes in "Etruscan" (i.e., Tuscan) dialect. There can be no doubt about the subject of his evaluation. After reading a large portion of the translation, he found that Landino added some things to Pliny, omitted other things, and misrepresented the sense of many passages. He asked Ferrante to relieve him of the charge to correct the translation—a task almost impossible to accomplish, Brancati said, because of the large and damaged volumes that contained its text, and because of the translator's difficult "Etruscan" idiom. (Brancati was a native of Policastro, deep in Calabria, near Cosenza.) Indeed, Brancati said he would prefer to translate all of Pliny afresh rather than review and correct Landino's work. He quickly attempted to avoid a major new commitment, however, arguing the general insignificance of vernacular literature: "I derive far more pleasure from a single verse of Latin than from all the books translated in this fashion." He approved vernacular translations only for dull, unlearned men, and he encouraged Ferrante to improve his command of Latin rather than rely on Italian versions of important works.

Brancati's ploy did not succeed. Ferrante altered his charge and directed Brancati to produce a fresh translation of Pliny rather than a correction of Landino's work. This is clear from a second epistle in which Brancati reported progress on his work. He had recently translated a section on bees that prompted moral reflection on the contrasting qualities of animals and men. Unlike men, bees exhibited no tendency toward ambition, envy, or cruelty. Meanwhile, Brancati said, Ferrante merited praise because of his special virtues: he deserved recognition as king of men, whom he ruled in harmony, just as the king of bees rules the insects in his

---

Pliny's *Historia naturale*, trans. C. Landino (Venice, 1535), among other editions. Cf. de Marinis, *La biblioteca*, 1.190 n. 28; 2.130–31.

own realm. (Renaissance bees were governed always by kings, not queens.)

Brancati translated Pliny not into Tuscan, but into *napoletano misto*—"mixed Neapolitan"—a refined form of Neapolitan dialect spoken at court and employed by a few writers, such as Diomede Carafa. He justified his use of dialect by the example of Livy and by his conviction that *napoletano misto* stood inferior to no language. Yet Brancati clearly did not enjoy his work. When he had completed his translation, he dedicated it to Ferrante with an epistle that emphasized the extreme difficulty of the task, but that affirmed Brancati's readiness to obey Ferrante, no matter how laborious the charge.[44] Thus from the beginning to the end of his work, Brancati made clear his lack of enthusiasm for the Italian translation of Pliny. Ferrante presumably suggested and perhaps even insisted that Brancati undertake and complete the project.

Other works, too, survive to illustrate Ferrante's preference for reading Italian rather than Latin. Giovanni Albino, for example, prepared a work for Ferrante excerpting the lives of famous men from Plutarch. For each figure included, Albino presented both a Latin and an Italian translation of Plutarch; two letters to Ferrante, one each at the beginning and at the end of the work, appear only in Italian.[45] Finally, an anonymous author and translator made even more clear the connection between the vernacular language and the pursuit of patronage during Ferrante's reign. The author had experienced Ferrante's generosity—so he said in his letter of dedication—and decided to send Ferrante an Italian translation of the so-called Aristeas' letter on the translators of the Sep-

[44] Brancati's first two epistles survive in the manuscript of his works cited above, Valencia, BU, MS 774, fols. 99v–121r and 121r–129r. Giovanni P. Carratelli edited excerpts representing the largest part of the letters in "Due epistole di Giovanni Brancati su la 'Naturalis historia' di Plinio e la versione di Cristoforo Landino," *AAP*, n.s. 3 (1949–50), 179–93. For Brancati's dedication of his completed translation to Ferrante, see Pliny's *Storia naturale*, trans. G. Brancati, ed. S. Gentile (Naples, 1974), 1.5–13.

[45] The work survives in two manuscripts: Biblioteca Nazionale di Firenze, MS Palatino 689; BNN, MS XII. E. 34.

tuagint. He stated openly that he intended for the work to serve the common good by appealing to men without Latin. After lauding Ferrante's justice, wisdom, and liberality, the author mentioned also another motive for his work, his hope to obtain a place at Ferrante's court:

> With a joyful heart, then, you will accept this book, which I send you as proof of my goodwill. In return I hope to receive from your majesty a reward much greater and more distinguished than my own gift. I do not hope for gold or silver—it is well known that you are liberal and magnanimous in sharing wealth with all the world, wheresoever and whenever there is need—but for an even greater and more precious reward. And this is that by your humanity you deign to receive me in the number of your faithful and benevolent servants.[46]

No other work known to me makes such an undisguised appeal for Ferrante's support, but a great deal of evidence shows that Ferrante geared his cultural patronage to his personal interests.

This point holds particularly true in the case of music. Alfonso had certainly supported musicians at court: he employed among others the highly talented Spanish composer, Juan Cornago, to whom he awarded the generous salary of three hundred ducats per year. Furthermore, he had pieces composed for both sacred and secular ceremonies: Cornago and others prepared new compositions for the celebrations at the Castelnuovo during Holy Week, and Alfonso ordered psalms composed by court musicians to be sung before and after battles.[47] Yet Alfonso clearly appreciated literary more than musical culture. Panormita said in one place that Alfonso sometimes dismissed his trumpeters in order to concentrate on his reading of Livy, and in another place that Alfonso oc-

---

[46] BAV, Ottob. lat. 1558, esp. fols. 2r and 4r of the letter of dedication.

[47] See Allan W. Atlas, *Music at the Aragonese Court of Naples* (Cambridge, 1985), esp. pp. 62–69 on Cornago; also Isabel Pope and Masakata Kanazawa, eds., *The Musical Manuscript Montecassino 871: A Neapolitan Repertory of Sacred and Secular Music of the Late Fifteenth Century* (Oxford, 1978), esp. pp. 45–46, 69–71.

casionally became so absorbed in his reading that he seemed not to hear the music of flutes and the sounds of dancers around him.[48]

Ferrante's interest in and commitment to music, by contrast, left no doubts in the minds of contemporaries. The Florentine humanist Aurelio Brandolini, who had taught letters briefly at Capua from 1478 to 1479, dedicated a poetic work in praise of music (*De laudibus musicae*) to Ferrante as the most enthusiastic of all ancient and modern devotees of music.[49] Aurelio's younger brother Raffaele also briefly served the Aragonese—he tutored Duke Alfonso of Bisceglie, an illegitimate son of King Alfonso II, about 1493 to 1495—and recorded Ferrante's interest in music. In a treatise of 1513 on music and poetry, Raffaele recalled the musical tastes of several fifteenth-century princes, including Borso d'Este, Lorenzo and Giovanni de' Medici, and Pope Pius II, besides Alfonso the Magnanimous and Ferrante. Of all these connoisseurs and patrons of music, Ferrante received by far the largest portion of Raffaele's attention for his various efforts: he had hired the best musicians from all over Europe at the highest salaries; he had sponsored public musical ceremonies; and he had maintained a private collection of all musical instruments, which he conserved in a large hall adorned also with paintings and sculpture. Though a native of Florence and a seeker of Medici patronage—Pope Leo X appointed him professor of rhetoric at the University of Rome and a chamberlain (*cubicularius*) in his own household—Raffaele described Lorenzo de' Medici in his treatise as an imitator of Ferrante's musical patronage.[50]

[48] Panormita, *De dictis et factis*, pp. 6, 11.

[49] See the letter of dedication to this work, edited from the manuscript at Lucca, in de Marinis, *La biblioteca*, 1.75–76. On his career see the DBI, 14.26–28; and Elisabetta Mayer, *Un umanista italiano della corte di Mattia Corvino: Aurelio Brandolini Lippo* (Rome, 1938), esp. pp. 11–16 for the Neapolitan portion of his career.

[50] The manuscript of the work *De musica et poetica* survives in Rome, Biblioteca Casanatense, MS 805; see esp. fols. 16v–18r on Ferrante. Adrien de la Fage edited excerpts from this manuscript in his *Essais de diphthérographie musicale* (Paris, 1864), pp. 61–67. On Raffaele Brandolini's career see the DBI, 14.40–42.

A certain amount of documentary evidence survives to demonstrate the basic truth of Raffaele's characterization of Ferrante as musical enthusiast. In late 1466 or early 1467 Ferrante recommended one Giovanni Orca, a trumpeter, for a position at the court of the duke of Modena. The reason for Orca's interest in Modena is unknown, but fifteenth-century musicians often moved from one court to another for a wide variety of personal and professional reasons. The duke of Modena declined Orca's services, however, and in January 1467 Ferrante expressed his disappointment that the duke had snubbed a musician whom Ferrante had attempted to aid. He addressed a formal, Latin letter to the duke that with withering irony "thanked" him for accepting Orca into his service:

> For your humanity and consideration, illustrious Duke, you place us greatly in your debt, so that we owe you many thanks. Not because of Giovanni, a man afflicted by disgusting and contemptible habits and therefore unworthy of your house, but rather because of the law of friendship that you so diligently and scrupulously observe toward us, so that not even in the smallest matters do you neglect to discharge your duties.

A few months later Ferrante addressed the interests of current, not former clients: upon learning that his trumpet corps did not cut a handsome figure, he sent two carefully packed silk banners for them to use on formal occasions.[51]

More significantly, Ferrante employed some of the most distinguished musicians and musical theorists in all of Europe. Franchino Gaffurio, one of the foremost musical humanists of the Quattrocento, spent several years in Naples during the late 1470s and early 1480s. While there he composed his *Theorica musicae* (published in 1480), in which he sought to revive classical musical

---

[51] Both documents appear in Trinchera, ed., *Codice aragonese*, 1.14, 185.

theory.[52] Meanwhile, Iohannes Tinctoris, a Flemish singer of note and one of the most important music theorists of the entire Renaissance period, spent about twenty years (ca. 1472–ca. 1492) at Ferrante's court. Like the humanists at Naples during Ferrante's reign, he served the king in several capacities. In 1475, at Ferrante's request, he translated the constitution of the Order of the Golden Fleece from French into Italian. Tinctoris held a degree in law, and it seems that he also provided Ferrante with legal advice from time to time. Most of his efforts, however, were devoted to music. He served as cantor at Ferrante's court, and he composed twelve theoretical treatises as well as numerous musical works during his Neapolitan residence. He dedicated two of his treatises to Ferrante, including one especially important work on counterpoint. He served also as musical tutor to Ferrante's daughter, Beatrice, to whom he dedicated three of his other theoretical treatises.[53] Ferrante obviously placed a great deal of confidence in Tinctoris' musical judgment, as is clear from a set of diplomatic instructions dated 15 October 1487 in which Ferrante sent Tinctoris to France and Burgundy to seek out an accomplished singer and bring him back to Naples, where he would assume a position in the royal chapel.[54]

Yet another set of documents illustrates Raffaele Brandolini's point that Ferrante offered extraordinarily generous salaries to attract the best musicians from all over Europe. The documents all concern the Fleming Alexander Agricola, one of the leading singers and composers of the late fifteenth century, a man whose talent

[52] On Gaffurio, see Claude V. Palisca, *Humanism in Italian Renaissance Musical Thought* (New Haven, 1985), esp. pp. 166–78, 191–232, 293–98; and Carlo Vecce, ed., *Gli umanisti e la musica: un'antologia di testi umanistici sulla musica* (Milan, 1985), pp. 83–95, esp. pp. 88–89 for the *Theorica musicae*.

[53] On Tinctoris' life, see Ronald Woodley, "Ioannes Tinctoris: A Review of the Documentary Biographical Evidence," *Journal of the American Musicological Society*, 34 (1981), 217–48. For a survey of his works, see the introduction to Tinctoris' *Opera theoretica*, ed. A. Seay (Rome, 1975), 1.7–26, esp. p. 7. I wish to thank Pamela Starr for drawing my attention to Tinctoris' significance.

[54] Volpicella, ed., *Instructionum liber*, p. 168.

placed him in the same class as Josquin des Prez and Heinrich Isaac. In 1491 he deserted his post at the court of King Charles VIII of France and traveled without permission in search of patronage in Florence and Naples. At King Charles's request, Ferrante returned him to France in June 1492. But he had listened with great pleasure to Alexander's singing, he said in his reply to Charles's request, and he expressed his interest in regaining the singer's services in the future. Over the next fifteen months Ferrante corresponded several times with his ambassador in Paris concerning Alexander. At first he offered 300 ducats per year for Alexander's services. By contrast, Josquin des Prez earned 200 ducats annually and Heinrich Isaac 120 ducats, both at the court of Ferrara, and most musicians of the period earned considerably less than these luminaries. Alexander evidently accepted the offer, but he never returned to Naples. By June 1493 Ferrante's diplomatic isolation forced him to devote all his resources to military preparations. Thus he wrote at least three times asking his ambassador to stall Alexander gently until Ferrante called for his transfer to Naples.[55] The rapidly degenerating political situation of 1493, Ferrante's death the following January, and the French invasion of 1494 all combined to thwart the arrangement. Ferrante's willingness to pay Alexander three hundred ducats per year, however, demonstrates the fundamental truth of Raffaele Brandolini's point: that Ferrante used high salaries to entice the best musicians to his court.

Personal taste explains Ferrante's encouragement of Italian

[55] See the documents in Trinchera, ed., *Codice aragonese*, 2.1.119, 282; 2.2.60, 202, 229. On Alexander's Italian career, see Martin Picker, "A Letter of Charles VIII of France Concerning Alexander Agricola," in Jan LaRue, ed., *Aspects of Medieval and Renaissance Music: A Birthday Offering to Gustave Reese* (New York, 1966), pp. 665–72; and Allan W. Atlas, "Alexander Agricola and Ferrante I of Naples," *Journal of the American Musicological Society*, 30 (1977), 313–19. For the salaries of other musicians in the late fifteenth and early sixteenth centuries, see Atlas, *Music at the Aragonese Court of Naples*, pp. 66–67. Once again, I wish to thank Pamela Starr for drawing my attention to the recent scholarly literature on Agricola.

translations and musical talent, but political considerations also influenced his cultural patronage. Ferrante's need for professional administrators and bureaucrats led to the reopening of the Studio of Naples, the most important institutional beneficiary of his cultural investments. With the resumption of instruction in 1465, the Studio became more integrated than ever before into the political life of the Regno. Humanists such as Giuniano Maio and Francesco Pucci taught literature, to be sure, but the new Studio in general emphasized legal education under the tutelage of lawyers like Alessandro d'Alessandro, against whom the humanist Giovanni Pontano lodged numerous complaints in later years. In 1478 Ferrante tightened his control over the institution in two ways: he made his confessor or chaplain responsible for the direct governance of the Studio, and he began to review and approve the roster of professors and subjects offered at the beginning of each academic year.[56] By these arrangements, Ferrante gained the opportunity to gear the programs of the Studio more directly toward the political and administrative needs of the kingdom.

Meanwhile, the early Neapolitan press benefited both indirectly and directly from Ferrante's policies. Sisto Riessinger set up the first printing shop in the Mezzogiorno about 1470, when he moved from his native Strasbourg to Naples. In the earliest days, Neapolitan printers flourished because of the demand for textbooks created by the Studio. The printers turned out hundreds of works of medicine, grammar, literature, astrology, theology, and philosophy, most of them intended for use by students. Legal textbooks and collections of laws, however, dominated the press in Quattrocento Naples. It goes without saying that the only sizable market for such works consisted of students pursuing degrees in law.[57] Thus Ferrante's support for the Studio redounded to the benefit of the early Neapolitan printers.

[56] Besides Cannavale, *Lo Studio di Napoli*, and Filangieri, "L'età aragonese," see also Santoro, "La cultura umanistica," pp. 145–58; and Carlo de Frede, *Studenti e uomini di leggi a Napoli nel Rinascimento* (Naples, 1957), esp. pp. 13–25.

[57] For biographical sketches of the fifteenth-century Neapolitan printers and

Some Neapolitan printers also benefited in more direct fashion from Ferrante's support. Sisto Riessinger and Arnold of Brussels both received citizenship at Naples, and Riessinger also obtained royal protection for the works he printed.[58] The career of Francesco del Tuppo, however, best illustrates the potential of the fifteenth-century press to benefit both the monarchy and the printer. After his early education in Alfonso's library, Francesco probably studied law. By 1473 he had established a partnership with Sisto Riessinger; by 1481 Riessinger had left Naples for Rome; Francesco then ran his own business until his death about 1501. He remained loyal to the Aragonese dynasty, and several documents illuminate the mutual advantages that Francesco and Ferrante derived from their relationship. In 1480 Ferrante granted Francesco a privilege that entitled him to sell his books anywhere in the Regno without hindrance of tolls or any other barrier to their free commerce. In 1487 Francesco received 120 ducats for printing in two hundred copies an account of the trials of Antonello Petrucci, his two sons, and Francesco Coppola, the principal leaders of the second barons' revolt. Between 1488 and 1490 he received a further 495 ducats for publishing one thousand copies of a work that presented transcripts from the interrogations of rebel barons arrested after the execution of the Petrucci and Coppola. In 1498 he received sixteen ducats for two smaller commissions, the printing and distribution of 102 royal laws (*pragmatiche*) and 150 complaints (*proteste*) of King Federico against the former prince of Salerno.[59]

---

bibliographies of their works, see Fava and Bresciano, *La stampa a Napoli*, esp. 2.1–127 for bibliographies of the most important printers. For a splendid analysis of the early printing industry at Naples, see Mario Santoro, "I primi decenni della stampa a Napoli e la cultura napoletana," in *Primo convegno dei bibliotecari dell'Italia meridionale* (Naples, 1956), pp. 13–28.

[58] Fava and Bresciano, *La stampa a Napoli*, 1.10–27, 47–56.

[59] On Francesco's life and career see Mauro, *Francesco del Tuppo*. See also the documents on his relations with Ferrante and Federico in Mauro's appendix, esp. nos. 15, 17–20, 34–35, pp. 231–34, 243. See also a recent and provocative argument that the early Italian printers in general depended heavily on patronage

Francesco's connections and loyalty to the Aragonese dynasty clearly helped him to secure the long-term benefits that successive kings bestowed upon him. Yet it bears pointing out, too, that the Aragonese kings of Naples recognized political opportunity offered by the press, even in these earliest days of the printing industry. Francesco's publication of transcripts from the rebel barons' trials and interrogations represents one of the earliest uses of the press for purposes of political propaganda. A later chapter will explore this episode in more detail, but for the moment it serves to demonstrate the point made earlier, that Ferrante encouraged the work of early Neapolitan printers partly because of the political advantages the press made available to him.

Like Alfonso, Ferrante gained significant benefits for his public and political relations by his patronage of humanists and other cultural figures. Particularly among Florentines Ferrante enjoyed an impressive reputation. Several Florentine cultural figures lived in Naples during Ferrante's reign: Francesco Pucci taught at the Studio and served as librarian from 1485 to 1501; Lorenzo Bonincontri lived in Naples from 1456 to 1475, during which time he and Giovanni Pontano developed a close friendship because of their mutual interest in astrology; Francesco Bandini spent only about two years in Naples, from 1474 to 1476, but he praised Naples and Ferrante in an elegant epistle (discussed in a later chapter) to an unnamed friend in Florence.[60] Ferrante's reputation extended not only to expatriates, but also to permanent residents of Florence. Ferrante enjoyed close relations with Vespasiano da Bisticci, for example, and he carried on a long personal correspondence with Lorenzo de' Medici.[61] In 1478 Marsilio Ficino sent two epis-

---

rather than the market: M. D. Feld,"A Theory of the Early Italian Printing Firm" *Harvard Library Bulletin*, 33 (1985), 341–77; 34 (1986), 294–332.

[60] On Pucci, see Santoro, *Uno scolaro del Poliziano a Napoli*; on Bonincontri, the *DBI*, 12.209–11; on Bandini, Paul O. Kristeller, "An Unpublished Description of Naples by Francesco Bandini," in his *Studies in Renaissance Thought and Letters* (Rome, 1969), pp. 395–410.

[61] For his relations with Vespasiano, see Trinchera, ed., *Codice aragonese*, 1.133–34, 359, 371, 403, 420; for his correspondence with Lorenzo, Ernesto

tles, along with moral and philosophical writings, to Cardinal Giovanni d'Aragona, Ferrante's third son. The second letter is especially charming: it describes a recent, miraculous "encounter" of Ferrante, Ficino, and Alfonso the Magnanimous, in which the late king delivered in angelic language a short philosophical oration. Ficino "translated" the work into a human tongue—Latin, specifically—and sent it to Naples. He asked Cardinal Giovanni to read the treatise and then to submit it to Ferrante. The work does not present advanced philosophical arguments, but rather summarizes Ficino's Neoplatonic views on a variety of topics, such as God, angels, the immortality of souls, providence, free will, and the like.[62] Still, it helps to prove the point that among Florentines, Ferrante enjoyed a highly favorable reputation—one that he could hardly have earned without his patronage of humanists and other cultural figures.

Cultural Patronage Under the Later Aragonese Kings of Naples

Alfonso II ruled Naples for only one year before he abdicated, Ferrandino for less than two years before he died, and Federico for less than four years before he surrendered to the French. During their brief reigns, all three men faced a continuous political and military threat compounded of French dynastic interests backed up by invasions, Spanish hopes of gaining influence through the tactic of fishing in troubled waters, and the Neapolitan barons' independent ambitions that led many to ally with one foreign invader or the other. As a result of these pressures, none of the last three Aragonese kings of Naples had the opportunity to develop or implement a coherent policy of cultural patronage. Yet a few sources survive to show that in spite of the difficulties they confronted, Al-

---

Pontieri, "La dinastia aragonese di Napoli e la casa de' Medici di Firenze (dal carteggio familiare)," *ASPN*, n.s. 26 (1940), 274–342; n.s. 27 (1941), 217–73.

[62] Marsilio Ficino, *Opera omnia* (Turin, 1959), 1.812–13, 816–20. I wish to thank Paul O. Kristeller for pointing this passage out to me.

fonso II, Ferrandino, and Federico continued in the tradition of Alfonso the Magnanimous to support humanists and other cultural figures.

All three men had humanists as tutors, advisers, secretaries, and diplomats. Giovanni Albino, mentioned above for his services to Ferrante, actually spent most of his Neapolitan career in the employment of the younger Alfonso. Albino and Panormita collaborated in Alfonso's education. While Panormita devoted most of his other efforts to Ferrante, Albino continued to serve Alfonso as secretary and diplomat. After 1481 he held the post—evidently a sinecure, in view of his many other duties—of chief librarian for Duke Alfonso's personal library. For his loyalty to the Aragonese dynasty even during the darkest days of the first French invasion, in 1497 he received as a benefice and reward the royally patronized church of Santa Maria de Corte in Castelluccio. While duke of Calabria, Alfonso chose the humanist poet Gabriele Altilio to educate his son Ferrandino. Altilio undertook numerous diplomatic journeys on behalf of Aragonese interests; and in 1494 he assumed the post of political secretary when Ferrandino became duke of Calabria. He also served King Ferrandino loyally until the French occupation of Naples. At that point he retired from politics, moved to Policastro, and even gave up poetry in favor of theology. Meanwhile, Ferrandino's uncle Federico received his education from the humanist Luigi Galluccio, better known as Elisio Calenzio. Originally a student of law at Naples, Calenzio abandoned the Studio when his father died. He spent several years in Rome studying literature, then returned to Naples about 1465 and began to tutor Federico, whom he later served also as political secretary and treasurer.[63]

[63] On Albino, see Percopo, "Nuovi documenti," 20 (1895), 283–97; and the *DBI*, 2.12–13. On Altilio, see Percopo, "Nuovi documenti," 19 (1894), 561–74; the *DBI*, 2.565–66; and Bruno Maioli, "Una gloria di Caggiano rinverdita: l'umanista Gabriele Altilio (1436–1501)," *Humanistica lovaniensia*, 32 (1983), 358–66. On Calenzio see Felice Rossi, *Elisio Calenzio* (Lauria, 1924); and especially Liliana Monti Sabia, "L'*humanitas* di Elisio Calenzio alla luce del suo epis-

Thus Alfonso II, Ferrandino, and Federico all patronized men of culture as Alfonso the Magnanimous and Ferrante had done before them. Tammaro de Marinis shows further that each of the last three kings contributed in some way to the Aragonese library in Naples. He lists forty-five manuscripts prepared especially for Duke Alfonso and points out that a fair number of other works known to have been produced for him are now lost. He also mentions three manuscripts prepared for the young Ferrandino and six for Federico. The library unfortunately did not survive the Aragonese dynasty, at least not intact. A large number of volumes went to Paris in the baggage of Charles VIII, and most of the remainder traveled to Valencia with Federico's son Ferrante, the last Aragonese duke of Calabria, after Gonsalvo de Córdoba captured him and packed him off to Spain. This last Duke Ferrante continued to care for the library, and he had many books rebound after arriving in Spain in 1502. But he also lent them out on excessively generous terms, so that they did not return. Many of them went eventually into the library of Philip II at the Escorial—some survive there even today, though most of them perished in the great fire of 1671—while most of the remaining volumes survive in the university library in Valencia.[64]

The unfortunate paucity of documentation makes it impossible to characterize with any precision the cultural policies of Alfonso II, Ferrandino, and Federico. Occasionally, however, a source throws at least a bit of light on the problem. Lancellotto Macedonio's preface to his short *History of St. Paris*, for example, makes it clear that Federico actively encouraged cultural enterprise. Macedonio, a Hieronymite, encountered Federico at Teano, a small town near Naples and Gaeta. Federico traveled there for reasons of piety: he wanted to venerate the fount of St. Paris, who according to legend had rescued the terrified inhabitants of Teano from the ravages of a dragon, a bear, and a lion. While there, Federico pre-

---

tolario," *Annali della facoltà di lettere e filosofia dell'Università di Napoli*, 11 (1964–68), 175–251.

[64] De Marinis, *La biblioteca*, 1.97–99, 103–4, 117–22, 198.

vailed upon Macedonio to prepare a written account of St. Paris' deeds.[65] Thus like Alfonso the Magnanimous and Ferrante—no doubt also Alfonso II and perhaps even Ferrandino—Federico promoted scholarship that appealed to his personal tastes.

While scarcity of documentation does not permit a full characterization of cultural policy under the last three kings, there can be no doubt that the Aragonese dynasty as a whole profoundly influenced the development of Renaissance culture in Naples and Italy. Later chapters that analyze the content and themes of writings produced in Renaissance Naples will demonstrate the novel approaches taken by humanists and other cultural figures not only toward literature, learning, and scholarship, but also toward ethics, politics, and public morality. To some extent, the Neapolitans drew the inspiration for their works from the general cultural climate created by Renaissance humanism. But the Aragonese monarchs also played a role of considerable importance in the process of cultural and intellectual change by way of their cultural patronage. Whether motivated by personal taste or political needs or a combination of the two, the Aragonese kings encouraged and materially supported the men who transformed medieval into modern culture.

This point must not obscure the fact, however, that the Neapolitan humanists looked after their own interests as well as those of their royal patrons. The following chapter will examine the personal and professional benefits that several especially prominent humanists derived from their relationships with the Aragonese kings of Naples.

[65] Lancellotto Macedonio's *Historia sancti Paridis* is preserved in Valencia, BU, MS 730 (formerly 760). For the preface, see fol. 1r.

3

Clientage and Career

F IFTEENTH-CENTURY humanists depended upon the goodwill and generosity of private patrons to a degree difficult to
imagine today. Institutional means of support, such as universities, could provide positions only for a small minority of humanists. Meanwhile, no fifteenth-century writer could have supported
himself through the fledgling press, since a large, literate, book-
buying public did not emerge until the later sixteenth century.
The literary and scholarly production of Quattrocento humanists
thus naturally reflected the needs and interests of their patrons, as
preceding pages have shown in the case of Renaissance Naples.

Yet humanists eagerly sought positions with prominent patrons
and willingly entered their service. Even while addressing their
patrons' needs and interests, the Neapolitan humanists for the
most part found their posts comfortable and their work congenial.
The present chapter does not analyze the humanists' writings—an
effort reserved for the following two chapters—but instead examines the material and professional relationships between patrons
and clients in the cases of five humanists whose careers at the Aragonese court are illuminated by a large body of evidence. Study
of these careers will demonstrate that humanists enjoyed opportunities to benefit financially, professionally, and intellectually
from their relationships with the Aragonese kings of Naples.

Panormita (1394-1471)

Antonio Beccadelli, better known as Panormita, was one of the
first humanists to enter the service of Alfonso the Magnanimous.

84

He remained in Naples after Alfonso's death and served Ferrante faithfully, if not always happily, for thirteen more years. His career illustrates probably better than any other the opportunities open to Italian humanists in the mid-fifteenth century.

The Beccadelli family had its origins in Bologna, but in the early fourteenth century Antonio's ancestors had fled to Sicily because of civil disorders. Thus in 1394 Antonio was born in Palermo—*Panormus* in Latin, whence the cognomen Panormita.[1] In 1420 he went to study law at Bologna; later he traveled throughout northern and central Italy. During these years, the mid-1420s, he composed and published the most notorious work of his time, the *Hermaphroditus*, a collection of suggestive and salacious verses that won widespread approval for their literary qualities but equally widespread condemnation for their scandalous moral tone. In 1429 he obtained an appointment as court poet to the duke of Milan, Filippo Maria Visconti, who dispatched him to teach rhetoric at the University of Pavia during the academic year 1430 to 1431 and again from 1432 to 1433. The high point of Panormita's early career came in May 1432, when Holy Roman Emperor Sigismund crowned him poet at Parma.

Dismayed by a reduction in his salary, Panormita left Pavia early in 1434 and returned to his native Sicily, where he entered the service of Alfonso the Magnanimous. His first duty was to oversee Alfonso's library, housed at that time in the Ziza castle of

---

[1] The best biography of Panormita is that of Michele Natale, *Antonio Beccadelli detto il Panormita* (Caltanisetta, 1902); but Vicenzo Laurenza provides a better account of his Neapolitan career, "Il Panormita a Napoli," *AAP*, 42 (1912), 1–92. Alan Ryder adds some very interesting information to Laurenza in "Antonio Beccadelli: A Humanist in Government," in C. H. Clough, ed., *Cultural Aspects of the Italian Renaissance: Essays in Honour of Paul Oskar Kristeller* (Manchester, 1976), pp. 123–40. Ryder draws heavily on Aragonese archives in Barcelona, but unfortunately he devotes barely one page to Panormita's career during Ferrante's reign. See also Mario Santoro's nicely balanced portrait of Panormita as a cultural figure and propagandist for the Aragonese kings of Naples: "Il Panormita 'aragonese,' " *Esperienze letterarie*, 9 (1984), 3–24. Gianvito Resta, *L'epistolario del Panormita* (Messina, 1954), also contains a large amount of useful information.

Palermo, but he also accepted political responsibilities from the earliest days of his Neapolitan career. Already in July 1434 Alfonso named him administrator (*gaito*) of the royal customs at Palermo—a sinecure, since Panormita obtained also the right to name an assistant and to draw his own salary without contributing any administrative services.[2] More importantly, after the death of Queen Giovanna II in 1435, Panormita accompanied and served Alfonso in his campaign to conquer the Regno. Thus during the siege of Gaeta (August 1435), Alfonso sent Panormita as ambassador to urge the inhabitants of the city to surrender. Despite his elegant oration, Panormita experienced only limited success in this mission. Commanders of the garrison stalled negotiations by frequent requests for a truce, which Alfonso refused to grant. One spokesman eventually went to Alfonso's camp and agreed to a surrender, but upon his return to Gaeta he found the defenders resolved on resistance to the death. As it turned out, the battle of Ponza and the destruction of the Aragonese fleet put an early end to the siege of Gaeta.[3]

Meanwhile, however, Panormita had undertaken the first in a long series of diplomatic assignments on behalf of the Aragonese kings of Naples. Even before the completion of Alfonso's conquest of the Regno, Panormita fulfilled at least two other such missions. In the spring of 1436 Alfonso feared the establishment of an alliance of Florence, Siena, Venice, and Genoa against Duke Filippo Maria Visconti of Milan, Alfonso's only reliable friend in Italy. He sent Panormita to Florence and Siena in an effort to discourage them from joining the suspected alliance. Panormita declared Alfonso's love for the Sienese and urged them to consider Duke Filippo Maria their protector. To the Florentines he relayed Alfonso's warnings about the Genoese, "a thoroughly unreliable people

---

[2] R. Starrabba, "Notizie concernenti Antonio Panormita," *Archivio storico siciliano*, n.s. 27 (1902), esp. pp. 119–23.

[3] Bartolomeo Facio narrates the mission and presents the text of Panormita's oration in his *De rebus gestis ab Alphonso primo neapolitanorum rege*; see the edition in Gravier, ed., *Raccolta*, 4.75–82, esp. pp. 79–82.

who are absolutely faithless when it comes to their promises." Despite Alfonso's promises and threats, which Panormita also communicated on this embassy, his mission did not succeed: in June 1436 the four cities manifested their concerns by leaguing against Milan.[4] Yet Alfonso retained confidence in Panormita's abilities. In May 1441 he sent Panormita to the besieged town of Caiazzo, where he persuaded the inhabitants to surrender and trust Alfonso's mercy rather than resist and experience his wrath.[5]

Besides serving on diplomatic missions, Panormita also undertook other kinds of duties for Alfonso before 1442 and the end of his battle for the Regno. Between 1437 and 1439 he executed numerous documents in his capacity as lieutenant of the royal protonotary (i.e., director of the king's secretarial staff), lieutenant of the royal logothete (i.e., the king's spokesman), and president (i.e., member) of the Sommaria, the council that audited accounts and oversaw royal finances in Naples.[6]

Panormita clearly had won the king's favor, and he benefited handsomely from his position even in the days before Alfonso completed the conquest of Naples. Between 1437 and 1439, Alfonso provided for Panormita an annual salary of 75 ounces of *carlini* (silver Sicilian coins), equivalent to 450 ducats. He justified the expense not only on the basis of Panormita's official services, but also because of his other merits—including poetic talent, rhetorical skills, knowledge of moral philosophy, and advice in military affairs—and even because of the profit he derived from Panormita's conversation and readings. He noted that instability in the realm had made it difficult for Panormita to collect his salary; thus he

---

[4] G. Zurita, *Anales de la Corona de Aragón*, 7 vols. (Saragossa, 1610–21), 3.236–37. See also Panormita's instructions in the ACA, Reg. 2694, fols. 11r–12r.

[5] Facio, *De rebus gestis*, in Gravier, ed., *Raccolta*, 4.137; Nunzio F. Faraglia, *Storia della lotta tra Alfonso V d'Aragona e Renato d'Angiò* (Lanciano, 1908), pp. 235–36.

[6] Laurenza, "Il Panormita a Napoli," docs. I–XXV, pp. 63–68. On the offices see Ryder, *The Kingdom of Naples Under Alfonso the Magnanimous* (Oxford, 1976), pp. 4, 191–205, 218–21; also Ryder's "Antonio Beccadelli," pp. 126–27.

ordered his administrator in Palermo to advance the stipend reliably out of wine, oil, and salt levies.[7] The year 1439 was an especially good one for Panormita: in October he received an exemption from the *quinta*, a tax on royal stipends; and in December Alfonso granted him the Ziza castle of Palermo. Panormita held the castle as private property, and he bequeathed it to his son Antonino, who in 1489 sold it to the Aragonese viceroy of Sicily.[8]

Panormita thus parlayed his talents into material success even before Alfonso completed his conquest of the Regno. Alfonso's victory over Naples in 1442 and subsequent consolidation of his position, however, opened the period of his career in which Panormita achieved his greatest personal and professional success. During Alfonso's reign Panormita continued to hold his seat on the Sommaria and his post as administrator of customs at Palermo, but he received larger salaries for his services. In February 1450, Alfonso increased Panormita's salary to one hundred ounces, equivalent to six hundred ducats.[9] Two months later he bestowed upon Panormita the honor of Neapolitan citizenship with all its rights and privileges.[10]

Panormita's influence and prestige reached their height during the 1450s. In 1451 Alfonso sent him as ambassador to Florence, Ferrara, and Venice, along with Luis Despuig and the young Giovanni Pontano. The mission had several sensitive political aims: first to detach the Florentines from their recent alliance with Francesco Sforza; then to seek neutrality if not positive support from Ferrara; finally to solidify the new Neapolitan alliance with the Venetians. The embassy completely failed in Florence, but basi-

---

[7] M. Catalano Tirrito, ed., *Nuovi documenti sul Panormita* (Catania, 1910), docs. VI–IX, pp. 182–89. See esp. docs. VI and VIII, pp. 183 and 189, for Alfonso's justification of Panormita's salary.

[8] For the documents of 1439, see ibid., docs. X–XI, pp. 189–91. On the later history of the Ziza castle, see Starrabba, "Notizie concernenti Antonio Panormita," pp. 129–33.

[9] Catalano Tirrito, ed., *Nuovi documenti*, docs. XIII–XVI, pp. 194–96; Laurenza, "Il Panormita a Napoli," doc. XXXIV, p. 73.

[10] Laurenza, "Il Panormita a Napoli," doc. XXXIII, pp. 71–72.

cally succeeded in Ferrara and Venice. Panormita delivered an elegant Latin oration to the Venetian Senate, alluded briefly to previous tensions between Alfonso and the Venetians, but emphasized praise of Venice and celebration of the current state of peace.[11] The embassy enabled Panormita to establish friendships with Pasquale Malipiero, the future doge of Venice, and with the eminent Venetian humanist, Francesco Barbaro, both of whom exchanged correspondence with him in later years. While returning from Venice, the diplomatic party stopped in Padua, where Panormita took possession of an arm bone from a recently discovered skeleton presumed to be that of Livy. Knowing of Alfonso's deep interest in Livy, the Paduans sent him the relic as a token of their friendship and their hopes for peace with Naples. Thus, quite apart from his monetary compensation—which in the case of this embassy amounted to 850 *alfonsini* (gold coins), equivalent to 1,275 ducats, intended no doubt largely for expenses[12]—Panormita gained the opportunity to advance his own career, since he dealt with men of power and made the acquaintance of others who could share his cultural interests.

In 1452 Alfonso sent Panormita on another mission, this one to greet Emperor Frederick III, who had come to Rome for his coronation.[13] In 1453 Panormita again took on a more political embassy. In October of that year, he received two hundred ducats to

---

[11] Facio mentions the embassy and presents the text of Panormita's oration: *De rebus gestis*, in Gravier, ed., *Raccolta*, 4.223–26. For an expanded and perhaps more accurate version of the oration, see Panormita's collection of epistles and orations he composed on behalf of Alfonso and Ferrante: BAV, Barb. lat. 2070, fols. 28r–31r.

[12] Panormita said he received 700 gold *alfonsini* (equivalent to 1,050 ducats) before departing on the embassy and an additional 150 (equivalent to 225 ducats) after his return: *Epistolarum libri V* (Venice, 1553), fol. 120r. It seems that Panormita considered the amount too small, since he complained in the same letter about additional assignments without adequate support.

[13] See Panormita's *Epistolarum libri V*, fol. 115v. The oration Panormita delivered to Frederick has appeared in several editions, most conveniently in Girolamo Donzellini, ed., *Epistolae principum, rerumpublicarum, ac sapientum virorum* (Venice, 1574), pp. 398–409.

travel to Genoa, where he delivered an oration urging the Genoese to join a general Italian alliance against the Turks.[14] A final indication of his increasing political importance comes from several documents executed between 1454 and 1469 that refer to Panormita as royal secretary. Even in the absence of the documents, one could infer Panormita's secretarial duties on the basis of two sources: a manuscript in which Panormita collected diplomatic correspondence and orations that he composed on behalf of Alfonso and Ferrante, and other copies of similar correspondence that survive in archival collections.[15] The letters that Panormita composed (discussed in detail in the next chapter) went largely to princes, popes, cardinals, and other important political figures whom Alfonso and Ferrante sought to influence. Panormita's literary skills obviously held considerable political value for his royal patrons.

During the 1450s Panormita benefited also by the accumulation of numerous financial rewards. In October 1454 Alfonso conceded to him for his lifetime the office of notary to the Sommaria, along with an annual salary of fifty ounces, equivalent to three hundred ducats.[16] In April 1455 Alfonso provided for Panormita to draw his notarial stipend in the amount of three hundred ducats from Sicilian revenues, in addition to his salary of one hundred

[14] For the payment of the two hundred ducats, see Laurenza, "Il Panormita a Napoli," doc. XXXVI, p. 74. For his oration see his *Epistolarum libri V*, fols. 124r–126r.

[15] The earliest surviving notice of Panormita's appointment as a secretary dates from 1 September 1455: see Nicola Toppi, *De origine omnium tribunalium*, 3 vols. (Naples, 1655–66), 3.266–69. But this document probably represents a renewal of Panormita's original appointment, since other documents refer to him as a royal secretary as early as April 1454. See C. Minieri Riccio, "Alcuni fatti di Alfonso I. di Aragona," *ASPN*, 6 (1881), 447; Laurenza, "Il Panormita a Napoli," docs. XXXVIII–LXVIIII, passim; and R. Sabbadini, ed., *Ottanta lettere inedite del Panormita* (Catania, 1910), p. 158. Panormita's own collection of diplomatic correspondence and orations is preserved in BAV, Barb. lat. 2070. The next chapter will discuss other items preserved in the Aragonese archives in Barcelona.

[16] Jole Mazzoleni, ed., *Regesto della cancelleria aragonese di Napoli*, (Naples, 1951), no. 151, p. 27, and appendix XII, pp. 214–16; see also Laurenza, "Il Panormita a Napoli," doc. XXXVII, pp. 74–75.

ounces, equivalent to six hundred ducats, as administrator of customs at Palermo.[17] By the mid-1450s, then, Panormita received a handsome income—amounting to no less than nine hundred ducats of regular annual salary—from his various offices and sinecures. His largest single reward came in 1456, shortly after he had completed his laudatory, anecdotal book of Alfonso's sayings and deeds, *De dictis et factis Alphonsi*. As compensation for his efforts, Alfonso awarded him an extraordinary grant of one thousand ducats.[18]

De dictis et factis Alphonsi represented the only major literary work that Panormita undertook during his period of service to Alfonso. He produced a few verses and numerous epistles, to be sure, but he collected and preserved them in haphazard fashion.[19] Yet other evidence makes it clear that Panormita played an active role in cultural affairs during the period 1434 to 1458. Indeed, on the basis of his prestige and influence at the Neapolitan court, Panormita himself became an arbiter and something of a patron of culture, to the extent that he had the power to advance or retard an individual's prospects at Alfonso's court.

The first known case of a humanist outside Alfonso's court seeking Panormita's aid occurred in 1436, barely two years after Panormita left Pavia for Palermo. During the first half of 1436, the Florentine Lapo da Castiglionchio the Younger (grandson of the elder Lapo, the famous Florentine humanist) sent several works to the Regno. To Alfonso he dedicated his Latin translation of Plutarch's life of Fabius Maximus. To Panormita he sent his Latin translations of Isocrates' orations, *Nicocles* and *Ad Nicoclem*, along with a dedicatory epistle. Finally, he addressed also to Panormita

---

[17] Catalano Tirrito, ed., *Nuovi documenti*, doc. xx, pp. 176–77.

[18] Minieri Riccio, "Alcuni fatti di Alfonso," p. 447. This summary does not mention the reason for the grant. In view of the chronology, however, it seems most accurate to equate the award with the thousand ducats that Pontano said Panormita received for his work on Alfonso. See Pontano's *De liberalitate*, in *I trattati delle virtù sociali*, ed. F. Tateo (Rome, 1965), p. 45.

[19] *Poesie latine inedite di A. Beccadelli detto il Panormita*, ed. A. Cinquini and R. Valentini (Aosta, 1907); and Resta, *L'epistolario del Panormita*, pp. 23–27.

a letter referring to the previous two submissions. Both of the letters to Panormita reveal clearly Lapo's interest in Alfonso's patronage. In the epistle dedicating his translations of Isocrates, Lapo praised Panormita for his literary and scholarly accomplishments. He expressed the hope that the two orations—one on royal administration, the other on the king's education—would prove useful for Panormita. If so, Lapo said, he hoped further to benefit from Panormita's humanity and benevolence. In the independent epistle, Lapo inquired eagerly about how Alfonso had received the translation of Fabius Maximus' life. He openly stated that he would gladly receive a work that Panormita might dedicate to him in reciprocation for the translations of Isocrates.[20] Lapo had clearly identified Panormita as a man of influence who might advance his cause at Alfonso's court. But the ploy did not succeed. Lapo obtained no position with Alfonso, and he soon rededicated his translations of Isocrates to Francesco Condulmer, nephew of Pope Eugenius IV.[21]

Panormita's cultural influence reached its height only in the 1450s. He sometimes exercised his influence in a negative way: it seems likely, for example, that bitter feelings between Panormita and Porcellio Pandoni had something to do with Porcellio's departure from Naples about 1453.[22] More generally, however, sur-

[20] Lapo's translation of Plutarch's life of Fabius Maximus appears in BAV, Vat. lat. 1875, fols. 294r–305r. His translation of Isocrates appears in BAV, Vat. lat. 3422. Partial transcriptions of the dedicatory epistles occur in F. P. Luiso, "Studi su l'epistolario e le traduzioni di Lapo da Castiglionchio, junior," *Studi italiani di filologia classica*, 7 (1899), 266–68, 288–90. Luiso also edits Lapo's independent epistle to Panormita, p. 222.

[21] Lucia Gualdo Rosa, *La fede nella "paideia": aspetti della fortuna europea di Isocrate nei secoli XV e XVI* (Rome, 1984), pp. 32–33 and n. 56. See also Antonio Carlini, "Appunti sulle traduzioni latine di Isocrate da Lapo da Castiglionchio," *Studi classici e orientali*, 19–20 (1970–71), 302–309.

[22] Erasmo Percopo, "Nuovi documenti su gli scrittori e gli artisti dei tempi aragonesi," *ASPN*, 20 (1895), 317–26; and Ennio I. Rao, "Alfonso of Aragon and the Italian Humanists," *Esperienze letterarie*, 4 (1979), pp. 46–47, 51. I disagree, however, with Rao's contention (p. 51) that Panormita drove Lorenzo Valla away from Naples. As a later section will show, when Valla left Alfonso's service in 1447, he had long sought an opportunity to return to Rome; indeed, it is possi-

viving evidence shows that supplicants could hope for favorable treatment from Panormita. In a pathetic letter written probably in 1455, Giacomo Curlo, the most talented copyist of the Neapolitan library, addressed Panormita as "my prince" and described the miserable state of his financial affairs. He could not meet his daughter's dowry requirement despite a loan from his nephew, Curlo said, and he did not even have enough money to buy bread and vegetables. Curlo reported progress on the copying of Panormita's "commentaries"—no doubt meaning *De dictis et factis Alphonsi*—which he expected to complete soon. Meanwhile, he pleaded with Panormita to have some work entrusted to him, so that he would not starve.[23]

In the following year, 1456, a major humanist bestowed upon Panormita a scholarly gift of high interest. Theodore Gaza, who enjoyed Alfonso's patronage from 1456 to 1458, dedicated to Panormita his translation of Aelian's work on military tactics, *De aciebus instruendis*. The letter of dedication included the obligatory praise of Alfonso, but also a generous estimate of Panormita's literary production. Panormita's *De dictis et factis Alphonsi*, Gaza said, matched Alfonso's own achievements. Indeed, it led him to the observation that great rulers and writers generally lead simultaneous lives: to prove the point, he cited the examples of Alexander and Aristotle, Augustus and Vergil, and by implication, Alfonso and Panormita.[24] Gaza did not request any specific favor in this letter, and he no doubt acted out of genuine respect when he dedicated his work to Panormita. It could not have escaped his attention, however, that good relations with Panormita would not harm his own position at Alfonso's court.

The most important and long-lasting effect of Panormita's cultural influence was the establishment and maintenance of a hu-

---

ble that he never thought of his Neapolitan post as anything more than a temporary position.

[23] Tammaro de Marinis edited the letter from a Vatican manuscript of epistles to Panormita: *La biblioteca*, 2.313–14, doc. 968.

[24] Ibid., 2.3–5.

manist literary academy in Naples. Very little information survives to illuminate the early days of this academy, but a letter of Francesc Martorell, chief secretary in Alfonso's chancellery, makes it clear that Panormita played the major role in its establishment. Writing probably in the first half of 1447, Martorell informed Panormita that he had discussed the prospect of founding an academy with Alfonso, who had enthusiastically endorsed the idea: the seed that Panormita had planted during conversation thus seemed about to take root. Martorell suggested that Panormita travel personally to see Alfonso and tend to the necessary details.[25] Thus around 1447 there came into being probably the first of the academies or sodalities that for almost a century zealously promoted humanist studies.[26] After Alfonso's death, Panormita continued to serve as leader of the academy, and he hosted its proceedings in his own villa. Toward the end of his life, he entrusted it to the guidance of Giovanni Pontano, whose name eventually became most closely associated with the sodality, the Accademia Pontaniana.[27]

[25] The letter occurs in a manuscript of epistles to Panormita, BAV, Vat. lat. 3372, fol. 109r. The date I derive from Martorell's allusion to Panormita's second marriage: he suggested that Panormita travel personally to talk with Alfonso "cum primum cura rei uxoriae te respirare sinet." Although Panormita began to make arrangements for his marriage to Laura Arcelli during the summer of 1444, the wedding did not take place until the spring of 1447; cf. Laurenza, "Il Panormita a Napoli," pp. 11–14. Alfonso spent most of the period from October 1446 through August 1447 in Tivoli directing the Tuscan campaign: cf. A. Gimenez Soler, *Itinerario del Rey Don Alonso de Aragón y de Napoles* (Saragossa, 1909), pp. 230–47. On Panormita's own movements during this period and on the likelihood that he spent about five years in Sicily from 1444 to 1449, see Ryder, "Antonio Beccadelli," pp. 130–31.

[26] C. Minieri Riccio ranks the Neapolitan academy as the first and dates its origin to 1442: *Cenno storico della accademia alfonsina istituta nella città di Napoli nel 1442* (Naples, 1875), pp. 7–8. Minieri Riccio did not know the letter of Martorell to Panormita (1447) and thus incorrectly identified the literary seances in Alfonso's library with the foundation of the academy proper. Michele Maylender doubted the priority of the Neapolitan academy, but did not cite firm evidence of an earlier academy: *Storia delle accademie d'Italia*, 5 vols. (Bologna, 1926–30), 4.328–29; cf. 2.317–18.

[27] On the character of the Neapolitan academy, see esp. Mario Santoro, "La

The cultural and political significance of humanist academies has captured the interest of numerous historians in recent years. On the one hand, a kind of cynical interpretation holds that during the fifteenth and sixteenth centuries, humanists and other intellectuals gathered in their academies, perhaps even at the instigation of princes, because they had no social or political role to play. Internal struggles and private jealousies consumed their energies and prevented humanists from returning to political activity.[28] On the other hand, some historians have advanced more generous assessments of the academies as organizations that enabled humanists to pursue their intellectual and cultural interests, even as they devoted most of their time to official duties as secretaries and advisers to popes, prelates, and princes.[29] The case of the Neapolitan academy clearly supports the second interpretation. Humanists accepted political duties during the whole course of the Aragonese dynasty of Naples. They played prominent roles in all of the most crucial difficulties confronted by the Aragonese kings—Alfonso's conquest of the Regno, Ferrante's struggle for the succession, the second barons' revolt, and the foreign invasions following 1494. The academy of Panormita and Pontano thus did not serve to distract Neapolitan humanists from political activity. Instead, it appealed to them as one of the benefits of clientage at the Aragonese court of Naples.

The death of Alfonso the Magnanimous brought an end to the halcyon days of Neapolitan humanism in general; for Panormita in

---

cultura umanistica," in *Storia di Napoli* (Naples, 1975–81), 7.159–71. See also C. Minieri Riccio, *Cenno storico della accademia pontaniana* (Naples, 1876), pp. 1, 12.

[28] For the most extreme expression of this interpretation, see Ruggiero Romano, *Tra due crisi: l'Italia del Rinascimento* (Turin, 1971), pp. 117–36, esp. 129–30. See also the interpretations of Marsilio Ficino and Poliziano in Eugenio Garin, *Portraits from the Quattrocento*, trans. V. Velen and E. Velen (New York, 1972), pp. 142–89; and idem, *Italian Humanism*, trans. P. Munz (Oxford, 1965), pp. 78–81.

[29] See especially D'Amico, *Renaissance Humanism in Papal Rome: Humanists and Churchmen on the Eve of the Reformation* (Baltimore, 1983).

particular the succession of Ferrante opened a period of discontent and financial pressure that lasted several years. Panormita retained the positions he had obtained during Alfonso's reign. Surviving fragments of Sommaria registers show that he continued as notary of that body in the early months of Ferrante's reign.[30] A large amount of diplomatic correspondence shows furthermore that Panormita continued to serve as royal secretary. He wrote numerous letters—some in the name of Ferrante, others on his own initiative—in the early stages of Ferrante's battle to retain his crown. Panormita was most busy during the period 1459 to 1460, during the first barons' revolt and following the rout of Ferrante's forces at Sarno. He sent letters to Duke Francesco Sforza of Milan, Doge Pasquale Malipiero of Venice, Duke Borso d'Este of Ferrara, Pope Pius II, Don Carlos de Viana, and King Juan II of Aragon, among others.[31] Finally, Panormita also undertook two important embassies during the early months of Ferrante's rule. In August 1458 or shortly thereafter, he traveled to Milan in order to thank Francesco Sforza for supporting Ferrante against the late pope Calixtus III. The following year he addressed Pope Pius II at the Congress of Mantua (June 1459 to January 1460) in an effort to justify and gain support for Ferrante's war against Genoa.[32] All these services harmonized perfectly with the general thrust of Neapolitan diplomacy in the first eighteen months of Ferrante's reign.[33]

Yet Panormita found much to complain about during the dif-

[30] *Fonti aragonese*, vol. 8, ed. B. Ferrante (Naples, 1971). These fragments cover the period from December 1458 to March 1459.

[31] See Panormita's *Regis Ferdinandi et aliorum epistolae ac orationes utriusque militiae* (Vico Equense, 1586), esp. pp. 305–327. Despite the misleading title, almost all the pieces in this volume were Panormita's work.

[32] Panormita's oration to Duke Francesco is preserved in his collection of diplomatic epistles and orations: BAV, Barb. lat. 2070, fols. 39r–41v; see also a transcription in Resta, *L'epistolario del Panormita*, pp. 135–36. The oration to Pope Pius at Mantua occurs in *Regis Ferdinandi et aliorum epistolae*, pp. 338–43.

[33] For documents that place Panormita's diplomatic efforts in context, see A. Messer, ed., *Le codice aragonese* (Paris, 1912), esp. nos. 124, 126, 204, 246; pp. 169–76, 267–69, 311–13. See the next chapter for a detailed discussion of Panormita's diplomatic activities during this period.

ficult early years of Ferrante's rule. In 1460 and 1461 he wrote several times to Ferrante's chief secretary, Antonello Petrucci, who followed Ferrante on the several campaigns (1460–1462) directed against Jean d'Anjou and the rebel barons. In two letters of 1460, Panormita complained that Ferrante and his aides in the field consistently neglected the suggestions offered by Panormita and his colleagues on a council of military advisers in Naples. In other letters of 1460 and 1461, Panormita informed Antonello of his extreme displeasure with the stinginess of Ferrante, who risked serious danger because of his lack of generosity toward meritorious men. Panormita even advertised his unhappiness abroad: in a letter to Theodore Gaza he lambasted princely avarice and parsimony, threatening in his own case to substitute malediction for praise unless literary men received proper rewards for their services.[34]

Other letters make it clear that Panormita seriously considered leaving Naples during Ferrante's struggle for the succession. In 1460 or 1461 he lamented to Pope Pius II the passing of the golden age: "after the death of the glorious King Alfonso, all the hopes of learned men are extinguished." As a result, Panormita announced his decision to go either to Palermo or to Spain in search of new patrons; but he held open the possibility of moving instead to Rome, in case a post should become available for him there.[35] About the same time, Panormita exchanged several letters with Cardinal Bartolomeo Roverella: he mourned the burial of the Muses along with Alfonso, mentioned his plans to depart for Sicily or Spain, and sought support for a position in the church. Roverella's response reveals a much sounder appreciation of the situation's realities than do Panormita's complaints. Roverella sympathized with Panormita's problems, but explained them as the result of unfortunate necessity: sometimes the Muses must give way before arms. Panormita, he said, should consider the future.

---

[34] *Regis Ferdinandi et aliorum epistolae*, pp. 336–37, 346–47, 366–67, 374–76.
[35] Ibid., pp. 355–56.

Sicily could not guarantee happiness and prosperity over the long term, and Roverella could think of nothing that could possibly attract Panormita to Spain. Rather than abandon his home and friends, Panormita ought to stay in Naples and contribute his talents to Ferrante's cause, knowing that improved conditions in the Regno would soon result in a more fortunate financial situation for Panormita himself.[36]

Before the situation improved, however, Panormita even flirted with Jean d'Anjou, Ferrante's rival for the crown of Naples. In 1460 or 1461, Jean addressed a letter to Panormita, requested a copy of his *De dictis et factis Alphonsi*, suggested a personal meeting between the two men, and offered his house and hospitality to the humanist. Panormita willingly offered a copy of the book on Alfonso in his reply to this letter, but politely declined Jean's offer of an interview and his hospitality. In fact, however, Panormita never dispatched this reply to Jean d'Anjou. Instead he submitted it to Antonello Petrucci with a request for advice. Panormita's next letter to Petrucci makes it clear that Antonello counseled no further correspondence with Jean d'Anjou. Panormita accepted Antonello's advice and proclaimed himself willing to follow wise and grave guides.[37] In the meantime, however, it looks very much as though Panormita took advantage of Jean's overture to improve his own position in Naples. While carefully avoiding any hint of treason, he indicated clearly to Petrucci his desire to correspond with Jean d'Anjou. The prospect of losing Panormita—the most important instrument of propaganda for the House of Aragon in Naples—to the Angevin cause would not have appealed to either Petrucci or Ferrante.

In any case, Ferrante's fortunes soon improved, as Cardinal Roverella had predicted, and Panormita almost immediately benefited. In several letters of 1462, Panormita congratulated Ferrante

[36] BAV, Vat. lat. 3371, fols. 173v–174r; Vat. lat. 3372, fol. 111rv.

[37] The letter of Jean d'Anjou that opened this correspondence does not survive, but its message can be inferred from Panormita's response. See *Regis Ferdinandi et aliorum epistolae*, pp. 377–78 for Panormita's letter (never sent) to Jean d'Anjou, pp. 379–80 for his letters to Antonello Petrucci.

on his victory (at Troia) over the Angevins and rebellious barons. At the same time he reminded Ferrante rather pointedly of his royal obligation to spend money lavishly and to exhibit liberality toward deserving men.[38] By the time Panormita wrote these epistles, Ferrante had already begun to reward him for his services. In January 1462 Ferrante granted Panormita a garden confiscated from Marino Marzano, the rebel prince of Rossano. In August Ferrante ordered payment of Panormita's secretarial salary for the years 1458 and 1459. In November Ferrante granted him an exemption from gabelle levies. In January 1463 Panormita received yet another monetary concession of fifty ounces, equivalent to three hundred ducats. Finally, in May 1463, Ferrante appointed him tutor to Duke Alfonso of Calabria at an annual salary of three hundred ducats.[39]

Another set of sources shows that Panormita retained his influence as cultural arbiter after Ferrante's stabilization of the realm. Panormita befriended a promising young humanist named Antonio Calcillo and helped him to gain a position in the household of Cardinal Roverella in the late months of 1463. In later months he used Calcillo as a messenger when dealing with the cardinal, and he perhaps also helped Calcillo to win a post at the Studio of Naples, where the young humanist taught rhetoric from 1466 to 1471. Though not a well-known figure, Calcillo exercised some scholarly influence of his own: he prepared perhaps the first Latin dictionary in Italy; Giuniano Maio later edited and published it under his own name; and Angelo Poliziano made extensive use of Maio's work.[40]

Apart from his epistles, Panormita undertook only one major literary effort during Ferrante's reign. In August 1469 he completed a short history of Ferrante's life from the time of his arrival

[38] Ibid., pp. 392–93, 403–407.

[39] Laurenza, "Il Panormita a Napoli," docs. LV–LXV, pp. 81–84.

[40] Roberto Ricciardi, "Angelo Poliziano, Giuniano Maio, Antonio Calcillo," *Rinascimento*, n.s. 8 (1968), esp. pp. 284–88 on Panormita's role in advancing Calcillo's career; and pp. 304–8 for the appendix of correspondence between Panormita, Roverella, and Calcillo, transcribed from BAV, Vat. lat. 3371 and 3372.

in Italy (1438) up to King Alfonso's death (1458). He planned a continuation that would carry the story through Ferrante's victory over Jean d'Anjou and the barons. His death in 1471 prevented him from completing the work, however, and the story of Ferrante's battle for the Neapolitan crown remained untold until Giovanni Pontano composed his account of the war in 1499.[41]

In truth, Panormita wrote very little during his Neapolitan residence. Yet he advanced his own cause and that of other humanists in several ways. His understanding and appreciation of classical civilization earned him the respect and support of Alfonso the Magnanimous. His rhetorical abilities led to his participation in several sensitive diplomatic missions. His literary talents qualified him to compose important pieces of royal correspondence. His cultural authority enabled him sometimes to retard, but more often to advance the careers of other men of culture. Finally, his affability won him the friendship of almost everyone he met. He showed that humanists could serve the kings of Naples as tutors, advisers, secretaries, and ambassadors. Furthermore, in doing so he showed that humanists could live in comfort and prosperity, and that they could pursue their own cultural and intellectual interests in the setting of the humanist academy. Panormita did not possess a brilliant intellect like that of his rival, Lorenzo Valla, though the next chapter will demonstrate that he often served Alfonso and Ferrante as a rather shrewd adviser. Yet the combination of his personal, literary, and diplomatic skills enabled Panormita to show by his own example how humanists could play an important role in society and gain in return the greatest possible material and intellectual rewards for their efforts.

Bartolomeo Facio (circa 1405–1457)

Bartolomeo Facio did not fill a post at Naples until long after Lorenzo Valla had arrived at Alfonso's court, but his close relationship with Panormita and his hostility to Valla make it most con-

---

[41] See the edition and marvelous introduction to Panormita's *Liber rerum gestarum Ferdinandi regis*, ed. G. Resta (Palermo, 1968).

venient to discuss his career next. Facio was born at La Spezia, near Genoa, early in the fifteenth century.[42] His family had a tradition of service as notaries at La Spezia, and Bartolomeo benefited from their fortune and political connections. The early stages of Facio's career are very poorly documented, but at least a few points have become clear. In the early 1420s he studied with Guarino at Verona. Later he tutored the three sons of the Venetian doge, Francesco Foscari. In 1429 he went to Florence to improve his Greek. During the 1430s he lived in Genoa and Lucca, perhaps also in Milan for a while. Only in 1441 does much documentation appear on Facio's career. In that year he served as chancellor to the Genoese admiral Francesco Spinola and as notary to the Genoese political and military figure Raffaele Adorno. In December 1442 these two men engineered the expulsion of Doge Tommaso Fregoso, and in January 1443 Adorno was elected the new doge.

This event marked the major turning point in Facio's career, for Adorno entrusted him with diplomatic missions that led to his assumption of a post in Naples. In September 1443 Adorno sent Facio as a nuncio to open negotiations for the establishment of peace between Genoa and King Alfonso. He spent about seven weeks with the king in the marches, as Alfonso drove Francesco Sforza out of papal lands. In February 1444 Adorno sent Facio to Naples, this time as chancellor of the commune, along with several ambassadors and a charge to draft a peace treaty. During this second mission, if not already during the first, Facio renewed his acquaintance with Panormita, whom he had met perhaps in Venice in 1427 and certainly in Florence in 1429. The two men got along

---

[42] The two best accounts of Facio's life and career are Ubaldo Mazzini, "Appunti e notizie per servire alla bio-bibliografia di Bartolomeo Facio," *Giornale storico e letterario della Liguria*, 4 (1903), 400–454; and Paul O. Kristeller, "The Humanist Bartolomeo Facio and His Unknown Correspondence," in C. H. Carter, ed., *From the Renaissance to the Counter-Reformation: Essays in Honor of Garrett Mattingly* (New York, 1965), pp. 56–74. The most recent biography adds little to these works: Claudio Marchiori, *Bartolomeo Facio tra letteratura e vita* (Milan, 1971). Indeed, Marchiori's querulous, uncritical work often plagiarizes Mazzini. Cf. Marchiori, pp. 13, 19–20, 63, and 64, with Mazzini, pp. 405, 411–12, 415–16, and 417, respectively, for a few examples.

well, and Panormita promoted Facio for a position at Alfonso's court. Little wonder, then, considering his friendship with Panormita and the fact that his Genoese chancellorship carried no salary, that Facio decided to remain in Naples. By mid-December 1445 Facio had received or expected to receive soon an appointment as tutor to Ferrante—he perhaps undertook his Italian translation of Isocrates (discussed in the previous chapter) with tutorial duties in mind—and he had already accepted enough money from Alfonso to rent a house and satisfy his creditors.[43]

Unlike Panormita, Facio undertook numerous literary projects during his residence in Naples. About 1445 or 1446 he composed a dialogue on the happiness of life, *De humanae vitae felicitate*, which he dedicated to Alfonso. Though not a work of originality, the dialogue helped to define several characteristic themes of Renaissance analyses of the human condition. About 1448 Facio produced another treatise on a similar topic, the excellence of man, *De excellentia ac praestantia hominis*. He wrote at the urging of a Benedictine monk, Antonio da Barga, who even provided him with a sketchy outline for an argument. Like the earlier work, this treatise exhibits little profundity, but it influenced the development of Renaissance thought by its theme. Only a few years after Facio completed his work, King Alfonso encouraged Giannozzo Manetti to undertake his famous and much more impressive treatise *On the Dignity and Excellence of Man*.[44]

Meanwhile, Facio's treatise on man's excellence helps to throw light on the condition of his own life in Naples. Facio dedicated the treatise to Pope Nicholas V, and he took great pains to see that the work reached its destination. He addressed several letters to the Genoese cardinal Giorgio Fieschi, for example, inquiring whether Nicholas had received the work and what he thought of

[43] See Facio's letter to his father in Florence, Biblioteca Nazionale, MS II. X. 31, fol. 168r, dated 15 December 1445.

[44] The texts of the two treatises are most conveniently found in Felino Sandeo, *De regibus Siciliae et Apuliae* (Hanau, 1611), pp. 106–48, 149–68. For an analysis of the works and the most balanced of modern interpretations, see Charles Trinkaus, *In Our Image and Likeness: Humanity and Divinity in Italian Humanist Thought*, 2 vols. (Chicago, 1970), 1.200–229.

it. He even wrote directly to the pope himself, asking whether the treatise had arrived, promising to send another if not, and offering to write other things at the pope's pleasure.[45]

The explanation for all this epistolary activity is Facio's desire to leave Naples in 1448. For something over a year, he had conducted a bitter, public quarrel with Lorenzo Valla. Furthermore, he had experienced problems in collecting his salary, as he complained in several letters. In the early months of 1447, Facio had portrayed his position in Naples as secure, his patron munificent, and his future bright.[46] Within a year, however, things had changed: in May 1448 he wrote to his father from Rome, where he had gone to promote his works, saying that Alfonso's war in Tuscany had resulted in the disappearance of money in Naples. Facio did not consider himself singled out to suffer, but his anxiety and financial insecurity emerge clearly in the letter.[47] Two months later he wrote to Panormita about a "most stubborn man," presumably a treasury official of some sort, from whom he could not extract even a coin.[48] Finally, four other letters written about the same time—two each to Facio's Genoese patron Giangiacomo Spinola (son of the admiral Francesco Spinola mentioned above) and to his friend Manuele Guarino—make it clear that Facio hoped to obtain a post in Rome. He had sent copies of his treatises to Nicholas V, he said, and he knew that learned men in Rome praised him before the pope. He admitted uncertainty about the reception of his works, since no one had reported the impression they made on the pope. But he spoke highly of the treatise on the excellence of man and clearly expected it to win him favor with the pope.[49]

[45] Valladolid, BU, Colegio Mayor de Santa Cruz, MS 227, fols. 5rv, 7v–8r, 10r–11r for the letters to Fieschi, fol. 4r for that to Nicholas.

[46] See the appendix of epistles in Facio's *De viris illustribus liber*, ed. L. Mehus (Florence, 1745), p. 80. Reference to the composition of his work on the war between Venice and Genoa confirms the date.

[47] Florence, Biblioteca Nazionale, MS II. X. 31, fol. 168v.

[48] See the appendix of Facio's unedited epistles in Ferdinando Gabotto, *Un nuovo contributo alla storia dell'umanesimo ligure* (Genoa, 1892), p. 279.

[49] G. B. Mittarelli, *Bibliotheca codicum manuscriptorum monasterii S. Michaelis Venetiarum prope Murianum* (Venice, 1779), cols. 372–73, 375–76, 379–80.

Facio's work did not succeed in this objective. He returned to Naples, disappointed no doubt, but still respected by numerous Italian humanists of the first rank. In 1451 Flavio Biondo sent him a section of his work *Italia illustrata*, requesting critical help in revising it.[50] In August of the same year Facio received a flattering letter from the Venetian humanist Francesco Barbaro, who had heard of him through Panormita during his embassy to Venice. Barbaro lauded Facio's forthcoming history of Alfonso's deeds as a work that would portray the king and his character in the most accurate possible way—indeed, as a work that merited comparison with the paintings of Apelles or the sculpture of Phidias.[51] Finally, Facio carried on a long correspondence with Poggio Bracciolini between 1447 and 1455. The early stages of the exchange dealt largely with the disparagement of their mutual enemy, Lorenzo Valla, and the question of compensation for Poggio's translation of Xenophon's *Cyropaedia*. Facio's intervention with Alfonso led to Poggio's eventual receipt of his handsome reward of four hundred *alfonsini*, equivalent to six hundred ducats.[52]

Facio also remained productive during the remainder of his Neapolitan career, which he dedicated largely to the writing of history. The first fruit of his efforts was an account of the war of Chioggia between Genoa and Venice in 1377. He had already prepared for this work while living in Genoa, since he used unpublished Genoese annals as sources, but he completed it only in 1448. A letter from April of that year shows him applying the finishing touches to the work: he wrote Panormita requesting a critical opinion on the work, along with advice on ancient Latin words unknown to him.[53]

Facio's major literary work, his account of King Alfonso's career

[50] Biondo, *Scritti inediti e rari di Biondo Flavio*, ed. B. Nogara (Rome, 1927), pp. 165–66.
[51] See the appendix of epistles in Facio's *De viris illustribus*, pp. 90–92.
[52] Ibid., pp. 81–83, 96–107; also Valladolid, BU, Colegio Mayor de Santa Cruz, MS 227, fol. 27v.
[53] See the appendix of Facio's unedited epistles in Gabotto, *Un nuovo contributo*, pp. 275–76.

from 1420 through 1455—the ten books of commentaries *De rebus gestis ab Alphonso primo neapolitanorum rege*—also derived from this period. Facio served as court historian as early as October 1446, when he received an annual salary of three hundred ducats for his historiographical services.[54] During the following years he shared the evolving history with Panormita, who praised Facio's work to Francesco Barbaro while serving as Alfonso's ambassador to Venice in 1451. Barbaro's generous estimate of Facio's literary skills evoked a response that throws light on two things: Facio's conception of his work and his progress on it. Facio emphasized that he considered the work a true history (*rerum gestarum narratio*), not a panegyric (*laudatio*) or biographical sketch (*vita*). The response also informed Barbaro that Facio had completed seven books of his work, taking the story from Alfonso's entry in Italy to his triumph over the city of Naples.[55] By late 1453 or early 1454, Facio submitted the eighth and ninth books of his history to Alfonso.[56] Finally, in a letter of April 1455, Facio reported to Poggio Bracciolini that he had the tenth book—and barring an expedition against the Turks, the last—of his work in hand.[57]

Facio benefited handsomely after presenting his completed history to Alfonso. In fact, the rewards he received in the next two years made him a wealthy man. Vespasiano da Bisticci reported that Facio's work delighted Alfonso so much that he granted the author a reward of fifteen hundred florins (equivalent to fifteen hundred ducats).[58] Facio himself referred in a letter to one thousand gold coins—no doubt one thousand *alfonsini*, the equivalent of fifteen hundred ducats—that Alfonso bestowed on him after receiving the ninth book of the history.[59]

[54] Minieri Riccio, "Alcuni fatti di Alfonso," p. 251.

[55] See the appendix of letters in Facio's *De viris illustribus*, pp. 90–92 for Barbaro's epistle, and pp. 93–96 for Facio's reply.

[56] Valladolid, BU, Colegio Mayor de Santa Cruz, MS 227, fol. 5v.

[57] Facio, *De viris illustribus*, p. 104 in the appendix.

[58] Vespasiano da Bisticci, *Le vite*, ed. A. Greco, 2 vols. (Florence, 1970–76), 1.92.

[59] Valladolid, BU, Colegio Mayor de Santa Cruz, MS 227, fols. 35v–36v.

Other evidence proves that Facio began immediately to enjoy his new wealth. Shortly after submitting his finished work to Alfonso, he wrote to a Venetian friend, Marco Aurelio, requesting a special variety of glass bowl trimmed with gold to keep his wine chilled during the summer. Facio specified that the gold should be so carefully applied that it would not wear off during handling or washing, and he promised to reimburse Aurelio for his expenses. In 1456 he ordered fine pewter vessels from England through his friend Teodoro Spinola of Genoa. He instructed Spinola to spare no expense, but to obtain products of the most choice material and the most beautiful craftsmanship.[60] If he needed more financial security, Facio received it in 1457. A document from 26 July notes that a prince ought to reward and honor those who increase the prince's own glory and dignity. Thus it provided for a permanent raise in Facio's salary from three hundred to five hundred ducats per year.[61]

This last-mentioned reward perhaps represented Alfonso's gratification for the short work *De viris illustribus liber*, a collection of biographical sketches that Facio presented to the king in 1456. Facio divided his subjects into nine categories—poets, orators, lawyers, physicians, painters, sculptors, private citizens, generals, and princes—and in seventy-eight pages he briefly commemorated ninety-two illustrious men of his day. Though not a work of profundity, art historians have found the sections on painters and sculptors important for the understanding of artistic taste in the fifteenth century.[62]

Thus Facio devoted himself to letters even after his career had provided him with considerable material comfort. Indeed, he continued his scholarly work until his final days. His last project was a translation of Arrian's life of Alexander the Great. Facio's work

---

[60] Ibid., fols. 42v–43r and 41r–42r, respectively.

[61] De Marinis, *La biblioteca*, 2.243–44, doc. 174.

[62] Michael Baxandall, "Bartholomaeus Facius on Painting: A Fifteenth-Century Manuscript of the *De viris illustribus*," *Journal of the Warburg and Courtauld Institutes*, 27 (1964), 90–107.

did not represent a fresh version as much as a revision of an earlier translation by Pier Paolo Vergerio. Humanists in the fifteenth century disparaged the earlier work because of its unadorned literary style. Vergerio had produced his translation for Emperor Sigismund, who possessed only a limited grasp of Latin; though well-endowed with literary skills, Vergerio had perforce to present Arrian in rather plain Latin dress. Enea Silvio Piccolomini sent a copy of the work to Naples in January 1454, and soon thereafter Alfonso requested Facio to revise it and cast it in more polished form. For three years Facio worked at the task, occasionally consulting the Greek text of Arrian with the aid of the two Byzantine refugees then residing at Alfonso's court, Theodore Gaza and Niccolò Sagundino. Facio unfortunately suffered an early and sudden death in November 1457, by which time he had completed about one-fourth of the revision. His devoted Genoese friend, Giacomo Curlo, the copyist in Alfonso's library, then assumed and completed Facio's work.[63]

Numerous critics have belittled Facio's works for their lack of profundity, originality, or intellectual coherence. Facio simply did not rank in the first order of Renaissance humanists. The hypercritical evaluation of his career, however, fails to do justice to Facio's positive accomplishments. He produced the first translation of Isocrates into Italian, and he at least began an improved version of Arrian into Latin. His two treatises on the condition of man helped to lend definition to a characteristic theme developed

[63] For Piccolomini's assessment of Vergerio's translation and his loan of a copy to Alfonso, see *Der Briefwechsel des Eneas Silvius Piccolomini*, ed. R. Wolkan, 3 vols. (Vienna, 1909–18), 3. 1.433–37. For Facio's views on Vergerio's work and his understanding of his own efforts, see his letter dedicating the revised translation to Alfonso in BAV, Urb. lat. 415, fols. IIr–IIIr. For Curlo's views on Vergerio and his account of Facio's work, see his letter to Arnau Fonolleda in the same manuscript, fols. 175v–176v. Facio's letter, but not Curlo's, appears also in printed editions of his translation. Both are transcribed in the contribution of Philip A. Stadter, "Arrianus, Flavius," in Paul O. Kristeller and F. Edward Cranz, eds., *Catalogus translationum et commentariorum* (Washington, D.C., 1960–), 3.1–20. See esp. pp. 5–12 on Facio and pp. 8–9 for the letters of Facio and Curlo.

by many later Renaissance humanists. His epistles throw light on the events and conditions of a humanist's life in fifteenth-century Italy. Finally, his biographical and historical compositions, especially the account of Alfonso's career, remain valuable even today as sources of information, if not as definitive treatments of Facio's subjects. His career differed in some respects from that of Panormita: he relied on literary talent rather than on the personal skills that served his senior colleague so well, and he devoted his efforts to scholarship rather than to politics and diplomacy. Yet like Panormita, Facio demonstrated the possibility of meeting the demands of client status while also pursuing a meaningful and prosperous career.

Lorenzo Valla (1407–1457)

The most talented of all the Neapolitan humanists was Lorenzo Valla.[64] Born at Rome in 1407, Valla enjoyed access to men of learning and fine educators through his family: an uncle, Melchiorre Scrivani, obtained a post as papal secretary, and other relatives served as curialists or lawyers. The young Lorenzo studied with Giovanni Aurispa and Leonardo Bruni, among others, and entertained hopes of developing his own career in the papal bureaucracy. Indeed, when his uncle Melchiorre died in 1430, Valla sought to succeed him in his secretarial post. His abrasive personality had already manifested itself, however, with the first but not the last unfortunate results for his career. Valla had alienated two of the most influential papal secretaries, Antonio Loschi and Poggio Bracciolini, who prevented him from succeeding his uncle.

[64] The standard biography is still that of Girolamo Mancini, *Vita di Lorenzo Valla* (Florence, 1891). Though not a formal biography, the recent work of Mario Fois is actually more useful as a guide to Valla's life and career: *Il pensiero cristiano di Lorenzo Valla nel quadro storico-culturale del suo ambiente* (Rome, 1969). Numerous general and specialized studies of Valla's thought have appeared in recent years, and two of them merit special mention as a works of exceptional insight: Salvatore Camporeale, *Lorenzo Valla: umanesimo e teologia* (Florence, 1972); and Trinkaus, *In Our Image and Likeness*, 1.103–70; 2.674–82.

Thus Valla sought employment elsewhere. In 1431 he obtained a post teaching rhetoric at the University of Pavia, largely through the aid of Panormita, who had met Valla in 1428, just before going to Milan as court poet. During the early days of Valla's residence in Lombardy (1431–1434), the two men developed a close friendship. Shortly after moving to Pavia, Valla cast Panormita in a role of significance as a major spokesman in the first edition of his dialogue *On Pleasure*. The work pleased contemporaries by its style and astonished them by its doctrine, especially by the extended and enthusiastic espousal of Epicurean values that stood at the heart of the dialogue.[65] This work by itself would have earned Valla a prominent position in the history of Renaissance moral thought, but it represented only the first of many treatises in which Valla took a fresh, creative approach to a traditional problem.

Valla's career at Pavia came to an abrupt end in 1433, when he composed a short treatise attacking the fourteenth-century lawyer, Bartolus of Sassoferrato. Faculty and students of law at Pavia reacted violently to the treatise, and Valla fled for his life. He taught for about a year at Milan, where he encountered the indefatigable world traveler Ciriaco d'Ancona, and perhaps also Bartolomeo Facio. His major literary effort during that period was a revision of the dialogue *On Pleasure*. Late in 1434 he went to Florence and sought a post from Pope Eugenius IV, who had fled from Rome after the outbreak of a rebellion there. Thus Valla hoped to return to his native city under papal auspices. Eugenius barely controlled the church, however, and certainly was in no position to bestow expensive honors on abrasive humanists. The continuing enmity of Poggio Bracciolini and Antonio Loschi toward Valla did not improve his chances of winning a post. Once again, then, Valla

---

[65] See the critical edition of Valla's *De vero falsoque bono*, ed. M. de P. Lorch (Bari, 1970). Valla himself was not an Epicurean—certainly not in any simple sense of the word—but rather employed Epicurean arguments in order to reject the Stoic ethics popular among his humanist contemporaries. See Trinkaus, *In Our Image and Likeness*, 1.103–50.

looked abroad for employment. This time he went south, entered the service of King Alfonso, and began the most productive period of his entire career.

The exact time of Valla's transfer to Naples remains unclear, along with the nature of his early duties there. Valla himself says that he accompanied Alfonso at the battle of Ponza (August 1435)—indeed, he probably went into captivity with Alfonso and others who fell into Genoese hands during the battle—and that he traveled with him on numerous other military expeditions as well.[66] He no doubt participated also in the literary activities at court, together with Panormita and other humanists as they arrived in the Regno. At least by 1438 Alfonso hoped to persuade Valla to write his deeds as court historian. Valla never became enthusiastic about the project, however, and Facio eventually won the commission that Valla had declined.[67] He perhaps also served as tutor to Ferrante after Alfonso called his son to Italy in 1438. During the summer of that year, while living at Alfonso's provisional court in Gaeta, Valla translated for Ferrante the first four chapters of Xenophon's *Cyropaedia*. The chapters he chose deal with the young Cyrus, whose early days Valla presented for Ferrante as a model of princely virtue.[68]

Valla undertook numerous literary projects during his Neapolitan residence, most of them works of genuine significance for

[66] See Valla's response to Poggio Bracciolini's first invective against him: *Antidotum primum*, ed. A. Wesseling (Assen, 1978), pp. 124–26. See also two of Valla's letters, one of which suggests strongly that Valla accompanied Alfonso in his Milanese captivity, while the other shows clearly that he was present for Alfonso's victory over Antonio Caldora and the city of Sulmona in July 1438: Lorenzo Valla, *Epistole*, ed. O. Besomi and M. Regoliosi (Padua, 1984), pp. 152–53, 163–64, 164–69.

[67] In a document of 1438 Alfonso said that Valla would write his deeds: ACA, Reg. 2830, fol. 104r. In a letter of 1444 Valla mentioned to Flavio Biondo that Alfonso had commissioned him to take on the work, but that he had not done so for lack of adequate source materials: see Valla, *Epistole*, pp. 253–54.

[68] David Marsh, "Lorenzo Valla in Naples: The Translation from Xenophon's *Cyropaedia*," *Bibliothèque d'humanisme et Renaissance*, 46 (1984), 407–20, including transcriptions of Valla's work on pp. 409–20.

their influence on the development of Renaissance culture. After going to Naples, Valla devoted his first efforts to his plan to provide a new foundation for western philosophy—to base logic, dialectic, and metaphysics squarely on grammar, rhetoric, and philology. The resulting work, known generally as the *Dialectical Disputations* (first redaction completed about 1438 or 1439), strikes most commentators as outrageous, but it illustrates well the humanists' high valuation of the literary arts.[69] Three other works undertaken during the next five years show that Valla also conceived religious and theological issues in a novel manner. The dialogue *On Free Will* (1439) asserted the absolute uselessness of philosophy for the clarification of moral and theological issues.[70] The dialogue on *The Profession of the Religious* (1442) argued—on philological as well as moral grounds—that monks did not excel laymen in the holiness of their lives. Indeed, he argued that laymen most likely excelled monks and probably would receive a richer heavenly reward than those under vows.[71] Finally, Valla turned his attention to the ultimate source of Christian doctrine, the New Testament. He produced the first redaction of his notes to the New Testament in 1442 or 1443, based on his comparison of the Latin Vulgate with the Greek text of the New Testament, a work of profound significance because of its influence on the biblical scholarship of Erasmus of Rotterdam.[72]

[69] See the new critical edition, *Repastinatio dialectice et philosophie*, ed. G. Zippel, 2 vols. (Padua, 1982).

[70] See the Latin edition, *De libero arbitrio*, ed. M. Anfossi (Florence, 1934), reprinted in volume 2 of Valla's *Opera omnia*, ed. E. Garin (Turin, 1962); also the English translation, "Dialogue on Free Will," by Charles Trinkaus in E. Cassirer *et al.*, eds., *The Renaissance Philosophy of Man* (Chicago, 1948), pp. 145–82.

[71] See the Latin edition, *De professione religiosorum*, ed. J. Vahlen, in *Sitzungsberichte der kaiserlichen Akademie der Wissenschaften* (Vienna), Phil.-hist. Klasse, 62 (1869), 99–137, reprinted in volume 2 of Valla's *Opera omnia*; also the English translation, *The Profession of the Religious and the Principal Arguments from the Falsely-Believed and Forged Donation of Constantine*, trans. O. Z. Pugliese (Toronto, 1985).

[72] See the Latin edition, *Collatio Novi Testamenti*, ed. A. Perosa (Florence, 1970).

Each of these three works illuminates a characteristic feature of Renaissance thought. The dialogue on free will contributed to the analysis of human nature and human powers that figured prominently in moral and theological debate from the thirteenth to the seventeenth centuries. Indeed, Martin Luther, John Calvin, and other Protestant reformers praised Valla's work for its ostensible rejection of human free will. The reformers did not know of Valla's dialogue on monastic vows, which lay in manuscript until the nineteenth century, but they most surely would have applauded its denial that the monastic profession involved any special sanctity or merited any special reward. Apart from a few exceptional passages, the notes on the New Testament rarely addressed theological issues, yet they too exercised a powerful influence on Renaissance culture. In revised form (prepared after 1453), Valla's notes inaugurated a veritable revolution in scholarship: he insisted that students of the New Testament base their work on the Greek text, and he demonstrated how philological criteria could lead to improved texts, translations, and explanations of Scripture. Through his influence on Erasmus he helped to initiate the modern tradition, based on precise philological analysis, of New Testament scholarship.[73]

Several other works that Valla undertook in Naples show that he must have devoted all his energies there to literary affairs. He had begun sketches of his famous dissertations on Latin elegance before 1435 and only published them after returning to Rome in 1448, but he composed the bulk of the enormous *Elegantiae linguae latinae* in Naples. About 1445 or 1446 he completed also the first history of the reign of Ferdinand of Antequera, King Alfonso's father. This work served as instigator of a bitter controversy that pitted Valla against Panormita and Facio and that led Valla to compose a series of invectives against Facio. Sometime after 1444 he

---

[73] For studies that emphasize the importance of these works, see Trinkaus, *In Our Image and Likeness*, 1.165–70; 2.571–78, 674–82; and Jerry H. Bentley, *Humanists and Holy Writ: New Testament Scholarship in the Renaissance* (Princeton, 1983), pp. 32–69.

completed a second revision of his dialogue *On Pleasure*. Valla also composed and sent numerous letters from the Mezzogiorno, some of them extremely important for the proper understanding of his thought.

Finally, though Valla did not take on political duties during his residence at Naples, as did his colleague, Panormita, he composed one work of major political significance—his *Declamation on the Donation of Constantine* (1440). The political context of the work was Alfonso's struggle for the crown of Naples. From the death of Queen Giovanna II in 1435, Pope Eugenius IV had favored Angevin claims to the throne. In 1436 Alfonso sent a delegation to the Council of Basel in an effort to place indirect pressure on Eugenius. In this and following years he organized various diplomatic initiatives in the hope of exercising more direct influence on the pope. None of his efforts succeeded, however, and in April 1440 Eugenius and the cardinals decided to provide military support to René d'Anjou. At just about the same time, Valla composed his work, which had obvious implications for Alfonso's policy. If Valla could prove the Donation of Constantine a forgery, Eugenius' right to dispose of the kingdom as feudal overlord would rest on slender legal foundation.[74]

In view of this context, I find it difficult to understand how one recent interpreter can deny the political significance of Valla's work. Wolfram Setz characterizes Valla's treatise as a work of rhetoric, canon law, and theology, but not of politics.[75] Valla's own words, marshaled by Setz, prove that Valla had literary, legal, and religious aims for his work. But Mario Fois has demonstrated conclusively that Valla's work dovetailed with Alfonso's diplomacy in

[74] See the critical edition of Valla's treatise, *De falso credita et ementita Constantini donatione*, ed. W. Setz (Weimar, 1976). An English translation exists, based on an earlier edition: *The Treatise of Lorenzo Valla on the Donation of Constantine*, ed. and trans. C. B. Coleman (New Haven, 1922). The best discussion of the political context of Valla's work is that of Fois, *Il pensiero cristiano di Lorenzo Valla*, pp. 296–324.

[75] Wolfram Setz, *Lorenzo Vallas Schrift gegen die konstantinische Schenkung* (Tübingen, 1975), esp. pp. 13–17, 43–75.

the late 1430s and early 1440s. He has shown specifically that Valla's treatise developed points very similar to those made in a set of diplomatic instructions entrusted in October 1436 to the Dominican Juan García, Alfonso's confessor, when he served as ambassador to Eugenius IV seeking support for Alfonso. Both the instructions and Valla condemned Eugenius for simony, financial extortion, and the unholy waging of war.[76] Thus it seems to me impossible to doubt the political implications of Valla's treatise. Indeed, from hints that Valla dropped in his letters, it seems highly likely that he composed the work reluctantly and under the pressure of King Alfonso.[77]

The traditional interpretation—that Valla's treatise played a role in Alfonso's diplomacy—thus still stands, along with the distinct possibility that Alfonso himself commissioned the work. Recognition of these points does not diminish the long-term significance of Valla's argument, which relied heavily on philological observations in exposing the Donation of Constantine as a forgery. Instead, it enriches the understanding of the process by which philological criteria came to dominate literary and historical scholarship. Valla's treatise illustrates better than any other work of the Neapolitan humanists the way the needs of a patron and the talents of a client could combine to produce a work of genius.

Valla's extraordinary productivity during his Neapolitan residence—his ability to write as much as he did and to turn out at least six works of significance and influence—was partly the result of Alfonso's generous patronage. Valla served as Alfonso's secretary from 1435, but he did not receive regular political or administrative assignments. He presumably drew a salary, though there exists no record of monetary compensation for Valla before 1442. In any case, he benefited by Alfonso's efforts to obtain ecclesiasti-

---

[76] Fois, *Il pensiero cristiano di Lorenzo Valla*, pp. 319–24, 332–45, and 346–50, where he excerpts and partially transcribes the instructions. Cf. esp. to the peroration of Valla's treatise, pp. 172–76 in the edition of Setz cited above, n. 74.

[77] Valla, *Epistole*, pp. 247–48; and Donzellini, ed., *Epistolae principum*, pp. 413–16.

cal rewards for him. In a series of documents from 1438, Alfonso sought several benefices for him, including a pension from the abbey of Santo Spirito outside Palermo and a canonry in Cremona.[78] In 1441 Alfonso awarded Valla the temporal administration of the abbey of San Bartolomeo in Candio, after promoting the former abbot to the archbishopric of Benevento (vacated when Alfonso captured the rebel incumbent in seizing the city). It is not certain that Valla actually benefited by this award: Alfonso sought approval for it from the Council of Basel, but no response survives; even if the council agreed with the arrangement, the Treaty of Terracina between Alfonso and Eugenius IV (June 1443) might well have reversed it.[79]

By 1442 at the latest, Valla received a regular salary from Alfonso. In February of that year, Alfonso established for him an annual pension of 50 ounces of *carlini*, equivalent to 300 ducats. Five months later, after taking the city of Naples, Alfonso increased this amount by 50 ducats, for a total salary, after commutation, of 350 ducats. In November 1443 Alfonso provided Valla with tax proceeds from six towns in Traietto and Castelforte instead of his regular salary. The following February, however, at the Parliament of San Lorenzo, Alfonso and the barons abolished the old levies in favor of a new hearth tax, so that the foundation of Valla's livelihood disappeared. Thus on 26 February 1444, Alfonso reestablished Valla's annual salary of 350 ducats and ordered it paid retroactively to 1 September 1443. Valla perhaps did not manage to collect his entire salary: a document of 31 December 1446 ordered payment to Valla of 100 ducats against his annual salary of 300 ducats (rather than 350).[80] But after 1442 he must have experienced considerable financial security.

[78] ACA, Reg. 2830, fol. 104rv; Reg. 2584, fols. 71v–72r, 107v; Reg. 2832, fol. 179rv. See also the discussion in Fois, *Il pensiero cristiano di Lorenzo Valla*, pp. 171–73.

[79] Ramon d'Alos-Moner, "Contribució a la biografia di Lorenzo Valla," in *Miscellanea Crexells* (Barcelona, 1929), pp. 2–5.

[80] For the arrangements of 1442 to 1444, see ibid., pp. 6–7. For the payment of 1446, see Minieri Riccio, "Alcuni fatti di Alfonso," p. 252.

Like Panormita, Facio, and other Neapolitan humanists, Valla developed friendships in Naples that provided a different kind of reward for his efforts there. He reencountered Panormita, of course, and for several years the two men got along reasonably well. They had grown unfriendly while they still lived in Lombardy—in the first revision (1433) of his dialogue *On Pleasure*, Valla pointedly removed Panormita as an interlocutor—but a letter of 1437 shows that Valla had resumed more or less normal relations with Panormita.[81] Valla certainly became friendly with Juan García, bishop of Lérida—not the Dominican Juan García mentioned earlier, King Alfonso's confessor and occasional ambassador—to whom he dedicated the dialogue *On Free Will* in 1439. A third companion was Juan Serra of Valencia, to whom Valla addressed in 1440 an extremely important epistle justifying his writings.[82] For about a year, 1444 to 1445, Valla also enjoyed the company of a young Spanish theologian, Fernando de Córdoba, who impressed Valla and others with his strong memory and who sided with Valla in his bitter controversy (1444) on the Nicene Creed.[83]

Valla's brash nature, his arrogance, and his lack of diplomatic skills indeed led him into numerous difficulties, and in Naples as elsewhere his enemies caused him enormous grief. In the spring of 1444, shortly before Fernando de Córdoba arrived in Italy, Valla became embroiled in a controversy over the Nicene Creed. During Lenten sermons, a popular preacher of the day, Antonio da Bi-

---

[81] A recently published letter of 1432 proves beyond doubt that Valla and Panormita had a falling out while at Pavia: see Valla's *Epistole*, pp. 132–33; for their relationship in 1437, see pp. 163–64.

[82] Valla, *Epistole*, pp. 193–209. For the identification of Juan Serra as Valla's correspondent, now positive after many years of debate, see Agostino Sottili, "Note biografiche sui petrarchisti Giacomo Publicio e Guiniforte Barzizza e sull'umanista valenziano Giovanni Serra," in Fritz Schalk, ed., *Petrarca, 1304–1374. Beiträge zu Werk und Wirkung* (Frankfurt, 1975), pp. 270–86.

[83] Adolfo Bonilla y San Martín, *Fernando de Córdoba (¿1425–1486?) y los orígenes del Renacimiento filosófico en España* (Madrid, 1911); also M. A. Morel-Fatio, "Maître Fernand de Cordoue et les humanistes italiens du XVe siècle," in *Mélanges Julien Havet* (Paris, 1895), pp. 521–33. Valla warmly praised Fernando in a letter to King Alfonso: see his *Epistole*, pp. 258–62.

tonto, had expressed the traditional belief that the Creed originated with Jesus' disciples, each of whom contributed one of the
Creed's twelve points. Valla could not resist the opportunity to
display his erudition and critical prowess: he attacked Antonio, arguing from silence in the early church fathers' writings that the
Creed emerged only during the fourth century at the Councils of
Nicaea and Constantinople. This initial confrontation probably
would have led to nothing more serious than simmering hostility,
except that Valla carried his attack one step further. He addressed
an epistle to the legal scholars of Naples, suggesting that they
emend the passage in Gratian's *Decretum* that proclaimed the apostolic origin of the Creed. The proposal to alter so authoritative a
text as the *Decretum* outraged theological conservatives in Naples,
and they immediately initiated proceedings against him with the
Inquisition of Naples. The document Valla composed in his defense makes it clear that his enemies did not limit their investigation to the Creed, but instead examined a broad range of his
opinions, including controversial views developed in the *Dialectical Disputations*, in the dialogues *On Pleasure*, *On Free Will*, and *The
Profession of the Religious*, and in other works as well. From Valla's
own accounts of the episode, it seems that the inquisitors forced
him to recant his "errors," perhaps without following proper judicial procedures.[84] Valla had espoused no heresy, of course, but
his enemies nonetheless seized the opportunity to repay the hu-
miliation he had often visited upon them.

Valla became engaged two years later in a less serious, but

[84] For recent accounts of the controversy, see Giovanni di Napoli, *Lorenzo
Valla: filosofia e religione nell'umanesimo italiano* (Rome, 1971), pp. 279–312; and
G. Zippel, "La 'Defensio quaestionum in philosophia' di Lorenzo Valla, e un noto
processo dell'Inquisizione napoletana," *Bollettino dell'istituto storico italiano per il
Medio Evo e archivio muratoriano*, 69 (1957), 319–47. Zippel has also edited Valla's
defense: "L'autodifesa di Lorenzo Valla per il processo dell'Inquisizione napoletana (1444)," *Italia medioevale e umanistica*, 13 (1970), 59–94. Valla's own accounts of his experience occur in his apologetic epistle to Eugenius IV (1444) and
his fourth invective against Poggio Bracciolini (1453), both published in Valla's
Opera omnia, 1.355–62, 795–97.

equally annoying controversy with Panormita and Bartolomeo Facio. Increasing tension between Valla and Panormita served as background to the controversy. On several occasions Valla's superior erudition or literary skills had led to the public embarrassment of Panormita.[85] Once the two men both composed verses intended to accompany a portrait of King Alfonso in the Castel Capuano. Alfonso attempted to limit ill will between them by deciding against the inclusion of any verses at all, thus avoiding the necessity of choosing one man's work over that of the other. Another time Alfonso positively preferred verses composed by Valla over those of Panormita to be inscribed on a statue of the sleeping Parthenope. By about 1443, these and other episodes had damaged the relationship so much that Valla denounced Panormita in a letter to Pier Candido Decembrio: he described Panormita as a treacherous man, boasted that he had made him look ridiculous before the king and others, and submitted for Decembrio's amusement two sets of verses he had recently composed against his enemy.[86] Panormita did not sit idly by during this time: he composed his own verses criticizing Valla's poetry and calling into doubt his ability to produce worthy verse.[87]

Shortly after assuming his position at Alfonso's court in 1445, Bartolomeo Facio joined Panormita in his hostility to Valla. Facio no doubt opposed Valla partly because he coveted the commission, then still entrusted to Valla, to write the history of Alfonso's deeds. But he soon came to hold other grudges as well. Like Panormita, Facio resented Valla's contemptuous attitude and his habit of publicly exposing the intellectual inferiority of other humanists at court. In a letter of 1447 to Poggio Bracciolini, he described Valla as an "arrogant man" who "in a certain sort of sick

[85] See Valla's account of these and other episodes in his *Antidotum in Facium*, ed. M. Regoliosi (Padua, 1981), esp. pp. 303–22.

[86] Valla, *Epistole*, pp. 238–41.

[87] BAV, Barb. lat. 2069, fols. 3v, 15v, 58v; also BNN, MS V. E. 51, fols. 8v, 14rv.

spirit and the most petulant manner inveighs against all learned men."[88] Facio had in mind recent sessions of the Neapolitan literary seance that dealt with the text of Livy. In 1444 Cosimo de' Medici had sent to Alfonso a handsome manuscript of Livy that Petrarch had partially emended, but that still presented a largely corrupt text. Alfonso assigned to Facio and his Genoese friend Giacomo Curlo the task of continuing the emendation begun by Petrarch. Armed with superior erudition and philological skills, Valla attacked Facio's emendations and provided better ones of his own. Modern scholars regard his emendations—many of them now confirmed in other manuscripts—as a scholarly tour de force.[89] But Valla's undiplomatic manner only annoyed Facio and Panormita, who thirsted for revenge.

Their opportunity arrived in 1446, when they obtained an early draft of Valla's history of Ferdinand of Antequera. Late in 1445 Valla had presented it to Alfonso, who had delivered it to his librarian, Tomas de Aulesa. Both Alfonso and Valla departed temporarily from Naples the following year; during their absence Facio and Panormita persuaded Aulesa to lend them the work. Facio examined it first and reported gleefully to Panormita that he had discovered more than two hundred errors in the first ten pages.[90] Upon the return of Alfonso and Valla to Naples, the conspirators waited for the opportune moment, then charged publicly that Valla commanded an insecure grasp of Latin style (!) and that he included unworthy materials in his history. Shortly thereafter Fa-

[88] See Facio's introduction to his *Invective in Laurentium Vallam*, ed. E. I. Rao (Naples, 1978), pp. 61–62; and his letter to Poggio in the appendix of epistles to his *De viris illustribus*, pp. 82–83.

[89] See Valla's account of these events along with his own emendations of Livy in his *Antidotum in Facium*, pp. 303–70, esp. pp. 322–27. For modern judgments of his work, see G. Billanovich, "Petrarch and the Textual Tradition of Livy," *Journal of the Warburg and Courtauld Institutes*, 14 (1951), 137–208; and Mariangela Regoliosi, "Lorenzo Valla, Antonio Panormita, Giacomo Curlo e le emendazioni a Livio," *Italia medioevale e umanistica*, 24 (1981), 287–316.

[90] See the appendix of Facio's unedited epistles in Gabotto, *Un nuovo contributo*, p. 275.

cio composed his four *Invectives* against Valla, where the slender basis for his accusations becomes all too clear. He sent copies to acquaintances throughout Italy, but did not supply one to Valla, who read the work only after a relative sent a copy from Rome. Thus Valla had to wait until 1447 to compose his response, the *Antidote* to Facio's poison; only then did he gain the opportunity to explain the context and events of the controversy, to defend his work against Facio's exaggerated charges, and to publish his emendations of Livy along with justifications.[91]

By 1447, however, Valla had but little time to remain in Naples. He had long desired the opportunity to return to his native Rome: he had sought a position in the curia just before going to Naples in 1435, as seen above; and within months of the Treaty of Terracina and the reestablishment of peace between Alfonso and Eugenius IV, he began to lay the foundations for his return to Rome. By November 1443 he began to address letters to cardinals, seeking specifically to remove his treatise on the Donation of Constantine as an obstacle to his return, and more generally to win their support for his plans.[92] At first Alfonso disapproved of Valla's intentions, but by August 1444 he agreed to release him and even provided letters recommending him for the service of Eugenius IV.[93] Valla addressed two apologetic epistles to Eugenius himself, seeking to remove lingering doubts about Valla's orthodoxy and continuing hostility because of his work on the Donation of Con-

---

[91] See the editions of these works cited above, notes 85 and 88. On the quality and limitations of Rao's edition of Facio's *Invective*, see Mariangela Regoliosi, "Per la tradizione delle 'Invective in L. Vallam' di Bartolomeo Facio," *Italia medioevale e umanistica*, 23 (1980), 389–97; and Riccardo Ribuoli, "Polemiche umanistiche: a proposito di due recenti edizioni," *Respublica litterarum*, 4 (1981), 339–54.

[92] Valla, *Epistole*, pp. 246–49, 254–57.

[93] On Alfonso's reluctance to allow Valla's departure in February 1444, see Valla's *Epistole*, pp. 257–58. Alfonso's letter of recommendation survives in the Aragonese archives and was published in Constantin Marinescu, ed., "Notes sur la vie culturelle sous le règne d'Alfonse *le magnanime*, roi de Naples," in *Miscel·lanea Puig i Cadafalch* (Barcelona, 1947–51), 1.306. Other unpublished recommendations survive in ACA, Reg. 2653, fols. 51r–52r.

stantine.[94] None of these efforts succeeded, however, at least not during the papacy of Eugenius IV. Only after the selection of Valla's friend Tommaso Parentucelli as Pope Nicholas V (1447–1455) did the way open for Valla to return to Rome.

Valla continued to work in his unconventional way after going back to Rome. During the last decade of his life he produced, among other less important works, an astonishing encomium of St. Thomas Aquinas, a work that ended by praising patristic theology at the expense of the Schoolmen; a clever sermon on the mystery of the Eucharist, which argued the irrelevance of philosophy for the explanation of divine phenomena; and a revision of his annotations to the New Testament. The last item ranks as an especially momentous work for the history of scholarship, since a manuscript of this second redaction of Valla's notes fell into the hands of Erasmus of Rotterdam, who derived considerable inspiration from it.

For present purposes, however, Valla's Neapolitan career is more important than his life at Rome. He seems to have lived comfortably in Naples, if not as splendidly as Panormita. He certainly enjoyed opportunities to indulge his literary and scholarly interests. Indeed, from the viewpoint of intellectual history, Valla ranks without doubt or question as the most important of the Neapolitan humanists. During his Neapolitan residence he powerfully influenced Renaissance moral thought (through the dialogue *On Free Will*), philosophy (through the *Dialectical Disputations*), Latin style (through the *Elegantiae*), and philology (through the *Elegantiae*, the treatise on the Donation of Constantine, and the annotations to the New Testament). He certainly experienced troubles while living in Naples: his overbearing personality led him into bitter disputes with Panormita and Facio, and his continual quarreling with other humanists must have caused problems even for Alfonso. Not enough, however, that Alfonso contented himself

[94] See Valla's *Opera omnia*, 1.795–800a; and Donzellini, ed., *Epistolae principum*, pp. 409–418.

easily with Valla's departure. Valla after all performed several useful functions for Alfonso: he served as an erudite literary scholar who could comment knowledgeably on matters of interest to Alfonso; he at least once lent his literary and philological skills to the support of Alfonso's policy by exposing the Donation of Constantine as a forgery; and he improved the image of the House of Aragon in general by his generous account of the deeds of Ferdinand of Antequera.

Despite his prickly nature, then, Valla developed a successful career at Naples, especially considering it from a professional rather than a personal point of view. No other Aragonese king of Naples enjoyed the service of a man possessing such sheer intellectual brilliance as did Valla. Other humanists performed political and administrative duties much more willingly and effectively than he did. But of all the men of culture who lived at the Aragonese court of Naples, Lorenzo Valla most profoundly influenced the development of Renaissance thought.

Giannozzo Manetti (1396–1459)

Giannozzo Manetti deserved recognition, according to his close friend Vespasiano da Bisticci, as one of those "singular men who have defined and adorned their age."[95] Manetti could not entirely make up for the loss of Lorenzo Valla at Naples, but his presence there lent the luster of an established and universally respected humanist to Alfonso's court.

Manetti did not go to Naples entirely of his own accord. Born into a family of successful merchants and bankers, Giannozzo followed his father's wishes and devoted himself to business until

---

[95] There is no modern biography of Manetti, but Vespasiano composed a short biographical sketch and a long commentary on Manetti's life: *Le vite*, 1.485–538; 2.513–627. The quotation occurs at 1.485. See also Heinz Willi Wittschier, *Giannozzo Manetti. Das Corpus der Orationes* (Cologne, 1968), pp. 2–26; and Lauro Martines, *The Social World of the Florentine Humanists, 1390–1460* (Princeton, 1963), pp. 131–38, 176–91.

adulthood. Only about 1421 did he begin to study Latin, which he soon supplemented with Greek and Hebrew. At the same time, he prepared himself for public service. He enrolled in the guild of bankers and money changers in 1425, and in 1429 he served as one of the Twelve Good Men, who composed a sensitive advisory council to the Florentine republican government. In later years he assumed numerous other positions important for the administration of Florence or for policy making. Beginning in the 1440s he received foreign as well as domestic assignments. He served as governor of several Florentine territories, and he traveled on at least twelve major diplomatic missions on behalf of the republic, most of them concentrated in the period 1448 to 1453. Early in the 1450s, however, Manetti fell foul of a powerful political clique allied with Cosimo de' Medici. As a result of his friendship with King Alfonso and his successful diplomatic efforts in Naples and Venice, Manetti's enemies charged him with treason and imposed upon him the crippling tax assessments that drove him out of Florence. Manetti went first to Rome, where he served for two years (1453–1455) as secretary under Pope Nicholas V, at an annual salary of six hundred ducats. Calixtus III confirmed his appointment as secretary in 1455, but after Nicholas' death, Manetti accepted King Alfonso's offer to assume a post in Naples.

Manetti and Alfonso had known each other since 1443, from the first of Manetti's four diplomatic missions to the king. They seem to have enjoyed a cordial personal relationship from the earliest days, though serious political differences divided them during the War of the Milanese Succession (1447–1453). In 1448 Manetti delivered two orations condemning Alfonso's policy. The first urged Siena to resist the Neapolitan thrust into Tuscany, specifically to aid the port of Piombino, then under Alfonso's siege. Manetti painted Alfonso himself in the blackest of colors, portraying him as an immensely ambitious man eager for domination and expansion, as a violator of divine and human law willing to lie and deceive in order to advance his interests. Shortly afterward Manetti addressed the citizens of Venice in similar fashion, but in even stronger terms. Here Manetti argued the need to drive Alfonso out of Italy altogether. He likened Alfonso to Hannibal in that he posed a threat to the independence of the entire peninsula, and he even called upon the Venetians to support the efforts of René d'Anjou to recapture the kingdom of Naples.[96]

Over the long term, however, Manetti and Alfonso developed an extraordinarily close friendship. In May 1445 Manetti served as Florentine representative at the wedding of Ferrante, then duke of Calabria, to Isabella di Chiaromonte. In his oration for the occasion, Manetti praised Alfonso for his patronage of learning, his merciful conquest of Naples, and his noble Spanish ancestors, including the Roman emperors Trajan, Hadrian, Theodosius, Arcadius, Honorius, and Theodosius II.[97] The oration enchanted Alfonso so thoroughly (as Manetti recalled on a later occasion) that he sat rapt and motionless through the entire speech, even though three flies crawled around the royal nostrils.[98] Manetti presented several other favorable and even flattering rhetorical portraits of Alfonso in succeeding years. In 1451 he delivered before Alfonso an oration praising the peace treaty that Manetti hoped would end hostilities between Florence and Naples. In 1452 he praised Alfonso himself in an oration (probably not delivered orally) congratulating the king on the visit of Emperor Frederick III. In 1455 Manetti lauded Alfonso as an ideal commander for a crusade in another oration (again probably never actually delivered) to Pope Calixtus III.[99]

Alfonso and Manetti drew especially close in 1451, when Manetti spent almost five months as Florentine ambassador in search

[96] The texts of these two orations appear in Wittschier, *Giannozzo Manetti*, pp. 142–75.

[97] Sandeo, *De regibus Siciliae et Apuliae*, pp. 169–75.

[98] Ibid., p. 177. Panormita also told this story in his *De dictis et factis*, pp. 15–16.

[99] For the oration on the praise of peace, see Sandeo, *De regibus Siciliae et Apuliae*, pp. 177–84. The other two survive only in manuscript; I rely on the copy that came from Manetti's personal library, BAV, Pal. lat. 1604, fols. 7v–22v, 22v–29v. On Manetti's orations in general, see Wittschier, *Giannozzo Manetti*.

of a peace treaty between Alfonso and Florence. During this period Manetti and Alfonso often held long conversations on cultural as well as political matters. One of their colloquies in fact led to Manetti's most enduring work, the treatise *On the Dignity and Excellence of Man*. During their talk Manetti mentioned Bartolomeo Facio's treatise on the excellence of man, and Alfonso asked him to compose another work on the same theme. Manetti completed the work and dedicated it to Alfonso the following year.[100] In a curious way, this treatise hastened Manetti's permanent departure from Tuscany: his Florentine enemies relied upon Manetti's dedication of the treatise to Alfonso and his obvious friendship with the king as foundations for their charges of treason against the republic.

In any case, Manetti recognized a foundation for his future in his close relationship with Alfonso. Already in March 1452 he wrote to Panormita with news of rumors that had begun to fly around Florence because of Alfonso's goodwill toward him; for his own part, Manetti expressed his desire to remain in the good graces of his Neapolitan friends.[101] When Pope Nicholas V died, then, Manetti was well placed to accept Alfonso's invitation to go to Naples. Vespasiano says that Alfonso awarded Manetti an annual salary of nine hundred ducats, further that he told him not to waste time at court, but rather to devote his time and talents to scholarship. A document of 1455 confirms Vespasiano: by 13 October of that year Alfonso had named Manetti a royal councillor and a president (i.e., member) of the Sommaria, and he assigned to him an annual salary of 150 ounces, equivalent to 900 ducats, for the remainder of his life.[102]

---

[100] See Manetti's letter dedicating his treatise to Alfonso in the recently published critical edition, *De dignitate et excellentia hominis*, ed. E. Leonard (Padua, 1975), pp. 1–2.

[101] BAV, Vat. lat. 3372, fols. 40v–41r. Cf. also Manetti's letter of December 1452 to Panormita in the same manuscript, fol. 41rv.

[102] Vespasiano, *Le vite*, 1.100, 532–33; 2.604–5. For the document, executed by Panormita, see Toppi, *De origine omnium tribunalium*, 3.261–63. Cf. a similar document dated 30 October 1455, published only in a rare edition of Vespasi-

Thus Manetti enjoyed an arrangement that provided him with considerable comfort and leisure. Little wonder, then, that Manetti wrote as prolifically as he did during his last four years of life. He dedicated to Alfonso a revision of his parallel lives of Socrates and Seneca (originally composed about 1440).[103] The earthquakes that struck the Regno in December 1456 prompted Manetti to sort out views on tremors developed by historians, philosophers, scientists, and theologians.[104] Manetti's most important projects during this period were perhaps his translations. He produced a new Latin version of Aristotle's *Nicomachean Ethics* and the first Latin translations of his *Eudemian Ethics* and *Magna moralia*. He intended to translate into Latin both the Old and the New Testaments. He translated the New Testament in its entirety, but completed only the Psalter from the Hebrew scriptures.[105] The latter work he justified against critics in a long apologetic treatise.[106] He composed the larger part of a theological work, *Contra iudeos et gentes*, that defended Christianity against Judaism and paganism.[107] Finally, he began but did not live to complete a work on the parallel lives of Philip of Macedonia and Alfonso the Magnanimous.[108]

Alfonso's death in June 1458 did not put an end to Manetti's Neapolitan career: Ferrante confirmed his position as a royal councillor, his seat on the Sommaria, and his salary of 150 ounces.[109]

---

ano's *Commentario della vita di messer Giannozzo Manetti*, ed. P. Fanfani (Turin, 1862), doc. 4, pp. 155–57.

[103] See the new edition of Manetti's *Vita Socratis et Senecae*, ed. A. de Petris (Florence, 1979), esp. pp. 9–11, 113–18.

[104] On the circumstances and plan of the work, see Manetti's letter dedicating it to Alfonso: BAV, Pal. lat. 1604, fols. 97r–98r.

[105] On Manetti's intention, see his letter dedicating the Psalter to Alfonso: BAV, Pal. lat. 41, fols. 2r–3r. The translation of the New Testament survives in BAV, Pal. lat. 45 and Urb. lat. 6.

[106] See the recent edition of Manetti's *Apologeticus*, ed. A. de Petris (Rome, 1981).

[107] BAV, Urb. lat. 154.

[108] See Vespasiano, *Le vite*, 2.508, 606.

[109] Ibid., 2.614. See also the document published as an appendix to Vespasiano's *Commentario* on Manetti's life, ed. Fanfani, doc. 5, pp. 158–59.

But illness plagued Manetti in his own last months and prevented him from devoting his time to scholarship. In fact, in almost exactly sixteen months, Manetti followed his royal patron to the grave (26 October 1459). The generosity of Alfonso, however, had succeeded eminently well in the case of Manetti. The most significant of all Manetti's works, most notably the oration *On the Dignity and Excellence of Man* and the biblical translations, emerged either at Alfonso's encouragement or with his material support. The oration ranks as probably the most important of all the works dedicated to the characteristic Renaissance theme of human dignity. The biblical translations did not exercise as much influence as the oration, since they survive even today only in manuscript. But scholars have nonetheless found Manetti's translations important as works that illuminate the intellectual environment within which Renaissance humanists carried out their scriptural scholarship. Thus once again a major Italian humanist found it possible to undertake work of great cultural significance because of the conditions of clientage he found at the court of Naples.[110]

Giovanni Pontano (1426–1503)

Better than any other Neapolitan humanist, Giovanni Pontano exemplified the ideal of the intellectual active in politics. He obtained a position at Alfonso's court at the tender age of twenty-one years, and he served the Aragonese monarchy and the city of Naples until his last days. Meanwhile, he found occasion to produce volumes of poetry, literature, astrology, moral philosophy, and history.

Giovanni Pontano was born 7 May 1426 in Umbria at Cerreto (near Spoleto) to a family traditionally active in politics.[111] His fa-

---

[110] For an analysis of Manetti's most important works and a discussion of their significance, see Trinkaus, *In Our Image and Likeness*, 1.230–70; 2.571–601, 722–34.

[111] The best biography is that of Erasmo Percopo, *Vita di Giovanni Pontano*, ed. M. Manfredi (Naples, 1938). See also two important studies of Pontano's

ther died young during an uprising in Cerreto, and his family lost much of its wealth in the aftermath. Giovanni studied at Cerreto and Perugia, but saw little future for himself in Umbria. Thus he began to seek patronage elsewhere. In September 1447 Alfonso the Magnanimous and his army invaded Tuscany in an effort to seize the lordship of Milan. During the conflict, Pontano presented himself to Alfonso and sought a post at the Neapolitan court. Evidently he impressed Alfonso, for he won his position and entered Naples with the king in October 1448. In the early days at Naples he continued his studies, concentrating especially on Greek and astrology. By the age of twenty-four years he had gained a reputation as a prodigy, and he began to receive assignments of some importance. He accompanied Panormita and Luis Despuig on their diplomatic mission of 1451 to Florence and Venice. His friendship with the important Neapolitan patron and secretary, Juan Olzina, led to a position as secretary in the chancellery. And during the years 1452 to 1457 he served as tutor to Alfonso's nephew, Juan of Navarre.

Pontano's more significant duties began after Ferrante's succession to the Neapolitan throne. He traveled with Ferrante during the war against the Angevins and rebel barons; at least two letters that Pontano composed on the king's behalf survive from this period.[112] By 1461 he had assumed posts as lieutenant to the great chamberlain and the royal protonotary, and the following year Ferrante named him a royal councillor. Pontano probably left Naples for two years (1466–1468) in order to teach in Perugia, but the active political life lured him back. In 1471 Ferrante granted Pontano Neapolitan citizenship, and by at least 1475 he had appointed him to the Sommaria.

---

thought: Giuseppe Toffanin, *Giovanni Pontano fra l'uomo e la natura*, 2d ed. (Bologna, 1938); and especially Francesco Tateo, *L'umanesimo etico di Giovanni Pontano* (Lecce, 1972). Finally, see also the insightful interpretative essay on Pontano's thought by Mario Santoro in his *Fortuna, ragione e prudenza nella civiltà letteraria del Cinquecento*, 2d ed. (Naples, 1978), pp. 27–69.

[112] *Lettere inedite di Joviano Pontano in nome de' reali di Napoli*, ed. F. Gabotto (Bologna, 1893), pp. 39–47.

By this time Pontano served not only Ferrante, but also Duke Alfonso of Calabria. He succeeded Panormita as Duke Alfonso's tutor, and he served as secretary both to the duke and to his wife, Ippolita Sforza. From May 1475 until January 1482 he worked almost exclusively on behalf of Ippolita. Most of the correspondence he wrote for her dealt with minor matters, but at times it touched on sensitive political issues. During November and December 1475, for example, both Ferrante and Duke Alfonso—the king and the heir apparent—fell seriously ill. Pontano composed a series of letters advising Ippolita's brother, Duke Galeazzo Maria Sforza of Milan, and her other relatives about the courses of the diseases. Concern for the Aragonese dynasty of Naples explains Pontano's detailed reports on the victims' symptoms, their doctors' treatments, and even on the content of Ferrante's stool. On another occasion, in January 1482, Pontano's last surviving letter for Ippolita expressed the hope that the duchess could serve as a link between Milanese and Neapolitan regimes, advancing the common interests of both.[113]

Succeeding events provide the explanation for this letter, as Milanese and Neapolitan forces cooperated in the War of Ferrara (1482–1484). By May 1482, and probably somewhat earlier, Pontano began to serve as secretary exclusively for Duke Alfonso, already engaged by that time in the first phase of the War of Ferrara. Pontano followed the duke and his army into the Abruzzi and Lombardy, where he composed all of Alfonso's military and political correspondence.[114] At the war's conclusion, Pontano figured as the prime source of inspiration for the Peace of Bagnolo (7 August 1484), which attempted to return Italy to the condition established thirty years earlier by the Peace of Lodi.

Pontano's service during the War of Ferrara proved his value to

---

[113] Ibid., pp. 47–122, esp. pp. 64–90, 120–22. For Pontano's correspondence for Isabella on a later, less serious occasion when Ferrante became ill, see Milan, Archivio di Stato, Autografi 150, letter of Pontano dated 19 October 1476.

[114] Ibid., pp. 122–335.

the Aragonese monarchy of Naples, and he assumed increasingly important political responsibilities in succeeding years. During the second barons' revolt he helped to formulate royal plans, and he accompanied Duke Alfonso on military campaigns. At war's end he served as ambassador to Pope Innocent VIII, the barons' chief Italian ally, with whom he negotiated the peace of 1486.[115] After the arrest and execution of Antonello Petrucci, Pontano became Ferrante's chief secretary and consequently the most important spokesman for the Regno. In that capacity he composed instructions to ambassadors justifying Ferrante's policy of repressing the barons, as well as almost all the more normal diplomatic correspondence of the realm.[116] He urged Ferrante continually to establish a normal diplomatic relationship with Pope Innocent, and in January 1492 he negotiated a definitive peace reducing the tension that for many years had plagued relations between Naples and Rome.

After Ferrante's death in January 1494, Pontano served as secretary to King Alfonso II, who placed high value on Pontano's political experience. Indeed, the Milanese ambassador in Naples reported that no one had more access to the new king or more influence on his thinking than Pontano.[117] After Alfonso's abdication, Pontano served briefly as secretary also to King Ferrandino. He worked feverishly to prevent the French invasion, but to no avail. The French occupation of Naples put an end to Pontano's regular political service. He delivered the keys of the Neapolitan fortresses to Charles VIII and sought guarantees that the invaders would not harm the city. But no evidence supports Francesco Guicciardini's tale that Pontano welcomed Charles to Naples in a warm oration that maligned the Aragonese kings. Pontano's consistent loyalty to his patrons and his equally consistent loathing of the French both argue against the story's probability.

[115] Fedele, "La pace del 1486," pp. 481–503.

[116] Volpicella, ed., *Instructionum liber*, pp. 53–195; Trinchera, ed., *Codice aragonese*, vol. 2, pts. 1 and 2.

[117] See the document of 11 February 1494 in Milan, Archivio di Stato, Sforzesco 252.

Very little information survives on the rewards Pontano received in exchange for his services. In July 1460, just before the battle of Sarno, at the most difficult point of his struggle to succeed King Alfonso, Ferrante assigned Pontano an annual salary of 40 ounces, equivalent to 240 ducats. The document by which he provided this salary made it clear that Ferrante held a deep and genuine respect for his young protégé: he praised Pontano's learning and intellect, and he remembered in especially warm terms the services Pontano had provided during the recent, difficult period of hostilities. In 1466 Ferrante raised Pontano's salary by 160 ducats, so that his total annual stipend amounted to 66 ounces and 20 *tarì*, equivalent to 400 ducats.[118] By 1490 Pontano was wealthy enough to own a villa and a townhouse, and he had begun to build a famous chapel in the city of Naples. Upon its completion, he endowed the chapel with a provision of 270 ducats per year, and he had transferred to a distinguished place beneath its altar the arm bone of Livy that Panormita had brought from Padua in 1452.[119] During the early days after Ferrante's death, King Alfonso II desperately sought to retain Pontano's loyalty and richly rewarded him as a result. According to the Milanese ambassador in Naples, the new king gave a galley to Pontano's son, who wanted to become a merchant, and bestowed upon Pontano himself a castle located some twenty-six miles from Naples and worth eight hundred ducats of income per year.[120]

Despite his wealth, Pontano occasionally had serious grievances to lodge against Ferrante. In a brief sketch of his own career composed about 1499, Pontano mentioned that he had resigned his position three times during Ferrante's reign, but that each time

---

[118] See the documents published by Toppi, *De origine omnium tribunalium*, 3.272–81; also by Percopo, *Vita di Giovanni Pontano*, pp. 309–12.

[119] Percopo, *Vita di Giovanni Pontano*, pp. 56–59. On the chapel see also R. Filangieri, "Il tempietto di Giovanni Pontano a Napoli," in *In onore di Giovanni Gioviano Pontano nel V centenario della sua nascita* (Naples, 1926), pp. 11–49.

[120] See the document of 31 January 1494 in Milan, Archivio di Stato, Sforzesco 252.

the king had refused to accept the resignation.[121] A surviving letter sheds light on one of these occasions. On his birthday, 7 May 1490, Pontano addressed to Ferrante a letter of undeniably insolent character—Pontano never minced words, even when addressing kings and popes—bitterly complaining about a new tax of twenty ducats per month charged against chancellery income. The new levy consequently exceeded by far the customary rate of 4 percent at which royal officials paid tax and required Pontano to pay 12, 15, or even 18 percent of his income into the treasury.[122] Besides allowing Pontano the opportunity to vent his outrage and display his considerable literary talent, this letter also makes it possible to calculate at least roughly the chancellery's income in 1490. Assuming the basic accuracy of Pontano's figures—a levy of twenty ducats per month and effective tax rates of 12, 15, and 18 percent—the chancellery would have earned between 111 and 167 ducats per month early in 1490. No doubt Pontano had expenses to meet out of these earnings. Still, chancellery income must have represented a considerable portion of Pontano's personal earnings following his appointment as Ferrante's chief secretary.

Pontano's letter did not achieve its goal—Ferrante persuaded him to continue in his post—and not until the French occupation of 1495 did Pontano gain release from his political chores. Yet his official duties did not prevent Pontano from occupying himself with literature. All through his adult life, from the 1450s onward, Pontano composed poetry. While tending to secretarial and diplomatic duties he also found time to compose works of literature and moral philosophy. Three of his dialogues, *Charon*, *Antonius*, and *Asinus*, derive from the period about 1467 to 1486, and while still politically active he at least began work on several moral treatises, including *De principe* (1468), *De obedientia* (1470), *De rebus coelistibus* (1475), *De fortitudine* (1481), *De liberalitate* (1493), and

---

[121] See Pontano's *De prudentia*, reprinted in his *Opera omnia soluta oratione composita*, 3 vols. (Venice, 1518–19), vol. 1, fol. 166rv.

[122] See E. Percopo, "Lettere di Giovanni Pontano a principi ed amici," *AAP*, 37 (1907), pp. 32–34.

De beneficentia (1493). Finally, following the death of Panormita in 1471, Pontano also presided over sessions of the Neapolitan academy, which in fact often met in his house. Dozens of political, literary, religious, and philosophical thinkers frequented the academy during the years that Pontano guided its discussions. Conversations in this period focused on political and moral problems as well as on literature, and occasionally members also presented public readings of their poetic compositions. Under Pontano's guidance, the academy became the most influential institutional exponent of humanist culture in all the kingdom of Naples.[123]

His retirement from politics in 1495 enabled Pontano to cultivate more diligently than ever before the contemplative rather than the active life: only in his last years did he concentrate all his energies on literature and scholarship. After his retirement he prepared most of his works for publication; wrote two new dialogues, *Actius* and *Aegidius*; composed eight new treatises on moral and philosophical themes, including *De magnificentia*, *De splendore*, *De conviventia*, *De magnanimitate*, *De prudentia*, *De immanitate*, *De fortuna*, and *De sermone*; and produced his only work of history, *De bello neapolitano*, on Ferrante's struggle to succeed Alfonso.[124]

And yet even in these last years, Pontano occasionally per-

[123] On the academy under Pontano's guidance, see Percopo, *Vita di Giovanni Pontano*, pp. 106–19; and Santoro, "La cultura umanistica," pp. 159–71. For biographical sketches of many (though not all) of its habitués, see Minieri Riccio, *Biografie degli accademici alfonsini*.

[124] All of Pontano's literary and scholarly works appear in his *Opera omnia*, but many are available also in better and more convenient editions: *I dialoghi*, ed. C. Previtera (Florence, 1943); *I trattati delle virtù sociali*, (cited n. 18 above); *De magnanimitate*, ed. F. Tateo (Florence, 1969); *De immanitate liber*, ed. L. Monti Sabia (Naples, 1970); *De sermone libri sex*, ed. S. Lupi and A. Risicato (Lugano, 1954); and the edition of *De principe* in Eugenio Garin, ed., *Prosatori latini del Quattrocento* (Milan, 1952), pp. 1021–63. I wish to mention also two especially important studies of Pontano's works: Francesco Tateo, "Le virtù sociali e l'"immanità' nella trattatistica pontaniana," *Rinascimento*, n.s. 5 (1965), 119–54; and Mario Santoro, "Il *De immanitate*: testamento spirituale del Pontano," *La partenope: rivista di cultura napoletana*, 1 (1960), 5–16.

formed political services on behalf of his adopted land. Indeed, the very last writing known to have come from Pontano's hand sought to protect the interests of the city of Naples. On behalf of the city fathers, Pontano addressed a letter in mid-May 1503—only a few months before his death in September or October—to King Louis XII of France. He pointed out that as the troops of Gonsalvo de Córdoba advanced on the city, the French garrison had deserted Naples, leaving it without defenses or food. The city thus had no choice except to surrender to the *gran capitán*. Without saying it in so many words, Pontano evidently wanted to convey the impression that the city of Naples had not willfully betrayed the French, but surrendered only for utter lack of alternatives. By implication, then, the city would deserve no punishment if the French managed to regain their hold on it.[125]

No single document expresses better than this last epistle of Pontano the confusion and frustration that reigned in Italy after 1494. Occupied by one foreign power until almost the moment that Pontano composed his letter, Naples was to serve as host to another parasitic army within a matter of days—but could not safely rule out the possibility that the first invader might return. Little wonder that the theme of fortune loomed so large in Italian political writing and reflection during the late fifteenth and sixteenth centuries.

At the same time, however, the letter to Louis XII offers unimpeachable evidence that Pontano possessed a powerful sense of civic duty. Aged just over seventy-seven years, the old humanist picked up his pen to write one last time on behalf of his beloved city. No other secretary or diplomat or minister—perhaps not even any governor or ruler—ever served the city and kingdom of Naples as well or as thoughtfully as Giovanni Pontano.

---

[125] Liliana Monti Sabia publishes the text of Pontano's epistle along with a splendid introduction and analysis: "L'estremo autografo di Giovanni Pontano," *Italia medioevale e umanistica*, 23 (1980), 293–314.

Patronage and Clientage in Renaissance Naples

Civic patriotism and professional rhetoric: for two decades, terms like these have helped historians to define their conceptions of Renaissance humanists as social and political animals. Did the humanists genuinely recognize a duty to contribute their intellectual talents to their states? Or did they seek to sell their literary skills to the highest bidder? If conceived exclusively in this way, the problem takes on all the characteristics of the classic false dichotomy.[126] Few historians today, however, would voluntarily abandon the entire spectrum of interpretative possibilities in favor of the two exaggerated extremes. More recent interpretations do not directly address the issues raised in earlier debates. Yet they often reflect the influence of earlier concerns by arguing that humanists rather cynically allied themselves with men of power in order to advance their own interests.[127]

The study of patron–client relationships must figure prominently in any effort to characterize the humanists' political and social lives. In the case of Naples, humanists served their royal patrons with impressive loyalty. Indeed, the extent of their good faith toward the Aragonese monarchy and their efforts on its behalf will become apparent only in the next chapter, which discusses several episodes that place the humanists' services in especially clear light. Even during difficult times the humanists devoted themselves to the royal interest: Panormita wrote vigorously on behalf of Ferrante during the darkest days of the period 1460 to 1462, even as he vented his frustration over his salary and openly considered leaving Naples; despite his three attempts to resign, Pontano served the Aragonese continuously for more than forty

---

[126] For the most famous debate on this issue, see Jerrold E. Seigel, " 'Civic Humanism' or Ciceronian Rhetoric?" *Past and Present*, 34 (1966), 3–48; and Hans Baron, "Leonardo Bruni: 'Professional Rhetorician' or 'Civic Humanist'?" *Past and Present*, 36 (1967), 21–37.

[127] See for example Romano, *Tra due crisi*, pp. 117–36; and Martines, *Power and Imagination*, pp. 191–217.

years, working absolutely at fever-pitch during especially tense moments such as the aftermath of the second barons' revolt and the period preceding the French occupation of 1495. As subjects of a monarchy rather than citizens of a self-governing republic, the Neapolitan humanists of course did not develop the republican strain of civic patriotism associated with the humanists of the Tuscan city-states. The authenticity of their loyalty to the Aragonese dynasty, however, and even their sense of duty to the entire kingdom, will bear no doubt or question.

At the same time, the humanists benefited handsomely from their work on behalf of the dynasty. They did not simply serve as intellectual tools for the Aragonese kings, but rather provided very well indeed for themselves and their families: for their services they received generous financial compensation, which enabled them to live comfortably, acquire property, and leave handsome legacies for their heirs. Panormita, Manetti, and Pontano received especially liberal compensation—indeed, few humanists in all of Renaissance Italy enjoyed such munificence—while Valla and Facio lived in considerable comfort, if not in luxury.

Yet their material rewards represented only a portion of the benefits that attracted humanists to the Regno. Their positions at the Neapolitan court made available to them a range of rewarding opportunities inconceivable elsewhere in Italy, excepting only Rome and perhaps Florence. During the reign of Alfonso at least, humanists enjoyed the leisure necessary to devote themselves seriously to literature or scholarship. When this opportunity fell to a man of exceptional talent, such as Valla or Manetti, the results could prove momentous for the culture of the entire Renaissance period of European as well as Italian history. Most if not all of the humanists also participated in the life of the Neapolitan academy, where they could indulge their cultural and intellectual interests without dedicating all their time to study. Finally, humanists with the requisite talents also gained the opportunity to influence events through their activities as secretaries, advisers, and diplomats. The cases of Panormita and especially of Pontano serve as the clearest illustrations of this point.

Thus no single explanation accounts for the humanists' activities as social and political animals. The humanists did not act purely as patriots, nor as mercenary intellectuals. Only a complex web of motives—dynastic loyalties, professional opportunities, cultural interests, personal desires, financial considerations, and perhaps others as yet unidentified—can explain a humanist's decision to seek a certain opportunity, accept a certain post, or fulfill his duties in a certain way. In any case, the Neapolitan humanists in general clearly found it possible to lead a reasonably balanced existence: while serving the political needs or satisfying the cultural tastes of the Aragonese kings of Naples, they also pursued careers that provided them both with material rewards and with opportunities to indulge their literary and scholarly interests.

4

The Foundations of a Realistic Political Ethic

MACHIAVELLI rejected metaphysics, theology, idealism. The whole drift of his thought is toward a political realism, unknown to the formal writing of his time." Thus Max Lerner captured the essence of the matter.[1] Machiavelli has commanded the attention of thoughtful people during the past four hundred years for one prime reason: better than his contemporaries or anyone else who lived within several centuries of his time, Machiavelli understood and described the role of power in political relationships.

Recent scholarship has largely cast Machiavelli's analysis of power in the shade, focusing instead on his biography, education, vocabulary, language, understanding of history, and other topics. The recent studies have without doubt contributed significantly to the understanding of the whole of Machiavelli's thought: they have disclosed fresh evidence, explored new ideas, and introduced a high degree of precision into the analysis of Machiavelli's work. Yet the theme of realism and power politics continues to demand attention. Along with the writings of Han Feizi and other Legalists of ancient China, Kautilya's *Arthasastra*, and Thucydides' Melian dialogue, to name only a few pertinent examples, Machiavelli's works illuminate one of the classic universal issues—how to establish and maintain a powerful state. Machiavelli certainly did

[1] See Lerner's introduction to *The Prince and the Discourses*, trans. L. Ricci and E. R. P. Vincent (New York, 1950), esp. p. xxxi for the quotation.

not invent or discover the theme of power.[2] His treatment of it, however, remains important as the best-developed Renaissance expression of the universal theme, also as a barometer indicating something about the character of politics and the quality of political thought in the Renaissance.

The question naturally arises: to what extent did Machiavelli's thought reflect his intellectual milieu? Granted that Machiavelli himself dealt most acutely with the theme of power politics, did other Renaissance political thinkers anticipate or perhaps even contribute to Machiavelli's view of things? A surprisingly small body of scholarship has addressed these questions. Allan H. Gilbert and Rodolfo de Mattei pointed to numerous parallels between Machiavelli's thought and that of other Renaissance political thinkers. Felix Gilbert offered a brilliant analysis of Machiavelli in the context of fifteenth-century humanist thought. More recently, Quentin Skinner has provided a systematic study of Machiavelli in the context of both civic humanism and scholastic political theory.[3] While admitting numerous individual points of coincidence between Machiavelli and other Renaissance political thinkers, these studies in general emphasize the idealistic quality of the humanists' political thought against the hard-headed realism of Machiavelli. Skinner asserts several times, for example, that humanist political theory prescribed cultivation of the traditional cardinal virtues and Christian virtues as the chief or even sole obligation of the prince who wanted to maintain his state and acquire

---

[2] For excellent studies of western European variations on this theme, see Felix Gilbert, "Machiavellism," in his *History: Choice and Commitment* (Cambridge, Mass., 1977), pp. 155–76; and Gaines Post, *Studies in Medieval Legal Thought* (Princeton, 1964), pp. 241–309. On the Legalists, see Benjamin I. Schwartz, *The World of Thought in Ancient China* (Cambridge, Mass., 1985), pp. 321–49; on Kautilya, R. P. Kangle, *The Kautilya Arthasastra: A Study* (Bombay, 1965).

[3] Allan H. Gilbert, *Machiavelli's "Prince" and Its Forerunners* (Durham, N.C., 1938); Rodolfo de Mattei, *Dal premachiavellismo all'antimachiavellismo* (Florence, 1969); Felix Gilbert, "The Humanist Concept of the Prince and *The Prince* of Machiavelli," in his *History: Choice and Commitment*, pp. 91–114; and Quentin Skinner, *The Foundations of Modern Political Thought*, 2 vols. (Cambridge, 1978), esp. 1.23–65, 113–38.

honor, glory, and fame. Machiavelli insisted instead that the prince develop whatever skills the situation required him to exhibit. In short, from Skinner's point of view, the humanists confused moral virtue with political *virtù*. Machiavelli did not.[4]

Skinner has provided perhaps the most penetrating analysis ever directed toward the political thought of the Italian Renaissance, and I wish to record here my profound respect for his achievement. Yet the case of Naples suggests some modifications to the traditional view that Skinner's work has so ably supported. The argument of the following pages does not depend on formal political treatises, the chief category of sources studied by Skinner, but rather on another kind of source that does not figure in most other works. The following account relies primarily on various kinds of ad hoc writings—diplomatic correspondence, political memorandums, and personal correspondence—that throw considerable light on the humanists' understanding of specific political and military issues. Supplemented occasionally by reference to the humanists' formal works—political treatises and moral treatises with political implications—these ad hoc writings will support the thesis of this chapter: from Panormita through Pontano, the Neapolitan humanists exhibited an increasing willingness to take, if not an immoral or amoral, at least a hard-headed approach toward political problems. None of these humanists carried their line of thought as far as Machiavelli did a few decades later, but several of them anticipated Machiavellian positions and consequently warrant analysis for their efforts to rethink western political ethics.

The chapter begins not with the humanists themselves, but with Diomede Carafa, a prominent military and political figure of

[4] Skinner, *Foundations of Modern Political Thought*, 1.126–28, 131, 134, 138. For a similar argument, see also Skinner's *Machiavelli* (New York, 1981), pp. 21–47. The other scholars cited above basically agree with the characterization of the humanists as idealist thinkers and of Machiavelli as a realist. See Allan Gilbert, *Machiavelli's "Prince,"* pp. 231–37; Felix Gilbert, "Humanist Concept of the Prince," pp. 98–105, 109–14. Of the four, de Mattei most closely approaches the interpretation advanced in the following pages; but cf. also *Dal premachiavellismo all'antimachiavellismo*, pp. 3–6.

Aragonese Naples. The section on Carafa serves two functions: it suggests first the fallacy of associating political realism exclusively with the name of Machiavelli; at the same time it illustrates some of the features of practical political realism in Renaissance Naples, against which it is possible to evaluate the humanists as political analysts. The chapter continues with four sections on the humanists' activities as political advisers, diplomats, spokesmen, and analysts.

Diomede Carafa (ca. 1406–1487) and Political Realism

Born into a noble family traditionally active in Neapolitan politics, Diomede Carafa attached himself very early to the cause of Alfonso the Magnanimous.[5] He left Naples in 1423, when Angevin forces drove the Aragonese out of Italy. He accompanied Alfonso on military campaigns in Spain (1429–1430), the island of Jerba (1432), and eventually in the conquest of the Regno (1435–1442). In fact, Carafa led one of the companies of men that entered Naples by way of a forgotten aqueduct and subsequently secured the city: he probably planted the first Aragonese standard inside Naples, and during the assault he certainly suffered a leg wound that bothered him all the rest of his life. Yet he continued to provide military services in succeeding years. He helped Alfonso drive Francesco Sforza out of the marches (1443); he perhaps accompanied Alfonso on his first Tuscan campaign (1447–1448); and he certainly helped Ferrante conduct the second one (1452–1453). He aided Ferrante in a political and diplomatic if not also a military capacity both during the war of succession (1458–1462) and

---

[5] The literature on Carafa includes Tommaso Persico, *Diomede Carafa: uomo di stato e scrittore del secolo XV* (Naples, 1899); and Franca Petrucci's short but accurate sketch in the *DBI*, 19.524–30. See also J. D. Moores, "New Light on Diomede Carafa and His 'Perfect Loyalty' to Ferrante of Aragon," *Italian Studies*, 26 (1971), 1–23; and Lucia Miele, "Tradizione ed 'esperienza' nella precettistica politica di Diomede Carafa," *AAP*, n.s. 24 (1975), 141–51.

during the second barons' revolt (1485–1486). He served Ferrante also in peaceful times as political adviser, diplomatic agent, and chief financial administrator of the Regno. As rewards, he accumulated numerous grants and privileges, most notably the concession of large land holdings and the title count of Maddaloni. Always exceptionally loyal to the Aragonese dynasty of Naples, Carafa died on 17 May 1487, a few days after the executions of Antonello Petrucci and Francesco Coppola, the prime leaders of the second barons' revolt.

Carafa merits attention not only as a man of action, but also as a man of contemplation. He did not have an impressive education, to be sure: he began the study of letters in his early years, but interrupted it in favor of the military life, then resumed it only after an interval of about forty-five years. Thus when he began to write political and military treatises about 1467, he did not command the literary and stylistic skills of the humanists. He composed his works in *napoletano misto*, the refined version of Neapolitan dialect spoken at the Aragonese court, though within 150 years several of his treatises had found their way into Latin or standard Italian translations. Yet Carafa was a thoughtful man, and he knew how to learn from experience. An undistinguished literary facade thus conceals military and political doctrines of high interest for students of the Italian Renaissance.

The most important of Carafa's works is a treatise on the duties of the prince (entitled *I doveri del principe* not by Carafa himself, but by the first editor of the work).[6] Between 1473 and 1476, Carafa dedicated the work to Ferrante's elder daughter, Eleonora, who in 1473 married Ercole d'Este, duke of Ferrara. Carafa did not intend this work to be a creative or innovative contribution to the science

---

[6] Persico first published the surviving portions of Carafa's original text as an appendix to his *Diomede Carafa*, pp. 261–96. Franca Petrucci is currently preparing a new critical edition of all Carafa's writings, a much anticipated work. In its absence I cite Carafa according to the best existing manuscript or edition. See also Franca Petrucci, "Per un'edizione critica dei Memoriali di Diomede Carafa: problemi e metodo," *ASPN*, 4th ser. 15 (1977), 213–34.

of statecraft, and he certainly did not exhibit the literary or intellectual flair that enliven Machiavelli's *Prince* and *Discourses*. Yet the treatise stands on a foundation of sound common sense more realistic in many ways than the sensational thought of Machiavelli—in that Carafa's sober principles of government would more likely result in the effective maintenance of the state than would many of Machiavelli's specific pieces of advice.

Carafa divided his treatise into four parts, which dealt successively with the maintenance of order, the dispensation of justice, the administration of resources, and the welfare of subjects and cities. In some ways Carafa took a traditional, moralistic approach to statecraft throughout his treatise, but at the same time he kept in view the practical results of his advice. Throughout the treatise, for example, Carafa insisted upon the prince's duties before God, but in many cases he found that observance of these duties coincided with the prince's political interests. Thus he urged the establishment of special advocates for the poor and just treatment of foreigners as policies especially pleasing to God—but also as measures likely to win popular goodwill and ensure the safety of the prince's own subjects traveling in alien lands. Like almost all political writers of the Renaissance, Carafa also addressed the traditional question whether the prince should inspire love or fear in his subjects. Governance based on love he considered not only more laudable than rule founded on fear, but also more effective, since subjects will come to a beleaguered prince's aid most willingly when they believe he has their own interests at heart.[7]

In other places Carafa addressed equally traditional questions, but in his response projected a practical realism foreign to earlier theorists. A very interesting section of his treatise, for example, deals with counsellors and ministers. Carafa advised selection of men who lacked prudence over those who lacked fidelity, since he considered the faithless more likely to turn their talents to perni-

---

[7] For Carafa's arguments on these issues, see his treatise *I doveri del principe* in Persico, *Diomede Carafa*, pp. 266–67, 278–81.

cious or traitorous activities. He advised few rather than many ministers, the better to maintain the confidentiality of state secrets. He insisted on counsellors of foresight and intelligence: men who could prepare for the flood before it arrives; who not only could distinguish a good from a bad thing, but also could select the better of two goods or the lesser of two evils. Carafa's advice on state security sprang from this same sober appreciation of political reality. Although he advised the prince to rule through love rather than fear, he pointed out specifically that the presence of soldiers in the land marvelously encouraged obedience and dissuaded subjects from acting on evil thoughts.[8]

Apart from the rather general political advice that dominates his treatise on princely duties, Carafa devoted noteworthy attention to several specific issues. No doubt his most creative advice dealt with economic affairs. Indeed, in an age in which princes generally sought to extract as much tax revenue as possible from their subjects, Carafa developed stunning insights into the wealth of principalities. He urged the prince not to compete with his subjects in business, lest he threaten or ruin private entrepreneurs and consequently undermine the economic foundations of his land. Instead, he encouraged the prince to provide positive support for trade, industry, and agriculture, since economic aid to subjects represented less a royal expenditure than a public investment with large political implications: "when the lord has rich subjects, he himself cannot be poor." Carafa spoke highly of Ferrante's enlightened economic policy: Ferrante provided merchants with ships he had built himself, and he helped to establish the wool industry in the Regno.[9] Several surviving documents testify to Ferrante's support for merchants and entrepreneurs. Indeed, in view of Carafa's political and administrative influence, it does not seem unlikely that he played a role in framing Ferrante's economic policy.[10]

[8] Ibid., pp. 263–66, 270.

[9] Ibid., esp. pp. 286–87, 290–91. The quotation appears on p. 291 in the context of Carafa's point that the prince should support industry.

[10] See, for example, Trinchera, ed., *Codice aragonese*, 3.37–38, 209–13. For a

While not as innovative as his economic advice, Carafa's military thought reflected accurately the major features of fifteenth-century warfare and military affairs. He touched briefly on the need for an army in his treatise on princely duties, but he developed his military thought most clearly in other works. The most important of these was a memorial written in July 1478, perhaps in Ferrante's name, to Duke Alfonso of Calabria as he prepared to lead Neapolitan forces into Tuscany. In this memorial Carafa addressed issues that went far beyond those raised by the immediate campaign. He urged that the commander make permanent provisions for soldiers so that they did not lack support during intervals between wars. In other words, he called for the establishment of a permanent military force, even as states both in Italy and beyond the Alps resorted to standing armies. Carafa placed great faith in heavy artillery, without considering it a substitute for intelligence in strategic planning. He strongly counseled tactical caution and thus adhered to the school of the *Sforzeschi*, who emphasized discipline and prudence over the daring strikes and unexpected maneuvers favored by the rival *Bracceschi* tacticians. Even in the matter of military intelligence Carafa reflected the practices of his day: like other fifteenth-century theorists, he devoted considerable attention to the techniques of recruiting and deploying spies, then to the task of evaluating the information they obtained.[11]

---

fuller discussion of Carafa's economic thought in the context of Neapolitan economic policy, see G. Ricca Salerno, *Storia delle dottrine finanziarie in Italia*, 2d ed. (Palermo, 1896), pp. 47–56.

[11] Piero Pieri edited this memorial along with one by Carafa's contemporary and colleague, Orso Orsini: "Il 'Governo et exercitio de la militia' di Orso degli Orsini e i 'Memoriali' di Diomede Carafa," *ASPN*, n.s. 19 (1933), 99–212. For the points referred to here, see esp. pp. 180–91, 198–200, 207–9. For a fuller discussion of Carafa's military thought, see Pieri's introduction to the works of Orsini and Carafa, pp. 99–125; also his article, "L'arte militare italiana della seconda metà del secolo XV negli scritti di Diomede Carafa, Conte di Maddaloni," in *Ricordi e studi in memoria di Francesco Flamini* (Naples, 1931), pp. 87–103. Finally, for an analysis of the state of military affairs in Italy during the fifteenth century, see Piero Pieri, *Il Rinascimento e la crisi militare italiana* (Turin, 1952),

Finally, Carafa's advice to courtiers and ambassadors mirrored the realities of politics in the late fifteenth century, the quintessential age of princes. During the late 1470s, Carafa dedicated several treatises to prospective courtiers—to his own son, Giantommaso, and to King Ferrante's second and fourth sons, Federico and Francesco—as well as one to an unnamed ambassador. They all urge absolute devotion to the interests of the prince. The treatise to the ambassador survives only in a fragment that offers only a few details as to the emissary's proper behavior. The memorials to courtiers, however, allow considerable insight into Carafa's conception of princely service. Several times he stressed the value of conservative qualities like caution, prudence, and taciturnity as those most conducive to a successful career. The courtier must learn the prince's will and promptly implement it in order to win his benevolence and obtain rewards. Carafa's emphasis on external and sometimes superficial behavior—exhibition of courtesy and affability, maintenance of an honorable reputation, and constant concern to please the prince—have encouraged interpreters to portray Carafa as a predecessor of Baldassare Castiglione and Giovanni della Casa, who in the sixteenth century developed an art, or even a science of courtiership.[12] Whatever his significance as precursor of these men, Carafa clearly demonstrated in his own treatises an

---

esp. pp. 234–319; and two works by Michael Mallett: *Mercenaries and Their Masters: Warfare in Renaissance Italy* (Totowa, N.J., 1974), esp. pp. 3–5, 107–80; and "Diplomacy and War in Later Fifteenth-Century Italy," *Proceedings of the British Academy*, 67 (1981), 267–88.

[12] I cite only the most useful edition of the treatises to Giantommaso, Federico, and Francesco, each of which has appeared in print at least twice: Carafa, *Dello optimo cortesano*, ed. G. Paparelli (Salerno, 1971); Petrucci, "Per un'edizione critica dei Memoriali," pp. 227–34; Antonio Altamura, ed., *Testi napoletani del Quattrocento* (Naples, 1953), pp. 35–49. For alternatives to these sometimes rare editions, see Petrucci, "Per un'edizione critica dei Memoriali," pp. 214–22. See also the fragment of Carafa's treatise to the ambassador in Naples, Biblioteca della Società Napoletana di Storia Patria, MS XX. C. 26, fol. 66rv. Interpretative literature includes E. Mayer's introduction to Carafa, *Un opuscolo dedicato a Beatrice d'Aragona, Regina d'Ungheria* (Rome, 1937), esp. pp. 6–12; and Paparelli's introduction to the edition of Carafa's *Dello optimo cortesano*, esp. pp. 37–49.

awareness of the degree to which princes had captured the initiative in Italian politics in the later fifteenth century.

The Neapolitan humanists certainly did not match all of Carafa's insights. They did not possess his experience in financial administration and thus did not share his sophisticated understanding of economic matters. They did not devote major portions of their careers to the military life and thus could not speak with authority to the details of military affairs. Yet in various ways the humanists exhibited a sense of political realism similar to that of Carafa. The effort to sustain this thesis begins with an analysis of Panormita's political career.

Panormita as Adviser, Secretary, and Diplomat

Ever since the publication of the *Hermaphroditus* in the 1420s, Panormita's reputation as a poet has preceded him. In fact, the image of the genial, slightly raucous humanist has largely obscured the less romantic but more accurate truth of things: Panormita spent the greater part of his adult life tending to various legal, political, and administrative chores in the kingdom of Naples.[13]

To some extent, Panormita deflected attention from his more mundane duties and promoted an image of himself as a refined and sophisticated intellectual. To the extent that he acknowledged his role in day-to-day affairs, he portrayed himself as a humanist moralist, one who employed his rhetorical skills to justify the righteousness of his own prince's policy and to encourage the prince to

[13] Only a few studies deal seriously with Panormita's career as a functionary. Michele Natale, *Antonio Beccadelli detto il Panormita* (Caltanisetta, 1902), presents a detailed review of his role as political adviser and secretary. Vicenzo Laurenza, "Il Panormita a Napoli," *AAP*, 42 (1912), 1–92, brings an enormous amount of documentary evidence to bear on his administrative career. Most recently, Alan Ryder, "Antonio Beccadelli: A Humanist in Government," in C. H. Clough, ed., *Cultural Aspects of the Italian Renaissance: Essays in Honour of Paul Oskar Kristeller* (Manchester, 1976), pp. 123–40, adds a great deal of additional information from Aragonese archives on Panormita's services to Alfonso, though he says little about the continuation of Panormita's career under Ferrante.

observe high standards of conduct. Panormita seems to have placed special value on one composition that conveys this impression, for he included it in three of his works. The writing in question is an oration that Panormita composed for Alfonso the Magnanimous to deliver to Ferrante as he prepared to lead Neapolitan forces into Tuscany in 1452. Despite Alfonso's obvious ulterior motive—he hoped to gain peninsular influence by meddling in the already confused state of affairs in Lombardy—Panormita's oration justified the impending campaign as a reluctant response to numerous Florentine provocations. Diplomacy and arbitration had failed to curb the Florentines' treachery, so that recourse to armed intervention remained the only option open to Alfonso. Ferrante would command an experienced army, but the oration insisted that he place his confidence in divine aid rather than human skill. God grants victory and imposes defeat, after all, so that military affairs leave little room for human boasting. Still less should Ferrante allow free rein to his troops' cruelty, greed, or lust, for his object was to reconcile the Florentines to friendship, not to annihilate them.[14]

This sense of righteousness and high moral standards, found in many other published writings of Panormita besides this oration, does not extend to all of Panormita's political compositions. Sources both published and unpublished make it clear that military theory deeply interested Panormita, that he sometimes advised Alfonso and Ferrante to adopt harsh policies, and that he represented their political interests on several sensitive embassies. More importantly, a large amount of material, most of it still in manuscript, demonstrates that he played a crucial role in the rough world of Neapolitan foreign policy, especially during the

---

[14] The oration appears with only minor variations in Panormita's *De dictis et factis Alphonsi regis* (Basel, 1538), pp. 89–92; *Regis Ferdinandi et aliorum epistolae ac orationes utriusque militiae* (Vico Equense, 1586), pp. 298–300; and *Liber rerum gestarum Ferdinandi regis*, ed. G. Resta (Palermo, 1968), pp. 99–101. Bartolomeo Facio attributed a similar discourse to Alfonso in his *De rebus gestis ab Alphonso primo*, in Gravier, ed., *Raccolta*, 4.232–34.

difficult decade 1455 to 1464, from the papacy of Calixtus III through Ferrante's victory in his war to succeed Alfonso.

Panormita's correspondence with the Venetian humanist, Francesco Barbaro, throws light on his interest in military theory. During the spring and summer of 1451, the two men shared texts of a dozen Greek military treatises, including works of Aelian, Onosander, Mauritius, Hiero, and other lesser-known authors. In correspondence prompted by the treatises, Barbaro pledged to study them as works of literature rather than field manuals, while Panormita took the opportunity in his reply to praise peace and emphasize the inherent riskiness of warfare.[15] The letters of both men thus reflected the newly established alliance between Naples and Venice, but they also betrayed a deep interest in ancient military theory. In the case of Panormita, other sources testify to the same point. In 1456, for example, Theodore Gaza dedicated to Panormita his Latin translation of Aelian's tactical treatise, *De aciebus instruendis*. The dedication shows in and of itself that Gaza recognized Panormita's interest in military theory. More importantly, perhaps, the prefatory epistle mentions Panormita's work on his own treatise on military affairs (*de re militari*). The treatise unfortunately does not survive—Panormita perhaps never completed it—nor does any detailed characterization of the work survive. From what Gaza said, it seems safe to say only that the work concentrated on the military career of Alfonso the Magnanimous.[16] In any case, the information proves Panormita's interest in modern as well as ancient military affairs.

Other sources show that Panormita regularly offered political and military advice. As early as 1437 Alfonso cited understanding of military affairs as one of the justifications for raising Panormita's

[15] The letters appear in Panormita's *Epistolarum libri V* (Venice, 1553), fols. 115v–117v. Vittore Branca provides precise identifications of the Greek military treatises at issue: "Un codice aragonese scritto dal Cinico," in *Studi di bibliografia e di storia in onore di Tammaro de Marinis*, 4 vols. (Verona, 1964), 1.213–15.

[16] Gaza's prefatory letter survives in manuscripts but not in published editions of his translation of Aelian. Cf. BAV, Vat. lat. 3414, fols. 33r–35v. De Marinis has also published the text of the letter in *La biblioteca*, 2.3–5.

annual salary.[17] Panormita himself mentioned an example of his counsel in his collection of Alfonso's sayings and deeds. During the siege of Gaeta (August 1435) food supplies ran so low that the city's defenders expelled children and elderly inhabitants, forcing them to fend for themselves in the no-man's-land between the locked city gates and Alfonso's army. In the ensuing debate, Panormita agreed with a group of advisers who urged Alfonso to ignore the plight of the involuntary refugees. He himself pointed out that military law did not require Alfonso to shelter the unfortunate group. On this occasion, Panormita said, Alfonso overruled his advisers with the observation that he preferred never to hold Gaeta than to capture it in a cruel manner.[18] Panormita continued to provide political and military counsel during Ferrante's reign. Several letters dating from the war of succession show that he collaborated with a group of men who sent regular advice from Naples as Ferrante and his army campaigned against Angevins and rebellious barons. Unfortunately, Panormita complained, his sage counsel often went unheeded.[19] Indeed, after Ferrante's victory, Panormita argued in a letter to Giovanni Pontano that his advice could have prevented the war altogether. In late 1458 or early 1459, he said, Ferrante raised the question whether he should take up arms against the prince of Taranto, Giovanni Antonio Orsini del Balzo. Panormita argued enthusiastically that Ferrante should seize the opportunity and move against the faithless prince. His prophetic foresight went for naught, however, and the Regno suffered great misery before Ferrante secured his position.[20]

Apart from the advice he gave, Panormita also provided diplomatic services for kings Alfonso and Ferrante. He failed to bring about the surrender of Gaeta in 1435, as seen in the previous chap-

[17] M. Catalano Tirrito, ed., *Nuovi documenti sul Panormita* (Catania, 1910), doc. VI, pp. 182–88, esp. p. 183.

[18] *De dictis et factis Alphonsi*, pp. 4–5; cf. also p. 8.

[19] See for example *Regis Ferdinandi et aliorum epistolae*, pp. 336–37, 391–92.

[20] Ibid., pp. 389–90. The letter also appears in Percopo, "Lettere di Giovanni Pontano a principi ed amici," *AAP*, 37 (1907), 67–68.

ter, but early in 1436 Alfonso nonetheless dispatched him on an important mission to Siena and Florence. In his instructions, Alfonso directed Panormita to convey his goodwill for the Sienese and his promise to support them militarily if the need should arise. To the Florentines, Panormita delivered an amicable warning not to ally with the faithless Genoese, but to remain friendly with Alfonso's own ally, Duke Filippo Maria Visconti of Milan.[21] Once again the mission failed: nervous about the power of Milan and Naples, the republics of Siena, Florence, Genoa, and Venice concluded a league in June 1436. Panormita's most complicated diplomatic assignment came in February 1451, when Alfonso directed him to accompany Luis Despuig on a long embassy through central and northern Italy. The instructions called for the diplomatic party to go first to Rome and Siena, express Alfonso's goodwill, and offer an opportunity to join the recently concluded alliance of Naples and Venice against Milan. The ambassadors had orders to proceed then to Florence, where they would emphasize the defensive nature of the alliance and warn the Florentines not to oppose it, lest their merchants in Naples suffer as a result. Alfonso sent his emissaries next to Ferrara, where they would seek to gain a new ally, and failing that, to obtain assurances that Ferrara would remain neutral in any eventual conflict. Finally, Panormita and Despuig would go to Venice, where they would offer congratulations on the conclusion of the new league and conduct detailed political and military negotiations.[22]

These examples show that Panormita tendered political and military advice on the basis of the existing political and military situations, without necessarily adjusting his counsel according to moral criteria, also that Alfonso had enough confidence in his political judgment and diplomatic skill to send him on several sensitive embassies. His realistic approach to affairs of state perhaps accounts for the high degree of independence that both Alfonso

[21] ACA, Reg. 2694, fols. 11r–12r.
[22] ACA, Reg. 2697, fols. 81v–89r.

and Ferrante allowed him as political secretary. Several letters illuminate the procedures Panormita followed when conducting correspondence for his royal patrons. The king determined the addressee and the basic message; Panormita composed the requested epistle, then submitted it for review by the king, or his chief political secretary, or both.[23] In one especially interesting letter, Panormita indirectly confirmed his responsibility for drafting official letters, because he justified the tone he employed when composing correspondence for Ferrante. The letter in question served as dedicatory epistle—to Cardinal Oliviero Carafa of Naples—to that portion of Panormita's correspondence which derived from Ferrante's early years on the throne. Adverse fortune mandated that Panormita cast official correspondence from that period in a humble, sometimes pleading tone, he explained, since an arrogant or haughty manner would more likely have brought ridicule than the aid that Ferrante so desperately needed.[24]

Documents refer to Panormita as royal secretary from April 1454, but I know of no surviving correspondence he composed before the elevation of Calixtus III to the papacy (8 April 1455). By the summer of 1455, tensions between Alfonso and Calixtus had already placed great strains on their relationship. The difficult business of justifying Alfonso's policy before the pope and other Italian states fell to Panormita, the only active figure in the Neapolitan chancellery who commanded general Italian respect. Thus Panormita represented the interests of Alfonso just as the humanist chancellors of Florence—Salutati, Bruni, Poggio, and others—served as spokesmen for their republic.

The most important source of information on his secretarial duties is a manuscript in which Panormita himself collected some of

---

[23] See Panormita's letter to Alfonso in his *Epistolarum libri V*, fol. 111r, and his letter to Antonello Petrucci in *Regis Ferdinandi et aliorum epistolae*, p. 333. See also another letter to Alfonso, which shows that Panormita composed his oration to Emperor Frederick III according to a similar procedure: *Epistolarum libri V*, fol. 115v.

[24] BAV, Vat. lat. 3371, fols. 134r–35v.

the epistles and orations he composed on behalf of both Alfonso and Ferrante.[25] Though not archival documents, the letters Panormita collected unquestionably represent genuine diplomatic correspondence. In many cases, letters in his manuscript agree precisely with copies of Neapolitan correspondence surviving in archives or reported by reliable intermediaries. In the pages that follow I cite both Panormita's manuscript and archival sources whenever possible. When lacking other confirmation, however, I have not hesitated to rely exclusively on Panormita's collection, since its authority seems to me well validated by its widespread agreement with archival documents.

The bulk of surviving correspondence Panormita composed for Alfonso fell in the period from August 1455 to August 1456. This correspondence had as its major aims the maintenance of pressure on Pope Calixtus and the acquisition of support for Alfonso's policies from other Italian states. In pursuit of these aims, Panormita dealt most importantly with three closely related issues: the conditions under which Alfonso would lead or participate in a crusade against the Turks, the activities of the condottiere Jacopo Piccinino in central Italy, and the continuous hostility between Alfonso and Genoa.

The next section will examine Panormita's view on the crusade in the context of other humanists' thought on the issue. But the question of an expedition against the Turks arose so frequently in the diplomatic correspondence of this period that it deserves at least a general comment here. Panormita and Alfonso basically raised hopes for a crusade—always the dearest policy of the near-fanatic Calixtus—in order to extract concessions from the pope. Alfonso could not consider embarking on a crusade while Calixtus

---

[25] BAV, Barb. lat. 2070. The only published discussions of this work are Michele Natale's short article, "Due codici inediti di Antonio Beccadelli," *Archivio storico siciliano*, n.s. 25 (1900), 396–400; and Gianvito Resta's brief mention in *L'epistolario del Panormita* (Messina, 1954), pp. 35–37. Though interested primarily in Panormita's familiar letters, Resta adds new information concerning his diplomatic correspondence, including notice of three manuscripts besides the one cited above, pp. 35–36, n. 34.

made war against Piccinino, so Panormita argued, or while Genoa threatened the stability of the entire peninsula. Panormita occasionally became somewhat offensive in correspondence addressed to the pope on this issue. Thus in the first draft of a letter that he wrote in the king's name, Panormita acknowledged receipt of the papal bull naming Alfonso leader of a crusade. The letter suggested that Calixtus direct his bulls to all Christian princes; it continued in a rather insolent tone by pointing out that a crusade required not only bulls, but also men, arms, horses, ships, equipment, and money, among other things. The letter soon underwent revision, and Calixtus received a more gently worded response to his bull.[26] The two drafts illustrate well, however, the way Panormita and Alfonso could turn Calixtus' dream of a crusade to the advancement of Neapolitan interests, not to mention the value of Panormita's literary talents for the task of representing those interests.

The same drafts as well as other letters also show how Alfonso and Panormita exploited the turmoil that plagued central Italy in those days. The Peace of Lodi and League of Italy had resulted in loss of employment for the former Venetian and Neapolitan condottiere, Jacopo Piccinino, who then began to seek his own fortune. After a series of abortive thrusts in the papal state, Piccinino turned his attention toward the republic of Siena. At Calixtus' urging, most Italian states opposed Piccinino's brazen efforts, but Alfonso provided him with both material and diplomatic support. Alfonso secretly encouraged Piccinino, allowed the condottiere to use his castle at Castiglione della Pescaia, and sent supplies when the castle came under siege. Alfonso even suggested that the Italian states hire Piccinino as leader of a crusade. The proposal was not well received. Meanwhile, responsibility for diplomatic contacts fell largely to Panormita. In numerous letters to the pope and

[26] The first draft of this letter, dated 16 August 1455, occurs in BAV, Barb. lat. 2070, fols. 57r–60v. A marginal note on fol. 57r points out that the letter was "softened" before it went out to Calixtus. The second draft, dated 29 August 1455, occurs in the same manuscript, fols. 3v–6r.

to other Italian political figures, Panormita lambasted Calixtus' policy of fomenting war against the Christian Piccinino rather than the infidel Turk, and he repeatedly insisted on peace in Italy as the indispensable prerequisite for a crusade.[27] Only in the spring of 1456 did the various parties involved resolve the issue by paying Piccinino to withdraw his forces into the Regno—a movement he delayed carrying out until the following September.

By that time, however, Alfonso's Genoese policy had introduced new complications into peninsular politics. Perennial strife between aristocratic factions in Genoa offered Alfonso yet another opportunity to satisfy his expansionist ambitions. In 1450, after an absence of seven years, the Campofregoso faction ousted the Adorno party and returned to power in Genoa. Alfonso intrigued with the new exiles with the double aim of reinstating the Adorno group (always less hostile to the Aragonese than the Campofregosi) and of increasing his influence in Corsica (long dominated by Genoa, but coveted equally as long by the Aragonese). His policy led in 1455 to skirmishes at sea and Genoese raids on Aragonese garrisons in Corsica. In the summer of 1456, Alfonso escalated the conflict when he sent a fleet of ships—including at least six galleys

---

[27] Besides the drafts cited in the previous note, see also letters Panormita wrote to King Charles VII of France, Duke Francesco Sforza of Milan, the doge and senate of Venice, and the Florentine condottiere Simonetto Capitano, in BAV, Barb. lat. 2070, fols. 6r–7r, 8r–10r, 17r. The letters to Duke Francesco and Simonetto survive also in the ACA, Reg. 2700, fol. 98rv, and Reg. 2661, fol. 99r, except that in the archives the latter is addressed not to Simonetto, but to Bernardo de' Medici, a distant relative but close friend of Cosimo de' Medici who had served as ambassador to King Alfonso during his Tuscan campaign of 1447 to 1448. Cf. also Panormita's letters composed at the conclusion of the period of tension: ACA, Reg. 2661, fols. 120v–21r. Alan Ryder has transcribed these last two letters in "Antonio Beccadelli," pp. 136–37. Information on Simonetto and Bernardo de' Medici appears in Facio's *De rebus gestis ab Alphonso primo*, in Gravier, ed., *Raccolta*, 4.208. The best account of Alfonso's policy in this period is that of Pontieri, *Alfonso il Magnanimo re di Napoli (1435–1458)* (Naples, 1975), pp. 329–40. Though implacably hostile to Alfonso, Ludwig von Pastor's account is also valuable for some of the details it presents from archival sources: *History of the Popes*, trans. F. I. Antrobus, 40 vols., 2d ed. (St. Louis, 1913–53), 2.359–66.

and one other ship that Pope Calixtus had fitted out for service against the Turks—to ravage the Genoese coast. The ensuing outcry, largely the work of Calixtus and the Genoese, once again raised the need for Panormita's literary talents as spokesman for Neapolitan policies. In letters to the pope and leaders of various other states, Panormita denied the charge that Alfonso sought to exploit the tensions caused by Genoese factions, and he blamed the most recent hostilities exclusively on the Genoese raids in Corsica.[28] In a letter to Doge Pietro Campofregoso himself, Panormita took a slightly different tack. He continued to blame Genoese raids in Corsica for the current hostility, but he openly acknowledged Alfonso's support for "the best and most noble citizens" of Genoa, men who deserved to return to power. He made up for the admission, however, by heaping abuse on the Genoese republic. He accused Genoa of perfidy and faithlessness, and he likened the republic to a shameless strumpet who, having lost her own sense of honor, sought only to lure modest women into a life of vice.[29]

None of the Italian states held a monopoly either on political virtue or on political vice during the years following the Peace of Lodi and the establishment of the League of Italy. Yet Alfonso's policies during the pontificate of Calixtus III—particularly his support for Jacopo Piccinino and his renewed vendetta against Genoa—rank as some of the more cynical ones of the entire fifteenth century. Panormita's enthusiastic efforts to explain and justify Alfonso's policy demonstrate eloquently the point made earlier: when addressing practical political problems, Panormita did not recognize the validity of prior moral standards, but acknowledged instead the reality of power and the potential of propaganda.

[28] BAV, Barb. lat. 2070, fols. 20v–21r, preserves such a letter to Calixtus. A letter with an almost identical text, but addressed to Duke Francesco Sforza, survives in ACA, Reg. 2661, fol. 136r, and is now published in Ryder, "Antonio Beccadelli," p. 137.

[29] BAV, Barb. lat. 2070, fols. 21r–24r. The letter is also published in Agostino Giustiniani, *Annali della Reppublica di Genova*, ed. G. B. Spotorno, 2 vols. (Genoa, 1854), 2.385–89. The Genoese response survives in ibid., 2.389–94.

The death of Alfonso the Magnanimous (27 June 1458) greatly altered the political situation of the Italian peninsula, but it did not change Panormita's basic approach to problems of practical politics and statecraft. In July 1458, Panormita wrote numerous epistles to political leaders announcing Alfonso's death and affirming Ferrante's desire to seek peace in Italy and harmony with the papacy. In the first surviving letter that he wrote in Ferrante's name to Calixtus, Panormita recalled how the future king and future pope had traveled together, in the same ship, from Valencia to Italy. Evidently he hoped that, combined with pledges of current loyalty to the church, a personal appeal based on a relationship of long standing would move Calixtus to recognize Ferrante as king of Naples.[30] The ploy did not succeed, however, and by late July Panormita found it necessary to compose letters in a different tone. He wrote directly to the college of cardinals, asking them to pressure Calixtus into acceptance of Ferrante's succession, as well as to various Italian princes, from whom he sought diplomatic support. If the pope must encourage fighting, Panormita said, let him direct it against the Turks![31] Eventually he resorted to sharp language when addressing the pope himself: "I [Ferrante] am King of Sicily by grace of God, paternal kindness, papal concession, and general consensus of the peers and people [of Naples]. I am king by a right equally as perfect as that by which you are pope." Thus Panormita represented Ferrante's view of things in the draft of a letter that went to Calixtus in only slightly more conciliatory form.[32]

[30] See the letters to Emperor Frederick III, the college of cardinals, Enea Silvio Piccolomini, Duke Francesco Sforza, Cosimo de' Medici, and others in BAV, Barb. lat. 2070, fols. 42r–48r. See especially the letter to Calixtus, fol. 43rv.

[31] BAV, Barb. lat. 2070, fols. 48r–49r. The letters survive also in A. Messer, ed., *Le codice aragonese* (Paris, 1912), pp. 20–22, 29–30, where they are attributed to Tommaso de Girifalco rather than to Panormita. Messer's edition also represents the addressee of one epistle as Marquis Luigi Gonzaga of Mantua rather than Duke Francesco Sforza, as in the manuscript. A note at the end of the text in Messer makes it clear, however, that similar letters in fact went to other princes as well.

[32] BAV, Barb. lat. 2070, fols. 49v–50r. A marginal note in the manuscript

The death of Calixtus (6 August 1458) brought a temporary respite for Ferrante, since Pope Pius II immediately recognized his claim to the Neapolitan throne. Soon thereafter Panormita undertook a diplomatic mission to Milan, where he delivered an elegant oration thanking Duke Francesco Sforza for supporting Ferrante. His stand helped to preserve peace in Italy, Panormita said, and earned the duke the gratitude of the entire kingdom of Naples, its towns, fields, and even brute animals.[33]

Within a year's time, however, the invasion of Jean d'Anjou and the rebellion of the barons had placed Ferrante once again in difficult circumstances. Once again, too, Panormita's literary and diplomatic skills played a crucial role in the effort to secure Ferrante's position. He wrote letters to princes in all parts of Italy emphasizing the faithlessness of the Angevins and rebel barons, not to mention their threat to the peace of the entire peninsula.[34] After the debacle at Sarno (7 June 1460) that nearly stripped Ferrante of his kingdom, Panormita did not scruple to play on any fear he could identify in his search for military support. Thus in two letters to Doge Pasquale Malipiero of Venice, he emphasized the danger of foreign intervention in Italian affairs: the French presence threatened serious disruption of the peace of Italy, so that Venetian interests lay in the recognition of Ferrante and exclusion of foreigners from peninsular affairs. At precisely the same time, however, Panormita desperately solicited aid from King Juan II of Aragon and his son Don Carlos, prince of Viana. In the absence of Aragonese aid, Panormita predicted, Ferrante's monarchy would immediately collapse. Only France and Genoa—traditional and visceral enemies of the Aragonese—would benefit by Ferrante's fall. Aragonese interests thus lay precisely in their immediate military intervention in peninsular affairs.[35]

---

points out that the first letter was not sent, implying that the second one went out in its place.

[33] BAV, Barb. lat. 2070, fols. 39r–41v; available in transcription in Resta, *L'epistolario del Panormita*, pp. 135–36.

[34] *Regis Ferdinandi et aliorum epistolae*, esp. pp. 305–327; also BAV, Vat. lat. 3371, fols. 140r–41r.

[35] *Regis Ferdinandi et aliorum epistolae*, pp. 313–22.

Ferrante's best ally during the war of succession was Pope Pius II. Ferrante had cooperated with Pius from the earliest days of his papacy. In a letter written by Panormita (23 November 1458), for example, the king promised to observe whatever requests Pius made of him, pledging specifically the restoration of ecclesiastical towns that Alfonso had earlier invested. Several months later a letter from Pius to Ferrante (5 May 1459) shows that the pope had in fact regained control of Benevento, long a source of contention between popes and Neapolitan kings.[36] Thus Ferrante turned naturally to Pius when seeking support against his Angevin and baronial enemies. In a series of letters Panormita informed the pope about the progress of Ferrante's enemies, the attempt on the king's life by Marino Marzano, and the disaster at Sarno.[37] As a result of their close relations, Pius responded with both military aid and diplomatic support for Ferrante. He encouraged the king to remain optimistic and resolute. He urged the prince of Taranto, leader of the rebellious barons, to resolve his disagreements with Ferrante in a peaceful manner. And he subjected the French ambassadors to a lengthy lecture explaining why he recognized Ferrante rather than Jean d'Anjou as king of Naples.[38]

Panormita figured in the Neapolitan diplomacy of this period not only as a secretary, but also, for one last time, as an ambassador. On 1 June 1459 Pius II opened the Congress of Mantua, which he hoped would lead to composition of Italian quarrels and organization of a crusade against the Turks. Several sources make it clear that the oration Panormita delivered in Mantua harmonized perfectly with the general features of Neapolitan diplomacy.

---

[36] BAV, Barb. lat. 2070, fol. 51rv; ASV, Reg. brev., Arm. XXXIX, 8, fol. 55r. Cf. also *Regis Ferdinandi et aliorum epistolae*, pp. 301–2. For the extent of Pius's anxiety over Benevento, see also the letter he addressed to Bartolomeo Roverella in September 1461: A. Ratti, "Quarantadue lettere originali di Pio II relative alla guerra per la successione nel Reame di Napoli (1460–63)," *Archivio storico lombardo*, 3d ser. 19 (1903), p. 286.

[37] *Regis Ferdinandi et aliorum epistolae*, pp. 304–5, 310–12, 322–27.

[38] ASV, Reg. brev., Arm. XXXIX, 9, fols. 14rv, 22r, 138r–39v, 148rv; *Regis Ferdinandi et aliorum epistolae*, pp. 304–5; and Ratti, "Quarantadue lettere," pp. 282, 285. On the last point see also Pastor, *History of the Popes*, 3.91–94.

In precongress correspondence, Pius II had urged Ferrante to seek a speedy resolution to his quarrels with princes and states both inside and outside the Regno, since Italian disunity made it impossible to deal with the Turkish menace.[39] Diplomatic instructions to the official Neapolitan ambassadors to the pope and the congress show that in the second half of 1459, Ferrante repeatedly cited internal uneasiness and peninsular disorder as obstacles to his participation in a crusade. On at least two occasions he adduced the lesson of Constantinople in making his case for papal aid: Pope Nicholas V had delayed his support for Constantinople too long, and the city consequently fell to the Turks; the obvious implication was that Pius must provide immediate aid for Ferrante, lest the kingdom of Naples fall to her own enemies.[40]

Panormita's oration at Mantua sought to explain Ferrante's involvement in peninsular squabbles, thereby excusing him from immediate participation in a crusade. Ferrante inherited from Alfonso a conflict with the unstable Sigismondo Malatesta, Panormita said, as well as a more serious war with Genoa. He devoted the bulk of his oration to condemnation of Genoese treachery, particularly as manifested in their alliance with the French. Ferrante desired nothing more than peace in Italy and war against the Turks, Panormita said, but the presence of French forces in Italy made it impossible to think seriously about a crusade. Ferrante had no choice but to protect Italy and his kingdom from French aggression. Ferrante would eagerly accede to the Italian peace that Pius sought to promote—provided that the French leave Italy and the Genoese accept Ferrante as a friend. Only on those conditions did it make sense to plan an expedition against the Turks.[41]

Panormita's political activity under Alfonso and Ferrante illus-

---

[39] ASV, Reg. brev., Arm. XXXIX, 9, fols. 21v, 23rv, 25v–26r. On the Congress of Mantua, see Pastor, *History of the Popes*, 3.45–101.

[40] Messer, ed., *Le codice aragonese*, esp. pp. 267–69, 274–75, 311–19, 335–37, 339, 367–69. The references to the fall of Constantinople occur on pp. 312 and 369.

[41] *Regis Ferdinandi et aliorum epistolae*, pp. 338–43.

trates two important points. In the first place, his faithful service demonstrated the depth of his loyalty to the Aragonese dynasty of Naples. This is particularly true for his work during Ferrante's reign. The previous chapter showed that Panormita became disenchanted with the conditions of his employment during the years 1458 to 1462—precisely the period of greatest danger in Ferrante's struggle to succeed Alfonso—and that he entertained the notion of improving his lot by going to Rome, Sicily, or even Spain. Yet during those same dark days he worked furiously as adviser, secretary, and ambassador, striving to save Ferrante's crown. In the light of these efforts, it seems ungenerous to characterize Panormita as a professional rhetorician interested only in selling his talents to the highest bidder. In the second place, Panormita's political experience helps to clarify also the character of humanist political thinking. Like many of his humanist contemporaries and political theorists from other ages as well, Panormita generally cast his public discussion of political questions in moralistic terms. Indeed, the next chapter will examine his political ideals in the context of other humanists' political thought. When he dealt directly with practical political problems, however, Panormita abandoned his public idealism and worked according to the dictates of the real world of politics. Already developed at some length in the last few pages, this point will emerge yet again in the next section, which examines the thought of Panormita and other humanists on how best to deal with the Turks.

The Turkish Threat and the Question of a Crusade

During the course of his reign, Alfonso the Magnanimous received a great deal of unsolicited advice concerning the Islamic world, and especially concerning the desirability of a crusade. Perhaps the first such counsel came in the form of an exhortation by the Greek émigré, George of Trebizond. Writing in 1443, shortly after Alfonso's victory in Naples and a full decade before the fall of Constantinople, George urged Alfonso to mount an expedition to Egypt and Syria with the aim of recovering the Holy Land of "Judaea" for Christianity. He briefly cited the menace of the Turks as another argument for a crusade. Yet in this oration, George consistently envisioned liberation of the Holy Land from Arab Muslims as the ultimate goal of a crusade, even in revisions of his work prepared as late as 1452.[42] The fall of Constantinople brought sharper focus to calls for a crusade: most advocates after 1453 urged an expedition specifically against the Turks, not a vaguely planned campaign to the Levant; and they hoped to safeguard Italy and Christianity, not to liberate a Holy Land long since fallen into Muslim orbit. Thus about 1454 Pope Nicholas V initiated a diplomatic campaign calling for Alfonso to lead a united Christian effort against the Turks, and he dispatched Cardinal Domenico Firmano at the head of a delegation to encourage the project.[43] After the conclusion of the Tuscan war and the reestablishment of communications between Naples and Florence, Poggio Bracciolini addressed letters to the same effect both to Alfonso and to Bartolomeo Facio.[44]

For the most part, Alfonso received inferior advice from humanists urging him to lead a crusade. Apart from the effusions of Poggio and George of Trebizond, numerous exhortations came to him at the instigation of Pope Calixtus III, who initiated a veritable

[42] John Monfasani, ed., *Collectanea Trapezuntiana: Texts, Documents, and Bibliographies of George of Trebizond* (Binghamton, N.Y., 1984), pp. 422–33. On the place of this oration in George's apocalyptic thought, see Monfasani, *George of Trebizond: A Biography and a Study of His Rhetoric and Logic* (Leiden, 1976), pp. 50–53. In other works George substituted Constantinople for the Holy Land as target for a crusade, and in 1465 he even traveled to Constantinople in hopes of converting Sultan Mehmed II to Christianity: cf. ibid., pp. 128–31, 141, 184–94.

[43] Lucio Marineo, *De primis Aragoniae regibus* (Caesaraugusta, 1509), fols. xlii v–xlvi r.

[44] Poggio, *Epistolae*, ed. T. Tonelli (Florence, 1832–61), 3.158–65 (republished along with the other volumes in Poggio's *Opera omnia*, ed. R. Fubini, 4 vols. [Turin, 1963–69], vol. 3); Facio, *De viris illustribus liber*, ed. L. Mehus (Florence, 1745), appendix of epistles, pp. 101–4.

literary as well as diplomatic campaign to push Alfonso into action. Thus in June 1456, the humanist Niccolò Perotti, recently appointed to a post as papal secretary, praised Alfonso for his various qualities and requested him to contribute fifteen triremes to the papal fleet about to depart Rome.[45] About the same time, Orazio Romano composed and dedicated to the king a long poetic exhortation deploring Turkish cruelty and identifying Alfonso as the only hope for the survival of Europe and Christendom.[46] In the same year Andrea Contrario delivered before Alfonso an oration to the same effect.[47] Whatever their literary merits, these works provided only a shallow justification for Alfonso's participation in a crusade—and necessarily so, since the authors failed to appreciate the political and military realities of the situation. Advice of this sort basically shows the extent to which the crusading ideal had captured the attention of Quattrocento Italy. However cynically they might behave, humanists and rulers alike responded readily to the depiction of their age as a time of epochal, even eschatological conflict between Christendom and the infidel.

Only two lobbyists—the Greek humanist and émigré, Niccolò Sagundino and the Italian humanist historian Flavio Biondo—offered Alfonso truly intelligent advice for a crusade. Sagundino possessed a great deal of experience with the Turks: he had spent thirteen months as a prisoner after the fall of Thessaloniki (March 1430); he had observed the fall of Constantinople from the vantage point of Chalcis in Euboea; and he had served as Venetian ambassador to Sultan Mehmed II.[48] Pope Nicholas V selected him as one

[45] Giovanni Mercati, *Per la cronologia della vita e degli scritti di Niccolò Perotti* (Rome, 1925), pp. 44–46, 148–50.

[46] Tammaro de Marinis and Alessandro Perosa, eds., *Nuovi documenti per la storia del Rinascimento* (Florence, 1970), pp. 105–14.

[47] BAV, Ottob. lat. 1677, fols. 1v–7v. Andres Soria provides a transcription in *Los humanistas de la corte de Alfonso el Magnanimo* (Granada, 1956). pp. 309–19.

[48] On his life see two works of Franz Babinger: "Nikolaos Sagoundinos, ein griechischer-venedischer Humanist des 15. Jahrhunderts," in Χαριστήριον εἰς Ἀναστάσιον Κ. Ὀρλάνδον (Athens, 1964), pp. 198–212; and *Johannes Darius (1414–1494)* (Munich, 1961), pp. 9–52.

of the diplomats in his campaign to organize a crusade, and in that capacity Sagundino delivered an oration to Alfonso early in 1454. Sagundino despised the Turks and deplored their cruelty, as did every other Christian who wrote about them in the fifteenth century, but he offered an impressive understanding of Turkish history and reliable information on Sultan Mehmed II. He characterized Mehmed as a cruel and ruthless man implacably hostile to Christianity, but also as an intelligent, grave, diligent, and highly capable ruler. Sagundino took seriously the fear, then circulating around Europe, that Mehmed intended to use his recent conquest, Constantinople, as a staging point for expansion into Christendom, beginning with Italy. Sagundino's evaluation of the Turkish threat no doubt carried a greater sense of authority than the views of other contemporary commentators, but his emphasis on Mehmed's military and political competence could not have made Alfonso enthusiastic to challenge the sultan.[49]

Flavio Biondo did not possess Sagundino's direct experience with the Turks, but his historical and geographical interests enabled him to frame a reasonable argument on behalf of a crusade. This point emerges most clearly from a long treatise that Biondo composed and dedicated to Alfonso three weeks after news arrived in Rome that Constantinople had fallen. Biondo carefully reviewed the progress of the Turks against the Byzantine Empire under Sultans Bayezid I, Murad II, and Mehmed II. He reminded Alfonso also of the extensive lands in the Balkans and southeastern Europe that Mehmed either ruled directly or controlled as tributary states. As for strategy, Biondo urged a coordinated offensive by both land and sea. Crusading forces on the land would ally with

---

[49] The oration survives in several manuscripts, including BAV, Ottob. lat. 1732, fols. 20r–23r; Venice, Biblioteca Nazionale Marciana, MS lat. XIV. 244 (= 4681), fol. 1r–13v; and Florence, Biblioteca Medicea Laurenziana, MS Ashburnham 270, fols. 7r–13v. N. Iorga published the most interesting passages from yet another, Milanese manuscript in his *Notes et extraits pour servir à l'histoire des croisades au XVe siècle*, 6 vols. (Paris, 1899–1902, and Bucharest, 1915–1916), 3.315–23. See also an account of Turkish history that Sagundino later prepared for Pope Pius II: *Rerum turcarum liber* (Louvain, 1553).

discontented Christians in lands subject to the Turks, as John Hunyadi had sought to do in the 1440s and early 1450s, and would hope to exploit internal divisions among the Turks themselves. Meanwhile, Christian naval forces—vastly superior to those of the Turks, who in fact had negligible naval experience before the siege of Constantinople—would seek to interrupt Turkish lines of supply. Though excessively optimistic about the prospects for Christian unity, Biondo outlined a feasible plan for an expedition against the Turks, thanks largely to an appreciation of geographical and political realities far superior to that of most other humanists.[50]

Yet Alfonso never exhibited any serious interest in leading or even contributing to a crusade. Indeed, a recent article by Alan Ryder has argued that Alfonso did not consider the Turks a genuine threat to Italy.[51] Alfonso's eastern policy thus did not reflect fear of the Turks as much as Aragonese diplomatic and dynastic interests in the Balkans and Catalan economic and mercantile interests in the Mamluk sultanate of Egypt. Neither Alfonso nor any other fifteenth-century European could openly disavow the crusade, but Alfonso sought consistently to impede an expedition that would divert resources from his other projects. His diplomacy thus unfolded on two levels: while publicly endorsing the crusading ideal, Alfonso privately interposed every necessary obstacle to ensure that the ideal did not travel very far down the road to reality.

Ryder based his argument quite properly on the analysis of archival documents, without investigating humanists' writings on

[50] Biondo, *Scritti inediti e rari di Biondo Flavio*, ed. B. Nogara (Rome, 1927), pp. 29–58. Cf. also shorter treatises sent later to Genoa and Venice, pp. 59–89; also a short, unconvincing oration he delivered before Alfonso and Emperor Frederick III in April 1452, pp. 107–14. On the Turks' military capacities under Sultan Mehmed II and particularly on their inexperienced navy, see Franz Babinger, *Mehmed the Conqueror and His Time*, trans. R. Manheim (Princeton, 1978), pp. 128–34, 444–50.

[51] Alan Ryder, "The Eastern Policy of Alfonso the Magnanimous," *AAP*, n.s. 28 (1979), 7–25.

the crusade. The interesting thing for present purposes is that much of what he says about Alfonso applies equally well to Panormita. As secretary to both Alfonso and Ferrante, Panormita often affirmed the kings' enthusiasm for a crusade. In official correspondence, however, he called for large concessions on the part of other princes while avoiding specific or substantial Neapolitan commitments. Furthermore, in one remarkable personal letter to Alfonso, he advised caution and delay as the wisest policy for the king to take with respect to the crusade.

One of the very first letters Panormita composed as Alfonso's secretary addressed the college of cardinals on the issue of the crusade. Panormita deplored the fall of Constantinople, denounced the barbarism of the Turks, and declared Alfonso's readiness to expel them from Greece, even to pursue them beyond Europe.[52] During the years 1455 to 1458 Panormita sent numerous official letters portraying Alfonso as more zealous for a crusade than the archfoe of the Turks, Pope Calixtus III himself. In the early days of Ferrante's reign he affirmed to Francesco Sforza and Pope Pius II the new king's eagerness to confront the Turks. The last surviving piece of Panormita's official correspondence repeated this point to Pope Paul II (1464–1471).[53] Thus Panormita clearly recognized the importance of the crusading ideal in the political consciousness of Quattrocento Italy, and from the beginning to the end of his secretarial career, he publicly represented Alfonso and Ferrante as Christendom's foremost promoters of the expedition to smite the Turk.

In doing so, however, he attempted to establish such preconditions for the kings' participation that they would never actually take up arms. By one ploy, for example, Panormita demanded on Alfonso's behalf that all European princes, including the pope,

[52] BAV, Barb. lat. 2070, fols. 2r–3v. The letter is dated 1 April 1454, i.e., just over six months after the fall of Constantinople.

[53] For these letters on Ferrante's behalf see BAV, Barb. lat. 2070, fols. 55v–56v; and *Regis Ferdinandi et aliorum epistolae*, pp. 301–2, 440–41.

contribute 10 percent of their resources to the cause of a crusade.[54] For months Panormita argued in various state letters that Pope Calixtus himself hindered the enterprise by making war against the Christian Jacopo Piccinino—who of course was able to campaign in Tuscany only because of Alfonso's aid—and that Alfonso could prepare and lead a crusade only after the establishment of a stable peace in Italy.[55] Meanwhile, Panormita avoided making significant commitments of Neapolitan resources. In one particularly illuminating letter written on Alfonso's behalf, Panormita solicited the contribution of a fleet from the king of Portugal, promising only that Portuguese ships could put in at Neapolitan ports and take on provisions on the same terms available to Alfonso's own fleet.[56] The war of succession largely removed pressure from Ferrante to take action against the Turks. Yet even in the early years of Ferrante's reign Panormita occasionally linked aid for the new and embattled king with the threat of the Turks and the prospect of a crusade.[57]

Panormita's own understanding of the Turkish threat emerges most clearly not in diplomatic correspondence, however, but in a personal letter that he addressed to King Alfonso. The text of the letter makes it clear that Panormita composed it in the period between late June and early August 1456. During that summer the commander of the papal fleet, Cardinal Lodovico Trevisan—often but inaccurately called Scarampo—tarried in Naples en route to the Aegean Sea and action against the Turks. He stopped at Naples in order to augment the fleet with fifteen galleys that Alfonso had promised, but did not contribute to the crusading forces. Trevisan and Alfonso knew each other quite well, and they spent so much time together that Panormita had to submit advice in written form rather than in person. In his letter he urged Alfonso to think critically and realistically about Trevisan's enterprise. As

---

[54] BAV, Barb. lat. 2070, fols. 11v–12r.
[55] BAV, Barb. lat. 2070, esp. fols. 3v–10r.
[56] BAV, Barb. lat. 2070, fols. 19v–20r.
[57] Cf. *Regis Ferdinandi et aliorum epistolae*, pp. 319–22, 338–43.

the unofficial but obvious leader of Christian military forces against the Turk, Alfonso must think of the interests of all Christendom. He specifically must not attack the Turks with inadequate forces—meaning no doubt Trevisan's insignificant fleet, which probably numbered only sixteen galleys. Panormita warned Alfonso against provoking the Turks into preparation of their own large naval force, which they could then turn against the Neapolitan fleet. He advised Alfonso to strengthen his military forces and to inform the pope that he intended to defer an expedition until he had assembled a fleet equal to the demands of a crusade.[58] Both official and private correspondence thus show that Panormita's thought on a crusade closely resembled Alfonso's policy: both men supported the idea of a crusade in public, but recognized that military and political realities dictated a policy of caution, perhaps even of hindrance to an expedition against the Turks.

The unfortunate loss over the centuries of Neapolitan archival sources makes it impossible to determine the extent to which later humanists continued to view the Turkish threat and the question of the crusade in Panormita's realistic way. Particularly unfortunate is the absence of documents that might have shed light on the work and thought of humanists who played roles in Neapolitan politics and diplomacy during the period of the Turkish siege of Rhodes (1480) and occupation of Otranto (1480–1481). Pontano often referred to the Turkish threat in diplomatic correspondence composed during the 1490s, but no information survives to illuminate his conception of the issue as clearly as the items of Panormita examined above. Meanwhile, however, other issues of the 1470s and 1480s generated documentation that survives and demonstrates beyond question the capacity of Neapolitan humanists to deal with political and diplomatic problems in a supremely realistic way.

[58] See Panormita's *Epistolarum libri V*, fols. 118v–20r. On Trevisan's naval expedition see Pastor, *History of the Popes*, 2.368–76; and Kenneth M. Setton, *The Papacy and the Levant (1204–1571)*, 4 vols. (Philadelphia, 1976–84), 2.168–71, 184–90.

The Justification of Ferrante's Policies

Humanists at Ferrante's court supplied him with numerous intellectual, literary, and diplomatic services, as much of this book demonstrates. During one difficult decade of Neapolitan history, the years from 1478 to 1488, these services concentrated largely on the effort to explain and justify Ferrante's unpopular policies. The period opened with the Pazzi conspiracy and subsequent war that pitted Florence against Naples and Rome (1478–1480): for the first time since his pacification of the Regno in 1462, Ferrante engaged the kingdom of Naples in open war, thanks largely to his alliance with the martial Pope Sixtus IV. The campaign to recover Otranto from Turkish invaders followed almost immediately (1480–1481), then the War of Ferrara (1482–1484). Finally, there came the barons' revolt and Ferrante's repression of the rebel leaders (1485–1487). Except for the operation against the Turks, all these conflicts led to serious diplomatic problems, beyond the Alps as well as in Italy. A fair amount of documentation survives to show how three humanists—Giovanni Brancati, Giovanni Albino, and Giovanni Pontano—helped to defend Neapolitan policies during this period.

Brancati played a role of some importance in the cultural history of Renaissance Naples: he served as chief of the royal library, as translator of Pliny into the vernacular, and as an orator who publicly praised Ferrante and his family on several momentous occasions. The fortuitous survival of two letters shows that from time to time he also assumed more purely political duties. Dated 15 August 1478, as Ferrante and Duke Alfonso of Calabria prepared to enter Pope Sixtus's war against Florence, the first letter responded to a Milanese protest against Neapolitan provocations in central and northern Italy. The Milanese complaint charged Ferrante with the waging of an unjust war, secretly aiding the Turks, and encouraging Genoa to rebel against her Milanese lords. It recalled the considerable support that Duke Francesco Sforza had provided in helping Ferrante to secure his hold on the Regno, and it warned darkly that Ferrante's heirs would need Milanese friend-ship to retain the crown of Naples. In his reply, Brancati blamed the chief Milanese counsellor, Cicco Simonetta, for poor relations between Milan and Naples; he denied that Ferrante had intrigued with the Turks; he explained Neapolitan intervention in Genoa as Ferrante's effort to aid a political ally unjustly persecuted by Si-monetta. Brancati pointed out that Ferrante had aided the young duke of Milan, Galeazzo Maria Sforza, in his bid for power, and he lamented the shift in Milanese policy toward Naples, from tradi-tional friendship to current hostility. Finally, Brancati charged that under Simonetta's tutelage Milan stood for the violation of treaties, the destruction of alliances, the ruin of Italy, the perver-sion of law, and the triumph of tyranny, even as Ferrante promoted liberty and piety.[59]

Brancati's second letter dealt with an even more delicate mat-ter—the threat of renewed conflict between Naples and France. About mid-September 1478, King Louis XI hinted in a state let-ter to Naples that he might come to the aid of Florence, traditional peninsular ally of France. Brancati replied about the end of Sep-tember, portraying Ferrante as a lover of peace and an obedient ser-vant of Pope Sixtus IV. He refuted once again the allegation that Ferrante had become friendly with the Turks, and he justified Fer-rante's reluctant intervention in Genoese affairs as an unfortunate but necessary effort to protect his own legitimate interests. Bran-cati went to great lengths to deny the charge that Ferrante sought to establish Neapolitan hegemony over all Italy: he pointed to sev-eral specific occasions, for example, when Ferrante had declined earlier opportunities to take advantage of Milanese and Florentine difficulties. He admitted that Duke Alfonso of Calabria had re-

---

[59] The letter survives in a manuscript of Brancati's works, Valencia, BU, MS 774 (formerly 52), fols. 172r–89v. Unaware of Brancati's manuscript, Giulio C. Zimolo published the text of the two letters—the original Milanese complaint and Brancati's response—from Milanese archives: "Le relazioni tra Milano e Na-poli e la politica italiana in due lettere del 1478," *Archivio storico lombardo*, 64 (1937), 403–34. De Marinis first pointed out Brancati's authorship of the letter in *La biblioteca*, 1.185, 191 n. 30.

cently taken an army into Tuscany, but defended the measure as a response to papal appeal. Ferrante had long suffered in silence, he said, as Venice, Milan, and Florence threatened the peace of Italy by breaking treaties, disrupting alliances, and generally fishing in troubled waters. Only at the pope's call did he take up arms. In closing, Brancati once again portrayed Ferrante as a promoter of liberty and religion, as opposed to his enemies, who stood for servitude and impiety.[60]

Brancati succeeded in constructing a handsome mask for Ferrante's policies, but he neglected to mention several important points and seriously distorted the truth of matters as a result. In fact, Ferrante had long considered the possibility of allying with the Turks as a way of gaining support against Venice, and by 1482 at the latest he had opened serious negotiations with Istanbul. Furthermore, Ferrante's encouragement of Genoese rebels had much to do with his fear that Milan was moving toward a Venetian alliance. Finally, Ferrante entered the war against Florence largely out of concern over the progressive consolidation of a strong Florentine state in Tuscany. Ferrante certainly did not envision the establishment of Neapolitan dominion in all of Italy, as his enemies charged, but he had long sought to increase his influence in central Italy, particularly in Siena, and he continued to do so during the war following the Pazzi conspiracy.[61] Brancati's defense of Ferrante's policies strongly suggests that he subscribed to a principle later espoused openly by various humanists and political thinkers, beginning with Pontano: interests of state excuse dissembling and a certain amount of diplomatic dishonesty.

The wars of Otranto and Ferrara initiated Giovanni Albino into

---

[60] Carlo de Frede published this letter from the Valencia manuscript of Brancati's works: "Un memoriale di Ferrante I d'Aragona a Luigi XI (1478)," *Rivista storica italiana*, 60 (1948), 403–19.

[61] The best guide to Neapolitan policy in this period is Pontieri, *Per la storia del regno di Ferrante I d'Aragona redi Napoli*, 2d ed. (Naples, 1969), pp. 277–303. On Ferrante's negotiations with the Turks, see also Franz Babinger, "Sechs unbekannte aragonische Sendschreiben im grossherrlichen Seraj zu Stambul," in *Studi in onore di Riccardo Filangieri*, 3 vols. (Naples, 1959), 2.107–28.

the difficulties of Neapolitan politics in the late fifteenth century. A humanist and man of culture like Brancati, Albino served as librarian to Duke Alfonso of Calabria, and he later composed six books on the deeds of the Neapolitan kings in the late Quattrocento. Yet he also served as a diplomat on numerous missions. He helped to organize support for Duke Alfonso's campaign against the Turks at Otranto, and he played an especially important role during the War of Ferrara. In December 1483 King Ferrante sent Albino into Lombardy in an effort to stabilize the league of Naples, Milan, Rome, and Ferrara against Venice. Duke Alfonso had threatened the alliance by his aggressive maneuvers and unwise talk. He had even announced his desire to have someone murder the Venetian condottiere, Roberto Sanseverino. Ferrante entrusted to Albino the message that Duke Alfonso's irresponsible conduct compromised Neapolitan strategy. Considering the unreliability of his own allies and the expanded campaign planned for the following year by the Venetians, Duke Alfonso should say kind things about Sanseverino—especially in light of Ferrante's hopes of luring the condottiere into Neapolitan service![62]

Undoubtedly the most difficult task that fell to the humanist spokesmen for the kingdom of Naples was justification of the measures taken by Ferrante in the aftermath of the second barons' revolt. Despite their alliance with Pope Innocent VIII and diplomatic support from abroad, the barons did not coordinate their efforts successfully and thus could not withstand Duke Alfonso of Calabria and his experienced forces. Within ten months of the outbreak of hostilities—expulsion of the Aragonese garrison at Aquila took place on 26 September 1485—Duke Alfonso had largely pacified the Regno. By 11 August 1486 Pontano had negotiated a treaty of peace between Ferrante and Pope Innocent.

---

[62] See the collection of diplomatic materials compiled by Giovanni Albino's nephew, Ottavio Albino, ed., *Lettere, istruzioni, ed altre memorie*, in Gravier, ed., *Raccolta*, 5.12–90, esp. 71–79. Giovanni Albino occasionally referred to his own diplomatic services when recounting the history of this period: cf. his *De gestis regum neapolitanorum ab Aragonia*, in Gravier, ed., *Raccolta*, 5.42–46.

The pact called for Ferrante to pardon the rebel barons, restore their holdings that Duke Alfonso had seized, honor the papacy, pay the annual tribute traditionally expected of Neapolitan kings, and observe other less important provisions as well.[63] Yet already on 13 August Ferrante violated the agreement when he arrested Antonello Petrucci and his two sons, along with Francesco Coppola and other former conspirators. Exactly three months later, 13 November, a tribunal publicly read sentences of death in the cases of the three Petrucci and Coppola. Within one month, 11 December, Francesco and Giovanni Antonio Petrucci had suffered execution; Antonello Petrucci and Francesco Coppola languished in the dungeon of the Castelnuovo until their public beheading, 11 May 1487. But the troubles had not yet come to an end. A large number of barons continued to conspire against Ferrante even after the establishment of peace. According to confessions taken later, they encouraged intervention in Neapolitan affairs by Roberto Sanseverino, now chief papal condottiere, and by Duke René of Lorraine, who claimed the kingdom of Naples as a part of his Angevin inheritance. Thus Ferrante moved once again against the barons. On 12 June and again on 4 July 1487 he ordered new rounds of detentions, and numerous other barons suffered imprisonment, trial, and deprivation of their holdings as a result.[64] Thus, far from pardoning the barons and restoring their possessions, Ferrante repressed them absolutely and confiscated their estates. Meanwhile, he honored Pope Innocent with disobedience, and he refused to submit the annual tribute that the peace of 1486 obliged him to pay.

Ferrante's policy is not particularly difficult to justify in purely political terms. The barons, after all, had allied with Ferrante's

[63] For the official, papal text of the treaty, see Volpicella, ed., *Instructionum liber*, pp. 196–210. See also P. Fedele, "La pace del 1486 tra Ferdinando d'Aragona ed Innocenzo VIII," *ASPN*, 30 (1905), 481–503.

[64] For the details of Ferrante's repression, see Notar Giacomo, *Cronica di Napoli*, ed. P. Garzilli (Naples, 1845), pp. 159–64; and Riccardo Filangieri, ed., *Una cronaca napoletana figurata del Quattrocento* (Naples, 1956), pp. 48–50, 58–66, 71–74.

most dangerous enemies, including the republic of Venice and Duke René of Lorraine. Pope Innocent also had seriously menaced the stability of Ferrante's monarchy. He maintained close relations with the rebel barons throughout their revolt, and he actively solicited support for their cause from the Holy Roman Emperor, the German princes and cities, and the kings of France and Spain.[65] Ferrante's enemies thus left him with no realistic alternative to a powerful military and political response.

In moral and diplomatic terms, however, Ferrante's policy was much more difficult to explain, particularly so after the later rounds of arrests in June and July 1487. When news of the new detentions reached Rome, Pope Innocent mounted a vigorous diplomatic campaign designed to force Ferrante to release the barons and observe the peace of 1486. Already on 18 July he dispatched a letter that reached Naples the very next day, inquiring as to the reasons for the new detentions, complaining because no one had consulted him on the matter, and insisting that Ferrante delay proceedings until Innocent could send his representative to Naples.[66] Shortly thereafter he dispatched Bishop Pietro Vicentino of Cesena as a special emissary, demanding the explanation for Ferrante's action and calling for him to deliver the detainees into papal hands until neutral judges could investigate their alleged crimes.[67] Innocent then sought external support for his policy. On 4 September 1487 he sent an ambassador to Florence and Milan with instructions to ask for their aid against Ferrante. The instruc-

[65] See numerous surviving instructions to ambassadors and pieces of diplomatic correspondence Innocent directed to rebel barons: ASV, Reg. brev., Arm. XXXIX, 19, esp. fols. 62r, 113v, 123v, 127rv, 136v–37r, 236r, 249v, 291rv, 303v–4r, 366v–67r, 370v, 425rv, 469v–70r, among others. See also letters seeking support from Germany, Spain, and France, in ibid., fols. 162rv, 188v–189r, 250rv. See finally the report of the Milanese ambassador in Naples, which shows that already in April 1485 the fact of Innocent's letters to the barons had become common knowledge: Milan, Archivio di Stato, Sforzesco 247, dispatch of 21 April 1485.

[66] Ottavio Albino, ed., *Lettere, istruzioni ed altre memorie*, in Gravier, ed., *Raccolta*, 5.132–33, esp. 133.

[67] ASV, Misc. Arm. II, 20, fols. 141r–42r; Misc. Arm. II, 56, fols. 419r–21r.

tions provided for the ambassador to explain that Innocent did not seek support from Ferdinand and Isabella of Spain—recognized in the treaty of 1486 as guarantors of the peace, along with the duke of Milan and the republic of Florence—because he hoped to keep foreigners out of Italian affairs. A further set of secret instructions, however, provided for the ambassador to inform the Florentine and Milanese leaders that Innocent planned to enforce the peace of 1486 and would accept aid from any source whatever—a clear allusion to Innocent's trump card, the possibility of calling for Spanish assistance if Italian states did not adequately support his policy.[68] Twelve days later, on 16 September, Innocent sent letters to Spain, Venice, Milan, and Florence, explaining his position once again and calling for Ferrante to return to obedience.[69]

Pope Innocent's diplomatic offensive placed enormous pressure on Ferrante, who found it necessary to engage a great deal of his kingdom's intellectual and diplomatic resources in the defense of his policy. A remarkable treatise of 1487 throws unusually clear light on the kind of thought and discussion that took place during the early days of Innocent's diplomatic campaign. The anonymous work survives in one manuscript with a Spanish text (perhaps a translation of an Italian or Latin original) edited some years ago by Benedetto Croce.[70] The author was obviously a lawyer: the treatise developed technical legal arguments—studded with direct citations and allusions to Bartolus, Baldus, Irnerius, and other medieval lawyers—to prove five main points. The author argued first that Ferrante had accepted the treaty of 1486 only under duress: he stood in danger of losing his entire realm and agreed to terms only in order to forestall the ruin and destruction of his kingdom. Agreements made under duress are invalid and unenforceable, however, so that the treaty of 1486 was null and void. The argument from duress served as the basis also for the author's second

[68] ASV, Misc. Arm. II, 56, fols. 141r–45r.
[69] ASV, Misc. Arm. II, 56, fols. 517r–20r.
[70] Benedetto Croce, ed., *Prima del Machiavelli: una difesa di Re Ferrante I di Napoli per il violato trattato di pace del 1486 col papa* (Bari, 1944).

point, which argued that Ferrante's oath to observe the treaty had no force, as well as the third, which held that Ferrante's letters and documents of ratification similarly bound him to nothing. The fourth argument justified Ferrante's continued repression of the barons in spite of the treaty. He pardoned them in August 1486 for offenses committed until that time; their renewed machinations fully warranted the new rounds of detention and confiscation that took place in the summer of 1487. Finally, the author argued that quite apart from the treaty's invalidity, the pact did not oblige the Catholic kings of Spain to intervene on the matter of the tribute. The treaty called for the guarantors—the Spanish kings, the duke of Milan, and the republic of Florence—to oversee only Ferrante's pardon of the barons, not his payment of the tribute. In sum, the treatise argued that the treaty of 1486 was invalid, that Ferrante had no need to observe its terms, that in any case he had not violated it by moving against the barons, and that the guarantors of the peace had no cause to intervene.

The narrow, legalistic reasoning of the anonymous treatise of 1487 bespeaks clearly the moral and diplomatic discomfort that Neapolitan spokesmen experienced in the period following Ferrante's renewed repression of the barons. For immediate purposes, its prime significance lies in the fact that several of its arguments found their way into Neapolitan diplomacy of the period. The response to Pope Innocent's diplomatic campaign against Ferrante—largely coordinated by Giovanni Pontano, who became chief royal secretary shortly after the arrest of Antonello Petrucci—employed similarly legalistic reasoning and sometimes depended on genuinely deceptive arguments. By chance, a fair amount of diplomatic documentation survives from the period 1486 to 1488. Instructions to Neapolitan ambassadors, almost all of them written by Pontano, show that Ferrante's response to Pope Innocent's challenge dealt with four main issues.

Most of the surviving materials addressed the major cause of tension between Ferrante and Pope Innocent, the new arrests of barons in June and July 1487, the legal proceedings against them, and the confiscation of their estates. To some extent, Neapolitan diplomacy for several months had prepared the way for these measures. Already in 1486 Ferrante had demanded that certain barons turn over their castles and fortresses to him, under penalty of facing Duke Alfonso's army for failure to comply. During the first half of 1487, Pontano and others explained this measure as a response to the barons' continuing conspiracy: since the peace of 1486, they had treated with Duke René of Lorraine, Roberto Sanseverino, and even the Turks.[71] After the detentions of June and July had precipitated Pope Innocent's diplomatic offensive, Pontano went to great lengths to justify Ferrante's actions. As early as 6 July 1487 he addressed a long, eloquent letter of instructions to the humanist Giovanni Albino, then Neapolitan ambassador to Virginio Orsini, lord of Bracciano. Ferrante had attempted to deal gently with the barons, Pontano said, but their perverse nature forced him to adopt harsher tactics. Instead of offering them pleasant food, he had no alternative but to treat them with unpleasant medicine, since they resembled patients who were grievously, desperately, and even incurably ill. (Medical metaphors appear frequently in Pontano's writings.) Specifically, the barons had continued to plot with Ferrante's enemies outside the realm, including even the Turks; Ferrante imprisoned some of them for no other reason than to preserve peace in the Regno and in Italy as a whole. Pontano's letter was accompanied by a memorial outlining some of the specific charges against the barons—including the allegation that their conspiracy numbered Cardinal Giuliano della Rovere (later Pope Julius II) among its external allies—and promising early delivery of the official proceedings against them.[72]

Pontano later justified Ferrante's policy in other courts besides that of Virginio Orsini. He explained Ferrante's measures in very similar terms—though not at such great length or with such eloquence as in the letter to Albino—in diplomatic instructions ad-

[71] Volpicella, ed., *Instructionum liber*, pp. 53, 62–66, 81–82, 87, 114–15.

[72] Ottavio Albino, ed., *Lettere, istruzioni ed altre memorie*, in Gravier, ed., *Raccolta*, 5.120–27.

dressed to Neapolitan ambassadors in Rome, Florence, Milan, Spain, and Hungary.[73] Beginning in early August 1487, ambassadors received from Pontano not only their instructions, but also copies of the proceedings against the barons, including depositions and confessions of the guilty parties themselves.[74] About one year later, as mentioned already, Francesco del Tuppo published one thousand copies of the proceedings, as Neapolitan spokesmen conducted an increasingly public justification of Ferrante's policies.[75]

A second issue Pontano addressed in diplomatic writings of this period was the annual tribute money that Pope Innocent demanded of Ferrante. In the spring of 1487, Milanese ambassadors inquired as to Ferrante's intentions with respect to the tribute, prompting Pontano's most lengthy discussion of the issue. He argued that Ferrante had spent so much money defending his realm against the barons and preparing it for possible conflicts with the Turks that he could not afford to pay the tribute. He claimed a bit weakly that Ferrante had inherited exemption from the tribute as part of his legacy from Alfonso. He argued further, like the anonymous lawyer, that the treaty of 1486 did not oblige Ferrante to pay the tribute, since his representatives agreed to terms solely in order to persuade Innocent to lay down his arms. In any case, Pontano said, Ferrante himself never agreed to make the annual pay-

[73] Ibid., pp. 132–37; Volpicella, ed., *Instructionum liber*, pp. 127–28, 131–32, 141–46, 170–75.

[74] Volpicella, ed., *Instructionum liber*, pp. 132, 141, 171–75. For an account of the presentation of these proceedings to Pope Innocent, see Ottavio Albino, ed., *Lettere, istruzioni ed altre memorie*, in Gravier, ed., *Raccolta*, 5.142–44, 146–48.

[75] See Alfredo Mauro, *Francesco del Tuppo e il suo "Esopo"* (Città di Castello, 1926), docs. 19 and 20 in the appendix, pp. 233–34, for the payment of 495 ducats del Tuppo received for his work. For a reprint of the proceedings, see the old edition of Camillo Porzio, *La congiura de' baroni*, ed. S. d'Aloe (Naples, 1859), pp. CXLI–CCLXXIII of the appendix. Del Tuppo's edition of the proceedings against Antonello Petrucci, his sons Francesco and Giovanni Antonio, and Francesco Coppola had become available 14 July 1487. D'Aloe also provided a reprint of this work: pp. I–CXL of the appendix.

ments.[76] In another place Pontano attempted to shift blame for the tribute disagreement onto the pope. Ferrante's representatives—meaning primarily Pontano himself, who negotiated the peace of 1486 on the king's behalf—did not agree to the article calling for tribute payments, indeed had no power to do so. Pope Innocent added numerous items to the articles approved by Ferrante's representatives, Pontano said, including the one specifying annual tribute payments.[77] On this point the documents simply do not support Pontano. It is true that the pope circulated a more elaborate peace treaty than Pontano had negotiated. Provision for the tribute, however, appears not only in the official text of the treaty released by Pope Innocent, but also in a preliminary draft of the treaty's articles endorsed by Pontano himself.[78]

Yet Pontano continued to make his argument as late as 1489. On 1 May of that year, the Venetian, Florentine, and Milanese ambassadors in Naples attended a meeting at the Castelnuovo where Ferrante called on Pontano to justify the king's refusal to pay the annual tribute. The foundation of his case remained the allegation that a papal scribe inserted provisions into the peace treaty that the negotiators had not agreed to. Although it sheds no new light on the political issue, this episode nevertheless has the incidental value of demonstrating the high degree of confidence that Ferrante placed in Pontano's diplomatic skills. Although Ferrante and Duke Alfonso both attended the meeting, the Milanese ambassador reported that Pontano outlined the Neapolitan position, with occasional contributions by the king or the duke.[79]

Besides defending Ferrante's repression of the barons and denying his obligation to pay tribute, Pontano argued also that guarantors of the treaty of 1486 had no warrant to intervene on behalf

[76] Volpicella, ed., *Instructionum liber*, pp. 113–15.

[77] Ibid., pp. 171–72, 178–79.

[78] P. Fedele published the text of the preliminary draft in "La pace del 1486." See esp. pp. 499, 503 for Pontano's agreement to the article on the tribute. The official treaty released by Pope Innocent appears in Volpicella, ed., *Instructionum liber*, pp. 196–210.

[79] See the dispatch of 2 May 1489 in Milan, Archivio di Stato, Sforzesco 247.

of Pope Innocent, at least not under conditions prevailing in 1487. He maintained in several places that the cosignatories to the treaty—the duke of Milan, the republic of Florence, and the Catholic kings of Spain—had obliged themselves to guarantee only three things: that Ferrante would pardon the barons, keep the peace, and not make war against the pope. Since Ferrante did not break the peace or move against the pope, and since the demands of security justified his new repression of the barons, the guarantors had no cause to support Innocent against Ferrante. In instructions to ambassadors going to Spain, Pontano emphasized also the political troubles that popes had often caused. Their traditional hostility to non-Italians, their viciousness, their tendency to resort quickly and lightly to arms, their unbridled ambition, their drive to enlarge the papal state by means both fair and foul, and their attempts to introduce turbulence into Italian affairs, even when all other states lived in quiet and stability—all these characteristics of papal policy explained current tensions between Ferrante and Innocent.[80] Pontano no doubt calculated that no European monarch of the fifteenth century—and certainly not Ferdinand and Isabella of Spain—could resist the appeal of his antipapal tirade.

Pontano counted on Spanish endorsement also for his position on the last and ultimately the most important of the four main issues he addressed in diplomatic correspondence of 1487—the question of papal jurisdiction in secular, political affairs. The issue arose because of Pope Innocent's attempt to take charge of Ferrante's new proceedings against the barons. Surviving documentation shows that Innocent instructed his ambassador to Naples, Bishop Pietro Vicentino of Cesena, to suggest that Ferrante deliver the barons into neutral (papal) hands, prior to investigation of the charges against them by the guarantors of the treaty of 1486.[81] From information that Pontano provided to ambassadors going to Spain, however, it seems that Vicentino threatened excommuni-

---

[80] Volpicella, ed., *Instructionum liber*, pp. 113–14, 144–45, 171–75.
[81] ASV, Misc. Arm. II, 20, fols. 141r–42v; Misc. Arm. II, 56, fols. 419r–21r.

cation and nullification of the proceedings unless Ferrante conducted them on papal terms, pointing out also that popes had even deposed emperors and kings in the past.[82] Pontano responded vigorously to the papal challenge, casting his argument in quite general terms: "There is no one so ignorant as not to know that kings, princes, and lords have jurisdiction over the crime of lèse majesté." Pontano developed his position most clearly in a set of instructions for Loise di Casalnuovo, Neapolitan emissary to Rome who responded to Vicentino's demands. Ferrante desired earnestly to serve the church as a loyal son, Pontano said, but the bishop of Cesena grossly exceeded his authority in attempting to intervene in the king's proceedings against the barons. Ferrante ruled on the basis of his own thirty years of experience and his ancestors' thousand years of rule. He had loved the barons as sons, borne numerous affronts in patience, and moved against them only out of dire necessity. Pontano several times cautioned Loise to present Ferrante's case in a sober and civil manner, so as not to offend the pope, and always to portray the king as eager for reconciliation. But he also instructed the ambassador to convey the unambiguous points "that jurisdiction over rebellions and crimes of lèse majesté pertains to kings and secular princes, that His Holiness should leave the government of temporal states to those to whom God has given them, and that in the matter of temporal jurisdiction His Holiness does not possess such power as some have led him to believe."[83]

Thus Pontano employed frank speech when conducting business with pontiffs, no less than when he addressed sovereigns. Like his humanist colleagues Brancati and Albino, Pontano had ample opportunity to learn about the difficulties that fifteenth-century politics caused for Italian princes. Whether as secretaries, spokesmen, or representatives of Ferrante, all three men recognized the impossibility of conducting Neapolitan diplomacy according to

[82] Volpicella, ed., *Instructionum liber*, pp. 142–44, 170–71, 174–75.

[83] Besides the passages cited in the previous note, see also ibid., pp. 147–50. The quotations occur on pp. 174 and 148, respectively.

the standards of an absolute, abstract morality. No less than Diomede Carafa or Niccolò Machiavelli, Brancati, Albino, and Pontano carried out their diplomatic duties according to the prevailing standards of the real political world.

Pontano as Secretary, Diplomat, and Political Analyst

Scholars have long recognized the importance of Pontano's political services to the Aragonese dynasty of Naples. Erasmo Percopo long ago provided a basic chronological survey of Pontano's career, and Mario Santoro argued more recently that Pontano's political experience decisively influenced his moral and ethical thought.[84] Yet there exists no analysis of Pontano's life in politics.

The following pages do not deal with Pontano's entire political career, but concentrate instead on the period that he served the Aragonese kings as chief royal secretary. A fair number of materials survive from Pontano's days as secretary to Duke Alfonso of Calabria and his wife, Ippolita Sforza. Those produced during the War of Ferrara show that Pontano had been exposed to the brutal side of war and that he could discuss in detail such mundane matters as maneuvers, money, provisions, strategy, engagements, spies, and even atrocities.[85] These items do little, however, to illuminate Pontano's own conception of political and diplomatic problems. Letters, memorials, and documents that he composed after 1486 shed a great deal more light on this topic than his earlier writings. Furthermore, after the barons' revolt, Pontano exercised much more influence in Neapolitan politics than before. He dealt with

[84] Erasmo Percopo, *Vita di Giovanni Pontano*, ed. M. Manfredi (Naples, 1938), esp. pp. 28–92; Mario Santoro, *Fortuna, ragione e prudenza nella civiltà letteraria del Cinquecento*, 2d ed. (Naples, 1978), pp. 27–69.

[85] Pontano, *Lettere inedite di Joviano Pontano in nome de' reali di Napoli*, ed. F. Gabotto (Bologna, 1893), pp. 122–338, esp. pp. 135–41, 171–73, 184–98, 201–4, 250; also Erasmo Percopo, "Nuove lettere di Gioviano Pontano a principi ed amici," in *In onore di Giovanni Gioviano Pontano nel V centenario della sua nascita* (Naples, 1926), esp. pp. 117–25.

Ferrante and his successors on a daily basis and thus had the opportunity to press his view of matters in a consistent manner.[86] Several pieces of correspondence survive to show that Ferrante had a high opinion of his secretary's literary and diplomatic talents, and that after establishing the basic points of a document, he entrusted its composition to Pontano.[87]

The loss of Neapolitan archives places severe limits on the historian's ability to reconstruct Pontano's assessment of Italian political problems in the 1480s and 1490s. Regular documentation of his diplomatic work simply does not survive; never will historians understand the thinking behind Neapolitan policy as they do in the case of Florence. Yet the situation is not entirely hopeless. A series of diplomatic correspondence—largely the work of Pontano—survives from the crucial period between the autumn of 1491 and the death of Ferrante in January 1494. Combined with several pieces of his personal correspondence, this material shows that in discharging his responsibilities, Pontano advocated two chief policies. Probably by the late 1480s he urged Ferrante to develop close and friendly relations with the papacy. After the establishment of a definitive peace between Rome and Naples in 1492, Pontano argued both at home and abroad for measures that would maintain the stability of Italy and that would protect it specifically from threats posed by the French and the Turks. Early in 1494 it

[86] Although his chronicle of the years 1484 to 1491 recorded the activities of Duke Alfonso of Calabria, not King Ferrante, Joampiero Leostello da Volterra often mentioned business or working sessions of Pontano with Ferrante or Duke Alfonso or both: *Effemeridi delle cose fatte per il Duca di Calabria (1484–1491)*, in Gaetano Filangieri, ed., *Documenti per la storia, le arti e le industrie delle provincie napoletane*, 6 vols. (Naples, 1883–91), vol. 1, esp. pp. 30, 65–66, 217–18, 247, 260–61, 273–74, 284, 287, 289, 296, 300, 306, 343, 380, 403, 405.

[87] Trinchera, ed., *Codice aragonese*, 2.1.106–7, 110–11, 128–31, 151–53, 156–57, 164, 166. In 1907, Erasmo Percopo doubted that Pontano actually composed diplomatic correspondence: "Lettere di Giovanni Pontano," pp. 1–2. By 1926, however, he had become convinced that Pontano was responsible for dictating or composing almost all official Neapolitan correspondence from the fall of Antonello Petrucci through the reign of Ferrandino: "Nuove lettere di Gioviano Pontano," pp. 114–15.

became clear that diplomacy had failed to eliminate the French threat, and events forced Pontano to work furiously to limit the damage. At that point Pontano did not gear his advice or diplomatic efforts to any specific policy, but rather reacted as best he could to new situations and opportunities as they arose.

The barons' revolt and Ferrante's continuing repression of selected rebels placed Pontano and other Neapolitan spokesmen in an extremely difficult position. In defending Ferrante's policies, Pontano implicated the papal curia in the barons' new conspiracies, charged former pontiffs with irrational hostility toward the kingdom of Naples, and exercised his penchant for frank speech even when addressing Pope Innocent himself. At least by 1489, however, Pontano had come to realize the danger posed by long-term hostility between Naples and Rome.[88] Beginning in May 1489, Pope Innocent took steps to excommunicate Ferrante, depose him, and reclaim his kingdom as an escheated fief if the king did not begin to observe the treaty of 1486. Renewed war with the pope by itself would probably not have placed excessively severe strains on Neapolitan resources. The problem of 1489 was that Pope Innocent had no reliable Italian support for his opposition to Ferrante, but looked instead to King Charles VIII of France. In October 1489, even as Ferrante defied Pope Innocent and encouraged turmoil in the papal state, Pontano dispatched a soothing reply to a letter of warning from Charles VIII. Ferrante desired peaceful relations with the pope, Pontano said, and intended to display only piety and devotion in dealings with him. He denied the charge that Neapolitan forces currently threatened papal territory, but explained recent maneuvers as designed to defend the dignity and honor of the Holy See.[89]

Tension between Naples and Rome continued for two more years, but Ferrante and Pontano clearly recognized the danger of the French threat from 1489 at the latest. Their recognition led

---

[88] On the events of 1489—not represented in surviving Neapolitan records— see Pastor, *History of the Popes*, 5.271–87.

[89] Percopo, "Nuove lettere di Gioviano Pontano," p. 128.

ultimately to a definitive reconciliation between Ferrante and Pope Innocent. The process opened with a personal letter (20 October 1491) from Pontano to the pope. Pontano admitted that he had bad legs, but observed that the pontiff had none better. Nonetheless, if the two of them walked the proper road—that is, by establishing peace between Naples and Rome—they would both find rest not only for their tired feet, but also for the rest of their aged bodies.[90] In December Pontano traveled to Rome, and by 7 February 1492 he had negotiated peace between Ferrante and Innocent. The treaty remitted Ferrante's duty to pay annual monetary tribute to the pope, but obliged him to continue to send the white horse, also to supply the pope with two triremes and three hundred men at arms. The instrument recognized Duke Alfonso of Calabria as Ferrante's legitimate heir, but provided that he would pay fifty thousand ducats for his bull of investiture. Of the agreement's remaining provisions, the most notable called for neutral parties to dispose of the cases still pending against rebel barons.[91] In fact, Pope Innocent had little opportunity to implement the pact: already aged and weakened by illness, he died on 25 July 1492, less than six months after the treaty's publication.

The question naturally arises: did Pontano influence Ferrante in his reconciliation with Pope Innocent, or did he simply implement policy that the king developed independently? Archival losses make it impossible to offer a definitive answer to this question, but several sources surviving from the early 1490s suggest that Pontano urged a papal alliance on an unenthusiastic Ferrante. Pontano of course followed his orders and represented Neapolitan policy as Ferrante directed. But he did not overlook opportunities to press his own views on the king. Thus in instructions for Neapolitan ambassadors composed during the summer of 1491, he portrayed Ferrante as having nothing to do with troubles caused

<hr>

[90] Percopo, "Lettere di Giovanni Pontano," p. 35.

[91] The text of the treaty is published in Angelo Mercati, ed., *Raccolta di concordati su materie ecclesiastiche tra la Santa Sede e le autorità civili*, 2d ed., 2 vols. (Vatican City, 1954), 1.222–33.

by the citizens of Ascoli, who had invaded the papal state, besieged Fermo, attacked a papal governor in the marches, and killed a papal legate. In fact, Ferrante had sent Virginio Orsini, his captain-general, to aid the Ascolani against the forces Pope Innocent sent to restore order, and Pontano himself helped to bail them out of their diplomatic difficulties even as he negotiated peace between Innocent and Ferrante. In the spring of 1492, however, he scolded Ferrante for his role in "the madness of Ascoli," which had brought him no benefit in Rome.[92]

Private letters that Pontano wrote on 1 January 1492, as he negotiated the peace of 1492 in Rome, show beyond doubt that he pressed for reconciliation as Ferrante stalled. The letters went to Duke Alfonso of Calabria and Ferrante's wife, Queen Giovanna of Naples; Pontano said that he sent similar messages also to Ferrante himself and to the king's second son, Federico. In both of the surviving letters he complained because of the niggling doubts and objections that Ferrante's counselors raised during the process of negotiation. All the lawyers' quibbles mortified him, he said, and he threatened resignation if the next envoy from Naples brought fresh complications for his task. Finally, he offered to show his work to anyone, so as to dispel the suspicion that he did not adequately represent Neapolitan interests.[93] Pontano of course did not resign, but successfully negotiated a peace treaty. Yet he had not come to the end of his experience with diplomatic dilatoriness and delay on Ferrante's part. Between May and October 1492, he spent time intermittently at Rome tending to various pieces of Neapolitan business. Once again he found it necessary to remonstrate, this time to Ferrante himself, against the obstacles that royal counselors placed in the way of his work. Even Ferrante's most distinguished lawyers—Pontano named Nicolantonio de' Monti and Antonio d'Alessandro—had not accomplished as much

[92] Trinchera, ed., *Codice aragonese*, 2.1.1–16, 21–22. For Pontano's diplomatic aid on behalf of the Ascolani and for his criticism of Ferrante's duplicity in the matter, see Percopo, "Lettere di Giovanni Pontano," pp. 38–39, 40–41.

[93] Percopo, "Lettere di Giovanni Pontano," pp. 36–37.

for him as had Pontano, not to mention the lesser lights who never left the city of Naples. Ferrante would do better to avoid wasting money on unnecessary salaries and spare Pontano the inconveniences visited upon him by the stream of notaries from Naples.[94]

Pontano's clearest advice concerning papal relations came in an impressive and insightful memorial he submitted to Ferrante on 26 April 1492. Pontano pointed out that differences with popes in the past had brought Ferrante nothing but anguish and infamy, while close relations resulted in profit and a good reputation. When Ferrante and the pope get along well, the other Italian states become nervous. Yet Ferrante seemed determined to poison the political atmosphere precisely when he needed a papal alliance. Once again Pontano indulged his habit of forthright speech: "You do not know how to judge the situation (pardon me for saying so)." Ferrante's best Italian ally, Lorenzo de' Medici, had recently died; Ludovico il Moro of Milan had developed into a formidable enemy of Naples; Pontano did not need to remind Ferrante of the traditional and continuing hostility of Venice toward the Regno. Pontano recently negotiated a peace that cost Ferrante nothing in money, land, or military obligations—yet the king accepted it in a resentful spirit, and he continued to treat with Rome in desultory, dilatory fashion. Pontano sought to move Ferrante to a more sensible policy by putting the matter in down-to-earth terms: "You have been plucked and caponized by all the other Christian princes; now that you have the opportunity to be a cock, you refuse to crow."[95]

Necessity eventually brought about the rapprochement that Pontano urged on Ferrante. Eloquent testimony to this point survives in the original, autograph letter that King Alfonso II addressed to Pope Alexander VI on 26 January 1494, one day after Ferrante's death. In his own hand, the new king humbly commended himself to the pope, pledged his devotion, promised filial

---

[94] Trinchera, ed., *Codice aragonese*, 2.1.106–76; Percopo, "Lettere di Giovanni Pontano," pp. 45–46.

[95] Percopo, "Lettere di Giovanni Pontano," pp. 39–43.

obedience, and offered himself, his son, his state, and his faculties to the Holy See.[96]

As Pontano encouraged close papal relations in his advice to Ferrante—and no doubt also in that to Alfonso II and Ferrandino—he advocated the maintenance of stability in Italy both in domestic counsel and in diplomatic correspondence. For Neapolitan purposes, the maintenance of stability in Italy implied the exclusion of French influence from peninsular affairs and the establishment of a common defensive effort against the Turks. Pontano did not develop these points for the first time: an earlier section of this chapter showed that Panormita had argued along similar lines, for example, at the Congress of Mantua in 1459. In the 1490s, however, the increasing diplomatic isolation of the Regno forced Pontano to present the Neapolitan view of things more insistently than any earlier spokesman had done.

Emphasis on the stability of Italy became especially prominent in Neapolitan diplomacy about the time that Lorenzo de' Medici died (8 April 1492), depriving Naples of her best peninsular ally. Upon receiving news that Lorenzo had fallen gravely ill, Pontano drafted instructions to Ferrante's ambassador in Rome, charging him to persuade Pope Innocent to prevent the introduction of turbulence or changes into Italian affairs. So strong was his desire to maintain stability that Ferrante even placed his captain-general, Virginio Orsini, at the pope's disposal. Within a month of Lorenzo's death, new Turkish movements raised the specter of a threat to Italian peace from a different quarter. Acting sometimes as secretary and sometimes as a special emissary to Rome, Pontano sought aid from the pope as well as other European princes for the common defense of Christendom.[97]

Neither the transfer of leadership in Florence nor the move-

[96] ASV, A. A. Arm. I–XVIII, 5020, fol. 29r. Cf. similar letters that went to Milan, one in Alfonso's own hand to Duke Giangaleazzo, the other in another hand to Ludovico il Moro: Milan, Archivio di Stato, Sforzesco 252, documents of 26 January 1494.

[97] Trinchera, ed., *Codice aragonese*, 2.1.74–75, 97–108, 124–27, 130–31.

ments of the Turks led immediately to political problems for the kingdom of Naples. In the following spring, however, a truly unsettling development encouraged Pontano to emphasize once again the advantages of stability in Italy. By April 1493 news had reached Naples that Ludovico il Moro had organized a military league between Milan, Venice, and Pope Alexander VI. The announced purpose of the alliance was protection of the papacy. The principal threat to papal security in 1493 came from the efforts of Virginio Orsini to absorb several territories in the Roman Campagna into his already substantial land holdings. Research has shown that Ferrante did not support Orsini's ambitions, but rather subjected his captain-general to considerable pressure in order to minimize the damage to his relations with Pope Alexander.[98] Nonetheless, Orsini's close relationship with Ferrante and his bellicose attitude during the affair of 1493 enabled Ludovico il Moro to organize all the major Italian states against Ferrante. In diplomatic correspondence he composed during the spring and summer of 1493, Pontano pointed out the menace to Italian peace and stability posed by the league, also the potential for foreign intervention should peninsular tensions lead to war. He especially emphasized the fickleness of the French, who governed themselves by whim rather than reason, he said, and who made very poor neighbors.[99]

In a remarkable memorial of 12 October 1493, Pontano presented an analysis of Italian politics to Ferrante, stressing once again the insecurity of Naples. All Italy conspired against Ferrante, Pontano warned, and planned to call in Duke René of Lorraine in order to bring him down. According to Pontano's assessment, Ferrante's enemies feared the power and independence of King Charles VIII, but expected to control Duke René while still overthrowing the Aragonese dynasty in Naples. The Florentines especially favored this plan, Pontano said, because Piero de' Med-

[98] On Neapolitan diplomacy with respect to the affair of Virginio Orsini, see Pontieri, *Per la storia del regno di Ferrante*, pp. 527–90.

[99] Trinchera, ed., *Codice aragonese*, 2.1.371–84; 2.2.75–76.

ici anticipated great profits for the Medici bank and the Florentine cloth industry. The Venetians resented loss of their markets in Apulia and would already have moved against Ferrante except for fear of the Turks. The pope had no love for Ferrante, but sought primarily to build a power base for his son, Jofrè. Finally, Ludovico il Moro wanted to consolidate his usurpation of the duchy of Milan, and he considered the ruin of Naples necessary for the achievement of his goal. Thus he planned not only to ally with Duke René of Lorraine, but also to incite the prince of Salerno and various Neapolitan towns to rebellion. Pontano reported that on the very day he composed his memorial, the Milanese ambassador in Naples had spoken of Ludovico's schemes with the Florentine representative. As counter-measures, Pontano urged Ferrante to foresee and divert his enemies' plans, and especially to bring about a rapprochement with Pope Alexander, a move that would enable him to send his foes scattering. Most of all, Pontano impressed upon Ferrante the need for immediate action, since the king's customary delaying tactics would not save him in the current situation. The Italian states, France, Spain, and the Turks all either had positive designs on Naples or would gladly take advantage of turmoil in the Regno. Only tough, decisive action would enable Ferrante to save his realm from the multiple threats posed to it by so many enemies.[100]

Ferrante surely recognized many of these points even before Pontano's memorial. It is notable, however, that during the autumn and winter of 1493 to 1494, Neapolitan diplomacy sought zealously to mend political fences and emphasize the double threat of France and the Turks to Italian stability. Within two days of his memorial, Pontano dispatched instructions calling for ambassadors to make these points in Rome, Venice, and Florence. In one set of instructions dated 15 December 1493, Pontano directed the Neapolitan ambassador in Rome to propose that Pope Alexander ally with France's natural enemies, England and the Holy Roman

---

[100] Percopo, "Lettere di Giovanni Pontano," pp. 47–51.

Empire, in order to discourage Charles VIII from invading Italy. Barely one month later, Pontano instructed the same ambassador to remind Pope Alexander of the danger a French invasion would pose to the papacy itself: the French had never entered Italy without leaving it in ruins, he said, and in the event of victory, Charles VIII would seek to dominate not only Naples, but all the rest of Italy as well, including the papacy. Neapolitan diplomacy in this period even attempted a reconciliation with the republic of Genoa. In January 1494 Pontano composed two elegant Latin epistles to the Genoese seeking improved relations. The second of them— dated 23 January, only two days before Ferrante's death—announced that in the name of friendship Ferrante had liberated an unspecified number of Genoese prisoners held in Naples.[101]

After the ascension of King Alfonso II, Pontano continued his diplomatic efforts to forestall the French invasion, seeking to mollify potential adversaries both within and outside the Regno. By the spring of 1494, however, his surviving diplomatic writings deal increasingly with military preparations undertaken by the new king in defense of his realm.[102] By early summer the drift of events had become clear. In a letter of 20 June, Pontano informed the Milanese ambassador in Naples that the bad faith of Ludovico il Moro forced Alfonso II to take over administration of Ludovico's holdings in the Regno. Ten days later he expressed regret at the lack of meaningful communications and sent the ambassador back to Milan: "You may leave freely and follow your road."[103]

Felix Gilbert has pointed out that for several reasons, Italian statesmen did not take the French threat seriously in 1494. Some thought they could control a foreign ally; others did not believe the French would actually intervene, or at least that they would

[101] Trinchera, ed., *Codice aragonese*, 2.2.271–79, 322–31, 348–56, 380–83, 389, 393–401, 411–14, 421–31, 437–38.

[102] Percopo, "Nuove lettere di Gioviano Pontano," pp. 133–37; also Carlo de Frede, "Alfonso II d'Aragona e la difesa del regno di Napoli nel 1494," *ASPN*, 3d ser. 20 (1981), esp. the document published on pp. 210–19.

[103] See Pontano's *Lettere inedite*, pp. 352–57.

not do so on a large scale; all dismissed Pontano's diplomatic work as serving Aragonese rather than Italian interests. Only after the second French invasion of 1499 and the Spanish occupation of Naples of 1501 did Italians begin to think of the events of 1494 as a turning point in their history.[104]

Whatever the attitudes of other statesmen, a few surviving pieces of political and diplomatic correspondence show that Pontano did not take the French threat lightly, but rather exhausted every possible option in an effort to thwart Charles VIII. In a memorial of 11 July 1494 he advised Alfonso II to send a fleet and army to seize Genoa, thus depriving the French of their gateway into Italy. Alfonso II largely incorporated Pontano's advice into Neapolitan military strategy for the summer of 1494, though with modifications. The plan did not succeed—Ludovico il Moro strengthened the Milanese garrison in Genoa by three thousand troops, and Federico's fleet suffered defeat at Rapallo—but Pontano's memorial demonstrates an impressive grasp of the military realities of the situation, also of the means by which Alfonso II might gain useful support from Pope Alexander and the Florentines.[105] (The humanist Gabriele Altilio conducted much of the military and diplomatic correspondence from the field during these days, since he served as political secretary to his former pupil, Ferrandino, now duke of Calabria, who directed the Neapolitan land forces in Tuscany and Romagna.[106]) Some months later, after the abdication of Alfonso II, Pontano wrote in the name of the new king, Ferrandino, desperately seeking military aid from the Catholic kings of Spain.[107] By 9 February 1495, as Charles

[104] Felix Gilbert, *Machiavelli and Guicciardini: Politics and History in Sixteenth-Century Florence* (Princeton, 1965), pp. 255–59.

[105] The memorial appears in Percopo, "Lettere di Giovanni Pontano," pp. 52–54, but a better edition, along with a short introduction, is available in Erasmo Percopo, "Pontaniana," *Studi di letteratura italiana*, 3 (1901), 199–207.

[106] See the correspondence composed by Altilio in ASV, A. A. Arm. I–XVIII, 5020, fol. 67r; also in Pontieri, "La dinastia aragonese di Napoli e la casa de' Medici di Firenze," esp. n.s. 27 (1941), 251–70.

[107] Percopo, "Nuove lettere di Gioviano Pontano," pp. 137–38.

VIII made his way toward Naples, Pontano had no specific advice, but only general encouragement to offer. In a memorial of that date to Ferrandino, he argued the virtues of stiff resistance. He urged Ferrandino to make effective use of his experienced army and knowledge of the Neapolitan terrain, confident in the conviction that French impetuosity and disorder would make it impossible for them to endure a long and difficult campaign. Caution, cleverness, and stratagem would enable Ferrandino to prevail, as the inherent difficulties of their enterprise would condemn the French to failure.[108] Indeed, by the end of May, Charles VIII had left Naples, along with a large part of his army. Shortly thereafter Ferrandino regained his throne, and in September 1495 Pontano sought to gain official recognition of the young king's return by having the kingdom of Naples admitted into the League of Venice, organized the previous March with the intention of driving the French out of Italy.[109]

In the end, Pontano's efforts failed. No matter that Pontano had responded intelligently and realistically to the challenges faced by the Regno, diplomacy alone simply could not save the Aragonese dynasty of Naples. Pontano's political experience had significant cultural repercussions, however, since it encouraged him to reconsider traditional western political ethics. The next chapter will examine his political thought as developed in Pontano's formal compositions, which enabled him to express himself in more careful and reflective fashion than was possible in his day-to-day writings.

Meanwhile, their various ad hoc writings—diplomatic instructions, foreign correspondence, political memorials, and personal correspondence—demonstrate clearly that from the time of Panormita forward, the Neapolitan humanists in general conceived political problems and responded to them in realistic fashion. And little wonder, considering the turbulent political experience of fifteenth-century Naples, afflicted not once but several times by for-

---

[108] Percopo, "Lettere di Giovanni Pontano," pp. 56–58.
[109] Percopo, "Nuove lettere di Gioviano Pontano," pp. 138–40.

eign invasion, internal rebellion, peninsular warfare, Turkish menace, and papal conflict. No Neapolitan humanist or any other figure could have survived for long in any sensitive public post without possessing or developing a reasonably hard-headed approach to political problems.

Their experience as secretaries, diplomats, and advisers educated the humanists in the uses of power and in the occasional necessity of violating inherited norms of political morality. Their experience served also as the indispensable foundation for the construction of a new political ethic, one that began to emerge already in the formal moral treatises of Giovanni Pontano. In short, Niccolò Machiavelli held no monopoly on political realism, but rather shared a hard-headed assessment of the political world with numerous other men, humanists and nonhumanists alike, who tended to matters of statecraft and diplomacy in Renaissance Italy.

5

The Implications of Humanism
for Renaissance Political Thought

THE NEAPOLITAN humanists accurately reflected the political realities of Quattrocento Italy, to the point, in fact, that the difficult business of Renaissance politics encouraged them to develop realistic conceptions of political and diplomatic problems. But the Neapolitan humanists were not mere passive recipients of political influence. Instead, as this chapter argues, they left their mark on the emerging secular political consciousness of early modern Europe. They did not do so in the same way that some of their Florentine and Venetian colleagues did, by developing the republican tradition of constitutional thought, but rather by addressing other issues more pertinent to the Neapolitan experience. In the first place, since the Regno had a monarchical rather than aristocratic or republican constitution, they elaborated a set of values appropriate for princes or kings. Furthermore, they produced historical interpretations geared sometimes to the interests of a newly established monarchy, other times to the more general need to explain difficult political experiences in convincing secular terms. Finally and perhaps most importantly, they sought to identify the principles that explained the workings of the political world, that accounted for the turbulent experience of Renaissance Naples, and that suggested how best to respond to the challenges posed to administrators by political change.

The sources that best illuminate these themes include formal treatises, orations, and historical writings—works that enabled the humanists to develop most clearly their reflections on the pertinent issues—though occasionally pieces of private or diplomatic correspondence also throw light on a particular point. Before turning to a direct analysis of the Neapolitan humanists' contribution, however, it will be useful to discuss the issue of civic humanism, which ranks as the most influential category by which historians today understand the relationship between politics and humanism in the Italian Renaissance.

The Question of Civic Humanism

Scholars have long associated the concept of civic humanism with the impressive development of political and moral thought in Florence during the first half of the fifteenth century. The association of course derives from Hans Baron's penetrating analyses of the political and cultural experience of early Quattrocento Florence. Baron interpreted the political, moral, and social thought of Tuscan humanists in the context of the Florentine political experience, and he developed a vision of civic humanism as a distinctive cultural movement of the early Quattrocento. The most important elements of this civic strain of humanism included a new humanist historiography, a lay-oriented social ethic, a fresh appreciation of vernacular literature, and a profound commitment to republican political values.[1]

Baron demonstrated brilliantly how to analyze the interaction between politics and culture in Renaissance Italy. Yet his work generated a great deal of critical response. Jerrold Seigel, for example, cast doubt on some of the precise connections that Baron drew between the world of events and the realm of ideas.[2] More pertinent for present purposes is the critique of Quentin Skinner,

[1] See especially Hans Baron, *The Crisis of the Early Italian Renaissance*, 2d ed. (Princeton, 1966).

[2] See Jerrold E. Seigel," 'Civic Humanism' or Ciceronian Rhetoric?" *Past and Present*, 34 (1966), 3–48. Baron restated his views but did not succeed in dismissing many of Seigel's objections, in his reply, "Leonardo Bruni: 'Professional Rhetorician' or 'Civic Humanist'?" *Past and Present*, 36 (1967), 21–37.

who sought not to challenge, but to broaden the notion of civic humanism by associating it with developments beyond the narrow spatial and chronological confines of early Quattrocento Florence. Baron's civic humanists continued a tradition of republican political thought long cultivated during the Middle Ages—so Skinner argued—and furthermore, humanists in other city-states developed ideas quite similar to those of Baron's Florentine civic humanists.[3] The concept of civic humanism thus has application far beyond the city walls of Florence.

Humanism was a cosmopolitan cultural movement, after all, and individual humanists employed their talents in the service of multiple causes. Some humanists devoted their efforts to their Christian faith, for example, so that it makes sense to speak of Christian humanism as a subcategory of Renaissance humanism in general.[4] Others sought to advance the interests of the papacy and the Roman Catholic church as an institution.[5] It was only natural, then, for yet other humanists to place their peculiar skills in the service of their city-states. Venetian humanists worked tirelessly as administrators, ambassadors, and propagandists for their aristocratic republic.[6] Milanese humanists likewise provided political services, expressed intense pride in their city, and glorified the Visconti and Sforza dynasties.[7] The question thus naturally arises: To what extent did Neapolitan humanists develop a strain of civic

[3] Quentin Skinner, *The Foundations of Modern Political Thought*, 2 vols. (Cambridge, 1978), 1.26–28, 41–48, 53–56, and esp. 69–112.

[4] See Charles Trinkaus, *In Our Image and Likeness: Humanity and Divinity in Italian Humanist Thought*, 2 vols. (Chicago, 1970); Jerry H. Bentley, *Humanists and Holy Writ: New Testament Scholarship in the Renaissance* (Princeton, 1983); and John W. O'Malley, *Praise and Blame in Renaissance Rome* (Durham, N.C., 1979).

[5] John F. D'Amico, *Renaissance Humanism in Papal Rome: Humanists and Churchmen on the Eve of the Reformation* (Baltimore, 1983).

[6] Margaret L. King, *Venetian Humanism in an Age of Patrician Dominance* (Princeton, 1986), esp. pp. 37–49, 76–91.

[7] See Eugenio Garin's two articles: "La cultura milanese nella prima metà del XV secolo," in *Storia di Milano*, 16 vols. (Milan, 1953–66), 6.554–56, 566–69, 581–82, 604–8; and "La cultura milanese nella seconda metà del XV secolo," ibid., 7.554–56, 577–80, 591–93.

humanism comparable to that of their Florentine, Venetian, and Milanese counterparts?

In some respects, Neapolitan humanism developed along lines analogous to the pattern of civic humanism in central and northern Italy. In Florence, for example, nonhumanist patriots cultivated an intense civic pride, which their humanist contemporaries adapted and expressed in characteristic humanist idioms. So also in Naples. This book opened with an extended discussion of the unpolished yet charming praise of Naples by Loise de Rosa, but many others could have stood in his place. Thus in 1474 Angelo Catone, a professor of philosophy and astronomy at the Studio, lauded Naples on various grounds: it boasted a beautiful environment, ideal climate, enviable mineral resources, and abundant agricultural production. Little wonder that ever since the days of Pythagoras, brilliant minds had flowered in the sunny southern realm! Catone made special mention of Thomas Aquinas, but did not neglect to point out that at least three hundred learned men currently lived in the city of Naples.[8] About 1476 the Florentine exile Francesco Bandini echoed Catone's praise and added new considerations as well. Bandini called attention not only to Naples' healthy climate, fertile earth, and learned community, but also to her paradisiacal surroundings, fresh water, noble citizens, magnificent buildings, splendid gardens, awesome Castelnuovo, and triumphal arch. Most notably, Bandini praised Naples for her political stability and general prosperity—the result, he said, of Ferrante's justice—which he contrasted favorably to the sedition, corruption, and perennial turmoil that afflicted his native Florence.[9] Constantine Lascaris—the refugee from Constantinople who eked out a precarious existence in Messina for the last thirty-

[8] Catone's praise occurs in the preface to his edition of Matteo Silvatico's *Liber pandectarum medicinae*. See the edition of this preface in Mariano Fava and Giovanni Bresciano, eds., *La stampa a Napoli nel XV secolo*, 3 vols. (Leipzig, 1911–13), 2.71–76. On Catone's career, see ibid., 1.146–47.

[9] Paul O. Kristeller, "An Unpublished Description of Naples by Francesco Bandini," in his *Studies in Renaissance Thought and Letters* (Rome, 1969), pp. 395–410.

five years of his life—prepared for Duke Alfonso of Calabria a brief catalog of eminent Greek philosophers and literary figures who sprang from Calabrian soil in ancient times.[10]

In view of the long tradition of civic praise developed in all parts of Italy during the Middle Ages, it does not seem surprising that humanists at court also expressed their pride in the city and kingdom of Naples.[11] Thus in an oration of 1472, Giovanni Brancati praised King Ferrante for his quality of magnificence in benefiting and beautifying his realm: as cases in point he mentioned Ferrante's establishment of a public school in Naples, presumably the Studio, which earlier kings had shamelessly neglected; his foundation of a hospital for victims of the plague; and his renovation of the ports of Naples and other cities, which, according to Brancati, deserved more praise than a temple to God.[12] About 1492, Giuniano Maio emphasized the beauty as well as the safety provided by city walls that Ferrante had repaired and refurbished.[13] At century's end, Giovanni Pontano himself reflected on the glory of Naples, singling out her buildings, aqueducts, and walls for special mention, while recalling also the efforts to beautify and glorify the city of Naples from the time of the Roman emperors up to the day of Duke Alfonso of Calabria. He emphasized the natural beauty and healthy environment of the Neapolitan realm and took special pride in the flowering of letters, scholarship, and science that had occurred in his own day. His highest praise, however, he reserved for King Ferrante, who for thirty years had provided the Regno with peace and stability, so that he deserved to be ranked among the best of all princes.[14]

The Neapolitan humanists reflected broader Italian interests

[10] J. P. Migne, ed., *Patrologia graeca* (Paris, 1857–1904), vol. 161, cols. 923–28.

[11] For a survey of the tradition, see J. K. Hyde, "Medieval Descriptions of Cities," *Bulletin of the John Rylands Library*, 48 (1966), 308–40.

[12] Valencia, BU, MS 774 (formerly 52), esp. fols. 9v–12v.

[13] Giuniano Maio, *De maiestate*, ed. F. Gaeta (Bologna, 1956), pp. 197–200.

[14] See Pontano's *De bello neapolitano*, in Gravier, ed., *Raccolta*, 5.139–48, esp. 145–48.

also in their social thought: like their counterparts in Tuscany and elsewhere, they glorified and justified the active life in the world as opposed to the contemplative existence idealized in the Middle Ages. Even before going to Naples, Lorenzo Valla had presented a spirited defense of natural worldly delights—though Valla did not necessarily endorse the views of his Epicurean spokesman—in his famous dialogue *On Pleasure*. Later, during his residence at Alfonso's court, he justified the laic lifestyle in his dialogue *On the Profession of the Religious* and denied that the cloister bestowed any special virtue on its inhabitants. By the 1490s, Giovanni Pontano could assume the respectability of the layman's existence and devote his energies to the clarification of various social virtues: thus his series of treatises on liberality, beneficence, magnificence, splendor, conviviality, and magnanimity. In these works Pontano addressed himself basically to the issues of money and influence and their proper uses in society. He offered no especially original observations in these treatises, but largely followed the lead of Aristotle's *Ethics*.[15] His work shows clearly, however, that a lay-oriented social ethic had taken firm root in Naples during the course of the fifteenth century.

The Neapolitan humanists thus responded to many of the same intellectual currents—such as the increasing emphasis on laic or secular values—that influenced thought in other parts of Italy and Europe. Like their counterparts in central and northern Italy, the Neapolitan humanists also developed senses of patriotism and political loyalty, so that they dedicated their talents enthusiastically to the cause and the honor of king and country. Clearly, then, there emerged in Renaissance Naples a set of values that closely

[15] Giovanni Pontano, *I trattati delle virtù sociali*, ed. F. Tateo (Rome, 1965), and *De magnanimitate*, ed. F. Tateo (Florence, 1969). See also Francesco Tateo, "Le virtù sociali e l' 'immanità' nella trattatistica pontaniana," *Rinascimento*, n.s. 5 (1965), 119–54, which interprets Pontano's work as a reflection of the aristocratic society of Renaissance Naples; and the more general interpretation of Charles Trinkaus, "Themes for a Renaissance Anthropology," in his book of collected essays, *The Scope of Renaissance Humanism* (Ann Arbor, 1983), esp. pp. 372–85.

paralleled the strain of civic humanism that developed in other parts of Italy.

Yet several important differences distinguished the course of civic humanism in Naples from its analogues in central and northern Italy. Civic humanists in Florence largely appreciated vernacular literature, for example, while Neapolitan humanists encouraged the cultivation of Latin letters in a rather elitist way. Bartolomeo Facio and Giovanni Brancati both urged Ferrante to study Latin rather than Italian, though both also produced vernacular translations for their royal patron. Brancati went as far as to translate Pliny into *napoletano misto* and to justify his use of that dialect because of its inherent beauty. For the most part, however, all through the fifteenth century and well into the sixteenth, Neapolitan humanists preferred Latin to Italian as a literary language; and when employing the vernacular, Neapolitan literary figures generally wrote in Tuscan, imitating Dante, Petrarch, or Boccaccio, rather than developing independent literary traditions for the southern dialects.[16] In short, Neapolitan humanists did not seek to broaden the social and linguistic base of their movement, as did Leonardo Bruni and his Florentine contemporaries, but rather sought to maintain a monopoly on high culture in Renaissance Naples through their mastery of Latin and Tuscan, the tongues of an elite minority.

More significantly, different political contexts led to the development of different styles of civic humanism in the various Italian states. Princely regimes in Milan and the despotic states of northern Italy produced a variety of humanism reasonably similar to that of Renaissance Naples. But a republican administration governed in Florence, an aristocratic order in Venice, and a papal court in Rome. Politically active humanists in those cities naturally devoted a great deal of their attention to republican, aristo-

---

[16] The best work on vernacular literature in Renaissance Naples is that of Antonio Altamura. See especially his *L'umanesimo nel Mezzogiorno d'Italia* (Florence, 1941); and "La letteratura volgare," in *Storia di Napoli*, 10 vols. (Naples, 1975–81), 7.293–361.

cratic, or ecclesiastical values. Of all the Italian states in the fifteenth century, only Naples had a monarchical constitution. Neapolitan humanists who reflected on political issues therefore naturally geared their thought to problems of monarchy and especially to the virtues that the prince ought to bring to his office.

The Qualities of the Prince

In his treatise *De obedientia*, Giovanni Pontano advanced a spirited justification for a monarchical rather than republican form of government. He associated the rule of a single man with peace, stability, and harmony, while portraying republics as hotbeds of sedition, faction, and insurrection. Nature itself, he said, taught the wisdom of monarchical rule: a single deity governs the universe, and a single king (*sic*) holds sway over all the other bees. Meanwhile, abundant experience taught the folly of a republican constitution: the selfish pursuit of private interests and the inevitable elevation of incompetent men to positions of authority led eventually to the triumph of tyranny. Only in a monarchy could individuals enjoy true liberty, which Pontano defined as obedience to the law, observation of social responsibilities, and behavior according to the dictates of reason.[17]

Pontano's defense of monarchy stood almost alone among the political writings of the Neapolitan humanists. The next chapter will show that during the difficult years following 1494, Neapolitans devoted some thought to alternative forms of government. But during most of the fifteenth century, it must have seemed supremely idle for Neapolitans to speculate on constitutional issues, since the Aragonese kings had successfully consolidated their dynasty. In fact, the establishment of princely regimes was a peninsular phenomenon with general implications for Italian political

[17] Pontano, *Opera omnia, soluta oratione composita*, 3 vols. (Venice, 1518–19), vol. 1, fols. 29v–32r.

thought in the Quattrocento.[18] The extension of princely rule, whether by conquest or by subversion, naturally drew the attention of political thinkers to the figure of the prince himself. As a practical matter, the most promising means of exercising effective political influence seemed to lie in the ability to persuade the prince to govern in a certain way.

Like their counterparts in central and northern Italy, then, the Neapolitan humanists largely refrained from reflection on constitutional or institutional questions during the second half of the fifteenth century. Instead they assumed the fact of monarchy and sought to influence the behavior of kings and princes by adapting two traditions to their uses. In the first place, they outlined the qualities of the ideal prince in works that fall into the genre of the *speculum principis*, the mirror of the prince. In the second place, they depended on the revived tradition of classical rhetoric, particularly epideictic, to place emphasis on the virtues most pertinent to the prince. The two traditions did not exercise their influence to the point of mutual exclusion. Instead, they often combined forces, as in numerous cases of epideictic orations that praised princely qualities long recognized as staples of *speculum principis* literature. Indeed, the influence of the two traditions extended also to historiography (discussed in the next section). For analytical purposes, however, it will be worthwhile to distinguish between the two influences, then to examine some of the more prominent qualities the Neapolitan humanists urged on their kings.

The genre of the *speculum principis* exercised its influence from the earliest days of western political reflection. Isocrates, Plato, Aristotle, Cicero, Seneca, Plutarch, St. Augustine, Isidore of Seville, John of Salisbury, St. Thomas Aquinas, Erasmus of Rotter-

---

[18] Cf. Felix Gilbert's classic essay, "The Humanist Concept of the Prince and *The Prince* of Machiavelli," in his *History: Choice and Commitment* (Cambridge, Mass., 1977), pp. 91–114; also Skinner's brilliant analysis of humanist political thought geared toward the problems of princely government, in *Foundations of Modern Political Thought*, 1.113–28.

dam—sometimes writing in abstract terms, other times addressing an individual prince—all these men devoted some thought to
the qualities appropriate to the prince. Not even Machiavelli entirely escaped the attraction of this tradition: his treatise on *The
Prince* faithfully mirrored the form, if not always the content, of
the typical *speculum principis*.[19] In view of its ubiquitous influence,
it is hardly surprising that this genre should help to determine the
characteristics of political thought in Renaissance Naples.

The Neapolitan humanists employed several different literary
forms to convey the qualities of the ideal prince. Though ostensibly a work of history, Panormita's *De dictis et factis Alphonsi* illustrated laudable princely virtues through the sayings and deeds of
Alfonso the Magnanimous. Indeed, lest the reader miss his point,
Panormita equipped each anecdote of his work with an adverb, indicating how Alfonso had behaved "bravely," "justly," "mod-
estly," "prudently," "wisely," "humorously," "gravely," "pa-
tiently," "mercifully," "piously," "faithfully," "diligently,"
"liberally," "humanely," or otherwise virtuously in each instance.
Neapolitan humanists often resorted also to the form of the epistle
when urging virtues on their princes. About 1462, for example,
toward the end of the war of succession, Panormita addressed to
Ferrante two letters that together amount to a brief *speculum principis*. He congratulated Ferrante for his recent victories in Apulia,
then offered advice on the proper administration of his newly regained realm. In the first letter, Panormita concentrated on the
kind of ministers Ferrante should select: he recommended just,
chaste, moderate men of virtue as those best qualified to preserve
the realm. In the second he advised Ferrante himself to cultivate
the qualities of gratitude, kindness, humanity, liberality, and justice. Despite their rather self-serving character—Panormita urged
Ferrante to exhibit liberality and gratitude especially to those who
had faithfully served the king himself—the two letters constitute

---

[19] Allan H. Gilbert, *Machiavelli's "Prince" and Its Forerunners* (Durham, N.C.,
1938).

a reasonably well-rounded, if brief discussion of princely virtues.[20] Between about 1463 and 1476, Elisio Calenzio composed a series of epistles which he hoped would instill desirable virtues in his royal pupil, Federico. In discussing justice, liberality, mercy, and other virtues, Calenzio in effect offered a *speculum principis* under the guise of a collection of epistles.[21] No doubt the most unusual literary vehicle for a *speculum principis* in Renaissance Naples was a set of diplomatic instructions (dated 4 April 1487) prepared by Giovanni Pontano for Ferrandino, then prince of Capua at nineteen years of age, as he prepared to assume a royal governorship in Apulia. All virtue derives from fear of God and observance of the divine cult, Pontano began, so that Ferrandino should conspicuously attend religious services while engaged in his mission. He must administer justice fairly, render grave, impartial sentences, and do so expeditiously. He must behave in public with both authority and dignity, so as to command both the love and the fear of his subjects. He must maintain strict discipline among his men at arms and ensure that the civilian population suffered no physical or financial harm at the hands of military forces.[22] This remarkable document stands out conspicuously from all the others in the series, which dealt with details of administrative, diplomatic, and military affairs in the wake of the second barons' revolt. The peculiar literary form itself testifies eloquently to the extent of the

[20] BAV, Vat. lat. 3371, fols. 192r–93r, 195rv. These letters appear also in *Regis Ferdinandi et aliorum epistolae ac orationes utriusque militiae* (Vico Equense, 1586), pp. 403–7, but in altered form. The edited version of the first letter in particular contains long additions not present in Panormita's manuscript. The additions presumably represent the work of the pious sixteenth-century editor of Panormita's letters. Gianvito Resta has shown that this editor consistently altered Panormita's text so as to make it conform to the ideals of the Counter-Reformation: *L'epistolario del Panormita* (Messina, 1954), pp. 104–9.

[21] Elisio Calenzio, *Opuscula* (Rome, 1503), esp. the epistle to King Ferrante explaining Calenzio's purpose, fol. C6v. For an analysis of Calenzio's letters, see Liliana Monti Sabia, "L'*humanitas* di Elisio Calenzio alla luce del suo epistolario," *Annali della facoltà di lettere e filosofia dell'Università di Napoli* 11 (1964–68), 175–251.

[22] Volpicella, ed., *Instructionum liber*, pp. 105–7.

influence exercised by the *speculum principis* tradition in Renaissance Naples.

Two especially important contributions to the *speculum principis* genre appeared in the more familiar form of the political treatise. The first was Pontano's short work *De principe*, which he composed in 1468 for Duke Alfonso of Calabria. Some of Pontano's advice consisted of principles of governance. Thus he urged Duke Alfonso to listen to wise counsel, gain the loyalty of his servants, and elevate the best, most frugal, diligent, and industrious subjects to positions of authority. The greater part of the treatise, however, dealt with the qualities that Pontano thought most important for princely rule. He considered a reputation for justice and piety useful for winning popular support; liberality and clemency similarly helped the prince to gain his subjects' goodwill and even the respect of his enemies; moderation and self-control would help him to overcome difficulties imposed by fortune. If a prince did not positively exhibit the virtues of liberality and humanity, he at least must avoid acquiring a reputation for greed and cruelty.

The single quality that Pontano most strongly emphasized, however, was majesty, which he considered the preeminent princely attribute. Majesty had its roots in human nature, according to Pontano, but it was subject to cultivation if a prince worked diligently at the task. Majesty served to increase a prince's glory and authority, but it made numerous demands in return. It required the prince to exhibit gravity, constancy, and circumspection in his public behavior. A majestic prince listened and reflected much, but spoke little, briefly, and cautiously. He exhibited perfect courtesy in dealings with ambassadors from other states, and he absolutely never lost his composure or self-control. He took care not to betray his feelings, at least not immediately, except perhaps before a few counselors. He endured inconveniences without complaint, and he indulged only moderately in food, drink, and physical pleasure. Pontano placed special emphasis on the prince's general bearing. Majesty required him to refrain from all excess in movement, gesture, laughter, and the like, lest he seem ridiculous and undignified. The majestic prince selected dress appropriate for the place, the season, and the occasion, but avoided a silly and vain concern with fads in fashion. Finally, the prince carefully cultivated his speech. Pontano considered speech the best index of one's personality and advised development of skills that represented the prince's urbanity, circumspection, honesty, good judgment, and humanity.[23]

The theme of majesty also played a large role—indeed, it served as the organizing principle—in the *speculum principis* of Giuniano Maio, *De maiestate*. Maio had taught rhetoric in the Studio of Naples from 1465 to 1488; since 1490 he had served as tutor and courtier in Ferrante's household. In 1492 he composed the *De maiestate* as a work that enabled him to expound on the various qualities appropriate to the prince and at the same time to laud his patron and celebrate the royal house of Naples during the last years of Ferrante's reign. The bulk of Maio's work consists of brief discussions of twenty virtues that represent aspects of majesty; for each of the subqualities, Maio presented a general description, illuminated by classical moral thought, then an illustration of the virtue drawn from the experience of King Ferrante. Maio devoted some attention to heroic virtues: his first discussion dealt with courage, which he exemplified with the exciting story of Ferrante's

---

[23] This treatise is most conveniently available in Eugenio Garin, ed., *Prosatori latini del Quattrocento* (Milan, 1952), pp. 1021–63. Most of the second half of the treatise deals with the quality of majesty. Studies of Pontano's treatise include Michele Romano, *La trattatistica politica nel secolo XV ed il "De principe" di G. Pontano* (Potenza, 1901); and especially Lucia Miele, "Tradizione letteraria e realismo politico nel 'De principe' del Pontano," *AAP*, n.s. 32 (1983), 301–21. Miele argues that both classical thought and contemporary political interests shaped Pontano's thought; his treatise thus retained traditional values even as it foreshadowed the modern political science of the sixteenth century. Miele perhaps exaggerates the political realism of Pontano's *De principe*: his ad hoc writings (discussed in the previous chapter) and his later treatises (examined toward the end of the present chapter) demonstrate much more clearly than *De principe* Pontano's fundamentally realistic conception of Quattrocento politics. Yet Miele's formulation serves as an accurate general characterization of Pontano's political thought as a whole.

successful self-defense in 1460 against the assassination attempt organized by Marino Marzano. He included other typically princely qualities such as liberality, magnificence, and glory in his work. Yet most of his dissertations treated moral virtues. In Maio's conception, majesty was composed of such qualities as clemency, kindness, self-control, honesty, gratitude, modesty, and piety. Like Pontano, he placed great emphasis on the public behavior of the prince. Thus he devoted one chapter to modesty in speech, another, longer one to modesty in bearing, and a third to the heavy obligations that devolved upon the prince because of his public persona.[24]

Thus Pontano and Maio both adapted the tradition of the *speculum principis* to the conditions of the later Quattrocento. As princes consolidated their regimes in all parts of Italy, and as monarchs increased their authority in all parts of Europe, Pontano and Maio provided an up-to-date portrait of the ideal prince. The modern prince possessed not only the time-honored virtues of the *speculum principis* tradition—justice, liberality, clemency, and the like—but also more peculiarly princely qualities, like magnificence and especially majesty, calculated to increase his stature and authority.

The revival of interest in classical rhetoric worked alongside the tradition of the *speculum principis* to influence the political thought of Renaissance Naples, as it also helped to provide definitive shape to Renaissance culture in general. In classical times, the rhetorical tradition had developed along three lines. Judicial rhetoric was geared to the courtroom and sought to prove guilt or innocence in cases at law; deliberative rhetoric was geared to the political forum and sought to persuade an audience to adopt or reject a certain course of action; epideictic rhetoric was geared to the broader so-

---

[24] Maio, *De maiestate*. Cf. also Franco Gaeta's perceptive introduction to this edition. Gaeta's interpretation supersedes that of Diomede Lojacono, who read Maio's treatise as a call for a modern, absolutist monarchy: "L'opera inedita *De maiestate* di Giuniano Majo," *Atti della reale accademia di scienze morali e politiche di Napoli*, 24 (1891), 329–76.

ciety and sought to instill admiration or contempt by praising or condemning a person, value, or some other object. During the fifteenth century, humanists revived the tradition of classical rhetoric, put its precepts into practice, and turned it to uses that historians have only begun to chart. Classical rhetoric exercised an enormous formal influence not only on oratory and speechmaking, but also on the composition of epistles, orations, and sermons in Renaissance Europe. Perhaps more importantly, it influenced also the themes, values, and methods developed by Renaissance historians, theologians, moralists, political thinkers, literary figures, and logicians.[25] In the absence of any general or systematic study of the topic, the following pages seek to explore in the case of Naples the influence that the tradition of classical rhetoric worked on Renaissance political thought.

Though best suited to a state in which assemblies of men made political decisions, deliberative rhetoric in the classical style made at least occasional appearances in fifteenth-century Naples. Several of Panormita's diplomatic orations fall into this category, including most notably his effort in 1435 to induce the inhabitants of Gaeta to surrender before the forces of Alfonso the Magnanimous.[26] By far the best example of deliberative rhetoric, however, was Giannozzo Manetti's oration to Pope Calixtus III urging the selection of King Alfonso as commander of a crusade. Manetti prepared the ground for his main point by arguing briefly for the absolute necessity of a large war against the cruel and infidel Turks, who already held Greece, the Balkans, and large parts of Hungary, and who threatened the apostolic see and the Christian religion.

---

[25] For a survey of classical rhetoric and its influence during the Renaissance, see George Kennedy, *Classical Rhetoric and Its Christian and Secular Tradition from Ancient to Modern Times* (Chapel Hill, 1980). For a sampler of recent studies, see James J. Murphy, ed., *Renaissance Eloquence* (Berkeley, 1983). Finally, for a brilliant analysis of epideictic rhetoric at the papal court, see O'Malley, *Praise and Blame in Renaissance Rome.*

[26] Bartolomeo Facio, *De rebus gestis*, in Gravier, ed., *Raccolta*, 4.79–81. Panormita perhaps delivered a similar oration while bringing about the surrender of Caiazzo in 1441: cf. ibid., 4.137.

He found Christendom unfortunately unembarrassed by military riches and nominated Alfonso as the only European prince who exhibited all four of the qualities necessary to the ideal commander. In the first place, Alfonso possessed a deep knowledge of military affairs, thanks to his experience making war both on land and at sea in Spain, Sicily, Italy, and other parts of the Mediterranean. Furthermore, Alfonso possessed all the virtues desirable in a commander: perseverance, courage, justice, prudence, and decisiveness, as well as other, moral virtues like temperance, faith, and humanity. In the third place, Alfonso's authority won him the respect of Christians, but would throw fear into the Turks. Finally, Manetti argued that fortune had singularly favored Alfonso, as witnessed his liberation from captivity and subsequent alliance with Filippo Maria Visconti after falling prisoner to Genoese forces in 1435.[27] The tradition of deliberative rhetoric thus enabled Manetti to celebrate the reputation of Alfonso the Magnanimous, whose court the humanist entered shortly after composing this work.

More appropriate for this purpose, however, was the epideictic tradition, which influenced humanism in Naples much more deeply than did the strain of deliberative rhetoric. The work of Giannozzo Manetti, the consummate orator, once again throws considerable light on the matter. Manetti actually delivered two epideictic orations before Alfonso: the first in May 1445, when he served as Florentine representative at the wedding of Ferrante,

[27] I rely on the text in BAV, Pal. lat. 1604, fols. 22v–29v. It is possible that Manetti never delivered this work orally, since some manuscripts refer to it as a hortatory epistle rather than an oration. But the work clearly depends upon the principles of deliberative rhetoric, so that it remains useful for the purposes of the present analysis. It is clear that Manetti composed the work before his own move to Naples (30 October 1455, at the latest), since he twice referred to himself as apostolic secretary (fol. 23r). But Manetti knew Alfonso well and had long considered a transfer to Naples, so that the composition has some significance for Renaissance Naples. For a discussion of other manuscripts and philological considerations bearing on this work, see Heinz Willi Wittschier, *Giannozzo Manetti. Das Corpus der Orationes* (Cologne, 1968), pp. 134–38.

then duke of Calabria; the second in January 1451, when he served as ambassador negotiating the end of the war in Tuscany. Furthermore, in 1452 he composed another long panegyric of epideictic character to congratulate Alfonso on the occasion of Emperor Frederick III's visit to Naples. Although he called the work an oration, Manetti probably never delivered it orally. Nonetheless, its thoroughly rhetorical nature renders the work valuable as one that clearly exhibits epideictic influence.

In the first oration Manetti naturally offered Florentine congratulations on Ferrante's wedding, but he devoted most of his efforts to the praise of Alfonso the Magnanimous. Though not yet well acquainted with Alfonso, Manetti found material to celebrate in the king's Spanish heritage, his physical and intellectual gifts, the military genius that enabled him to capture the city of Naples by employing Belisarius' tactic, and his mercy for sparing the city after conquering it. The second oration praised peace rather than Alfonso. Manetti called to witness numerous authorities—Hebrews, Greeks, Latins, and Christians; poets, orators, philosophers, prophets, evangelists, apostles, and doctors—in arguing the beauty of peace and outlining its benefits. Manetti did not seek to flatter Alfonso in this oration, but to instill in him such a profound admiration for peace that he would no longer wage war, except perhaps against the barbarous and inhumane infidels. His resort to epideictic rhetoric thus enabled Manetti in an indirect way to discourage Alfonso from further pursuit of the Tuscan war. The most interesting of Manetti's three epideictic works is the third. Ostensibly a congratulatory oration intended to celebrate the visit of Frederick III, the work amounts in fact to a long panegyric of Alfonso the Magnanimous. As in his oration of 1445, Manetti praised Alfonso for his noble Spanish lineage and for his physical and intellectual attributes. By 1452, however, Manetti had come to know Alfonso quite well, and he devoted most of the later work to praise of the king's numerous virtues. He concentrated on the public and princely virtues—justice, courage, gravity, liberality, and magnificence—illustrating them often with examples from

Alfonso's career. Yet he could not avoid paying some attention also to his private, moral virtues, including his piety, continence(!), devotion to learning, and encouragement of art and scholarship.[28]

About the same time that Manetti delivered the first of his orations, Bartolomeo Facio prepared two epideictic works in praise of Alfonso and Ferrante. Like Manetti, Facio emphasized the royal virtues when speaking of Alfonso. Only the qualities of justice, courage, gravity, and equanimity entitled a ruler to be considered a true king. Without them, a ruler becomes a rapacious beast and a plague on his people. Facio devoted most of his oration to praise of Alfonso's clemency and humanity, exemplified by the mercy he showed to the city of Naples in 1442. After overcoming resistance in the city, Alfonso ruled as a father rather than as a victor: he executed none of the defenders, and he prevented his forces from sacking houses, setting fires, or violating women. Indeed, Facio spent so much time on this theme that his oration has the air of an effort to persuade Neapolitans of their good fortune in having Alfonso as their recently victorious king. When praising Ferrante, Facio obviously had fewer solid achievements to mention, so he concentrated on the young prince's intellectual abilities and his promising potential. He lauded the vigor and acuity of Ferrante's mind, and he admired especially Ferrante's enchantment with the law, so that it seemed he always discussed legal arguments and cases. Without examining all his virtues, Facio congratulated Ferrante for possessing all the qualities a future king could want or need. In a concluding remark no doubt intended to spur the prince to high levels of accomplishment, Facio predicted that his natural gifts would lead to certain glory—unless Ferrante himself ruined his own future.[29]

[28] The first two orations appear in Felino Sandeo, *De regibus Siciliae et Apuliae* (Hanau, 1611), pp. 169–75, 177–84. The third work survives only in BAV, Vat. lat. 1604, fols. 7v–22v. For brief analyses of the three compositions, see Wittschier, *Giannozzo Manetti*, pp. 85–87, 107–9, 120–26.

[29] Valencia, BU, MS 443 (formerly 727), fols. 17r–20r, 20v–23r. These orations follow Facio's translation of Isocrates for Ferrante, which he completed in

Ferrante continued to win praise after succeeding Alfonso on the throne. One of the more active humanist orators at Naples during the later Quattrocento was Giovanni Brancati, who several times delivered polished addresses at ceremonial occasions in the 1460s and 1470s. In May 1473 he praised marriage and the principal parties at the wedding of Ferrante's daughter, Eleonora, to Duke Ercole d'Este; in 1477 he offered a similar oration in celebration of Ferrante's own second marriage to Juana of Aragon. More important for present purposes was a long oration that Brancati delivered in January 1472, praising Ferrante's virtues. Brancati attributed an impressive list of qualities to his patron: humanity, liberality, justice, clemency, courage, military skill, kindness, and piety. He devoted most attention to Ferrante's magnificence—exemplified by his reopening of the Studio and his building projects in Naples—and his promotion of peace in Italy and throughout Europe.[30]

Ferrante heard numerous such orations during the course of his long reign. The majority of them have disappeared, but the texts of at least a few survive in manuscript even today. An anonymous orator praised virtue in general and Ferrante in particular in 1463, when Ferrante conferred membership in the Order of the Ermine upon Federigo da Montefeltro.[31] A manuscript of Valencia preserves the texts of nine other orations delivered before Ferrante, and it illustrates well the variety of themes developed on ceremonial occasions in Renaissance Naples. Burgundian ambassadors delivered the first four of these orations during a mission to Naples in 1477. The anonymous orators did not command very impressive rhetorical skills: the first excused his lack of eloquence on his youth; the third apologized for speaking in Gallic fashion; and the

---

1444 or 1445. Cf. Lucia Gualdo Rosa, *La fede nella "paideia": aspetti della fortuna europea di Isocrate nei secoli XV e XVI* (Rome, 1984), pp. 35–38.

[30] These works survive in a manuscript of Brancati's epistles and orations: Valencia, BU, MS 774 (formerly 52), fols. 2r–25v, 25v–42v, 42v–69v. The oration in praise of Ferrante survives also in another manuscript in the same library, MS 735 (formerly 745), fols. 95r–114r.

[31] Venice, Biblioteca Nazionale Marciana, MS XI. 53 (= 4009), fols. 2r–9v.

fourth offered a speech utterly lacking unity or coherence, one that dealt at length with routine diplomatic business before progressing to the praise of Ferrante. Yet the four Burgundians evidently recognized the importance attached to rhetoric in Italy, and they consequently lauded Ferrante's military skills and general virtues to the best of their abilities. The fifth oration in the Valencian manuscript concentrated on the praise of philosophy, but recognized that Ferrante had generously advanced the cause of liberal studies in Naples; the sixth oration ostensibly celebrated the birthday of Roberto Malatesta, who from 1468 had served as a Neapolitan condottiere, but it too spent a great deal of time lauding Ferrante as an ideal ally for the Malatesta regime in Rimini. The last three orations all offered polished praise of Ferrante: the seventh dealt with his virtues in general; the eighth focused on his military skills and his efforts on behalf of peace; and the ninth was in fact Giovanni Brancati's praise of Ferrante discussed above, though like the other eight orations, it appears without attribution in the Valencian manuscript.[32]

An epistle from Giovanni Brancati to Antonello Petrucci demonstrates indirectly that the Neapolitan humanists took this sort of oratory very seriously indeed. Writing probably in the mid to late 1460s, Brancati presented a lengthy critique of an oration praising Ferrante by one Pietro Tarentino. The oration does not seem to survive today, but Brancati said that numerous learned men in Naples admired it so much that they had made copies of it for themselves. Though not present for Tarentino's delivery, Brancati had acquired a copy of the oration and read it avidly. He found to his dismay that the oration did not live up to its reputation. The author knew nothing of rhetoric and grammar, Brancati charged, so that he produced a clumsy, inept piece of work. His exordium unfolded at tedious length, but failed to capture the benevolence or sympathy of the audience. According to Brancati, in fact, Tarentino opened his oration with language that made it seem an unpleasant chore: "I am ordered [*iubeor*] today to enumerate [Ferrante's] immortal praises." Tarentino made a less than graceful exit from his exordium, Brancati said, as he moved toward the body of his oration; then before beginning the narration, he addressed a silly and pointless objection. These problems constituted proof for Brancati that Tarentino had no prudence, no taste, no sense of propriety. Besides problems of organization and development, Brancati objected also to a widespread abuse of Latin style, grammar, and usage that marred Tarentino's work. He descended to particulars at numerous points and corrected Tarentino's language, several times by reference to Lorenzo Valla's *Elegantiae*.[33] From the length and combative spirit of Brancati's critique, it seems likely that his differences with Tarentino involved more than an oration. In the absence of Tarentino's text, it is not possible to assess the fairness of Brancati's evaluation. But his objections establish one point with eloquence: Neapolitan humanists took their rhetoric seriously and paid attention to the form and style as well as to the content of public orations.

Epideictic rhetoric, then, obviously played a large role in the public and political life of Renaissance Naples. Like the tradition of the *speculum principis*, it lent itself naturally to humanists interested in emphasizing certain qualities that they considered appropriate for the ideal prince. The two such virtues most often examined by humanists in their oratory were liberality and justice, which through the influence of epideictic rhetoric gained wide currency also in other literary forms, such as epistles of dedication and moral treatises.

The prime beneficiaries of princely liberality were literature and scholarship, and Neapolitan humanists shrank from no opportunity to praise study as an enterprise eminently worthy of cultivation. The fifth oration in the Valencian manuscript discussed

[33] The letter survives in Valencia, BU, MS 774 (formerly 52), fols. 212r–42v. It has been partially edited in Giovanni P. Carratelli, "Un'epistola di Giovanni Brancati sull'arte retorica e lo scriver latino," *AAP*, n.s. 2 (1948–49), 109–23. Carratelli dates the letter to the period 1463 to 1471.

above, for example, outlines the numerous services and benefits made available to men by philosophy (understood in a loose sense as a collective term for the various disciplines of knowledge). By instilling love of God, encouraging piety, and engendering theology, philosophy renders men immortal. Through law it enables men to found and maintain stable governments. Other disciplines—medicine, mathematics, natural science, grammar, logic, and dialectic—serve men in various practical ways. Meanwhile, of the secular arts and sciences, rhetoric won the orator's highest praise, since it adorned all the other disciplines of knowledge and illuminated the deeds of illustrious kings like Ferrante.[34] In an oration of 1468 before Ferrante, Giovanni Brancati also praised letters and the study of antiquity as an almost divine activity that rendered men similar to God himself. Brancati considered literary learning indispensable for the organization of civil affairs and the maintenance of peace.

More surprisingly, perhaps, Brancati and others linked the arts and letters with military prowess. The Greeks and Romans easily defeated their barbarian enemies, Brancati noted, and the well-tutored Alexander the Great conquered the entire world. Indeed, Brancati made the point as explicitly as possible: arms grow in strength as men cultivate letters, and the effectiveness of arms diminishes as men lose experience in literary studies.[35] Somewhat later, while teaching at Capua (1478–1479), Aurelio Brandolini echoed this theme in an oration before Ferrante "On the Dignity, Affinity, and Praises of Military Affairs and Letters." Brandolini first acknowledged the importance of arms for the arts and letters, but later emphasized the necessity of learning for political stability and even for military success. All the outstanding commanders of the ancient world were learned men who relied on literary wisdom when making war, dispatching ambassadors, treating for peace, or rendering justice. The modern commander likewise needed a solid

---

[34] Valencia, BU, MS 735 (formerly 745), fols. 27r–39r.
[35] De Marinis, *La biblioteca*, 1.247–51.

grounding in letters, according to Brandolini: he needed especially the quality of eloquence in order to inspire his troops, but also a grasp of other disciplines like philosophy, geometry, and even astronomy—lest an unexpected eclipse frighten him into losing a certain victory.[36] Elisio Calenzio likewise insisted to Federico that success on the battlefield depended on a command of letters and eloquence, which he considered much more effective tools than brute force for the leadership of men at arms.[37]

Renaissance humanists knew very well indeed how to encourage princes to support scholarship. About the mid-1460s, Theodore Gaza addressed a letter to Panormita that dealt in plain terms with this question. Learned men can influence a prince's behavior, he said, by one of two means—praise or condemnation. Ordinarily, they will resort first to praise; but if princes despise scholars while embracing actors and brothel keepers, men of learning must turn to vituperation in hopes of improving the prince's wayward behavior.[38] The Neapolitan humanists for the most part found the tactic of praise suited to their needs, and they employed it both in its natural context of epideictic oratory and in other literary forms. On several occasions during the 1450s, for example, Giannozzo Manetti praised Alfonso the Magnanimous for his patronage of arts and letters.[39] Panormita likewise encouraged Alfonso to support scholarship, promising him immortality as a result and comparing him to Augustus for his liberality.[40] Giacomo Curlo and Francesco del Tuppo used the example of Alfonso's generosity to

[36] Paris, Bibliothèque Nationale, MS lat. 7860, fols. 5r–40v, with an Italian translation following on fols. 41v–83v.

[37] Calenzio, *Opuscula*, fol. C5r. See also Calenzio's more general endorsement of liberal education in another letter to Federico, fols. A3v–A4r.

[38] See the appendix in Francesco Filelfo, *Cent-dix lettres grecques de François Filelfe*, ed. E. Legrand (Paris, 1892), pp. 336–38.

[39] See most notably Manetti's oration on the occasion of the emperor's visit, BAV, Pal. lat. 1604, fols. 18v–20r; also his letter of dedication to the *Vita Socratis et Senecae*, ed. A. de Petris (Florence, 1979), pp. 113–18.

[40] See Panormita's *Epistolarum libri* V (Venice, 1553), esp. fols. 101r, 108v–9r.

inspire Ferrante to follow a similar cultural policy.[41] The difficulties of Ferrante's early reign, however, forced him to devote resources to security rather than to scholarship. Panormita resented the sudden austerity, but by 1462 Ferrante's fortunes had considerably improved. Thus Panormita pointedly advised Ferrante to spend his money wisely, since wealth would bring him no advantage without the goodwill of talented men.[42] Later sources make it clear that Ferrante in fact gained general respect for his liberality. Two anonymous orators praised him at length for reopening the Studio of Naples and for supporting all disciplines of learning.[43] Writing probably in the early 1480s, Joan Marco Cinico, the famous copyist in the Neapolitan library, ranked Ferrante ahead of all contemporary princes for his efforts to conserve works of literature and learning.[44] Meanwhile, Giovanni Pontano and Elisio Calenzio looked to the future. In his treatise *De principe* Pontano reminded Duke Alfonso of Calabria of the delight Alfonso the Magnanimous had taken in learned conversations and literary seances, and he issued to the young duke the challenge to outshine his illustrious grandfather in his love of letters.[45] Calenzio addressed a similar message to his own pupil, Federico: "Fortune has made princes not the guardians, but the distributors of things," he said, and the wise prince will dispense rewards liberally among the virtuous men around him.[46]

The humanists' universal call for literary patronage inevitably has a self-serving quality about it: the humanists essentially

[41] See Curlo's preface to his epitome of Donatus' commentary on Terence, in de Marinis, *La biblioteca*, 2.57–60; and de Marinis, *Supplemento*, 1.34–37. See also del Tuppo's letter dedicating to Ferrante his edition of Giovanni da Imola's *Repetitio de iure iurando*, in Fava and Bresciano, eds., *La stampa a Napoli*, vol. 2, esp. pp. 31–32.

[42] See Panormita's *Regis Ferdinandi et aliorum epistolae*, pp. 392–93.

[43] Valencia, BU, MS 735 (formerly 745), esp. fols. 67r–72r, 88v–91v.

[44] See especially his comment on Polybius in the *Elenco historico et cosmografo*, an annotated list of historical and geographical works in the Neapolitan library, which Curlo prepared for Ferrante, edited in de Marinis, *La biblioteca*, 1.240.

[45] Garin, ed., *Prosatori latini*, pp. 1032–35.

[46] Calenzio, *Opuscula*, fol. B2r.

sought to consolidate themselves as an elite intellectual class indispensable for the proper functioning of society. In developing the theme of justice, however, the humanists demonstrated a capacity to conceive issues from the point of view of the broader public interest. Once again, epideictic oratory helped to shape the humanists' expression of this theme, though the genre of the *speculum principis* also served as a natural vehicle for their thought on justice.

To the orators, justice meant the maintenance of public order and the equitable treatment of all subjects. In his oration celebrating the visit of Emperor Frederick III, Giannozzo Manetti praised the sense of justice that Alfonso manifested when he rewarded deserving subjects and punished criminals. The universal love of his subjects for their king served as confirmation for Manetti of Alfonso's justice.[47] In an oration addressed to Pope Calixtus III, Adamo di Montaldo praised Alfonso's accessibility to common subjects, who felt no fear of their social superiors because of the king's devotion to equity.[48] Two anonymous orators praised Ferrante on similar grounds: after pacifying the realm and consolidating his succession, the new king eliminated thieves, murderers, and other malefactors from the Regno and rewarded honest subjects. As a result, all Europe recognized Naples as a center of justice.[49] Toward the end of Ferrante's reign, Giuniano Maio also spoke of the civil harmony and security enjoyed by the kingdom of Naples. Ferrante, he said, had put an end to all the fraud, abuse, corruption, brutality, and violence that formerly had plagued the kingdom. He applauded Ferrante not only for maintaining order, however, but also for dispensing justice strictly according to the demands of equity rather than favoritism. Since all men have red blood, Ferrante held them all liable to measurement against the same stand-

[47] BAV, Pal. Lat. 1604, fol. 10v.

[48] See the edition of Adamo's oration in de Marinis, *La biblioteca*, 1.225–27, esp. 226.

[49] Valencia, BU, MS 735 (formerly 745), esp. fols. 62v–67r, 87v–88v.

ard of justice.[50] Elisio Calenzio devoted three of his epistles to the theme of justice, which he commended to Federico as "the prince of all virtues, the signal companion of the gods and of men, the ornament of all princes, the fortress of all cities and estates."[51]

A peculiar work of the copyist Joan Marco Cinico deals with a particular aspect of justice—the proper uses of mercy and punishment. Cinico recognized the importance of obedience to princes in his letter dedicating the work to King Ferrante; and the body of the work, which consists of excerpts drawn from classical and medieval authors, provided numerous illustrations of punishments imposed on rebellious or treasonous subjects. Yet the emphasis in this work fell on clemency, which led Tammaro de Marinis to suspect that Cinico composed his work around 1487 in the hope that it would induce Ferrante to show mercy to Antonello Petrucci and other conspirators involved in the second barons' revolt. Many of the extracts included in Cinico's work stressed the value of clemency and the problems that excessive cruelty or tyranny could pose for princes. In his concluding epistle, Cinico urged Ferrante to resort more readily to clemency—wherein there lay a true immortality that made men similar to God himself—than to severity. While acknowledging the need for rigorous justice, he considered the goodwill of one's subjects the only truly reliable source of security for a prince and his realm.[52]

Cinico thus made his case for mercy in somewhat tentative fashion, far removed from the straightforward manner of his contemporary, Pontano. In his last formal treatise—a work on inhumanity, *De immanitate*, written in 1501—Pontano dealt with many of the themes discussed in the last few pages, but explored them in his own peculiar way. In this melancholy, yet cautiously optimistic treatise, Pontano sought an explanation and a cure for the

[50] Maio, *De maiestate*, esp. pp. 201–13.

[51] Calenzio, *Opuscula*, fols. B1r, B1v, B6v. The quotation comes from fol. B1r.

[52] Cinico's work survives in BAV, Chigi L. VII. 269. The epistles of dedication and conclusion occur on fols. 9r–10r, 68rv. Cf. de Marinis, *La biblioteca*, 1.44, for the suggestion that Cinico hoped his work would win mercy for Petrucci.

transformation of rational men into feral beasts. He provided at discouraging length a catalog of bestial behavior, which he illustrated by examples both ancient and modern. Many of them concerned political outrages that exemplified the extremes of injustice. Thus Pontano condemned Sultan Mehmed II for the murder of his brother, Ludovico il Moro for disposing of his nephew, Swiss and Burgundian mercenaries for betraying Ludovico himself to the French in 1500, Ferrante for cruel incarceration of his enemies and for excessively harsh penalties imposed on those who poached his game, Duke Charles the Rash of Burgundy for destroying and razing Liège, and several condottieri for their sadistic and capricious murders. The cause of this sort of vicious behavior Pontano traced to a suspension of will and reason, which led to an unbridled lust to satisfy various appetites. As a cure for inhumanity Pontano recommended cultivation of the liberal arts and letters, which brought about refinement of the soul, respect for civilized manners, and the capacity to rule the passions and appetites by reason. The study of good letters, then, led directly to the cultivation of humanity itself.[53]

When relying on the tradition of epideictic rhetoric for guidance in the development of their political thought, most Neapolitan humanists resorted to the tactic of praise in order to encourage princes to observe high standards of behavior. Of all these men, only Pontano employed the more difficult tactic of condemnation in an effort to shame princes into proper behavior.[54] Yet even in

[53] Giovanni Pontano, *De immanitate liber*, ed. L. Monti Sabia (Naples, 1970), esp. pp. 14, 19, 21–22, 29, 40–41, 44–45 for the examples referred to here, and pp. 4–7, 41–42, 46–47 on the causes and cure of inhumanity. See also Mario Santoro's sensitive essay: "Il *De immanitate*: testamento spirituale del Pontano," *La Partenope: rivista di cultura napoletana*, 1 (1960), 5–16.

[54] Pontano's dialogue *Asinus* constitutes another example of this tactic. Although interpreters disagree as to Pontano's target in this dialogue, it is clear that he intended to censure the ingratitude of a prominent Neapolitan figure, probably King Ferrante. For the text, see Pontano, *I dialoghi*, ed. C. Previtera (Florence, 1943), pp. 289–308. For assessments, see Erasmo Percopo, *Vita di Giovanni Pontano*, ed. M. Manfredi (Naples, 1938), pp. 231–37; and Santoro, "La cultura umanistica," in *Storia di Napoli*, 10 vols. (Naples, 1975–81), 7.198, 279

his treatise on inhumanity, Pontano had positive goals in mind. He worked on the assumption that public virtues, such as justice, arise from more purely personal qualities. These qualities in turn develop only in individuals who seek to cultivate humanity, the most noble condition attainable by men using their natural powers. Finally, humanity itself stands on the foundation of a proper liberal education in the best thought and literature produced by men of wisdom and learning. From this point of view, support for literature and scholarship represented not only a kind of tribute designed to win praise from humanists, but also an intellectual and moral investment that promised handsome returns for the broader public interest.

Humanist Historiography in Renaissance Naples

Historiography in fifteenth-century Naples reflected no less than political thought the triumph of princely government. Already in 1443, when Alfonso the Magnanimous had barely consolidated his hold on the Regno, Flavio Biondo wrote to him, emphasizing the importance of history for kings who hoped to leave a favorable impression.[55] Biondo need not have worried, for Alfonso found history deeply engaging. He enjoyed hearing readings from Caesar and especially from Livy, and he encouraged humanists at his court to undertake a variety of historiographical projects. Furthermore, quite apart from his own interest, Alfonso needed the talents of men who could lend a sense of legitimacy to his new dynasty by recording his deeds in the currently fashionable idiom of humanist historiography.[56]

---

n. 82. Finally, for a highly interesting discussion of a similar, Roman case, see the study of Alexis Celadoni's funeral oration devoted to the shortcomings of Pope Alexander VI in John M. McManamon, "The Ideal Renaissance Pope: Funeral Oratory from the Papal Court," *Archivium historiae pontificiae*, 14 (1976), 9–70, esp. 54–70.

[55] Biondo, *Scritti inediti e rari di Biondo Flavio*, ed. B. Nogara (Rome, 1927), pp. 147–53.

[56] Two recent studies present different but complementary and supremely interesting analyses of historical writing in Renaissance Naples. While not neces-

Humanist historiography combined the influence of classical antiquity with the interests of Renaissance humanism. Its preeminent characteristic was imitation of an approved classical historian such as Livy or Caesar, though lesser lights like Suetonius or Xenophon also qualified as appropriate models for certain subjects. The influence of antiquity also dictated more general principles. Humanists were expected to cast their historical writings in refined literary style, for example, and adorn them periodically with appropriate speeches. Like their classical counterparts, humanist historians wrote on coherent political topics—battles, wars, rulers, cities, and states—rather than recording the jumbled hodge-podge of trivial and monumental information often found in medieval chronicles. Humanist historians universally recognized truth as their ultimate goal. As a result, they extracted information from new sources, like official documents, and they devised new, critical methods of evaluating their source materials. While searching more or less honestly for historical truth, the humanists thought of history as a discipline with tremendous didactic utility: they considered the historical record a great storehouse of examples that taught a variety of personal and political lessons.[57]

The seeds of humanist historiography fell on fertile soil in Renaissance Naples. Like their counterparts elsewhere in Italy, Neapolitan humanists respected classical literary monuments, including historical writings, and they sought ways to use their classical learning to illuminate and embellish contemporary issues. The composition of humanist history offered them the opportunity to satisfy their taste for antique culture while also addressing items

---

sarily subscribing to all the details of either study, I wish to record my debt to them both: Gianvito Resta's introduction to his edition of Panormita's *Liber rerum gestarum Ferdinandi regis*; and Eric Cochrane, *Historians and Historiography in the Italian Renaissance* (Chicago, 1981), esp. pp. 144–59. Both of these works supersede the older and completely unsympathetic account of Eduard Fueter, *Geschichte der neueren Historiographie*, 3d ed. (Munich, 1936), pp. 37–41, 98–99, 112–13 on the Neapolitan humanists.

[57] On Italian humanist historiography in general, see Cochrane, *Historians and Historiography*, esp. pp. xvi, 3–159.

on the political agenda of the later Quattrocento. Over a period of about fifty years, then, the dual influence of classical learning and contemporary needs helped to shape the distinctive features of humanist historiography in Renaissance Naples. In the early years after Alfonso's conquest of the Regno, humanists produced a brand of history that relied on the cachet of ancient models to lend glory and a sense of legitimacy to the new Aragonese dynasty of Naples. During the same period a somewhat atypical alternative emerged: employing a fine critical sense developed on the basis of profound classical learning, Lorenzo Valla rejected the impulse toward exaggerated glorification of the new dynasty and concentrated instead on devising means and methods of portraying the past in the most accurate terms possible. Finally, toward the end of the fifteenth century, humanists who had witnessed an enormous amount of political and military turmoil took the opportunity while writing history on the classical model to reflect on the roles of fortune and of human skills in the unfolding of history.

Though by no means the most impressive of the Neapolitan humanist histories, Panormita's works best exemplify the brand of historiography that placed classical learning in the service of the Aragonese dynasty of Naples. Panormita twice turned his hand to history: in 1455 he completed his anecdotal portrait of Alfonso the Magnanimous, the *De dictis et factis Alphonsi* often mentioned in previous chapters; and about 1469 he composed an account of Ferrante's life from the time of his arrival in Italy (1438) until the death of Alfonso (1458), the *Liber rerum gestarum Ferdinandi regis*. He unfortunately did not live long enough to continue this work, as he had originally planned, so that the story of Ferrante's battle to succeed Alfonso remained untold for another twenty-five years.

In *De dictis et factis Alphonsi* Panormita loosely followed the model of Xenophon's *Memorabilia*, which presented an anecdotal account of Socrates' sayings and experiences.[58] Panormita claimed

[58] Panormita himself referred to Xenophon as his model in the preface to the first book of his *De dictis et factis Alphonsi regis* (Basel, 1538), p. [a 6].

great authority for his work. In a letter of 1460 or 1461 to Jean d'Anjou—never sent because Antonello Petrucci advised against it—Panormita said he retold only episodes that he had witnessed himself or that he had learned through trustworthy testimony.[59] Indeed, previous chapters have shown that in at least a few cases, independent evidence confirms Panormita's account in *De dictis et factis Alphonsi*. Yet Panormita himself made it clear in other places that he intended for his work to have a kind of propaganda value. He referred to this goal in a letter of uncertain date to Giacomo Peregrino, who had encouraged Panormita to write something on Alfonso. He not only wanted to record Alfonso's glorious deeds and divine virtues, Panormita said, but also to entrust the memory of his generous patron to the permanence of letters and to praise him to the skies. For that reason he preferred not to write immediately—"for it was better to say nothing about Carthage than to mention only a few things"—but to wait until greater leisure afforded him the opportunity to prepare a fitting commemoration of the king.[60] In 1455 he dedicated the completed work to Cosimo de' Medici, in honor of the recent reconciliation of Florence, Milan, Naples, and other Italian states. In the letter of dedication Panormita promised that Cosimo would see Alfonso working and hear him speaking in the book, as the king demonstrated his gravity, justice, magnanimity, clemency, and urbanity, among other virtues.[61] Clearly Panormita had composed a work of flattery as well as history.

Indeed, *De dictis et factis Alphonsi* has the character of a literary hybrid influenced by both the tradition of anecdotal history and the genre of the *speculum principis*: while concentrating exclusively on the experience of Alfonso, the work's 227 short episodes attribute to him the qualities traditionally associated with the ideal prince.[62] Alfonso appears in *De dictis et factis Alphonsi* as a paragon

---

[59] Panormita, *Regis Ferdinandi et aliorum epistolae*, p. 378.

[60] BAV, Barb. lat. 2069, fols. 61v–62v, esp. fol. 62r.

[61] Panormita, *Epistolarum libri V*, fols. 117v–18r.

[62] In addition to the 220 chapters published in *De dictis et factis Alphonsi*, see

of piety, who had read through the Bible fourteen times, encouraged youngsters to study theology, and publicly washed and kissed the feet of paupers during Lent.[63] A man of culture as well as of faith, Alfonso diligently sought wisdom and understanding—even under difficult circumstances, such as those of illness or war—and he rewarded men of letters as well as men at arms.[64] Alfonso of course always had the interests of his subjects at heart: thus he exhibited liberality and clemency by preventing a sack of Naples after the city's fall in 1442; he once helped a peasant pull his ass from a ditch; he ensured that the powerful did not oppress the weak; and he preferred that his subjects did not fear him as much as fear for him.[65] In similar fashion, Alfonso worked on behalf of peace in all of Italy: he sought to conciliate his enemies with kindness; he drove Francesco Sforza out of the marches in 1443 out of sheer goodwill toward Pope Eugenius IV; and in 1447 he led his army into central Italy not because of his own political ambition, but solely in order to aid his faithful friend, Duke Filippo Maria Visconti.[66] Meanwhile, Alfonso refused to compromise his personal moral principles in order to advance his political fortunes: he rejected the offers of unnamed men to assassinate René d'Anjou and Francesco Sforza; he insisted on honoring a promise to deliver 30,000 ducats to Marquis Luigi Gonzaga of Mantua, even though it seemed likely that Gonzaga would use the money against Alfonso; and responding to a suggestion that he demand 200,000 ducats in order to make peace with Venice and Florence, Alfonso replied that he had the habit of giving peace, not selling it.[67] Such is the character of Panormita's *De dictis et factis Alphonsi* that a sev-

---

also 7 others first edited by Vicenzo Laurenza in his article, "Il Panormita a Napoli," *AAP*, 42 (1912), 91–92.

[63] *De dictis et factis Alphonsi*, pp. 41, 55–56, 107.

[64] Ibid., pp. 2–4, 6, 40, 57–60, 111, for a few examples of Alfonso's love of letters.

[65] Ibid., pp. 6–8, 20, 42, 117.

[66] Ibid., pp. 78–81, 85.

[67] Ibid., pp. 75–78.

enteenth-century editor published it under the title *Mirror of the Good Prince*.[68]

Panormita's work thus served the interests of a new dynasty by glorifying and legitimizing its founder. Although he cast his account of Ferrante's deeds in more traditional biographical form, his basic aims in the later work remained quite similar to those of *De dictis et factis Alphonsi*. Ferrante had engaged in more than five years of military and diplomatic struggles in order to secure his hold on the Regno, while popes and pretenders called the legitimacy of his reign into question. Thus Panormita again devoted his talents to the interests of the Aragonese dynasty by portraying its head as an ideal, virtuous prince. Though composed in the style of Suetonius, Panormita's biography of Ferrante once again betrayed considerable influence of Xenophon. The model in this case was not the *Memorabilia*, however, but Xenophon's *Cyropaedia*, his idealized, indeed fictional account of the education and upbringing of Cyrus, the future Persian king. Essentially a *speculum principis* concentrating on the education and qualities of the ideal prince, the *Cyropaedia* enjoyed a considerable vogue in Quattrocento Italy: Lorenzo Valla translated portions of it for the young Ferrante, and Poggio Bracciolini dedicated his Latin version of the entire work to Alfonso. It is hardly surprising, then, that Panormita chose to liken Ferrante in numerous ways to the young Cyrus.[69]

Panormita did not present a sophisticated account of Ferrante's early career, not even by the standards of the fifteenth century. He did not provide the detail that Facio offered in his history of Alfonso's deeds, for example, nor did he engage in the kind of thoughtful reflection that marks the work of Pontano. Indeed, he did not even present a continuous account of Ferrante's activities, but rather a kind of episodic survey that emphasized his manifold talents and virtues. Panormita began the work with Ferrante's ar-

[68] *Speculum boni principis*, ed. J. Santes (Amsterdam, 1646).

[69] See Resta's superb discussion of this point in his introduction to Panormita's *Liber rerum gestarum Ferdinandi regis*, pp. 36–48.

rival in Naples at seven years of age (1438). He made no mention of his subject's illegitimate birth, but associated him immediately with the authoritative figure of King Alfonso. Even as a child, Panormita's Ferrante possessed a constellation of virtues: besides modesty and taciturnity, he exhibited "reverence toward his father and relatives, all humanity toward the princes, kindness toward his peers, urbanity toward citizens, gentleness and benevolence toward all." At an unspecified age he rendered justice on a daily basis, emphasizing patience, moderation, and clemency, but resorting when necessary to severity. Soon, however, Ferrante sought military responsibilities from Alfonso, who accordingly entrusted to him leadership of the Tuscan campaign (1452–1453). Panormita devoted the longest section of his work to the prudence, bravery, and talent for arms and diplomacy that Ferrante manifested during this period. He closed the work with an account of the maneuvers undertaken by the barons during Alfonso's last illness—thus setting the stage for a history of Ferrante's war of succession, which Panormita did not live to write—and a report of the dying king's last speech to his son and heir.[70] Thus throughout his work, Panormita associated Ferrante with Alfonso and the new dynasty in an effort to legitimize his rule, all the while emphasizing the prince's personal and political virtues in an effort to enhance his reputation.

About the same time that Panormita completed *De dictis et factis Alphonsi*, Bartolomeo Facio submitted to Alfonso his ten books of commentaries on the king's deeds, *De rebus gestis ab Alphonso primo neapolitanorum rege*. Facio's work stands out as the most serious of the humanist histories that had as its main objective the glorification of the Aragonese dynasty of Naples. Facio worked for almost a decade on his monumental history, which he completed probably in the summer or autumn of 1455.[71] He exhibited an im-

[70] Panormita, *Liber rerum gestarum Ferdinandi regis*, esp. pp. 73–79, 90–91, 98–134 (on the Tuscan campaign), 136–43. The quotation occurs on p. 73.

[71] In a letter of 14 April 1455 Facio reported to Poggio Bracciolini that he was

pressive diligence in producing an enormously detailed work that remains even today the basic narrative source for Alfonso's reign.

As suggested by their title, Facio's commentaries follow the model of Caesar, and they concentrate almost exclusively on military and diplomatic history. Facio opened the work with Queen Giovanna's appeal for aid in 1420 and Alfonso's first experience with Neapolitan affairs. He continued with a chronological account of Alfonso's exploits, including his expulsion from Italy (1423), settlement of the civil war in Spain (1429–1430), conquest of Jerba (1432), siege of Gaeta (1435), campaign to subdue the Regno (1435–1442), expedition against Francesco Sforza in the marches (1443–1446), and his two ventures into Tuscany (1447–1448 and 1452–1453). The last pages of the work deal with Alfonso's continuous conflict with Genoa, the question of a crusade, and the death of Pope Nicholas V. The work does not so much conclude as simply stop in 1455, when Facio presented it to Alfonso. Though undistinguished in conception and organization, Facio's work furnished a useful narrative account of Alfonso's experiences. The author took seriously his obligation to present a truthful and accurate record, and when appropriate he drew upon documentary evidence: Facio's discussions of the Treaty of Terracina between Alfonso and Pope Eugenius IV (1443), the peace established between Naples and Genoa that Facio himself helped to negotiate (1443–1444), and the League of Italy (1455) represent only a few illustrations of passages in which Facio based his account on official documents.[72]

Yet Facio intended his work to do more than simply record the facts of history: he sought also to glorify his royal patron and endow him with a kind of literary immortality. Facio never presented an abstract or theoretical discussion of the purpose and uses of history, but several sources throw some light on the matter. In

---

working on the tenth and last book of his account: see the appendix of letters in Facio's *De viris illustribus liber*, ed. L. Mehus (Florence, 1745), p. 104.

[72] For the passages referred to here, see the standard edition of Facio's *De rebus gestis* in Gravier, ed., *Raccolta*, vol. 4, esp. 160, 184–85, 270–72.

1446, for example, he violently attacked Lorenzo Valla for recording unworthy things in his history of Alfonso's father, Ferdinand of Antequera. Valla had reported Ferdinand's hilarity when he witnessed the outlandish dress and arms of some Moorish forces captured in a skirmish; Facio scolded Valla for wounding Ferdinand's dignity, since he considered levity unbefitting kings and commanders. At another point, Facio criticized Valla because he did not attribute contempt for death to Ferdinand as he entered battle. Facio became most incensed, however, at Valla's reportage on Martin the Elder, last of the Catalan kings of Aragon. In one passage that Facio considered indecorous, Valla recorded that Martin had once snored while receiving French ambassadors. More scandalous was Valla's discussion of Martin's desperate efforts to produce a child and heir. Valla openly mentioned Martin's sexual problems and reported one occasion when an aide had helped the elderly king to achieve intercourse with his queen. Valla's accounts represented not so much a search for truth, Facio argued, as an inappropriate, unworthy characterization of dignified men.[73] Presumably, then, glorification of the historian's subject was for Facio a proper function, perhaps even an imperative of historiography.

Facio made this point in a more positive way in other places. Thus in a letter dating from about 1446, as he began work on his history of Alfonso's deeds, Facio expressed the hope that his efforts would prove worthy of the king's glory. He took comfort in the knowledge that the very magnitude of Alfonso's deeds would ensure that he produced a dignified work, but he pointed out also that the proper embellishment of the king's achievements called for rare learning and literary talent.[74] In a letter of 26 September

[73] For these passages, see Valla's *Gesta Ferdinandi regis Aragonum*, ed. O. Besomi (Padua, 1973), pp. 65, 75–76, 86, 93; and Facio's *Invective in Laurentium Vallam*, ed. E. I. Rao (Naples, 1978), pp. 82, 84, 96–97.

[74] See the appendix of epistles in Facio's *De viris illustribus*, pp. 89–90. Reference to Facio's *Invective* against Valla, of which he speaks as if he had recently completed them, dates the letter to about 1446.

1451 to Francesco Barbaro, Facio affirmed that insofar as his ability allowed it, he would continue his efforts to consecrate Alfonso
to eternity, as he had done already in the seven books of his work
so far completed.[75] These efforts were successful in the opinion of
Panormita, who clearly understood the propaganda value of Facio's history: after reading the first eight books of the work, he reported to Alfonso and Battista Platamone, royal vice-chancellor of
Sicily, that Facio had effectively expressed the king's praises, to
the point of rendering him immortal.[76]

Facio did not turn his history into a praise of the king's virtues,
as Panormita did in the cases of both Alfonso and Ferrante. But
Facio always kept Alfonso at the center of the story and portrayed
him as the most important agent of his times. More specifically,
he presented Alfonso as a man in perpetual contest with fortune.
The results did not always favor Alfonso, for fortune occasionally
dealt him difficult blows. In the end, however, fortune cooperated
with the most important of Alfonso's designs, and all the while
Facio's literary tactic resulted in an image of Alfonso as a vigorous
and dynamic force in history. Thus Facio spoke of Alfonso's challenge to fortune when he decided to attack the island of Jerba and
when he sought to make good his claim to the kingdom of Naples
after the death of Queen Giovanna II. The siege of Gaeta and the
naval defeat at Ponza fit neatly into the scheme: Facio ascribed Alfonso's loss largely to fortune, then portrayed Alfonso's subsequent liberation and alliance with the Milanese duke as genuinely
magnificent developments against the background of the debacle
at Ponza. Fortune dealt perhaps her cruelest blow in 1438, when
Alfonso's brother Pedro fell, mortally wounded, in an unsuccess-
ful siege of the city of Naples. But fortune finally opened the way
for Alfonso's forces to enter Naples when a mason informed them
of an unguarded aqueduct leading into the city. After describing
the subjugation of Naples, Facio could no longer withhold his

[75] See the appendix of letters in Facio's *De viris illustribus*, pp. 93–96, esp. p.
95.
[76] Panormita, *Epistolarum libri V*, fol. 104rv.

praise of Alfonso, who for twenty-one years had endured all the hardships of war with amazing courage and constancy, then exhibited unexampled mercy and clemency in taking his victory. To Facio it appeared that of all kings, only Alfonso had brought the power of fortune into his own possession.[77]

In its most extreme form, the kind of history that Panormita and Facio produced became subservient to the immediate demands of policy. Thus about the middle of the fifteenth century, Ciccolino Gattini composed a brief account of Alfonso's excursion into Tuscany following the death of Duke Filippo Maria Visconti of Milan. While praising Alfonso for his justice, piety, and other qualities, Ciccolino placed the blame for the conflict on Florentine aggression and provocation, which arose from the Tuscans' excessive pride.[78] Policy also shaped the writing of history during the reign of Ferrante. Thus in 1472 Giovanni Filippo de Lignamine published a short work on the life and virtues of Ferrante, whom he hoped to reconcile with the papacy. Born into a noble family at Messina, de Lignamine had spent much of his youth in Naples, where he perhaps even received some of his education alongside Ferrante. He opened a printing shop at Rome in 1469, and over the next fifteen years he published numerous editions of classical and humanist works. In 1471 his close friend, Cardinal Francesco della Rovere, became Pope Sixtus IV. De Lignamine recognized the opportunity of mending relations between Rome and Naples, which had suffered severe strain during the years of the prickly Pope Paul II, and he sought to bring about an alliance between his

[77] For the passages referred to here, see Facio's *De rebus gestis*, in Gravier, ed., *Raccolta*, 4.64, 68, 90–94, 115, 147, 151–55.

[78] Formerly in the library of Count Giuseppe Gattini of Matera, Ciccolino's manuscript work "De bello regis Alphonsi" is currently in the possession of Dottore Michele Gattini of Rome. I wish to express my appreciation for Dottore Gattini's efforts to locate the manuscript and provide me with a photocopy of it. For a few, sparse references to Ciccolino Gattini, see T. Pedio, *Storia della storiografia lucana* (Bari, 1964), p. 24; P. A. Ridola, *Memoria genealogico-istorica della famiglia Gattini da Matera* (Naples, 1877), pp. 18–19; and Giuseppe Gattini, *Saggio di biblioteca basilicatese* (Matera, 1903), p. 23.

childhood friend, Ferrante, and his curial patron, the new pope. The main instrument of his effort was de Lignamine's fulsome panegyric of Ferrante, dedicated to Sixtus. In fact, though he called his work the *Life and Praises* of Ferrante, de Lignamine endowed it with very little biography. He concentrated instead on the attribution to the king of prudence, piety, courage, moderation, justice, temperance, liberality, and all other manner of virtue—to the point that his work resembled epideictic rhetoric rather than history.[79]

Lorenzo Valla offered a clear alternative to this sort of history: he considered history a branch of scholarship rather than propaganda; he recognized as the historian's prime duty not the glorification of a patron, but rather the composition of an accurate record of the past. He put his principles into practice in his history of Ferdinand of Antequera, the *Gesta Ferdinandi regis Aragonum*, composed between April 1445 and February 1446.

In the famous preface to his work, Valla rated the discipline of history superior to philosophy and poetry. Historians possess more gravity and prudence than philosophers, he said, and they consequently attain to a more thorough and wise understanding of human affairs. Valla placed the emergence of history chronologically prior to the origin of poetry, but more importantly he argued that history was superior to poetry because it dealt with the truth of things rather than the products of the imagination. Valla's high ideal entailed serious obligations for the practicing historian: because of the discipline's difficulty, the historian must exercise ex-

[79] Giovanni Filippo de Lignamine, *Inclyti Ferdinandi regis vita et laudes* (Rome, 1472) survives in only one copy, preserved in Palermo at the Biblioteca Centrale della Regione Siciliana (formerly the Biblioteca Nazionale di Palermo). Pontieri published most of the work, however, excluding only a few passages, in *Per la storia del regno di Ferrante I d'Aragona re di Napoli*, 2d ed. (Naples, 1969), pp. 140–57. For an account of de Lignamine's life and an evaluation of his work, see ibid., pp. 105–39. For a recent assessment of de Lignamine as proprietor of a vanity press, see the provocative article of M. D. Feld, "A Theory of the Early Italian Printing Firm," *Harvard Library Bulletin* 33 (1985); 34 (1986). I wish to thank the author for allowing me to consult an early version of this work.

treme diligence in conducting research, employ sound judgment in evaluating his information, and present his findings with the aid of superior literary talent. Thus historians must command skills similar to those of a physician diagnosing a disease or a judge ferreting out the truth from testimony presented in a case at law.[80]

The history itself shows that Valla took seriously the obligations he imposed on the historian. The work falls into three coherent books: the first deals with Ferdinand's early career in Castile and his campaign against the Moors, culminating in his conquest of Antequera; the second reviews the internal political situation in Aragon and describes Ferdinand's accession to the throne by the Compromise of Caspe; the last discusses Ferdinand's reign in Aragon, as well as the early political experiences of Valla's patron, the future King Alfonso. Valla conscientiously sought Spanish sources of information for his work; he probably relied to some extent on documentary evidence; and he even based the speeches in his work on his primary sources of information.[81] Like the other humanist historians, Valla kept his subject in the forefront of his story, but unlike his colleagues, he made no effort to transform Ferdinand into a perfect specimen of royalty. Instead he sought to present the most accurate portrayal of Ferdinand that his sources would allow. Thus, for example, at the end of his work, while praising the king's justice, courage, modesty, and chastity, Valla frankly acknowledged that like the rest of the Spanish nobility of his time, Ferdinand had rather limited exposure to letters and learning.[82]

This sort of remark served as fuel for Valla's controversy with Bartolomeo Facio. To a large extent the polemic depended upon

[80] Valla, *Gesta Ferdinandi*, pp. 3–8.

[81] For a discussion of Valla's sources, see Besomi's introduction to his edition of Valla's *Gesta Ferdinandi*, esp. pp. xv–xxv. The royal library in Naples included several items that Valla could have consulted: see de Marinis, *La biblioteca*, 2.44–45, 117–18; and de Marinis, *Supplemento*, 1.32, 76–77. Valla himself asserted the authenticity of one oration in his work in his *Antidotum in Facium*, ed. M. Regoliosi (Padua, 1981), pp. 298–99.

[82] Valla, *Gesta Ferdinandi*, pp. 183–85.

Facio's personal and professional frustration: he loathed Valla and coveted his position as royal historiographer. Thus in the *Invectives* against Valla, he querulously—and almost always incorrectly—accused his enemy of committing hundreds of errors in Latin grammar, style, and usage. Yet some of his charges sprang from a different basic vision of history and its purpose. In Facio's view, the historian's task was to dignify and glorify the illustrious deeds of worthy men. Thus he faulted Valla on two substantive grounds: Valla employed inappropriate neologisms drawn from the vernacular languages rather than proper Latin words of classical origin; and he portrayed his subjects in a less than dignified way or failed to attribute noble qualities to them.[83]

Lorenzo Valla possessed superior polemical skills, and his response demolished Facio's rather silly objections. To be sure, Valla indulged in his own fair share of personal vituperation. He derided Facio for his Ligurian ancestry, denounced his father as a shoemaker for fishermen, condemned Bartolomeo himself as a lackey to the powerful Spinola family of Genoa, and addressed him throughout his work as "Fatuus." But Valla also cited hundreds of grammatical and literary sources to demonstrate overwhelmingly the lack of substance and erudition behind Facio's unwise attack, which, as Valla said in one place, argued "the wrong point, by the wrong reason, with the wrong words." More importantly, Valla rejected also Facio's understanding of the purpose of history. Valla justified his use of neologisms as a necessary adaptation to reality. The invention or discovery of new things, like cannons, calls for the employment of new words, like *bombarda*. No matter how elegant or how much approved by ancient authorities, the classical word *tormentum*, which Facio suggested in place of *bombarda*, failed to represent modern reality with accuracy. Valla also justified his selection and treatment of materials as a function of his concern for accuracy. Against Facio's charge that he had portrayed his subjects in an undignified way, Valla asserted the priority of historical

[83] Facio, *Invective*, pp. 73, 82, 84, 96–97, 115.

truth. Ferdinand in fact laughed riotously at his prisoners; old King Martin snored before the ambassadors; and Valla insisted on his right to report these facts. He likewise defended his report of the activities in and around Martin's marital bed, but argued also a further justification for this account: the old king's extraordinary measures served as corroboration for Valla's main point, which was to demonstrate that Martin sought in absolute desperation to produce a child and heir.[84]

Valla never developed a larger vision of history—one, for example, that encouraged the historian to advance a meaningful interpretation or explanation of the past—but his insistence on the priority of truth and accuracy stands out as perhaps the most courageous position taken by any of the fifteenth-century historians. Unfortunately, Valla's history of Ferdinand and his response to Facio exercised very little influence, either in his own day or in later times. Italian historians of the Quattrocento worked for the most part with the interests of a patron in mind, and they did not find it useful to imitate Valla in his spirited sense of independence. When historians of the sixteenth and later centuries again sought absolute accuracy as the highest goal of their work, they rarely referred to Valla's history of Ferdinand or to his controversy with Facio as influences on their thinking.

In other works, however, Valla contributed a crucial element to the historiography of the modern West. In his treatise on the Donation of Constantine and in his annotations to the New Testament, Valla demonstrated by example how to apply critical, philological reasoning to questions of history. In exposing the Donation of Constantine as a forgery, Valla employed a variety of historical and philological arguments. Some of them attacked the Donation on the grounds of its sheer implausibility: Constantine waged years of war to gain control of the Roman Empire, Valla

---

[84] Valla, *Antidotum in Facium*, pp. 3–5, 65, 106–7, 163–64, 236–37, 247–49, 253–57. See also an article that examines this controversy: Linda Gardiner Janik, "Lorenzo Valla: The Primacy of Rhetoric and the De-moralization of History," *History and Theory*, 12 (1973), 389–404.

observed, and it did not seem highly likely that he would suddenly grant half of it to the pope. But other, more certain arguments depended on Valla's deployment of his vast erudition. Thus he pointed out that no historical sources mentioned a transfer of imperial possessions; that the Donation employed words and expressions not used in Constantine's time; and that the spurious document exhibited historical anachronisms when it referred to the existence of Christian churches in Rome and a patriarchal see of Constantinople.[85] In his annotations to the New Testament Valla employed a similar kind of reasoning to establish the point that the man named Dionysius whom St. Paul converted on the Areopagus in Athens (Acts 17:22–34) was not the same man who wrote several works of Neoplatonic theology. Again he argued that a combination of improbability, anomaly, and silence in early historical sources mandated a distinction between the original Dionysius the Areopagite and the pseudo-Dionysius the Neoplatonist.[86]

Valla's philological arguments of this sort were significant not only for Italian, but also for European culture. Their most important effect was to encourage the cultivation of a sophisticated sense of history. Already from the time of Petrarch, Italian humanists had begun to recognize the fact that deep cultural changes took place during the course of history. Valla's superior erudition enabled him to frame arguments that emphasized in demonstrative fashion the historical and cultural differences between the age of Constantine and the time of the Donation of Constantine, or between the age of Dionysius the Areopagite and the era of the pseudo-Dionysius. These arguments worked a profound influence on later generations of European scholars, so that Valla figured as one of the most prominent founders of modern philological and

[85] Valla, *De falso credita et ementita Constantini donatione*, ed. W. Setz (Weimar, 1976), passim.

[86] Valla, *Collatio Novi Testamenti*, ed. A. Perosa (Florence, 1970), pp. 167–68; *Opera omnia*, ed. E. Garin, 2 vols. (Turin, 1962), 1.852.

historical scholarship.[87] In this light, the peculiar circumstances that pitted Alfonso the Magnanimous against Pope Eugenius IV during the early 1440s assume a large significance. Except for Alfonso's difficulties, he would not likely have pressured Valla to compose his work against the Donation of Constantine, which in turn could not have exercised its influence on European culture. Perhaps no other episode illustrates as clearly the long-range significance of the interrelation between politics and culture in Renaissance Naples.

Meanwhile, in the shorter term, other historians in Naples struggled to account for the kingdom's increasingly turbulent experience in the idiom of humanist historiography. Humanists active in the difficult years from 1478 to 1495 could not rely on the optimistic schemes adopted by Panormita and Facio, by which strong-willed kings performed glorious deeds, won the favor of fortune, and determined the direction of history. Giovanni Albino's historical works, which the author composed at various times between about 1480 and 1496, illustrate the difficulties faced by Neapolitan historians in the late Quattrocento. Albino wrote six books of history, of which four survive, on the experience of the kingdom of Naples between the war following the Pazzi conspiracy (1478–1480) and the first French invasion of Italy (1494–1495). Written in the style of Sallust, each of the four surviving books deals in coherent and well-integrated fashion with a single military conflict: the campaign against Florence, the war against the Turks at Otranto, the second barons' revolt, and the French invasion. Out of necessity, Albino placed less emphasis than his humanist predecessors on the Aragonese kings of Naples and more on the activities of their competitors, the Turks, the barons, and the French, as well as on the impersonal and unpredictable workings of fortune.[88] By the late 1490s, when Albino completed his

---

[87] For two recent studies in which the later influence of Valla's philology is an important theme, see Bentley, *Humanists and Holy Writ*; and Donald R. Kelley, *Foundations of Modern Historical Scholarship* (New York, 1970).

[88] On Albino's life and historical works, see the *DBI*, 2.12–13; and Lucia

work, it made little sense to pretend that the kings of Naples controlled their own destinies and the fate of their realm.

The most impressive effort of a Neapolitan humanist to interpret the bitter experiences of the Regno was that of Giovanni Pontano. In his dialogue *Actius* (1499), Pontano discussed history from a general and largely literary point of view. He advised the prospective historian to imitate Livy and especially Sallust in presenting a concise, fast-paced account, and he even prescribed a kind of general outline to govern the organization of materials.[89] Pontano's actual historical composition clearly reflects the influence of his theory: his language, description of events, and orations, for example, all follow the rules he established in the *Actius*. But Pontano's formal historical work also goes beyond his theory in its concern to explain, to render comprehensible the vagaries of history.

In fact, by the end of the fifteenth century Pontano had developed a vision of political history much more sophisticated and complex than his discussion in the *Actius* would suggest. His only formal historical work, *De bello neapolitano* (1499), reflects Pontano's understanding of the political process. Written under the influence largely of Sallust's model, this work provided an account of Ferrante's battle to consolidate his hold on the kingdom of Naples during the years 1458 to 1464. Like all the humanist historians, Pontano placed the emphasis on political and military events: the six books of his work divide the war of succession into coherent periods, according to Ferrante's shifting fortunes in the conflict. Pontano's work resembled those of the other humanist historians also in that he devoted the bulk of his attention to the efforts of King Ferrante, who obviously and inevitably served as protagonist of the work.

Gualdo Rosa et al., eds., *Gli umanisti et la guerra otrantina* (Bari, 1982), pp. 45–53. Albino's account of the war at Otranto is edited with an Italian translation in ibid., pp. 54–100. The Latin text of all his surviving books is available in Gravier, ed., *Raccolta*, 5.1–88.

[89] Pontano, *I dialoghi*, pp. 192–230, esp. pp. 208–30.

Like Albino, however, Pontano realized clearly that the kings of Naples did not determine the course of history by force of will. Thus he carefully outlined the interests of Ferrante's opponents and even of parties that maintained neutrality during the conflict. He opened his history with a survey of the political situation in all parts of the Italian peninsula, then focused attention on the major Neapolitan barons and their difficulties with Ferrante. He offered frank assessments of an individual's character or personality when relevant to his account. He acknowledged that even the young Ferrante had gained a reputation for dissimulation, which inclined the barons to mistrust the promises and gestures he made upon mounting the throne. He drew an impressive portrait also of Giovanni Antonio Orsini del Balzo, the prince of Taranto and leader of the rebellious barons, a personally timid man, yet one who envied Ferrante, loved conspiracy, and lusted for war. Pontano's understanding of the war depended also on a pessimistic vision of human nature at large. The invasion of Jean d'Anjou prompted masses of people in all parts of the Regno to forget the years of peace they had enjoyed under Alfonso and to rush to the standards of rebellion. "Especially at that time," Pontano observed, "it became possible to understand plainly that there is no faith, no constancy, no sense of gratitude in the hearts of men. They always resent the presence of government, crave a new state of affairs, place great hopes in the future, and take foolishness as their guide to the most extreme kinds of outrage."[90]

Thus Pontano composed a typical humanist history—modeled on a classical authority, divided coherently into books, equipped with eloquent orations, based when appropriate on documentary evidence and the author's first-hand experience[91]—but he also charged his work with a kind of thoughtful historical reflection rarely encountered in the humanist historiography of the Quattro-

[90] Pontano, *De bello neapolitano*, in Gravier, ed., *Raccolta*, 5.1–148. For the passages referred to here, see esp. pp. 3–16; the quotation occurs on p. 15.

[91] For Pontano's reliance on documents and his own efforts on Ferrante's behalf during the war of succession, see ibid., 5.104–5, 107–8, 111–14, 126.

cento. Pontano did not possess the historical vision of Guicciardini, but a half-century of life in the kingdom of Naples had led him to some understanding of human political affairs. He tacitly rejected the facile, patron-oriented historiography then produced in all parts of Italy and replaced it with an alternative that recognized the complexity of human affairs. Conflicts of will, the vagaries of fortune, the difficulties of managing men—these themes dominate Pontano's history. In view of the manifold influences at work in human affairs, in view of the innumerable possibilities offered by history, perhaps the ultimate result of the war of succession does not seem too outrageous: an unpopular king of suspect moral qualities evaded destruction, consolidated his position, and presented his realm with thirty years of peace and tranquility. For this political accomplishment—in spite of the well-known reservations he expressed in other works—Pontano ranked Ferrante among the best of princes.[92]

Humanist Efforts to Understand the World of Politics

Historians have often called attention to the point that after 1494 the concept of fortune loomed large in Italian political thought.[93] In an age in which French, Spanish, and imperial armies employed the Italian peninsula as a battleground, fortune represented all the uncontrollable forces that dominated political life in the various Italian states during the late fifteenth and sixteenth centuries. The theme of fortune exercised its influence so widely during the six-

[92] See esp. ibid., 5.7–8, 12–13, 14–16, 147–48.

[93] For a general discussion of the theme of fortune in western thought, see Vicenzo Cioffari, "Fortune, Fate, and Chance," in Philip P. Wiener, ed., *Dictionary of the History of Ideas*, 4 vols. (New York, 1973), 2.225–36. For two especially fine examinations of Renaissance variations on the theme, see Mario Santoro, *Fortuna, ragione e prudenza nella civiltà letteraria del Cinquecento*, 2d ed. (Naples, 1978); and Felix Gilbert, *Machiavelli and Guicciardini: Politics and History in Sixteenth-Century Florence* (Princeton, 1965), esp. pp. 28–45, 192–200, 267–70, 282–301.

teenth century, in fact, that it even suggested novel ways to compose music.[94] The fundamental instability of Italian politics during the late Quattrocento and the Cinquecento explains the heavy emphasis during that period on fortune and her mutations: political thinkers and historians resorted to the category of fortune in an effort to comprehend and account for a quantity of turbulence that reason alone could not explain.

Long before the French invasion of 1494, the kingdom of Naples experienced more than its fair share of turbulence. Indeed, intermittent violence punctuated the political life of the Regno all through the fifteenth century. Civil war during the last years of Queen Giovanna's reign, Alfonso's conquest of the kingdom, his subsequent adventures in central and northern Italy, Ferrante's war to succeed his father, his involvement in the wars of Pope Sixtus IV, the Turkish invasion at Otranto, the second barons' revolt, Ferrante's war with Pope Innocent VIII, and the increasing hostility of all the Italian states toward Naples during the 1490s—all these experiences encouraged Neapolitan humanists to invoke the theme of fortune even before external intervention began to dictate the terms of Italian political life.

During Alfonso's reign and Ferrante's early years on the throne, the Neapolitan humanists generally thought of fortune as an unpredictable force, to be sure, but as one whose effects the prince could withstand if he possessed the quality of perseverance. Indeed, fortune often enough favored a prince's designs. Thus in reporting to Panormita the complete victory of Neapolitan forces over a Florentine fleet at Piombino (July 1448), Bartolomeo Facio marveled that fortune accomplished whatever Alfonso wished, and he agreed with Panormita's characterization of the king as the "son of fortune."[95] In his *De principe*, Pontano advised Duke Alfonso of

[94] Edward E. Lowinsky, "The Goddess Fortuna in Music," *Musical Quarterly*, 29 (1943), 45–77.

[95] Facio's letter is published in the appendix of F. Gabotto, *Un nuovo contributo alla storia dell'umanesimo ligure* (Genoa, 1892), pp. 277–78. See also Facio's account of the battle in the *De rebus gestis ab Alphonso primo*, in Gravier, ed., *Rac-*

Calabria that princes must maintain their equanimity, even in the face of adverse fortune. God regulates human affairs, Pontano said, but sometimes does so in strange ways, so that he causes special difficulties for those whom he loves, while ensuring a favorable resolution of their troubles. Thus Alfonso the Magnanimous gained liberation on generous terms after falling prisoner to the Genoese and Duke Filippo Maria Visconti at the battle of Ponza in 1435; and upon hearing about the victory of his enemies at Sarno in 1460, Ferrante hardly changed his expression, but rather persevered and eventually triumphed.[96] Giuniano Maio argued a similar point as late as 1492: courage and patience often enable a prince to survive the uncertainties presented by fortune.[97]

Though not a profound thinker by any means, Panormita developed the most interesting conception of fortune advanced by any of the Neapolitan humanists before Pontano. The guiding theme of Panormita's thought was his identification of fortune with the will of God, which he then invoked in framing arguments concerning political or military affairs. In the summer of 1451, for example, after returning from his embassy to Venice, he corresponded with Francesco Barbaro, who had sent him a set of Greek military works. Barbaro had pledged jokingly to read the works for pleasure rather than practical guidance, lest all Italy suffer. In his reply, Panormita turned from a tone of light bantering to one of more serious reflection on the issue of war and peace. He considered victory in a war a most uncertain thing, one that came about not as the result of learned precepts or human power, but rather by divine providence. Thus he applauded Barbaro's wise decision not to implement the teachings of the Greek tacticians, but rather to prefer the existing state of peace to the uncertain prospect of military victory.[98] Barely a year after this letter, during the

---

colta, 4.215–16; and a documentary report of the same encounter in Alan Ryder, *Kingdom of Naples Under Alfonso the Magnanimous* (Oxford, 1976), pp. 301–2.

[96] See Pontano's *De principe*, in Garin, ed., *Prosatori latini*, esp. pp. 1028–33.

[97] Maio, *De maiestate*, esp. pp. 71–79.

[98] Panormita, *Epistolarum libri V*, fols. 115v–117v.

summer of 1452, Panormita associated fortune again with the will of God, but did so this time in justification of war rather than in praise of peace. The occasion was the departure of the Neapolitan army, under Ferrante's leadership, on Alfonso's second Tuscan campaign. Panormita composed an oration in Alfonso's name justifying the hostilities because of continual Florentine provocations and offering advice to Ferrante on how to conduct his forces. He especially emphasized the need for the wise commander to place his confidence not in his forces or his own talents, but rather in God, the author of all victory. Piety and innocence would win God's favor and consequently would lead much more surely to victory than would reliance upon arms or human bravery.[99] Several years later Panormita made a similar point in diplomatic correspondence, warning the republic of Genoa against war with Alfonso. No matter how strong their forces, he said, the Genoese could not count on victory, because God would preserve the party with justice on its side.[100]

Without doubt the most turbulent political and military experiences during Panormita's residence at Naples came during Ferrante's war to succeed Alfonso. In a letter of about 1465 Panormita referred to that period several times as one characterized by adverse fortune.[101] Yet he held to his understanding of fortune as the will of God. Already in 1452, in the oration to Ferrante as he departed on the Tuscan campaign, Panormita had pointed out that God sometimes punishes those whom he loves in order to improve them.[102] The war of succession provided abundant opportunity for

[99] The oration occurs in three of Panormita's works: *De dictis et factis Alphonsi*, pp. 89–92; *Regis Ferdinandi et aliorum epistolae*, pp. 298–300; *Liber rerum gestarum Ferdinandi regis*, pp. 99–101. Cf. also a similar speech attributed to Alfonso by Bartolomeo Facio, *De rebus gestis*, in Gravier, ed., *Raccolta*, 4.232–34.

[100] BAV, Barb. lat. 2070, esp. fols. 23v–24r; published also in Agostino Giustiniani, *Annali della Reppublica de Genova*, ed. G. B. Spotorno, 2 vols. (Genoa, 1854), 2.389.

[101] The letter serves as dedication, to Cardinal Oliviero Carafa, of the epistles that Panormita wrote for Ferrante during the war. It survives in BAV, Vat. lat. 3371, fols. 134r–35v.

[102] See the version of this oration in Panormita's *De dictis et factis Alphonsi* (completed in 1455), esp. p. 91.

Panormita to entertain this line of thought. "Fortune envies strong men and forces them into difficult straits," as Panormita observed in diplomatic correspondence with Pope Pius II, from whom he sought aid following Ferrante's defeat at Sarno.[103]

Fortune had favored Ferrante until the time of Alfonso's death—so Panormita explained things in his biography of Ferrante—but soon thereafter turned her face away. Ferrante had shown great generosity toward his adventurous cousin, Don Carlos de Viana, ever since the young prince's arrival in Naples in 1456. Yet Carlos intrigued against Ferrante in 1458, as Alfonso lay ill, allying with Spanish and Sicilian barons against the heir apparent. The parties would have come to blows at that time except that fortune—"which is precisely the will of God, against which all our designs are useless and ineffective"—destined Ferrante for the throne. Thus fortune caused an outbreak of the plague, which dispersed the conspirators and enabled Ferrante to gain control of the Neapolitan fortresses. Panormita promised a discussion of Ferrante's continuing difficulties, though he did not live to write an account of the war of succession.[104] Yet several pieces of his personal correspondence survive from the period of the war to show that he saw the hand of fortune behind Ferrante's experiences. In a letter to the king himself dating from the period after his victory at Troia in 1462, Panormita emphasized the role of fortune in bringing about Ferrante's success.[105] Two letters written after the death of the prince of Taranto (14 November 1463) made a similar point in even stronger terms. In the first, addressed to a certain theologian named Enrico, Panormita marveled at God's power to raise and crush men as he willed. Ferrante inherited a stable realm from Alfonso, then faced sudden and uni-

---

[103] *Regis Ferdinandi et aliorum epistolae*, p. 326.

[104] *Liber rerum gestarum Ferdinandi regis*, pp. 136–41. The quotation occurs on p. 139.

[105] BAV, Vat. lat. 3371, fol. 195rv. The pious, Counter-Reformation editor of Panormita's correspondence substituted the term *mutatio rerum* for *fortuna*. See *Regis Ferdinandi et aliorum epistolae*, pp. 406–7 for the published text of this letter; also Resta, *L'epistolario del Panormita*, pp. 104–9, for a discussion of the editor's treatment of Panormita's original text.

versal opposition; eventually the dynasty stood in danger of collapse, and Ferrante himself on the point of ruin. Then the death of one man—the prince of Taranto—brought confusion and defeat to Ferrante's enemies. Thus Ferrante owed his victory not to human skill or armed force, but solely to the will of God, who intervened to disperse the king's enemies.[106] About the same time, Panormita affirmed to Giovanni Pontano that human design, skill, and industry had exactly no effect on the fate of kingdoms, but rather that God governed the affairs of men and directed them in such a way as no one could predict.[107]

During the course of his own life at Naples, Pontano witnessed a great deal more turbulence than did his older friend, Panormita. The second barons' revolt and the tumultuous 1490s in particular impressed upon him the fundamental instability of Italian politics in the late Quattrocento. Not surprisingly, then, Pontano too invoked the category of fortune in his discussions of contemporary politics and history. On 17 January 1494, for example, he composed a remarkable set of instructions for the Neapolitan ambassador in Rome, ordering him to talk with Pope Alexander VI and seek to detach him from his alliance with Ludovico il Moro and the French. Among the numerous arguments that Pontano advanced to justify this advice, he included the point "that fortune brings about strange and various things, and it has happened very often in wars that those who began them were made the losers." As vicar of God, the pope should not subject himself to the risks of war, since those who initiated hostilities could not confidently hope to control their course.[108] Just over one year after Pontano composed this document, King Charles VIII departed Rome and made his way toward Naples. In a memorial of 9 February 1495 to the young King Ferrandino, Pontano explained the current situation as the work of the heavens. Like a river swelled beyond its banks

---

[106] *Regis Ferdinandi et aliorum epistolae*, pp. 384–85.

[107] Ibid., pp. 389–90. The letter also appears in Percopo, "Lettere di Giovanni Pontano," pp. 67–68.

[108] Trinchera, ed., *Codice aragonese*, 2.2.421–31, esp. 423–24.

that carries away everything in its path, the heavens order things to their liking when they find little resistance. The death of Ferrante and the unpopularity of Alfonso II rendered a weakened kingdom of Naples vulnerable to violent fluctuations brought on by celestial movements. [109]

Despite some similarities to the ad hoc reflections of Panormita, Pontano's thought on fortune differed in two important ways from that of his older friend. In the first place, Pontano could not accept the facile identification of fortune with the will of God: his experience with political and diplomatic disappointments forced him to think about fortune in a more sophisticated and systematic way than Panormita. In fact, he addressed the subject directly in one of his last formal compositions, the treatise *De fortuna* (1501). In this work, Pontano experienced more difficulty in defining and delimiting his subject than he had in any of his other treatises. He characterized fortune as a causal agent—a force that produced effects in the world—but he did not account very well for its origin. In the early pages of his treatise, he followed Aristotle in some basic observations: since it was neither good, ordered, intelligible, nor rational, fortune could not be the work of God, nature, intellect, or reason. Later in his work, however, Pontano clearly conceived of fortune as a kind of irrational but natural force. Finally, in the third book of his treatise, he made fortune a kind of subsidiary force to the power of fate. Essentially stellar influence working through the medium of air, fate ordered all earthly developments except those controlled by the human will. Moreover, Pontano placed celestial influence under the governance of God, so that fortune would seem to possess a providential as well as a natural character. [110]

---

[109] Erasmo Percopo, "Lettere di Giovanni Pontano a principi ed amici," *AAP*, 37 (1907), pp. 56–58.

[110] Pontano, *De fortuna*, in his *Opera omnia*, vol. 1, esp. fols. 264r–69v, 286r–87v, 299r–309v. On the moral dimension of Pontano's astrological thought, especially as represented in his *De rebus coelestibus*, see the excellent discussions in Francesco Tateo, *Astrologia e moralità in Giovanni Pontano* (Bari, 1960), pp. 28–

Whatever its precise origin, fortune exhibited certain traits and worked certain effects that Pontano outlined with reasonable clarity. The outstanding characteristic of fortune was its absolute inconstancy: irrational, immoderate, and indiscriminate, fortune was a transcendentally and quintessentially capricious force. As such, it produced effects that no one could predict in advance, but on the basis of hindsight and reflection, Pontano discerned patterns in the workings of fortune. He placed special emphasis on the role played by the "fortunate man" (*homo fortunatus*), the mortal upon whom fortune smiled, while using him as human agent through whom she worked her effects. Though eminently successful, the fortunate man owed his wealth or power not to his own virtue or honest endeavor, but rather to fortune herself. Moved by impulse or whim rather than reason or wise counsel, the fortunate man generally possessed a crude intellect and rude nature. He thus was a natural tool for fortune to use in her efforts to influence human affairs. Fortune drove or impelled her unwitting accomplice to success, leading him to victory in battles, wealth in commerce, fame for his writings, power in politics, or influence in the church. The actions of the fortunate man might produce either good or bad results for the broader society; the important consideration for Pontano was that his actions sprang not from reason or prudence, but rather from caprice.[111]

Pontano's thought on fortune differed from that of Panormita also in a second fundamental way. In identifying fortune with the will of God, Panormita portrayed it as a force against which men could strive only in vain. Pontano, however, viewed fortune as an influence that held sway only in the absence of reason and will, so that men with certain qualities could avoid, or at least minimize its effects. Thus from an early stage in his career until his last years, Pontano sought remedies for fortune, both on the theoreti-

---

35; and Charles Trinkaus, "The Astrological Cosmos and Rhetorical Culture of Giovanni Gioviano Pontano," *Renaissance Quarterly*, 38 (1985), 446–72.

[111] On the traits and effects of fortune, see Pontano's *De fortuna*, in his *Opera omnia*, vol. 1, esp. fols. 277r–84v, 292r–96r.

cal and on the practical level. In a way, the treatise *De principe* (1468) represents an effort to thwart fortune, since a prince who possessed the intellectual and moral qualities advocated there would prove difficult for fortune to control. More to the point, in the treatise *De obedientia* (1470), Pontano argued for disciplined obedience to king, country, or military commander. He did not refer specifically to the effects of adverse fortune in this work, but clearly had them in mind. Thus when one's homeland faced ruin, Pontano approved the adoption of policies that failed to meet rigorous moral standards: under extreme circumstances, he said, abuse of law and transgression of moral norms qualify as distasteful but necessary tactics. In general, for example, Pontano considered lies a kind of vicious, despicable fraudulence. Yet when a spokesman lied on behalf of an endangered king or country, Pontano called him not a liar, but a prudent man who knew how to balance the demands of necessity and morality.[112] In his treatise on courage, *De fortitudine* (1481), Pontano acknowledged the point that fortune often favors the rash, overconfident man, and he even conceded that audacity had certain valuable military uses. Nevertheless, he recommended the more moderate and sensible quality of courage—defined as a mean between the extremes of timidity and temerity—as more appropriate to the successful commander.[113]

Pontano not only thought about these issues in the abstract, but also urged application of his principles in actual cases. During the War of Ferrara, while serving as secretary to Duke Alfonso of Calabria, Pontano consoled the duke on the loss of an opportunity to defeat his opponent, the Venetian condottiere Roberto Sanseverino: despite the uncertainties and suspicions that always develop in war, Pontano said, reason and prudence must inevitably pre-

[112] Pontano, *De obedientia*, in his *Opera omnia*, vol. 1, esp. fols. 5r, 19rv, 35v–37r, 45r–48v. On this point, see also Charles Trinkaus, "The Question of Truth in Renaissance Rhetoric and Anthropology," in his collected essays, *The Scope of Renaissance Humanism*, pp. 437–49.

[113] Pontano, *De fortitudine*, in his *Opera omnia*, vol. 1, esp. fols. 51r–53r, 62v, 64r.

vail.[114] The vagaries of the 1490s provided Pontano with abundant opportunity to think about fortune and respond to its challenge. Thus in October 1493 Pontano addressed to Ferrante his striking memorial emphasizing the dangers that increasing diplomatic isolation brought for the kingdom of Naples. Toward the end of his long analysis, Pontano warned Ferrante to take immediate and effective action. He could not afford to employ his tactic of delay, since all Italy had designs on his realm; nor could he trust in God, who aided only those who helped themselves. Least of all could he rely on fortune, the habitual deceiver: for one thing, men have free will and can presumably benefit themselves better than fortune would do; but furthermore, of one hundred men upon whom fortune smiles (*uomini fortunati*), more than ninety come to a miserable end.[115] Sixteen months later, as the French army marched on Naples, Pontano urged a policy of prudent resistance on the new King Ferrandino. The heavens had taken advantage of Neapolitan weakness to propel Charles VIII—a "fortunate man" par excellence[116]—down the Italian peninsula. Ferrandino had no choice but to fight, but Pontano urged him to do so wisely. He must not tempt fortune or rush into a forced battle, but rather act with prudence and industry. The French, after all, had to deal with numerous problems, including poor morale and ignorance of the terrain, quite apart from their congenital impetuosity and disorganization. By relying on cleverness, caution, observation, and strategem, Ferrandino could maneuver the French into a disadvantageous situation, then bring the sword down upon them.[117] This

---

[114] Erasmo Percopo, "Nuove lettere di Gioviano Pontano a principi ed amici," in *In onore di Giovanni Gioviano Pontano nel V centenario della sua nascita* (Naples, 1926), pp. 122–23. For the background to this letter—high hopes on the part of Duke Alfonso and his allies that they would soon crush Sanseverino, followed by the condottiere's extrication of his forces from difficulty—see *Lettere inedite di Joviano Pontano in nome de' reali di Napoli*, ed. F. Gabotto (Bologna, 1893), pp. 135–44, 173–74.

[115] Percopo, "Lettere di Giovanni Pontano," esp. pp. 50–51.

[116] On this point, see Santoro, *Fortuna, ragione e prudenza*, pp. 44–45.

[117] Percopo, "Lettere di Giovanni Pontano," pp. 56–58.

memorial thus amounts to a lesson in the means by which Ferrandino could counteract the effects of adverse fortune in 1495.

After his retirement from politics, Pontano devoted more mature and systematic reflection to issues of this sort than he had ever done before, even in his works on obedience and courage. In his long treatise *De prudentia* (1499) he offered his most comprehensive discussion of the various qualities required for successful administration. Pontano considered prudence the queen of all the moral virtues because it best enabled men to live well in society, according to the Aristotelian ideal. Pontano recognized as "happy" (*felix*) only the man who loved civil society, lived in accordance with reason and virtue, and led a life of honest activity. Prudence made it possible to realize this ideal.[118] Thus in Pontano's view prudence was a supremely political virtue, one especially appropriate for administrators of public affairs. This point becomes especially clear in one section of his treatise where Pontano provided a catalog of various qualities that a man of true prudence possessed. The most important of these constituent qualities included the following: *consideratio*, the habit of reflecting diligently on affairs and of mastering all important detail; *providentia*, the ability to look ahead in order to avoid danger and win advantage; *perspicacitas*, the talent of discerning the hidden patterns of things; *versatilitas*, the flexibility to adapt to changing times and situations; *versutia*, the readiness to employ cunning and deception when required; *simulatio* and *dissimulatio*, the willingness even to misrepresent the truth through sham, hypocrisy, or lies when the variety and inconstancy of human affairs left no attractive alternative; *aestimatio*, the ability to exercise good judgment in appraising the times; *industria*, the capacity to work tirelessly and diligently at one's task; and *vigilantia*, the habit of careful, alert observation.[119]

[118] Pontano, *De prudentia*, in his *Opera omnia*, vol. 1, esp. fols. 149r, 150r, 153v, 157v, 171r, 209r. For excellent discussions of this treatise, see Mario Santoro, "Il Pontano e l'ideale rinascimentale del 'prudente,' " *Giornale italiano di filologia*, 17 (1964), 29–54; and his *Fortuna, ragione e prudenza*, pp. 27–69.

[119] Pontano, *De prudentia*, in his *Opera omnia*, vol. 1, esp. fols. 197r–207v.

The prudent administrator, then, possessed qualities that enabled him to respond effectively to whatever challenges the mutable, inconstant political world posed. Pontano's recognition of this need to respond leads once again to the theme of political realism. It hardly seems surprising that shortly after composing his treatise on *The Prince*, Niccolò Machiavelli—himself a close student of political mutations—discussed Pontano's views on fortune in correspondence with his friend, Francesco Vettori.[120] Indeed, in the light of their closely related patterns of thought, the surprising thing is that Machiavelli did not cite the treatises in which Pontano openly reconsidered western political ethics.[121]

Considering his times, Pontano had little alternative but to frame a morally flexible political ethic. He inhabited a world afflicted by extraordinary mutations, in which political principles derived from abstract moral or religious doctrine could lead only to ruin. Political survival in the late Quattrocento depended upon the implementation of effective, though sometimes morally ambiguous policy. Perhaps the most difficult but also most important of all Giovanni Pontano's tasks was his effort in *De prudentia* to bring into balance the varied imperatives of classical values, Christian norms, and contemporary experience.

[120] See Vettori's letter of 15 December 1514 and Machiavelli's reply dated five days later, in Niccolò Machiavelli, *Opere*, ed. S. Bertelli, 11 vols. (Milan and Verona, 1968–82), 5.354, 360.

[121] On parallels between Pontano and Machiavelli, see Rodolfo de Mattei, *Dal premachiavellismo all'antimachiavellismo* (Florence, 1969), pp. 3–24; and Allan Gilbert, *Machiavelli's "Prince" and Its Forerunners*, pp. 6, 11, 58–59, 84–85, 126–27, 170–71, 216–19, 236.

6

The Domestication of Humanism
in the Mezzogiorno

ALFONSO the Magnanimous actively recruited humanists and other cultural figures from abroad and brought them to Naples on generous terms. All five of the major humanists studied in this book—Panormita, Valla, Facio, Manetti, and Pontano—went to the Neapolitan court at Alfonso's call. The influence of these five and other humanists who worked in Naples made it possible for Ferrante to rely largely on natives of the Mezzogiorno for intellectual talent. He occasionally engaged the services of humanists from central Italy—Francesco Pucci and the Brandolini brothers, all natives of Florence, were the most important cases in point—and he sought diligently to recruit skilled musicians both from other Italian regions and from lands beyond the Alps. By the late fifteenth century, however, most of the humanists active in Naples were born and bred in the Regno: Giovanni Brancati, Giovanni Albino, Giuniano Maio, Gabriele Altilio, and Elisio Calenzio were all natives of the kingdom of Naples, and by 1471, Giovanni Pontano himself had taken Neapolitan citizenship and adopted the southern kingdom as his permanent home. This point illustrates one aspect of a general process by which humanism took root in the kingdom of Naples and developed along peculiar lines, according to the distinctive Neapolitan environment—a process that Mario Santoro has called the "Neapolitanization" of humanism in its southern manifestation.[1]

[1] Mario Santoro, "La cultura umanistica," in *Storia di Napoli*, 10 vols. (Naples, 1975–81), 7.117–27, 205–42.

All the Neapolitans studied in this book reflected the general interests common to Renaissance humanists—love of classical literature, cultivation of eloquence, concern with ethical and political questions, and the like. Already during the late fifteenth century, humanists like Pontano, Brancati, and Albino had energetically occupied themselves with the management and solution of local problems. During the early sixteenth century, the political difficulties and unpredictable future of the Regno encouraged a younger generation of thoughtful men to devote their efforts in an even more serious and fundamental way to public issues. As a result, Neapolitan humanism increasingly reflected political and social conditions in the kingdom of Naples. This chapter will examine briefly the political and moral thought of five men, all natives of the city or kingdom of Naples, who best illustrate how individuals of broad literary and humanist interests responded to the challenges of the early sixteenth century. The five include Pietro Jacopo de Jennaro, Andrea Matteo Acquaviva, his brother Belisario, Antonio de Ferrariis, and Tristano Caracciolo. The five men had vastly different educational experiences and political orientations, but each illustrates some aspect of the general effort to adapt the humanist culture developed originally in central and northern Italy to the political and intellectual environment of the Mezzogiorno. The following analysis will emphasize two concerns that figure especially prominently in their works. In the first place, during the unsettled days of the early sixteenth century, these humanists exhibited a fresh interest in constitutional questions, which their Quattrocento predecessors had almost entirely ignored. In the second place, having witnessed the collapse of the Aragonese dynasty of Naples and the contest between French and Spanish armies for Italian hegemony, the sixteenth-century humanists devoted a great deal of attention to the theme of fortune and her effects in the world.

In the final analysis, however, humanism failed to establish itself firmly in the kingdom of Naples. The Spanish viceregal regime exercised effective control over Neapolitan culture as well as politics, and by suppression or cooptation it eliminated all but a kind of narrow, academic humanism from the Mezzogiorno. The last section in this chapter, then, will discuss the developments that prevented humanism from consolidating itself as a permanent feature of Neapolitan society and culture.

Pietro Jacopo de Jennaro and the Constitution of the City of Naples

Neapolitan humanists of the fifteenth century paid no attention to constitutional questions, as the previous chapter argued, because they saw no realistic alternative to monarchy during the period of the Aragonese dynasty. But the French invasions of 1495 and 1501, the Spanish intervention of 1501, and the subsequent struggle between the two foreign powers brought about the disintegration of the dynasty. By late 1503 Gonsalvo de Córdoba had laid the foundations for a viceregal administration of the Regno, but no one could have foreseen then that Spanish viceroys would rule Naples well into the eighteenth century. It was only natural for humanists interested in politics to think about ways to improve the Neapolitan constitution during the early years of the sixteenth century.

The thought of Pietro Jacopo de Jennaro (1436–1508) illustrates the sort of intellectual experimentation that occurred in the period immediately following the fall of the Aragonese dynasty of Naples. Though best known as a poet who imitated the style of Dante and Petrarch, de Jennaro held numerous administrative posts in the Mezzogiorno during the late fifteenth century.[2] Born into a well-known noble family in Naples, he served Ferrante, Alfonso II, Ferrandino, and Federico as royal commissioner and fi-

---

[2] For the best account of his life, see the introduction to Pietro Jacopo de Jennaro, *Rime e lettere*, ed. M. Corti (Bologna, 1956), esp. pp. ii–xvi. See also Antonio Altamura, *L'umanesimo nel Mezzogiorno d'Italia* (Florence, 1941), pp. 77–83, 170–71; and Tommaso Persico, *Gli scrittori politici napoletani dal '400 al '700* (Naples, 1912), pp. 127–39.

nancial administrator in several provinces of Apulia, Calabria, and Basilicata. Among other activities, he served for some years as royal commissioner in Lecce (near Otranto in Apulia). In 1479 he directed a committee of ten men who reformed the government of Lecce in such a way as to undermine the power and influence of the feudal nobility. In order to qualify for government office, an individual had to reside in Lecce or hold property there; his wealth as reflected in *catasto* records then determined the kind of post the individual could occupy. The system provided for a large degree of popular influence: half of the twenty-four seats on the governing council went to men chosen from the wealthy urban classes, the other half to artisans. Meanwhile, the effective exclusion of feudal interests from local influence at Lecce resulted in tensions that persisted until the last days of the Aragonese dynasty.[3]

De Jennaro took great pride in his work at Lecce—a point he made clear in a treatise of 1504 entitled *Third Book on the Government of Men*. If de Jennaro in fact composed two previous books on his theme, they do not seem to have survived.[4] In any case, this third book he dedicated to Luis Sanz, treasurer-general of King Ferdinand of Spain, because of his concern for wise rule. In most of his treatise, de Jennaro presented a quite unexceptional endorsement of traditional political ethics and values, which he illustrated by examples drawn from ancient Roman history. Thus he argued that justice and civic harmony depended upon the love and veneration of God, as the career of Lucius Aemilius demonstrated; also that elders should instruct the young in political wisdom even as younger men respected their seniors, a point de Jennaro illuminated by the action of Marcus Fabius, who appointed responsible

[3] On de Jennaro's work at Lecce, see Pietro Palumbo, *Storia di Lecce* (Lecce, 1977), pp. 119–20. (Palumbo misidentifies de Jennaro, however, as "Gian Giacomo di Gennaro.") Some chronicles refer to de Jennaro's presence in Lecce as early as 1462: see G. B. Cantarelli, *Monografia storica della città di Lecce* (Lecce, 1885), p. 120.

[4] The only other surviving political work of de Jennaro is a summary and compendium of Egidio Romano's *De regimine principum*: cf. Corti's introduction to de Jennaro's *Rime e lettere*, p. xi.

young men to the Senate when war had decimated the ranks of
those with more experience. Occasionally de Jennaro geared his
ethical and historical commentary to issues of contemporary interest. After discussing Lucius Valerius' opposition to the *Lex Appia*
(a sumptuary law), for example, de Jennaro argued the usefulness
of a moderate law governing consumption in sixteenth-century
Naples, complaining bitterly about the lascivious and pretentious
dress affected by some inhabitants of the city, but also about the
uncontrolled sale of cheaply produced fabrics that encouraged poor
families to spend such sums of money on shoddy materials that
they could not supply themselves with food.[5]

In fact, de Jennaro registered several complaints about the current administration of the city of Naples. He identified the worst
abuses as the lack of supervision over merchants and their wares,
corrupt expenditures of alms funds, and fraudulent granting of gabelle contracts. The fundamental reason for these abuses he traced
to a pattern of office holding that he thought encouraged corruption. Each of the five noble districts, or *Seggi*, had either five or six
local representatives; known collectively as the Five and the Six,
these men selected six *Eletti* to serve as a board of governors for the
entire city. De Jennaro noted, however, that members of the Five
and the Six often conspired to have themselves named also to the
board of the *Eletti*. Then they ignored their local responsibilities
and used their amplified power to benefit themselves and their
clients. Since no official possessed both the power and the desire to
prevent corruption, the city and its inhabitants suffered the pre-
dictable effects of bad government, to wit, the abuses mentioned
above.[6]

De Jennaro modeled his plan for reform on his earlier work at
Lecce. Good government, he argued, depended upon the partici-

[5] De Jennaro's *Libro terczo de regimento dell'opera deli homini* survives in Palermo
as MS I. C. 17 of the Biblioteca Centrale della Regione Siciliana (formerly the
Biblioteca Nazionale di Palermo). For the passages referred to here, see esp. fols.
7r–10r, 23r–25v, 26r–34r.

[6] Ibid., fols. 18v–20v, 44v–48r.

pation of many good men elevated to office without respect to family, business, age, or social position. Thus, properly elected leaders of the Roman republic carried out their duties honestly and sought only to serve the general good, while dictators often abused their office and outraged Roman citizens by their lack of public morality. As a replacement for the current system, which enabled influential individuals to manipulate affairs in their own interests, de Jennaro advocated the selection of public officials by sortition. Wise elderly men would carefully consider the nature of public offices and the character of all Neapolitan citizens. They would draw up a secret list of all men suitable for each office. Taking no account of age, status, or trade, they would then introduce all the qualified names into sacks carefully sealed, locked, and guarded against tampering. On election days a child would draw names from the sacks in the presence of the city's elders and judges. Officials then would owe their positions not to personal influence and corrupt agreements, but rather to an honest and disinterested process. As arguments for the feasibility of his plan, de Jennaro cited the experience of other, unnamed cities that functioned smoothly under such a system; the precepts of Plato, Aristotle, St. Thomas, and Egidio Romano, whom he evidently read creatively; and most importantly his own experience in Lecce, where he had introduced a similar system that had eliminated bad government and won widespread popular approval.[7]

De Jennaro had no intention of introducing a republican constitution into the city or kingdom of Naples. He always located sovereignty in the monarchy and recognized the value of nobles as public leaders because of their learning, wisdom, and courage. He pointed out that caps go on the head, gloves on the hands, and shoes on the feet; popular rule he thought resembled the placing of caps on the feet, a silly practice that would lead to ruin for the entire commonwealth. De Jennaro in fact urged adoption of his

[7] Ibid., fols. 20v–21r, and esp. fols. 34r–42r.

new electoral procedures partly because of the honor it would bring to the prince: a well-ordered capital city would earn him a thousand years of praise from grateful citizens, whereas continued bad government would bring injustice and violence, tyranny and poverty, dissatisfaction and rebellion, among other unpleasant things.[8]

Yet de Jennaro's political advice illustrates the point that Neapolitan humanists of the early sixteenth century recognized a new obligation to address constitutional issues. Writing in 1504, after having witnessed nine tumultuous years of invasion, conquest, restoration, treachery, and radical uncertainty, de Jennaro properly insisted on the return of order and stability in Neapolitan affairs. Though unsystematic and incomplete, his treatise demonstrates at least two points. In the first place, de Jennaro not only railed against public abuse, but also reflected on the historical and institutional causes of corruption: years of disorder following the French invasion enabled unsupervised city officials to ignore the common welfare and organize affairs to the benefit of themselves and their clients. Thus at the very beginning of the new century, de Jennaro's thought reflected the same kinds of concerns that later moved Machiavelli, Guicciardini, and their compatriots to debate questions of constitution and good governance in the case of Florence. In the second place, in seeking solutions to the problems he identified, de Jennaro relied on the traditional humanist technique of bringing classical wisdom to bear on contemporary affairs: the experience of the Roman republic held some lessons for the administration of the city of Naples, even as Spanish viceroys attempted to establish a new political order throughout the Regno. Thus humanism held political implications not only for central and northern Italy, but could suggest solutions to the practical problems also of the Mezzogiorno.

[8] Ibid., fols. 12r–13v, 32rv, 34r–42r.

The Acquaviva Brothers and Feudal Humanism

Giulio Antonio Acquaviva stood out during the later fifteenth century as one of the most ferocious Neapolitan warriors, also as one of the most loyal to the Aragonese dynasty of Naples. For his efforts, King Ferrante granted him the right to call himself "Acquaviva di Aragona" and to attach the Aragonese royal seal to his own coat of arms. Though untimely, his death contributed significantly to the fame of his house: while serving with Duke Alfonso at the siege of Otranto in 1481, he led a small squadron into a daring attack on a Turkish raiding party; the enemy rushed reinforcements to the site; Acquaviva found himself confronted with a vastly larger force but refused to flee; Turkish cavalry surrounded and overpowered him, killed him, and took his head as a trophy.

Giulio Antonio Acquaviva himself provided the military education for his sons, Andrea Matteo (1458–1529) and Belisario (1464–1528), and it was only natural that like other Neapolitan barons of the late fifteenth century, they seriously pursued their military and political careers. Andrea Matteo fought with Duke Alfonso against the Turks at Otranto and against the Venetians at Gallipoli. He sided with the rebellious barons against Ferrante, for which he suffered loss of his titles; but later he received a pardon, regained his estates, and won the honorary office of grand seneschal. Ferrante's antifeudal policies put him again at odds with the monarchy, and in 1495 Andrea Matteo fought with Charles VIII against Ferrandino. He again lost his fiefs after the restoration of Aragonese rule, but regained them after the general amnesty promulgated by Federico in 1496. He fought for Federico in 1497 and 1498, but took the side of Louis XII after the joint French and Spanish invasion of 1501. He fell captive with seventeen wounds in 1503 and spent the next two years in the dungeon of the Castelnuovo. He won his freedom as the viceroys began to consolidate the Spanish grip on the Regno, and King Ferdinand of Spain himself saw to it that Andrea Matteo once again regained his dignities and possessions. Thereafter, however, he occupied himself only sporadically with politics, and he never challenged the new regime of the viceroys. Belisario Acquaviva pursued a much less complicated career than his brother. He supported the Aragonese dynasty of Naples against all of its enemies until its extinction, then sided with Gonsalvo de Córdoba against the French. His frequent military and political services won him a series of honors, most notably as count, then marquis, and finally as duke of Nardò, a small town deep in Apulia. He retired from politics in 1507 when Ferdinand suspected Gonsalvo's motives and recalled him to Spain.[9]

The Acquaviva brothers thus found abundant uses for the military and political education they received from their father. Unlike most barons of their time, however, the Acquaviva brothers had a formal literary education as well as instruction in practical affairs. Each had studied with Pontano and frequented the academy in Naples, and upon retirement from the active political life, each devoted his efforts to letters and scholarship. Andrea Matteo collected books and produced an edition and translation of Plutarch's treatise *On Moral Virtue*, which he equipped also with an erudite commentary. Perhaps more importantly, he helped the Neapolitan press to reestablish itself after the disruption caused by the decade of war and turmoil around the turn of the century. Thus he opened his own house to Antonio de Frizis, who published editions of Pontano and the poet Sannazaro, as well as Andrea Matteo's work on Plutarch.[10] Meanwhile, Belisario returned to his fief at Nardò and organized an Academy of the Laurel, where learned men of the area discussed letters and poetry.[11] Belisario's

[9] On the lives and careers of the Acquaviva brothers, see V. Bindi, *Gli Acquaviva letterati* (Naples, 1881), esp. pp. 6–124; and two short accounts in the *DBI*, 1.185–90.

[10] See the brilliant essay centering on Andrea Matteo as patron of the press and feudal humanist by Francesco Tateo, "Feudatari e umanisti nell'impresa tipografica," in his *Chierici e feudatari del Mezzogiorno* (Bari, 1984), pp. 69–96. See Pietro Manzi, *La tipografia napoletana nel '500*, 6 vols. (Florence, 1971–75), on the reestablishment of the Neapolitan press in the early sixteenth century (1.9–105) and on the work of Antonio de Frizis (1.167–220).

[11] On Belisario's Accademia del Lauro, see Michele Maylender, *Storia delle ac-*

own works included treatises on the education of princes' children, on military affairs, and on hunting and hawking, as well as a paraphrase of the pseudo-Aristotelian *Economics* and an exposition of the Lord's Prayer.

Both of the Acquaviva brothers exhibited the influence of humanism. They enjoyed an impressive command of classical literature and thought, and they took care to express themselves in an elegant Latin style. Yet neither of them displayed much interest in the values associated with the urban humanists of central and northern Italy—republican political ideals, nobility as a function of character rather than genealogy, the worthiness and usefulness of wealth, and the like. Instead, both of them deployed their humanist talents in such a way as to justify the values and interests of a feudal nobility.

Andrea Matteo Acquaviva enjoyed a solid grounding in Greek, as opposed to his brother, who possessed only the rudiments of the language, and his work on Plutarch afforded him ample occasion to display his knowledge of classical thought, both Greek and Latin. In his long commentary (138 folios), Andrea Matteo basically created an intellectual context for Plutarch's treatise by comparing his thought on various points with that of classical, Byzantine, and medieval western philosophers. This is particularly true for the first two books of his commentary, which dealt with metaphysics and natural philosophy. In the last two books he addressed moral and ethical questions and occasionally developed arguments reflecting the feudal values that had guided his life and career. Like Pontano, he took an Aristotelian approach to moral virtue, defining it generally as a golden mean between two extreme qualities. Thus, again like Pontano, he portrayed courage as the sensible middle way between timidity and audacity: those who fought out of fear or lust he did not consider courageous, since passion rather than reason motivated their actions. Unlike Pon-

---

cademie d'Italia, 5 vols. (Bologna, 1926–30), 3.403–4; and C. Minieri Riccio, *Notizia delle accademie istituite nelle provincie napoletane* (Naples, 1878), pp. 49–50.

tano, however, Andrea Matteo volunteered the opinion that those who fought valiantly in the face of certain peril on the battle-field—his father's example could not have been far from his mind—merited recognition as genuinely courageous men. The values of a feudal nobility influenced also Andrea Matteo's under-standing of justice. He affirmed that justice originally was tanta-mount to the royal will, insofar as it led to equity and fairness. Gradually, however, kings became tyrants who ruled through fear; contemporary princes, then, required the advice of lawyers, lest they lapse into unjust rule. But lawyers alone could not pre-vent unjust behavior: no matter how well they knew their laws and their books, Andrea Matteo said, they lacked practical experience leading men. Thus in order to rule justly, princes must consult with other prudent and wise men experienced in the business of meting out rewards and punishments.[12] Once again, Andrea Mat-teo's commentary clearly reflected the interests of the independent baronage of Renaissance Naples.

Though less learned and scholarly than his brother, Belisario Acquaviva developed his thought in more independent form. He cast only one of his four works in the form of a commentary—his explanation of the Lord's Prayer, not discussed here because it does not address political themes.[13] In another work Belisario offered a loose paraphrase of the pseudo-Aristotelian *Economics*, but couched it in such a way that he could emphasize points that particularly interested him while also displaying his knowledge of classical thought at relevant points. Belisario developed his ideas even more clearly in his treatises—*On Educating the Children of Princes*, *On Military Affairs and Individual Combat*, and *On Hunting and*

---

[12] See Plutarch's *De virtute morali*, ed. and trans. A. M. Acquaviva (Naples, 1526), published together with Andrea Matteo Acquaviva, *Commentarium in translationem libelli Plutarchi Chaeronei De virtute morali* (Naples, 1526). For the passages referred to here, see esp. fols. xcvii r–xcviii v, ci r–civ v. Cf. to Pontano's *De fortitudine*, in his *Opera omnia soluta oratione composita*, 3 vols. (Venice, 1518–19), vol. 1, esp. fols. 50v–53r, 62v–64r. The best discussion of Andrea Matteo's work is that of Tateo, *Chierici e feudatari*, pp. 79–91.

[13] Belisario's *Expositio orationis dominicae* survives in BNN, MS XVIII. 40.

Hawking—which afforded him a degree of flexibility that neither a commentary nor a paraphrase provided.[14] Thus Belisario's treatises will strike most historians as more interesting than his brother's erudite commentary, since they express more clearly and directly the values of feudal humanism.

Like his brother, Belisario provided abundant evidence in his works that humanism had deeply influenced both his general approach to literature and scholarship and his understanding of specific issues. He liberally studded his paraphrase of the pseudo-Aristotle and his treatise on education—and to a lesser extent also that on military affairs—with quotations and allusions to classical Greek and Latin literature. In outlining the qualities befitting a prince, Belisario reflected the *speculum principis* literature of the later Quattrocento: he emphasized the importance of traditionally recognized virtues like justice, prudence, liberality, temperance, courage, and clemency; he argued that princes must keep their faith and rule by means of love rather than fear; and he devoted considerable attention to the prince's bearing, speech, and dress in a discussion that closely resembled the advice of Pontano and Maio on princely majesty.[15]

Thus Andrea Matteo and Belisario both studied classical languages and literature, and they familiarized themselves with the issues and themes that most interested the Renaissance humanists in general. Their discussions of fortune help to define a bit more precisely the degree to which the Acquaviva brothers endorsed the views characteristic of Renaissance humanism. To some extent, both men adopted the somewhat pessimistic view of Pontano and other humanists of the late fifteenth century who saw fortune as a force that placed limits around human abilities, or that at least presented man with an awesome challenge to his will and talent.

[14] Belisario Acquaviva, *Paraphrasis in economica Aristotelis* (Naples, 1519); *De instituendis liberis principum* (Naples, 1519); *De re militari et singulari certamine* (Naples, 1519); and *De venatione et de aucupio* (Naples, 1519).

[15] For Belisario's understanding of the ideal prince, see his *De instituendis liberis principum*, esp. fols. IXr–XIIIv.

Andrea Matteo represented quite well the views of both men when he spoke of human free will as an agent of limited influence in a world governed largely by providence, fate, and chance.

Yet the theme of fortune also helps to show where the thought of the two brothers, particularly Belisario, diverged from that of the other Neapolitan humanists. Andrea Matteo, whose political and military experience no doubt encouraged him to reflect earnestly on fortune, affirmed that all the skill in the world would not enable a pilot to bring his ship safely to harbor without the aid of favorable winds. Likewise, men who administer public affairs require not only prudence, but also aid from fortune in order to govern successfully. Belisario addressed the theme of fortune in a specifically military context, when discussing the proper attitude for a military commander to display after victory or defeat. Fortune plays such a large role in determining the outcome of battles and wars, he said, that the wise commander will always maintain his composure. Defeat will naturally produce sadness, but does not mean inevitable ruin. The commander must not despair, because the vagaries of fortune ensure that all men experience victory as well as defeat. Meanwhile, the victorious commander must avoid excessive elation, and he certainly must treat his vanquished enemies with mercy and clemency. Belisario evidently considered harsh treatment of the defeated a temptation of fortune, who might then prepare more bitter experiences for a commander who took his success too seriously.[16] Thus, neither Andrea Matteo nor Belisario accepted Panormita's identification of fortune with the will of God, nor did they undertake a sophisticated moral, philosophical, and scientific analysis such as that Pontano devoted to fortune. Their discussions reflected instead the political and military experience of a feudal aristocracy.

Of the two brothers, Belisario best illuminated the convergence of feudalism and humanism. His treatise on military affairs stands

[16] See Andrea Matteo's *Commentarium*, fols. LXXXVIIIr–XCIv; and Belisario's *De re militari*, fols. VIv–VIIv.

265

out as the work that most completely blends Belisario's experience as a baron and feudal warrior with his cultural interests as a humanist and man of letters. Alongside technical discussions of such practical matters as the selection of campsites, organization of battle lines, and the direction of troops in combat, Belisario discoursed also on the qualities of the ideal commander and his comportment when directing an army. He transferred to the commander many of the qualities traditionally associated with the ideal prince—courage, temperance, magnanimity, and the like. Perhaps the most important one was prudence, the ability to think clearly about alternatives and to act according to wise deliberation. A prudent commander would behave in such a way, for example, that internal dissension did not afflict his forces, whether because of contempt, fear, jealousy, or pride, for his prudent leadership would prevent the development of such destructive emotions. Belisario placed special emphasis on the need to reward soldiers with regular stipends, lest men in the ranks develop doubts that might compromise their loyalty and willingness to fight. But the ideal commander also needed literary skills, in Belisario's opinion: the sounds of clashing arms and trumpets motivated men to some extent, but he considered nothing more effective than a stirring oration by the commander when the time came to inspire men and send them into battle.[17]

Belisario blended humanist, feudal, and military values also in other works. He put his literary talents to use in discussing the noble sports of hunting and hawking, also in outlining the law and etiquette governing behavior in personal feuds and duels.[18] More important, he included an education in letters as part of the preparation he considered necessary for men with public responsibilities. In the treatise *On Educating the Children of Princes*, Belisario advocated a curriculum that included hunting, horsemanship, art, and letters—but not music, which he thought had an

[17] See Belisario's *De re militari*, esp. fols. IIr–IIIr, IVrv, VIv–VIIv.
[18] See Belisario's *De venatione*, and the second book of his *De re militari et singulari certamine*, fols. IXr–XXr.

unfortunate, feminizing effect on young boys. He advised a set of studies, in short, that would encourage future princes to develop those qualities and skills that would enable them to exercise wise and successful rule over their subjects, whether in cities, republics, or kingdoms. In his paraphrase of the pseudo-Aristotelian *Economics*, Belisario emphasized the importance of literary studies also for future commanders. He granted that a commander could accomplish something without a literary education, but insisted that eloquence and a knowledge of letters vastly strengthened the hand of a military leader. He argued that a commander without letters lacked the basic intellectual wherewithal (*ingenium*) required by his profession and cited Plutarch's opinion that it made no more sense to assign a command to an unlearned man than to entrust wealth to a boy.[19]

Like other humanists, then, who placed their talents in the service of republican, aristocratic, monarchical, ecclesiastical, Christian, or some other set of values, the Acquaviva brothers deployed their literary and intellectual skills in such a way as to reinforce the values and way of life that they themselves most highly esteemed.[20] They did not establish a new school of humanism, and indeed probably had no intention or desire to do so. Only a few of their fellow barons developed anything more than a passing interest in humanism—though the Acquaviva family itself produced men of letters and learning well into the seventeenth century.[21] In

[19] See Belisario's *De instituendis liberis principum*, esp. fols. IIIr–Vr, VIIv–Xr, XIrv; and his *Paraphrasis*, esp. fol. VIIr.

[20] On civic humanism in Florence and Venice, see Hans Baron, *The Crisis of the Early Italian Renaissance*, 2d ed. (Princeton, 1966); and Margaret L. King, *Venetian Humanism in an Age of Patrician Dominance* (Princeton, 1986). On humanism geared to the interests of the Neapolitan monarchy, see the previous two chapters in this study. On Roman curial humanism, see John F. D'Amico, *Renaissance Humanism in Papal Rome* (Baltimore, 1983). On Christian humanism, among other works, see John W. O'Malley, *Praise and Blame in Renaissance Rome* (Durham, N.C., 1979); Charles Trinkaus, *In Our Image and Likeness: Humanity and Divinity in Italian Humanist Thought*, 2 vols. (Chicago, 1970); and Jerry H. Bentley, *Humanists and Holy Writ: New Testament Scholarship in the Renaissance* (Princeton, 1983).

[21] Bindi, *Gli Acquaviva letterati*, pp. 124–208.

any case, by the sixteenth century, humanism in general had become so closely associated with urban values that a new competitor such as the Acquavivas' feudal humanism would have faced considerable opposition from other already well-established interests—from humanists who devoted their talents to the interests of their state, church, religious faith, or some other cause. Yet the thought of the Acquaviva brothers points in a tantalizing way toward a strain of humanism that might have developed, had the humanist movement not disappeared from the Mezzogiorno during the later fourteenth century. Turmoil during the last years of the Angevin dynasty of Naples encouraged humanists to seek support in central and northern Italy, where humanism as a movement became closely associated with urban rather than feudal values. Had humanism consolidated itself in southern Italy during its formative period, it seems inevitable that it would have found spokesmen for the sort of values promoted by the Acquaviva brothers in the early sixteenth century. Feudal humanism, then, might well have emerged as an important subsidiary of the broader humanist movement.

In any case, the Acquaviva brothers' unusual blend of humanist interests and feudal values serves to make one point very clear: by the late fifteenth and early sixteenth centuries, humanism had penetrated the kingdom of Naples to such an extent that native-born intellectuals sought explicitly to adapt the broader cultural movement to the needs and conditions of the Mezzogiorno.

Galateo and the Transition to Spanish Hegemony in Italy

The work of Antonio de Ferrariis (1444–1517)—better known as Galateo, from his Apulian birthplace, Galatone—conveys remarkably well the confusion that must have afflicted most thoughtful Neapolitans during the late fifteenth and early sixteenth centuries. Galateo did not receive a humanist education during his early studies at Galatone and Nardò, but he gained a

solid understanding of Greek science and philosophy as a result of
the Byzantine cultural influence that still exercised its hold on fifteenth-century Apulia.[22] He went to Gallipoli about 1460 in order to study medicine, and later he acquired a reputation there as
a skilled practitioner. By 1471 he had gone to Naples, where he
frequented Pontano's academy and developed close friendships
with Neapolitan humanists and poets. In 1476 he went to Ferrara
in order to take his degree in medicine; during the next two years
he became friendly with the Venetian humanist Ermolao Barbaro
the Younger and came to admire the city of Venice itself. He returned to Apulia in 1478 and practiced medicine there for about
ten years. During that period he witnessed at close hand the dis-
turbances caused by the Turkish invasion at Otranto and the Venetian seizure of Gallipoli. By 1489 he had returned to Naples. In
1490 he won appointment as court physician, a post he held until
the end of the Aragonese dynasty. He left Naples in 1496 in order
to escape his enemies and detractors—he went to Lecce, where he
participated in the cultural activities of a small academy of learned
men—but returned to the capital city at King Federico's request
in 1498. Three years later he retired definitively to Lecce, where
he spent his remaining years practicing medicine, studying, writing, and keeping the company of learned men.

Galateo devoted his attention to a wide variety of topics.[23] He

---

[22] The best biography of Galateo is that of Angelo de Fabrizio, *Antonio de Ferrariis Galateo, pensatore e moralista del Rinascimento* (Trani, 1908). Ezio Savino's
work is querulous, arrogant, and often inaccurate: *Un curioso poligrafo del '400:
Antonio de Ferrariis (Galateo)* (Bari, 1941). There is no need here to cite all items
in the voluminous body of scholarly literature dedicated to Galateo. I wish to
mention instead only a few of the best and most thoughtful studies, which include those of Mario Santoro in his *Fortuna, ragione e prudenza nella civiltà letteraria
del Cinquecento*, 2d ed. (Naples, 1978), pp. 71–101; Francesco Tateo in his *Chierici e feudatari*, pp. 3–20; Benedetto Croce, "Antonio de Ferrariis detto il Galateo," *Humanisme et Renaissance*, 4 (1937), 366–82; Lucia Miele, *Saggi galateani*
(Naples, 1982); and Charles Trinkaus, "Themes for a Renaissance Anthropology," in his collected essays, *The Scope of Renaissance Humanism* (Ann Arbor,
1983), esp. pp. 369–72.

[23] The most complete edition of Galateo's works presently available is that of

composed a treatise on gout (ca. 1496), which included one of the first descriptions of syphilis.[24] He produced a descriptive geography of Apulia in several long letters, also more general geological treatises on the earth, its elements, rivers, and the seas.[25] His religious writings included a long exposition of the Lord's Prayer and a dialogue, *The Hermit*, which explored the need for pious reform in the Roman church.[26] Meanwhile, Galateo addressed numerous moral and cultural issues in his epistles, in which he offered short essays on themes like language, hypocrisy, education, human nature, religion, and nobility. Galateo's surviving works do not represent the entire range of his thought. He himself lost an indeterminate number of works during his various peregrinations, and since the mid-sixteenth century two manuscripts of his works have disappeared. One of them preserved at least thirty epistles otherwise unknown, the other a treatise on correct and corrupt procedure in philosophy.[27] Little wonder, then, that Mario Santoro has emphasized encyclopedism as a distinctive characteristic of Galateo's thought.[28]

Two features of Galateo's thought stand out with special clarity. In the first place, Galateo established such high moral and in-

---

Salvatore Grande, ed., *Collana di opere scelte edite e inedite di scrittori di Terra d'Otranto*, 22 vols. (Lecce, 1867–75), vols. 2, 3, 4, 18, 22. Most of his epistles are more conveniently available in Galateo's *Epistole*, ed. A. Altamura (Lecce, 1959). Francesco Tateo is currently preparing a new edition of Galateo's epistles, and his work promises to establish for the first time a reliable textual foundation for research on Galateo.

[24] See Galateo's *De podagra*, in Grande, ed., *Collana*, 3.195–294.

[25] See Galateo's *Epistole salentine*, ed. M. Paone (Galatina, 1974); and his treatises in Grande, ed., *Collana*, 4.1–90, 107–14.

[26] Grande, ed., *Collana*, 4.145–238; 18.5–104; 22.1–134. Large portions of the dialogue appear more conveniently in Eugenio Garin, ed., *Prosatori latini del Quattrocento* (Milan, 1952), pp. 1064–1125.

[27] Manfred E. Welti, "Il progetto fallito di un'edizione cinquecentesca delle opere complete di Antonio de Ferrariis, detto il Galateo," *ASPN*, 3d ser. 10 (1971), 179–91.

[28] See Santoro's "Scienza e humanitas nell'opera del Galateo," *La zagaglia*, 2 (1960), no. 5, pp. 25–40; no. 6, pp. 50–63; also his "La cultura umanistica," pp. 232–37.

tellectual standards for nobles and princes that few of his contemporaries could live up to the ideal. As a result, much of Galateo's political commentary gravitated between violent criticism of contemporary political leadership and a wistful, sometimes utopian yearning for a better world. In the second place, Galateo possessed a keen sense of change, to the point that he thought of the world in a Heraclitean way as the scene of continuous fluctuation. As a result, he found occasion to reflect on fortune as perhaps the prime agent driving history from the unstable present into the unpredictable future.

Galateo composed two long epistles on nobility, the first about 1488 and the other about 1495 or 1496. In both places he argued that true nobility depended on bearing rather than breeding. Education leads men to develop wisdom and justice, both of which Galateo considered preeminently moral qualities and signs of genuine nobility of character. He scorned the Neapolitan barons in general—he would no doubt have exempted his close personal friend, Belisario Acquaviva, from this charge—as scurvy barbarians who had outdone their fellows in crime and had thus catapulted themselves into positions that enabled them to tyrannize less perfidious men. Galateo thus measured nobles against the standard of philosophers, adducing in his behalf the view of a noted ancient sage who recognized as blessed only those republics in which philosophers ruled or rulers philosophized.[29]

Galateo established even higher standards for princes, from whom he demanded attributes appropriate for deities rather than philosophers. About 1496 he addressed to King Federico a short epistle that served as letter of dedication for his treatise on gout. There he explicitly characterized monarchy as a kind of divine power (*numen*), so that in addressing a king one should speak as though to God himself. He identified lèse majesté as the most heinous of all crimes, outranking even patricide and sacrilege, since it resulted in the dissolution of society, destruction of religion,

---

[29] Galateo, *Epistole*, pp. 104–16, 267–89.

and offense to the gods. Galateo's fear of novelty and instability explain the prayer with which he closed this letter: "May the gods preserve you, o good king, for your health is ours. May the gods preserve you, for your prudence is our liberty, and your integrity is our happiness. Long may you live, and happily as well. May the gods preserve you, Federico, and your house on behalf of us all."[30] Galateo sought to impress his high sense of princely duty also on Federico's son, Ferrante, the last of the Aragonese dukes of Calabria. In a short letter written at century's end (between about 1497 and 1500), he pointed out the difference between those born to serve and those born to rule: the former must learn to please their rulers and the gods, but the latter must bear in mind the obligations placed on them by the gods, their subjects, fortune and fame, their ancestors and descendants, their friends and allies, and even their enemies. Fortune in particular demands that princes lead a divine, unblemished life, against the risk of swift and savage destruction. Duke Ferrante inherited an astonishing collection of virtues from his ancestors, and Galateo presented a catalog of the qualities associated with the ruling princes of the House of Aragon from Ferdinand of Antequera through King Federico.[31]

For a man who craved stability and distrusted change as deeply as Galateo, the first few years of the sixteenth century represented the nadir of Italian civilization. His frustration appeared most clearly in a treatise *On Education*, which took the form of a long epistle to his friend Crisostomo Colonna, tutor to Duke Ferrante of Calabria. Galateo composed this bitter work between November 1504 and October 1505—after the death of the former King Federico in Tours and after the transfer of Duke Ferrante himself to Spain. The dominant theme of the treatise was not education so much as the new barbarism that Galateo saw prevailing over the forces of civilization in Italy during the early sixteenth century. Foreigners have always hated and envied Italy, Galateo said, which explained why contemporary Franks and Goths imitated their bar-

[30] Ibid., pp. 290–93, esp. p. 293.
[31] Ibid., pp. 81–84.

barian ancestors in despoiling the land of culture and learning. The modern French and Spanish barbarians, he charged, had introduced vile manners into Italy. The Spaniards he considered especially blameworthy: they had brought with them no learning, law, commerce, painting, sculpture, or other useful discipline, but instead imported usury, theft, piracy, galley-slavery, gaming, hooliganism, prostitution, pederasty, assassination, effeminate songs, Arab cuisine, hypocrisy, and feather beds, among other vanities. From Galateo's point of view, Duke Ferrante of Calabria represented Italy's only good hope in the early sixteenth century. Thus he pleaded that Crisostomo Colonna must ensure that the duke receive a proper Italian education. Colonna must see to it that Ferrante learn Latin rather than the barbaric Spanish tongue, that he love simplicity and truth rather than ostentation and corruption, that he embrace religion and honest living rather than superstition and hypocrisy.[32]

Did Galateo realistically expect Duke Ferrante to return and restore Italy to the status quo of the Quattrocento? Almost certainly not. In 1504, shortly before composing his treatise on education, he prepared a long exposition of the Lord's Prayer. Commenting on the clause, "[may] thy kingdom come," Galateo contrasted God's kingdom with the realms of men. The divine commonwealth offered joy instead of sorrow, happiness instead of misery. Fortune held no sway there. Men were judged by their virtue, not on the basis of wealth, lineage, fear, favor, or friendship. The kingdom of God had no place for vassals or rebels, lords or servants, creditors or debtors, but only for virtue, wisdom, the satisfaction of a well-lived life, and continuous spiritual discourse.[33] This utopian vision helps to point up the sense of utter frustration

[32] Grande, ed., *Collana*, 2.103–67. For the passages referred to here, see esp. 2.103–4, 108–22, 134–38, 141–45 (citing the Latin text rather than Grande's Italian translation). See also two important articles that deal with this treatise: Benedetto Croce, "Il trattato *De educatione* di Antonio Galateo," *Giornale storico della letteratura italiana*, 23 (1894), 394–406; and Vittorio E. Zacchino, "Il 'De educatione' di Antonio Galateo e i suoi sentimenti anti-spagnoli," in *Atti del congresso internazionale di studi sull'età aragonese* (Bari, 1972), pp. 620–33.

[33] Grande, ed., *Collana*, 4.184–85.

that pervaded Galateo's treatise on education. Knowing quite well that he would not see honest government again until he reached paradise, Galateo could only rail against the sad condition of mortal men and attribute to the new barbarians the invention of vices common to all the peoples of the earth.

Galateo thus remained profoundly disappointed by the events of the turbulent decade following 1494, which defied any attempt at rational explanation. To Galateo it seemed that the world was the site of eternal flux, where change occurred at the whim of unstable, capricious fortune. In 1495, after the abdication of Alfonso II and his miserable death in Sicily, Galateo composed an epitaph that portrayed the former king as a victim of fortune. Alfonso had possessed such military skill that he seemed invincible, witness his campaigns in Tuscany and Lombardy, against barons and Turks. But fortune always becomes jealous of good men and exalts the wicked. Thus she raised up the French and caused them to impose a yoke of servitude on Italian liberty.[34] During the same year, 1495, Galateo composed a short epistle on human inconstancy, a topic that resolved itself by his treatment into a Heraclitean view of the world. Not only do individual human natures differ profoundly, Galateo observed, but men constantly change their opinions and manners, sometimes at intervals of a few days or even a few hours. Galateo concentrated in this epistle on the personal and individual implications of his observation, but he also recognized its broader significance: "All nature is in continuous flux." This view of the world as a site of instability and mutation seems to have remained something of a constant in Galateo's thought: at a distance of almost twenty years, he echoed his short epistle of 1495, employing the same reasoning and almost the same language in explaining his own shifting views on the value and proper uses of education.[35]

In view of this Heraclitean view of the world, it perhaps does

[34] Galateo, *Epistole*, pp. 258–66.

[35] Ibid., pp. 124–27, also pp. 195–214, esp. pp. 205–6. The quotation comes from p. 126.

not seem especially surprising that Galateo eventually made his peace with the Spanish regime in Italy. In 1510 he addressed an epistle to King Ferdinand of Spain, whom he identified as an agent of God at work in the world. He congratulated Ferdinand for all his successful ventures, especially for his expulsion of the Moors from Spain and his concentration of military forces on heathen rather than Christian enemies. Galateo's main purpose in this epistle was to encourage Ferdinand to continue in the same vein, indeed to organize a campaign to recapture Jerusalem and restore the Holy Land to Christianity. God has favored Spain, Galateo said, transferring military might and empire into the hands of Ferdinand himself; the king must therefore take the opportunity at hand, extend the power of Spain, and swell the boundaries of Christendom.[36]

By 1510, however, Galateo had largely lost interest in this sort of large political question. After retiring to Lecce in 1501 he transferred his public loyalties to his beloved Apulia. In 1510 he composed a long treatise on the region, its history, geography, people, customs, and cities. A few years later he devoted a shorter but similar work exclusively to the town of Gallipoli.[37]

Galateo did not possess the practical political experience of Pontano and other Neapolitan humanists. Nor did he possess Pontano's talent for rigorous analysis of a problem. His epistles and treatises anticipate the genre of the essay in their idiosyncratic, sometimes quirky examinations of personal, political, moral, and cultural issues. Although he did not compose controlled, systematic reflections on political affairs, the immediacy of his writing conveys well the sense of frustration that plagued a sensitive and thoughtful man living through a period of political and military turmoil.

[36] Ibid., pp. 151–58.
[37] For the general treatise on Apulia, see Galateo's *Epistole salentine*, pp. 72–177. The description of Gallipoli appears both in the *Epistole salentine*, pp. 240–71, and in the *Epistole*, pp. 226–43.

Tristano Caracciolo and the Vagaries of Fortune

The biography of Tristano Caracciolo (1437–1528) was at least as unusual as those of the Acquaviva brothers and Galateo.[38] Eldest son in an urban noble family, Caracciolo assumed responsibility for managing the household's affairs upon the premature death of his father. The need to provide dowries for seven sisters caused the family considerable financial hardship and ensured that Tristano had little time for study. Only at age thirty-five, about 1472, did he begin to devote his attention to letters. He concentrated his efforts first on the classical historians, then on the grammarians; he frequented the Neapolitan academy and became friendly with Galateo and Pontano, among others. For more than fifty years he engaged in study and reflection, composing numerous works on political, moral, and religious themes. Caracciolo did not take care to publish his writings, or even to disseminate them widely in manuscript. Yet some twenty-four works survive and illustrate Caracciolo's ability to combine classical wisdom with practical experience and a realistic appraisal of contemporary conditions.[39] The following analysis concentrates on works that illuminate Caracciolo's understanding of Neapolitan politics during the late fifteenth and early sixteenth centuries.

In his earliest surviving work, the *Defense of the Neapolitan Nobility* (ca. 1480), Caracciolo expressed pride in his class, which he considered essential to good government in the city and kingdom of Naples. He composed the work largely in order to refute the accusations of Poggio Bracciolini, who in his treatise on nobility had charged that Neapolitan nobles wasted time, occupied them-

---

[38] Mario Santoro has provided a biography and study of Caracciolo's thought: *Tristano Caracciolo e la cultura napoletana della Rinascenza* (Naples, 1957). See also the chapter on Caracciolo in Santoro's *Fortuna, ragione e prudenza*, pp. 103–40.

[39] Thirteen of Caracciolo's works are published in L. A. Muratori, ed., *Rerum italicarum scriptores*, rev. ed., 34 vols. (Bologna, 1900–35), vol. 22, pt. 1. A few other works have appeared in print in an ad hoc fashion. Several important writings, however, survive only in manuscripts, of which the most important is MS IX. C. 25 of the BNN. Professor Mario Santoro is currently preparing a critical edition of Caracciolo's works.

selves with their horses, and in general led the lazy life. Caracciolo had no difficulty adducing examples of Neapolitan nobles who had served as archbishops, cardinals, and popes, and he argued the importance of Neapolitan military talent for current affairs in all parts of Italy, Europe, and the Mediterranean. He also portrayed the nobility as indispensable for the administration of justice and maintenance of order in the Regno. If Neapolitan nobles scorned mercantile careers, as Poggio had disdainfully observed, they did so for the very good reason that they devoted their efforts to support for the monarchy and maintenance of tranquility in the Mezzogiorno.[40]

Caracciolo obviously had developed a high view of the Neapolitan nobility and its importance for the smooth functioning of the kingdom's affairs. In fact, his faith in the Neapolitan nobility emerged regularly in his writings, and it ranks as one of the most prominent characteristics of his political thought. Caracciolo never directly addressed the question of the ideal constitution for the kingdom of Naples, but he clearly envisioned a large role for talented nobles in the making of policy and administration of affairs. This point helps to explain two of Caracciolo's biographies: the first (written in 1506), of his ancestor Sergianni Caracciolo, grand seneschal of the realm under Queen Giovanna II, whose prudence had led to the calling of Alfonso the Magnanimous into Italy; the second (written in 1518), of his son-in-law Giovanni Battista Spinelli, royal diplomat and adviser during the 1490s, whose discretion might have spared Italy her unpleasant fate if other men had recognized his wisdom.[41] Caracciolo's vision of the Neapolitan nobility thus helped to fashion his understanding of Neapolitan history; and his understanding of Neapolitan history had implications in its turn for present and future practice. In congratulating King Alfonso II on the occasion of his coronation, for example, Caracciolo found it necessary to qualify his praise of the first Al-

[40] Muratori, ed., *Rerum italicarum scriptores*, 22.1.141–48, esp. 145–48.
[41] Ibid., 21–40, 43–70.

fonso. Caracciolo granted that Alfonso merited genuine praise for his clemency—he executed no one after capturing the city of Naples and allowed fortunes to remain intact—but he faulted the former king for relying too heavily on his Aragonese followers for advice and administration, rather than accepting guidance and service from the Neapolitan nobility. Caracciolo placed high hopes in Alfonso II—a truly Neapolitan king, the first of his dynasty to be born and bred in Naples—and he clearly expected the new king to depend more heavily on the Neapolitan nobility than the first Alfonso and Ferrante had done.[42]

The events of the next few years, however, both disappointed his expectations and undermined the position of his class. The Spanish viceroys not only brought the Aragonese dynasty of Naples to an end, but also moved speedily to subordinate the Neapolitan barons to the new regime. Caracciolo recognized this point and reflected it in several writings. In 1507, for example, he composed an epistle on the condition of the city of Naples after the departure of King Ferdinand of Spain, who had visited the city from November 1506 through June 1507. He concentrated on the economic distress that afflicted the city to the point that merchants suffered, businesses closed, and "for rent" signs appeared in every quarter. The primary cause of these problems, he said, was the absence of the monarchy: the disappearance of the royal court resulted in much less wealth for the city's economy. But the habits of the nobility also helped to explain the economic problems of 1507. Neapolitan nobles had come to fear the future on the suspicion that some unpleasant turn of events would lead to deprivation of their goods. As a result, the nobility in general had ceased to cultivate the qualities of magnificence and liberality, preferring to accumulate wealth rather than spend it.[43] Thus already in 1507, in Caracciolo's view, changing times and political conditions had encouraged the Neapolitan nobility to alter its behavior.

[42] Ibid., 173–76, esp. 173–74.
[43] Ibid., 153–55.

Caracciolo found the new regime rather distasteful—he devoted a lengthy epistle to the heavy-handed but ultimately abortive effort of 1510 to introduce the Spanish Inquisition into the Regno[44]—but he was enough of a realist to adapt to the new political circumstances rather than resist a formidable power. This point emerges most clearly from two short treatises that Caracciolo wrote during the early days of the Spanish viceroyalty of Naples. He dedicated one, a collection of advice for the prospective courtier, to his own son; in the other, he counseled a distant relative, Giovanni Caracciolo, the young marquis of Atella, on the obligations imposed by his double role as prince of his own territory, but also subject of a more powerful lord ruling the entire Mezzogiorno. Caracciolo endorsed certain traditional values in both of his treatises: he argued the importance of education, especially one based on Latin literature and classical moral thought rather than the sophistical and argumentative works of the logicians; he advised the cultivation of self-knowledge, prudence, and the cardinal virtues, wisdom, justice, temperance, and courage; and he placed special emphasis on the need to fear God, develop faith, exhibit piety, and observe religious ceremonies. Other features of Caracciolo's advice in the two treatises seem to reflect the specific political conditions of the Regno in the early sixteenth century. Thus Caracciolo insisted on the need for proper and careful behavior at court. He advised his son to exercise close judgment in selecting friends at court: he must ally himself with virtue rather than ambition, and must cultivate worthy men without resorting to flattery and adulation. He warned the marquis of the various dangers awaiting him at court—envy, hatred, adulation, and calumny—and counseled him to seek by all means to capture the benevolence of the prince. He addressed both his son and the marquis on the need to maintain one's self-control: anger and lack of moderation would deform one's character and prevent successful dealings. In the treatise to his son—also in a separate work on the

[44] Ibid., 109–17.

abuses inflicted by contemporary courtiers and professionals on their speech—Caracciolo developed one implication of this general point in some detail. He denounced vain, vulgar, verbose, and especially dishonest speech, calling instead for circumspection, precision, economy, and honesty in communication. He repeatedly emphasized taciturnity as a prime quality for the prospective courtier: brief, pertinent speech offered at the appropriate time would serve him well at court.[45]

The same sort of changing circumstances that forced Caracciolo to alter his conception of the nobility and its role in Neapolitan politics encouraged him also to develop a pessimistic vision of human history. He expressed this vision most clearly in a treatise *On the Vagaries of Fortune*, the best known of all his works, which he composed during the latter years of his life. He argued the thesis in this work that the mutability of the present age proved the truth of King Solomon's dictum: all things human are works of vanity. Given the instability of kingdoms, principalities, wealth, beauty, and joy, Caracciolo thought it impossible to hope for temporal human happiness. Fortune mocked men's designs and intervened in affairs in order to expose the fragility of the human condition. By way of substantiating these points, Caracciolo reviewed the recent experiences of the most exalted men in the kingdom of Naples, demonstrating the personal or public ruin that fortune carefully prepared for each individual.

Caracciolo began his survey with the Aragonese kings of Naples. The dramatic and illustrious career of Alfonso the Magnanimous might suggest that he had won fortune's favor, but Caracciolo emphasized the difficulties of Alfonso's career in a way that earlier humanist historians had not. Amidst his triumphs, Alfonso faced civil war in Spain, suffered the death of his brother Enrico,

---

[45] Caracciolo's *Praecepta ad filium* and *Opusculum ad marchionem Atellae* survive in the BNN, MS IX. C. 25, fols. 121r–36r, 201r–11r. On the second work see also Giuliana Vitale, "L'umanista Tristano Caracciolo ed i principi di Melfi," ASPN, 3d ser. 2 (1962), 343–81. See also Caracciolo's treatise *De cuiusque vanitate in loquendo* in BNN, MS IX. C. 25, fols. 195r–200r.

experienced war in Italy and rebellion in the Regno, and struggled throughout his reign to ensure that Ferrante succeeded him as king of Naples. Indeed, during his last days, Alfonso had himself shuttled by litter from one Neapolitan castle to another in search of an accord on the matter of the royal succession. Thus even in the case of such a powerful king as Alfonso the Magnanimous, fortune demonstrated her ability to destabilize human affairs. Ferrante of course kept his throne and prevailed over papal, French, and baronial challengers, and Caracciolo recognized that earlier interpreters had judged him fortunate for evading the ruin that threatened him on numerous occasions. Caracciolo argued to the contrary that for each success or joy he experienced, Ferrante soon endured some countervailing sadness that either equaled or exceeded his pleasure. Thus during his lifetime Ferrante suffered the premature deaths of his sons Francesco and Giovanni (at twenty-four and twenty-nine years, respectively). After his own death, the miserable experiences of Alfonso II, Ferrandino, and Federico demonstrated on behalf of the Aragonese dynasty as a whole the futility and vanity of human affairs.

Caracciolo by no means limited his analysis to the Aragonese kings of Naples. He provided a similar, though briefer account of the Sforza dynasty of Milan, and he reviewed the fortunes of numerous Neapolitan barons and their families. He even included a section on misfortunes suffered by the republic of Venice as a whole. Perhaps the most emblematic of all his accounts were those of Francesco Coppola and Antonello Petrucci, leaders of the second barons' rebellion against Ferrante, whose careers strongly supported Caracciolo's thesis concerning the vanity of human affairs. Coppola rose speedily from obscurity to sublimity, and he won Ferrante's favor and the respect of powerful men. But he made the mistake of taking Ferrante for a dull, obtuse man rather than a shrewd, crafty, calculating monarch. His error in judgment led not only to his own instant ruin, but also to the destruction of his house, since Ferrante deprived his family of its noble status and confiscated its wealth. Son of a peasant gardener, Petrucci ascended to heights of power even more dramatically than did Coppola, but his conspiracy against Ferrante resulted in more complete ruin, indeed in the annihilation of his house. Arrested along with her husband and two sons, Petrucci's wife died in prison; shortly thereafter, Petrucci's sons suffered public execution; finally, Antonello himself was beheaded, along with Coppola. (Three other sons survived Petrucci, but they did not continue the family line: all three had taken holy orders and held high church positions.) Furthermore, needless to say, Ferrante confiscated the family's wealth upon the fall of Antonello.

Caracciolo thus offered a litany of misfortune and a catalog of vanity. From his case studies of men raised to giddy heights only to suffer perdition, Caracciolo drew moral lessons in characteristically humanist fashion. Men must not allow temporary success to blind them to the fundamental instability of human affairs. They must not assume falsely the mantle of excellence or felicity, lest they tempt fortune to turn the tables, mock their arrogant pretensions, and demonstrate yet once again the vanity of human affairs. Men currently enjoying the favor of fortune would do well to cultivate a sense of humility and vulnerability and avoid the temptation to oppress their weaker fellows. Finally, Caracciolo took the instability of human affairs and the misery of the human condition as signs of a better world. Only the prospect of unlimited future felicity could account for the mutability and suffering that afflicted this world. Thus he held temporal human pleasures in contempt when compared to the eternal joy promised by the Christian revelation.[46]

Humanists did not speak with one voice when addressing the theme of the human condition, but rather emphasized human dignity or misery, felicity or unhappiness in various ways.[47] Carac-

[46] Caracciolo's *De varietate fortunae* is published most conveniently in Muratori, ed., *Rerum italicarum scriptores*, 22.1.73–105. For the passages referred to here, see esp. pp. 73–80, 95–100, 104–5.

[47] For an analysis of several humanist investigations of the human condition, see Trinkaus, *In Our Image and Likeness*, 1.171–321.

ciolo certainly offered a more pessimistic vision of human affairs than those advanced by most other humanists, but he charged his work with the same kind of moral concern that characterized other humanist investigations of the human condition. Once again, the colloquy between classical wisdom, Christian values, and contemporary experience helped a Neapolitan humanist to make sense of a chaotic world.

Humanism and Neapolitan Society

The thought of local notables such as de Jennaro, the Acquaviva brothers, Galateo, and Caracciolo, among others, demonstrates the point that humanism resonated throughout the Mezzogiorno. Originally an alien import that flourished only at the court of Alfonso the Magnanimous, by the end of the Quattrocento humanism had penetrated by various routes into Neapolitan society. The Studio of Naples was one such route: though the Studio emphasized legal studies, professors of rhetoric and literature such as Giuniano Maio and Francesco Pucci helped to disseminate humanist tastes and develop humanist talents. For men of learning who lived in the city of Naples, the academy of Panormita and Pontano played an even more important role in the nurturing of southern humanism. Scores of Neapolitans—whose numbers were augmented by Greeks and Italian visitors from outside the Regno—took advantage of the opportunities the academy offered to men of letters and learning.[48] Belisario Acquaviva and Galateo even organized circles of learned men in Nardò and Lecce, respectively, in an effort to introduce the sophisticated pleasures of the capital city into the provinces.[49] By the end of the fifteenth century, the

[48] For a partial list of the academy's habitués, see C. Minieri Riccio, *Biografie degli accademici alfonsini detti poi pontaniani, dal 1442 al 1543* (Naples, 1881). For discussions of its activities, see Santoro, "La cultura umanistica," pp. 159–71; and Erasmo Percopo, *Vita di Giovanni Pontano*, ed. M. Manfredi (Naples, 1938), pp. 106–19.

[49] On Belisario's Academy of the Laurel at Nardò, see Maylender, *Storia delle*

printing press extended the reach of humanism even to towns that possessed no university or academy.

Thus humanism took root in the soil of the Mezzogiorno and produced a distinctively Neapolitan fruit. In order to survive over a long term, a cultural transplant such as humanism would require considerable cultivation—perhaps some occasional cutting back, but a great deal of careful nourishment as well. Humanism in Naples did not receive this sort of care over the long term. Although it flourished during the Quattrocento, Neapolitan humanism withered under the next century's difficulties: it suffered first from neglect and deprivation, later from a more calculated program of severe pruning that eventually killed the cultural transplant.

The first hardship encountered by Neapolitan humanism was the disappearance of the royal court. From the earliest days of the dynasty, the Aragonese kings of Naples had supported humanists and other men of culture. When the monarchy fell, the principal source of patronage for learned men disappeared, opening a void that the Spanish viceroys never sought to fill. Absence of patronage was bad enough in itself, but disappearance of the Aragonese court coincided also with the dispersal of the Neapolitan royal library. Much of the library went to Paris in the train of Charles VIII in 1495; most of the remainder went to Valencia with Duke Ferrante of Calabria in 1502. Carefully cultivated especially by Alfonso the Magnanimous and Ferrante, the library had served as a prime intellectual resource for the Neapolitan humanists. Its dispersal deprived them of access to a splendid collection of books, again opening a void that none moved to fill. Meanwhile, the libraries that remained in the hands of the Neapolitan barons were not large or sophisticated enough to support advanced study.[50]

---

accademie, 3.403–4; and Minieri Riccio, *Notizia delle accademie*, pp. 49–50. On Galateo's academy at Lecce, see his *Epistole*, pp. 147–50.

[50] Ferrante had absorbed the most impressive baronial libraries after the second barons' revolt. See de Marinis, *Supplemento*, 1.143–259. For a study of another, perhaps more typical baronial library, see Carlo de Frede, "Biblioteche e cultura di signori napoletani del '400," *Bibliothèque d'humanisme et Renaissance*, 25 (1963), 187–97.

The fall of the Aragonese dynasty thus dealt a double blow to Neapolitan humanism, depriving it both of patronage and of access to books.

The policies of the Spanish viceroys brought new pressures to bear on Neapolitan humanism. The viceroys attempted in sometimes heavy-handed fashion to ensure that Neapolitan thought and culture conformed to the Spanish understanding of Christian orthodoxy. Thus in 1510 and 1547 viceregal regimes attempted to introduce the Spanish Inquisition into the Regno—but failed both times because of massive and intense popular opposition. The viceroys experienced greater success in their efforts to patrol the press, which led to straitened circumstances for Antonio de Frizis, publisher of numerous humanist works, and for other printers who had established businesses in Naples after the difficult decade from 1494 to 1503.[51] Meanwhile, the viceroys kept a sharp eye also on the Studio of Naples. In 1507 the Studio reopened its doors—closed since about 1496 due to political and military turmoil—and it remained open almost continuously throughout the sixteenth and seventeenth centuries. But the viceroys carefully controlled the institution's budget, students, faculty, and curriculum. By the mid-sixteenth century, the Studio excelled in philosophy and the practical disciplines of law and medicine, but no longer in literature or rhetoric. Meanwhile, students and faculty almost never posed political or ideological challenges, but behaved in accordance with the conservative, orthodox ideals of the viceregal regime.[52]

The most serious blow to Neapolitan humanism fell in 1542 with the closure of the Neapolitan academy. During the early decades of viceregal administration, the academy had continued to provide a forum for men of letters and learning, including Pietro

[51] Manzi, *La tipografia napoletana*, 1.180–81. The subject of Neapolitan printing during the period of Spanish domination deserves a thorough study.

[52] See especially Nino Cortese, "Il governo spagnuolo e lo Studio di Napoli," in his *Cultura e politica a Napoli dal Cinque al Settecento* (Naples, 1965), pp. 31–119.

Summonte and Jacopo Sannazaro, the most talented Neapolitan poets of the sixteenth century. In 1542, however, the academy's last organizer, Scipione Capece, fell under suspicion of heresy, prompting Viceroy Pedro de Toledo to suppress the academy after almost a century of existence.[53] Founded by Panormita about 1447, skillfully guided by Pontano, sustained after his death by his friends Summonte and Sannazaro, the Neapolitan academy had long served as the most important exponent of humanism in the Mezzogiorno. Neapolitan humanism could hardly survive the suppression of this, the last effective institutional foundation of the movement.

Thus from the first decades of the sixteenth century, humanists exercised a continuously diminishing influence on Neapolitan thought. When cultural revival occurred at Naples during the late seventeenth and eighteenth centuries, the inspiration did not come from a continuing tradition of humanist thought, but either arrived from abroad, as in the case of the Cartesian rationalism that helped Pietro Giannone to frame his anticlerical vision of civic history, or arose sui generis, as in the case of the idiosyncratic reflections that enabled Giambattista Vico to develop his new science of society.[54]

Thus Renaissance humanism failed to become established as a permanent feature of Neapolitan culture and society. For a century and more, however—from Alfonso's patronage of Panormita, Valla, and others in the mid-1430s, through the careers of the Ac-

[53] Santoro, "La cultura umanistica," p. 171. Cf. also Benedetto Croce, *History of the Kingdom of Naples*, trans. F. Frenaye (Chicago, 1970), pp. 110–15.

[54] Some scholars view Lorenzo Valla as a precursor of Vico and other intellectual reformers of seventeenth-century Naples: see for example Nancy S. Struever, "Vico, Valla, and the Logic of Humanist Inquiry," in Giorgio Tagliacozzo and Donald P. Verene, eds., *Giambattista Vico's Science of Humanity* (Baltimore, 1976), pp. 173–85. I certainly do not intend to deny that humanists influenced later Neapolitan thinkers on individual issues, but rather to emphasize the point that by the mid-sixteenth century, the distinctive tradition of Neapolitan humanism had come to an end. On the revival of Neapolitan culture during the seventeenth and eighteenth centuries, see Croce, *History of the Kingdom of Naples*, pp. 147–89.

quaviva brothers and Caracciolo, and even into the 1540s until the closure of the academy—humanism figured as the most influential cultural movement of the Mezzogiorno. The next chapter will discuss the significance of Neapolitan humanism for the cultural history of Quattrocento Italy and of Renaissance Europe as a whole.

7

Neapolitan Humanism
and Renaissance Europe

URING THE LATE fourteenth and early fifteenth centuries,
humanists in central and northern Italy elaborated upon the
heritage of Petrarch and transformed it into a cultural movement
of considerable social significance. Petrarch's successors employed
their literary and analytical skills in discussing a wide range of social, political, and moral questions. They instituted an educational program that systematically imparted humanist interests
and values. They even established sophisticated literary and stylistic criteria for the conduct of political and diplomatic business.
Humanism was of course not a purely homogeneous phenomenon:
it naturally took on distinctive characteristics according to the peculiar environments in which the movement consolidated itself.
Thus aristocratic Venice, mercantile Florence, and curial Rome all
influenced the interests and values of humanists working there.
Yet humanists for the most part came from an urban, lay-oriented
world; and by the mid-fifteenth century, humanism clearly reflected the social and political conditions of central and northern
Italy.

The kingdom of Naples suffered sedition, invasion, and civil
war during the formative period of the humanist movement. No
advanced cultural movement could have survived the turmoil that
disturbed the Regno during the century before Alfonso the Magnanimous consolidated his grip on the kingdom. Thus only at a
late date in the course of its development did humanism, the cultural expression of an urban, lay-oriented society, enter the feudal,
agrarian world of the kingdom of Naples. More than any other

288

such movement, then, Neapolitan humanism manifested tensions between the cosmopolitan interests shared by humanists in general and the local problems peculiar to the Mezzogiorno. The Neapolitan humanists studied and appreciated classical literature, like their counterparts in central and northern Italy, and they cultivated rhetorical and literary talents in imitation of the ancients. Indeed, their presence in the humanist mainstream largely accounts for their attractiveness to the founders of a new dynasty. Once they assumed their new posts, however, the humanists found themselves confronted by a variety of problems and pressures peculiar to the kingdom of Naples. In addressing these problems they dealt with a range of issues far removed from the gamut of interests that engaged humanists in other parts of Italy and Europe.

Local conditions of the Mezzogiorno thus combined with the cosmopolitan culture of humanism to shape the thought of the Neapolitan humanists. The local influences helped to ensure that Neapolitan humanism was more than simply a derivative phenomenon, an unreflective southern imitation of a creative cultural movement originally developed in central and northern Italy. For the most part, to be sure, the Neapolitan humanists adapted the skills and strategies pioneered by earlier humanists and applied them to the conditions of the Mezzogiorno. Yet in several notable cases, a combination of cosmopolitan outlook and local experience encouraged Neapolitan humanists to develop an especially powerful line of thought. In these cases, the Neapolitan humanists again employed their sophisticated cultural talents in addressing an issue of immediate, local concern. But more importantly, they refracted their Neapolitan experience and blended it with the cosmopolitan interests of Quattrocento Italy in such a way as to make an enduring contribution to the culture of Renaissance humanism in general. Such is the argument of this last, brief chapter.

ALFONSO the Magnanimous brought foreign humanists to Naples partly because of his personal interest in the learned culture of the Italian Renaissance, but largely also because he recognized an opportunity to lend luster and a sense of legitimacy to his new dynasty by associating it with the humanist movement. Long before Alfonso consolidated his hold on the kingdom of Naples in the mid-fifteenth century, the states of central and northern Italy had entrusted their diplomatic business to humanist secretaries and ambassadors. Meanwhile, historians and rhetoricians drew upon humanist techniques when celebrating the experiences of city-states, the deeds of notable men, or the virtues of patrons. In order to participate in Italian politics on a par with other peninsular leaders, Alfonso would need spokesmen who could represent his interests and proclaim his accomplishments in the currently fashionable idiom of humanism. Thus Alfonso called into his service men of impeccable humanist credentials—first Panormita and Valla, then Facio, later Manetti and Pontano, as well as other, less prominent figures—men who had thoroughly absorbed the interests and developed the talents associated with humanism. Quite apart from the matter of his personal taste, which itself certainly inclined him toward humanism, Alfonso's political and diplomatic requirements strongly encouraged the new king to surround himself with well-known and widely respected humanists.

Panormita and Lorenzo Valla both entered Alfonso's service as men of wide renown, highly respected for their literary gifts, though also suspected by many on moral grounds. Bartolomeo Facio had fewer solid accomplishments than the other two men, but he had studied with Guarino, had served as a humanist tutor, had begun to work on his account of the war of Chioggia, and perhaps most importantly had become friendly with Panormita. Giannozzo Manetti's rhetorical skills had brought him fame and the respect of humanists throughout the Italian peninsula long before 1455, when he accepted Alfonso's invitation to live in Naples. Giovanni Pontano had not yet completed his studies when he first encountered Alfonso, but the king obviously recognized promise in the young man's talents, and he certainly invested wisely in providing Pontano with a post at his court. Like these five luminaries, other humanists who sojourned briefly in Naples also possessed impressive cultural credentials: Porcellio Pandoni, Pier Candido Decembrio, Francesco Filelfo, Flavio Biondo, Theodore Gaza, George of Trebizond—all stood in the front ranks of Italian humanism during the mid-Quattrocento. Perhaps only Leonardo Bruni—whom Alfonso sought to attract to Naples, though without success—could have significantly increased the brilliance of the humanist circle at Alfonso's court. Despite the continued presence of Panormita and Pontano, Neapolitan humanism lost much of its luster during Ferrante's reign. Nevertheless, men like Giovanni Albino, Giovanni Brancati, Giuniano Maio, Gabriele Altilio, and Elisio Calenzio possessed a solid command of humanist skills, even if they did not enjoy such fame as their predecessors.

Once established in their posts, the major Neapolitan humanists devoted much of their energies to the political and dynastic needs of the Aragonese kings of Naples. In some cases, royal needs coincided with typical humanist interests that the Neapolitan humanists held in common with their counterparts in central and northern Italy. In these cases, Neapolitan humanists took their cue from predecessors who had worked in other parts of Italy: they borrowed techniques that earlier humanists had developed and adapted them to the needs of the kingdom of Naples. Composition of history and biography, for example, strongly appealed to humanists in all parts of Italy. From the time of Leonardo Bruni forward, Italian humanists studied and imitated classical historians, applied their techniques to contemporary situations, and established a distinctive tradition of humanist historiography. Neapolitan humanists eagerly accepted the invitation to display their literary and rhetorical talents while also serving Aragonese dynastic interests. Valla's work on Ferdinand of Antequera implicitly legitimized the Aragonese dynasty by accounting for its origin in the Compromise of Caspe. Facio's detailed commentaries portrayed Alfonso the Magnanimous as the dynamic figure of his age, a genuine hero who seized opportunity, mastered fortune, and constructed a just political order where chaos had previously reigned.

Panormita's collection of anecdotes attributed all manner of virtue to Alfonso, while his account of the young Ferrante offered the reader a worthy prince equally vigorous and virtuous as his father. Through works like these, humanist historiography found a niche in Renaissance Naples approximately half a century after its emergence in central Italy.

Like history and biography, oratory strongly appealed to humanists in all parts of Italy, since it allowed them to display their learning and rhetorical skills while also serving some immediate cause. In the case of the Neapolitan humanists, oratory served a dual function as showcase of eloquence and vehicle of propaganda for the Aragonese dynasty of Naples. In the several diplomatic orations that he delivered for Alfonso and Ferrante, Panormita always supplemented his basic political message with an appropriately flattering characterization of his royal patron. Facio lauded Alfonso's clemency and Ferrante's intellect more straightforwardly in tributes praising the two men. In orations intended for popes, princes, emperors, and other notables, Manetti eulogized Alfonso the Magnanimous for his Spanish heritage, moral virtues, impressive learning, military genius, princely qualities, and signal generosity toward men of culture. At the court of Ferrante, Giovanni Brancati emerged as a worthy successor to Manetti. Brancati's work offered especially polished praise of Ferrante's virtues, but numerous other, anonymous orations survive to demonstrate the point that humanist rhetoric continued to flourish in Naples throughout the Aragonese dynasty.

In their political thought as in history and oratory, the Neapolitan humanists reflected their monarchical milieu. Italian humanists in general found special virtue in the constitutions of their own city-states: Florentines typically praised republican values, Venetians an aristocratic order, and Milanese a stable princely regime. The Neapolitan humanists similarly developed their thought within the framework of a monarchical constitution, and once again much of their work served to glorify the Aragonese dynasty. Pontano's treatise *De principe* associated Duke Alfonso of

Calabria with ideal princely virtues, and Giuniano Maio referred explicitly to the personal experience of King Ferrante in exemplifying each of the qualities he considered appropriate for the majestic prince. The monarchical environment of the Mezzogiorno continued to influence southern humanists even after the fall of the Aragonese dynasty. Tristano Caracciolo and the Acquaviva brothers perhaps hoped for greater influence of the nobility in Neapolitan affairs, but none of them challenged the basic assumption that some sort of monarchical regime would prevail in the Mezzogiorno. Meanwhile, Pietro Jacopo de Jennaro and Galateo both seemed positively eager for the continuation of a monarchical constitution.

If the Neapolitan humanists reflected their political environment in their works of history, oratory, and political theory, they responded even more directly to local conditions in fulfilling their secretarial and diplomatic duties. Humanists in Florence, Venice, Milan, Rome, and elsewhere offered elegant and able service as chancellors, secretaries, and ambassadors for their states. Likewise the Neapolitan humanists. Panormita composed state letters for both Alfonso the Magnanimous and Ferrante, and he represented Neapolitan interests on several especially sensitive embassies. After the second barons' revolt, Pontano became an indispensable figure in Neapolitan statecraft as secretary, spokesman, diplomat, adviser, and de facto prime minister of the realm. Without the services of these two men, the Aragonese kings of Naples simply could not have conducted their political and diplomatic affairs in accordance with the standards of statecraft that prevailed in Quattrocento Italy. Less prominent humanists like Giovanni Albino, Giovanni Brancati, and Gabriele Altilio undertook similar duties, though generally speaking they did not receive assignments of such moment as those entrusted to Panormita and Pontano.

In several important ways, then, Neapolitan humanists adapted the skills, talents, and interests common to humanists in general to the special conditions of the Mezzogiorno. The study of Neapolitan humanism thus helps to illustrate one route by which fifteenth-century men adapted a general, cosmopolitan movement to their own immediate and particular needs.

MORE importantly, analysis of the Neapolitan experience helps to account for several distinctive characteristics of Renaissance humanism in general. Neapolitan humanists not only adapted a cosmopolitan cultural tradition to their local needs, but also infused it with their own experience in such a way as to influence the development of the more general movement itself. Thus Neapolitan humanists made three contributions of special significance to Renaissance culture.

In the first place, they helped to create the science of philological analysis. Earlier humanists had already developed a considerable degree of philological awareness. Petrarch himself established high standards for textual critics and analysts, and some of his disciples, such as Coluccio Salutati and Poggio Bracciolini, continued to explore the vein that Petrarch had opened. Several of the Neapolitan humanists also had strong philological interests. Antonio Calcillo and Giuniano Maio both engaged in lexicographical studies: Calcillo prepared perhaps the first Latin dictionary in Italy, a work that Maio later edited and published and that Angelo Poliziano closely examined. Other Neapolitan humanists also engaged in textual scholarship: working with the aid of Giacomo Curlo and Panormita, Facio sought to emend a corrupt text of Livy, though his efforts reveal that he did not possess deep philological insight.

Most important of the Neapolitan philologists, however, was Lorenzo Valla, who indeed ranks as the single most crucial figure for the development of philological analysis in the entire Renaissance period. Valla produced his most important philological works during his Neapolitan residence. He completed most of the work for the *Elegantiae* in Naples, and he composed the first redaction of his annotations to the New Testament while there. He published the *Elegantiae* only after his return to Rome, and he prepared a second redaction of the annotations after he gained access to Roman manuscripts of the Greek New Testament. In both cases, however, he developed his basic analytical approach and conducted most of his work while employed at the court of Alfonso the Magnanimous.

In two other cases, Valla's Neapolitan experience directly influenced his philological work. His emendations to the text of Livy originated in the efforts of the Neapolitan humanists to display their erudition before King Alfonso and learned men at his court. Except for his need to reply to the four *Invectives* that Facio unleashed against his vexatious colleague, Valla would perhaps never have mentioned and certainly would not have presented explanations and justifications for his brilliant conjectural emendations to the corrupt text of Livy. More important and more influential than his work on Livy was Valla's exposé of the Donation of Constantine, a work that patently responded to the political situation of the early 1440s. King Alfonso found himself in an uncomfortable political and diplomatic position because Pope Eugenius IV refused to recognize his claim to the Neapolitan throne. It seems most likely that Alfonso commissioned Valla to attack the Donation of Constantine as part of a coordinated campaign to pressure the pope. In any event, Valla's work demonstrated an ability to place his humanist and philological talents in King Alfonso's political and diplomatic service.

Furthermore, and more significantly, Valla's work had implications that extended far beyond the issues of the moment. His exposé of the Donation of Constantine was in fact the first philological tour de force of the Renaissance. Valla demonstrated how the application of a broad erudition and an acute critical faculty might enable scholars to frame powerful historical and literary arguments. Valla's work deeply influenced later humanists, such as Angelo Poliziano, Guillaume Budé, and Erasmus of Rotterdam, who helped to establish philological scholarship as a hallmark of Renaissance culture. The combination of cosmopolitan humanist interests with local political pressures—joined by virtue of Valla's peculiar genius—thus helped to define one of the basic characteristics of Renaissance and modern western culture.

Renaissance humanists devoted themselves not only to analysis of words, but also to reflections on humanity. Here, too, the Neapolitan humanists made significant contributions to the thought of their age. Petrarch himself was the first humanist to address this concern with his penetrating, introspective self-analyses. By the early fifteenth century, his disciples, such as Coluccio Salutati, had devoted much of their thought to the human condition. When Bartolomeo Facio and Giannozzo Manetti addressed themselves to such themes as human happiness and dignity, then, they registered the influence of the cosmopolitan interest in the human condition on the Neapolitan humanist circle.

More important for present purposes were the reflections of the Neapolitan humanists on a more specialized theme—fortune and its role in human affairs. The tumultuous political experience of the Regno no doubt especially encouraged Neapolitan humanists to ponder this theme. Indeed, Neapolitans figured prominently in the ranks of those Italian humanists and moral thinkers who spoke of fortune during the late fifteenth and early sixteenth centuries.

In the early days of this period, to be sure, Neapolitan thought on fortune was not very profound or penetrating. Panormita and Facio enjoyed the luxury of identifying fortune with the will of God, since Alfonso I and Ferrante ultimately overcame the obstacles they confronted and consolidated their regimes. Later humanists, however, found fortune a less beneficent influence. Giovanni Albino thought of fortune as a force that took political and diplomatic initiative out of the hands of the Neapolitan kings. The Acquaviva brothers learned from abundant personal experience that fortune worked both benign and malign influences on any particular individual. Galateo saw the temporal world as the realm of fortune, the site of unpredictable, unpleasant, unceasing fluctuation. Tristano Caracciolo considered human existence itself a supreme vanity, since fortune made mock of all joy, all pleasure, all human effort of whatever sort.

The most thoughtful of the Neapolitan investigations of fortune, however, was that of Giovanni Pontano. During his last years, Pontano devoted much of his attention to fortune, its causes, effects, and remedies, drawing upon his forty years of experience as secretary, diplomat, and adviser to the Aragonese kings of Naples. Pontano viewed fortune neither as the providential guiding force appreciated by Panormita and Facio, nor as the malevolent, mocking minister of evil feared by Galateo and Caracciolo. Instead, Pontano took a cooler, more analytical approach, attempting first to clarify the relationship of fortune, fate, chance, and providence, then undertaking to characterize fortune itself and understand its role in human affairs. Most importantly, Pontano devoted special consideration to the human and moral dimensions of his subject. Fortune held sway only in the absence of human reason and will, he said, so that careful preparation of the intellect and proper execution of good judgment could negate even the best efforts of the capricious force.

Thus Pontano identified prudent and thoughtful action as the only human force that could render human affairs a meaningful pursuit rather than a chaotic congeries of irrational episodes. His thought certainly pointed in the direction of Machiavelli, who later developed a similar, though more fatalistic understanding of fortune's role in human affairs. More generally, Pontano's reflections have their place also in the larger, centuries-long debate on free will and the efficacy of human endeavor to lead a moral and meaningful life. Once again, then, a Neapolitan humanist drew upon personal experience to enrich the understanding of a theme of general interest to men of culture during the Renaissance.

A turbulent political experience did more than encourage Neapolitan humanists to think about fortune and its role in human affairs: it also forced upon them the necessity of reconsidering a venerable western tradition of political ethics. Humanists in other cities performed secretarial, diplomatic, and advisory duties very similar to those undertaken by Panormita, Pontano, and their Neapolitan colleagues. Antonio Loschi and Cicco Simonetta turned their humanist talents to the service of Milan; Francesco Barbaro and Bernardo Giustiniani rank as the best known of numerous politically active humanists in Venice; the public careers of Coluccio Salutati, Leonardo Bruni, and Poggio Bracciolini likewise demonstrated that humanists figured prominently also in Florentine politics. These humanists composed memorials, developed opinions, and offered advice on the most pressing political problems of their age. Research has shown that their practical political experiences brought several of these humanists to recognize the difficulty of exercising power within the limits established by traditional political ethics.

The Neapolitan humanists certainly learned to appreciate the ambiguities of their positions. Well tutored in classical and Christian moral thought, which they enthusiastically endorsed as an ethical ideal, they recognized that men of power did not regularly observe the strictures of abstract moral codes, further that political survival at least occasionally necessitated the adoption of unpleasant or even immoral policies. Panormita publicly portrayed Kings Alfonso and Ferrante as pious, virtuous monarchs who resorted to violence only when provoked beyond measure. His diplomatic and private correspondence, however, show that in his capacities as political secretary and adviser, Panormita understood the demands of the real political world and acted accordingly. He recognized the value of propaganda, loyally justified the morally ambiguous policies of his patrons, and tendered advice that contravened the lofty political ideals that he publicly espoused. Little information survives to illuminate the political understanding of Giovanni Albino and Giovanni Brancati, but at least a few materials suggest that they shared Panormita's realistic approach to problems of statecraft and diplomacy.

Once again, though, Giovanni Pontano expressed most clearly a line of thought only inchoately developed by earlier Neapolitan humanists. Pontano had even more experience than Panormita as political secretary, diplomat, and adviser, and he faced even more difficult political predicaments, including the second barons' revolt, war between King Ferrante and Pope Innocent VIII, the dangerous diplomatic isolation of the Regno in the 1490s, and ultimately the invasions that for a decade after 1494 plagued the kingdom, toppled the Aragonese dynasty, and led to the establishment of the Spanish viceregal regime in the Mezzogiorno. Like Panormita, Pontano served the Aragonese kings of Naples in thoughtful and loyal fashion, and the documents he executed demonstrate clearly that Pontano too adopted a supremely realistic frame of mind when acting in official capacity. More importantly, unlike the other Neapolitan humanists, Pontano devoted serious, systematic reflection to questions of political morality. The high moral standards prescribed in classical and Christian political thought certainly struck him as an attractive ideal. His practical political experience, however, forced Pontano to admit the necessity of adopting morally ambiguous, or even reprehensible policies in the interest of maintaining public order.

Thus in his treatises on courage, on obedience, and especially on prudence, Pontano inaugurated an effort—usually associated with the names of Machiavelli, Giovanni Botero, and later political theorists—to reconsider traditional western political ethics and revise them in the light of the principles that lead to success or failure in the real world of politics. It goes without saying that this effort figured prominently in the gradual development in early modern Europe of a secular, state-oriented political mentality.

THE SKILL of philological analysis, the examination of fortune and its influence in human affairs, and the realistic approach to problems of politics and statecraft—these rank as three of the most significant products of the Renaissance humanist imagination. Neapolitan humanists did not develop their thought on these themes in isolation from their counterparts in central and northern Italy: to the contrary, they drew inspiration from their predecessors and contemporaries who also embraced the cosmopolitan interests of the humanist movement. In each of the three cases, however, the peculiar experience of the Mezzogiorno directly influenced the Neapolitan humanists, enabling them to impart distinctive characteristics to a general intellectual concern of Renaissance Europe. In this way, the Neapolitan humanists contributed important elements to the culture of Renaissance humanism in general, and through it to the cultural stock of western civilization as a whole.

Bibliography

In the following bibliography I have listed only those manuscripts that struck me as especially illuminating for the foregoing study. Interested readers will find a wealth of information about other manuscripts that made up the Neapolitan royal library in the first two volumes of de Marinis, *La biblioteca*, also in the first volume of de Marinis, *Supplemento*. Since the printed literature on Renaissance Naples is so poorly known, I have chosen to err on the side of liberality rather than economy in listing published sources and secondary works. At several points, the study depends heavily upon research in archival collections, including the Archivo de la Corona de Aragón in Barcelona, the Archivio di Stato in Milan, and the Archivio Segreto Vaticano in Vatican City. The bibliography does not itemize the collections and their materials, but footnotes always provide complete data as to the source of material cited.

MANUSCRIPTS

Florence, Biblioteca Medicea Laurenziana
    Ashburnham 270: miscellany including Sagundino's oration to Alfonso
    Plut. 76, MS 42: translation of Onosander by Sagundino for Alfonso
Florence, Biblioteca Nazionale
    MS II. X. 31: humanist miscellany including letters of Facio
    Palatino 689: translations from Plutarch by Albino for Ferrante
London, British Library
    Add. 21120: translation of Aristotle including oration on the death of Alfonso
        by Carlos de Viana
Naples, Biblioteca della Società Napoletana di Storia Patria
    MS XX. C. 26: works of Carafa
    MS XXVI. C. 5: copies of Neapolitan diplomatic correspondence
Naples, Biblioteca Nazionale
    MS V. E. 51: poetry of Panormita
    MS IX. C. 22: history of Alfonso by Gaspare Pellegrino

MS IX. C. 25: works of Caracciolo

MS XII. E. 34: translations from Plutarch by Albino for Ferrante

MS XVIII. 40: Belisario Acquaviva's exposition of the Lord's Prayer

Palermo, Biblioteca Centrale della Regione Siciliana (formerly Biblioteca Nazionale di Palermo)

MS I. C. 17: de Jennaro's treatise on government

Palermo, Biblioteca Communale

MS 2. Qq. B. 28: epistles of Ludovico Saccano, including one on the death of Alfonso

Paris, Bibliothèque Nationale

MS ital. 447: treatise on government by Cola de Gennaro

MS ital. 616: translation from Plutarch by A. Brandolini for Ferrante

MS lat. 3615: treatise on human nature by M. de Striverio for Alfonso

MS lat. 7860: A. Brandolini's oration on military affairs and letters

Rome, Biblioteca Casanatense

MS 125: treatise of J. M. de Ferrariis on poisons for Alfonso

MS 805: treatise of R. Brandolini on music and poetry

Rome, Biblioteca Nazionale Centrale

Fondo gesuitico 404: epistle of L. Saccano on death of Alfonso

Rome, Library of Dottore Michele Gattini

Ciccolino Gattini, "De bello regis Alphonsi" (formerly in the library of Count Giuseppe Gattini of Matera)

Valencia, Biblioteca Universitaria

MS 215: instructions of King Federico

MS 375 (formerly 799): epistle of A. Contrario on Plato for Ferrante

MS 443 (formerly 727): Facio's translation of Isocrates

MS 450 (formerly 856): poem of O. Romano for Alfonso

MS 723: Sagundino's translation of Onosander for Alfonso

MS 730 (formerly 760): Macedonio's life of St. Paris

MS 731 (formerly 741): Poggio's translation of Xenophon's *Cyropaedia*

MS 735 (formerly 745): orations delivered before Ferrante

MS 757: poem by Bernardo Maria Aretino for Duke Alfonso of Calabria

MS 774 (formerly 52): works of Brancati

MS 839 (formerly 778): Facio's treatise *De proprietate verborum*

Valladolid, Biblioteca Universitaria, Colegio Mayor de Santa Cruz

MS 227: epistles and other works of Facio

Vatican City, Biblioteca Apostolica Vaticana

Barb. lat. 2069: epistles and verses of Panormita

Barb. lat. 2070: diplomatic epistles and orations of Panormita

Chigi L. VII. 269: treatise on government by Cinico

Chigi M. VIII. 159: list of historical works by Cinico

Ottob. lat. 1558: anonymous translation of Aristeas for Ferrante

Ottob. lat. 1677: includes epistle of Contrario to Alfonso

Ottob. lat. 1732: epistles and works of Sagundino

Pal. lat. 41: Manetti's translation of the Psalter

Pal. lat. 45: Manetti's translation of the New Testament
Pal. lat. 1604: works of Manetti
Urb. lat. 6: Manetti's translation of the New Testament
Urb. lat. 154: Manetti's defense of Christianity
Urb. lat. 415: Facio's translation of Arrian's life of Alexander
Urb. lat. 643: praise of Panormita by J. Pisanus
Urb. lat. 923: writings against the Turks, including one of Sagundino
Vat. lat. 1875: humanist translations from Plutarch, including da Castiglion-
    chio's version of Fabius Maximus' life for Alfonso
Vat. lat. 2906: miscellany, including letters of Facio
Vat. lat. 3371: epistles of Panormita to others
Vat. lat. 3372: epistles to Panormita
Vat. lat. 3414: translations of Aelian by Gaza and of Onosander by Sagundino
Vat. lat. 3422: translation of Isocrates by da Castiglionchio for Panormita
Vat. lat. 5567: P. Galatino's commentary on the Apocalypse, with description
    of the Turkish massacre at Otranto
Vat. lat. 7230: translation of Onosander by Sagundino
Venice, Biblioteca Nazionale Marciana
    MS lat. XI. 53 (= 4009): oration delivered before Ferrante
    MS lat. XI. 81 (= 4155): epistles including diplomatic correspondence be-
        tween Ferrante and Sixtus IV
    MS lat. XIII. 62 (= 4418): epistles and orations of Sagundino
    MS lat. XIV. 244 (= 4681): works of Sagundino

PUBLISHED PRIMARY SOURCES

Acquaviva, Andrea Matteo. *Commentarium in translationem libelli Plutarchi Chae-
    ronei De virtute morali.* Naples, 1526.
Acquaviva, Belisario. *De instituendis liberis principum.* Naples, 1519.
———. *Paraphrasis in economica Aristotelis.* Naples, 1519.
———. *De re militari et singulari certamine.* Naples, 1519.
———. *De venatione et de aucupio.* Naples, 1519.
Aelianus. *Tactica, seu de instruendis aciebus,* trans. T. Gaza. Leiden, 1607.
Altamura, Antonio, ed. *Otranto: testi e monumenti.* Galatina, 1955.
———. *Testi napoletani del Quattrocento.* Naples, 1953.
Arrianus, Flavius. *De rebus gestis Alexandri regis,* trans. B. Facio. Pesaro, 1508.
Barbaro, Francesco. *Centotrenta lettere inedite di Francesco Barbaro,* ed. R. Sabba-
    dini. Salerno, 1884.
———. *Epistolae,* ed. A. Quirini. Brescia, 1743.
Beccadelli, Antonio. *De dictis et factis Alphonsi regis.* Basel, 1538.
———. *Epistolarum libri* v. Venice, 1553.
———. *Epistolarum libri* v, ed. G. Riccardius. Naples, 1746.
———. *Hermaphroditus,* ed. F. C. Forberg. Coburg, 1824.
———. *Liber rerum gestarum Ferdinandi regis,* ed. G. Resta. Palermo, 1968.
———. *Ottanta lettere inedite del Panormita,* ed. R. Sabbadini. Catania, 1910.

Beccadelli, Antonio. *Poesie latine inedite di A. Beccadelli detto il Panormita*, ed. A. Cinquini and R. Valentini. Aosta, 1907.

———. *Regis Ferdinandi et aliorum epistolae ac orationes utriusque militiae*. Vico Equense, 1586.

———. *Speculum boni principis*, ed. J. Santes. Amsterdam, 1646.

Biondo, Flavio. *Scritti inediti e rari di Biondo Flavio*, ed. B. Nogara. Rome, 1927.

Bracciolini, Poggio. *Epistolae*, ed. T. Tonelli. 3 vols. Florence, 1832–61.

———. *Opera omnia*, ed. R. Fubini. 4 vols. Turin, 1963–69.

Bruni, Leonardo. *Epistolarum libri VIII*, ed. L. Mehus. 2 vols. Florence, 1741.

———. *Humanistisch-philosophische Schriften*, ed. H. Baron. Leipzig, 1928.

Calenzio, Elisio. *Opuscula*. Rome, 1503.

Cannavale, Ercole, ed. *Lo Studio di Napoli nel Rinascimento*. Naples, 1895.

Carafa, Diomede. *Gli ammaestramenti militari*, ed. F. Campanile. Naples, 1608.

———. *Memoriale a Beatrice d'Aragona, regina d'Ungheria*, ed. B. Croce. Naples, 1895.

———. *Memoriale a Federico d'Aragona in occasione della sua andata in Francia*, ed. L. Miele. Naples, 1972.

———. *Dello optimo cortesano*, ed. G. Paparelli. Salerno, 1971.

———. *Un opuscolo dedicato a Beatrice d'Aragona, regina d'Ungheria*, ed. E. Mayer. Rome, 1937.

Catalano Tirrito, M., ed. *Nuovi documenti sul Panormita*. Catania, 1910.

Commynes, Philippe de. *Mémoires*, ed. J. Calmette. 3 vols. Paris, 1924–25.

Croce, Benedetto, ed. *Prima del Machiavelli: una difesa di Re Ferrante I di Napoli per il violato trattato di pace del 1486 col papa*. Bari, 1944.

de Chaula, Thomas. *Gestorum per Alphonsum Aragonum et Siciliae regem libri quinque*, ed. R. Starrabba. Palermo, 1904.

de Ferrariis, Antonio. *Epistole*, ed. A. Altamura. Lecce, 1959.

———. *Epistole salentine*, ed. M. Paone. Galatina, 1974.

de Jennaro, Pietro Jacopo. *Dialogho chiamato plutopenia ad lo illustrissimo Don Frederico de Aragona*. Naples, 1471.

———. *Rime e lettere*, ed. M. Corti. Bologna, 1956.

———. *Le sei etate de la vita umana*, ed. A. Altamura and P. Basile. Naples, 1976.

de Lignamine, Giovanni Filippo. *Inclyti Ferdinandi regis vita et laudes*. Rome, 1472.

de Marinis, Tammaro, ed. *Per la storia della biblioteca dei re d'Aragona in Napoli*. Florence, 1909.

——— and Alessandro Perosa, eds. *Nuovi documenti per la storia del Rinascimento*. Florence, 1970.

de Rosa, Loise. *Napoli aragonese nei ricordi di Loise de Rosa*, ed. A. Altamura. Naples, 1971.

Donzellini, Girolamo, ed. *Epistolae principum, rerumpublicarum, ac sapientum virorum*. Venice, 1574.

Facio, Bartolomeo. *Invective in Laurentium Vallam*, ed. E. I. Rao. Naples, 1978.

———. *De viris illustribus liber*, ed. L. Mehus. Florence, 1745.

Ficino, Marsilio. *Opera omnia*. 4 vols. Turin, 1959.

Filangieri, Gaetano, ed. *Documenti per la storia, le arti e le industrie delle provincie napoletane*. 6 vols. Naples, 1883–91.

Filangieri, Riccardo, ed. *Una cronaca napoletana figurata del Quattrocento*. Naples, 1956.

Filelfo, Francesco. *Cent-dix lettres grecques de François Filelfe*, ed. E. Legrand. Paris, 1892.

————. *Epistolarum familiarium libri XXXVII*. Venice, 1502.

Fonti aragonese. Naples, 1957–.

Galateo. *See* de Ferrariis, Antonio.

Galluccio, Luigi. *See* Calenzio, Elisio.

Garin, Eugenio, ed. *Prosatori latini del Quattrocento*. Milan, 1952.

Gimenez Soler, A., ed. *Itinerario del Rey Don Alonso de Aragón y de Napoles*. Saragossa, 1909.

Giustiniani, Agostino. *Annali della Reppublica di Genova*, ed. G. B. Spotorno. 2 vols. Genoa, 1854.

Graevius, J. G., ed. *Thesaurus antiquitatum et historiarum Italiae*. 9 vols. Leiden, 1704–23.

Grande, Salvatore, ed. *Collana di opere scelte edite e inedite di scrittori di Terra d'Otranto*. 22 vols. Lecce, 1867–75.

Gravier, Giovanni, ed. *Raccolta di tutti i più rinomati scrittori dell'istoria generale del regno di Napoli*. 25 vols. Naples, 1769–77.

Gualdo Rosa, Lucia, I. Nuovo, and D. Defilippis, eds. *Gli umanisti e la guerra otrantina: testi dei secoli XV e XVI*. Bari, 1982.

Iorga, N., ed. *Notes et extraits pour servir à l'histoire des croisades au XVe siècle*. 6 vols. Paris, 1899–1902, and Bucharest, 1915–16.

Machiavelli, Niccolò. *Opere*, ed. S. Bertelli. 11 vols. Milan and Verona, 1968–82.

Maio, Giuniano. *De maiestate*, ed. F. Gaeta. Bologna, 1956.

Manetti, Giannozzo. *Apologeticus*, ed. A. de Petris. Rome, 1981.

————. *De dignitate et excellentia hominis*, ed. E. Leonard. Padua, 1975.

————. *Vita Socratis et Senecae*, ed. A. de Petris. Florence, 1979.

Marineo, Lucio. *De hispaniae laudibus*. Burgos, ca. 1500.

————. *De primis Aragoniae regibus*. Caesaraugusta, 1509.

Mazzoleni, Jole, ed. *Il "Codice Chigi": un regesto della cancelleria di Alfonso I d'Aragona, Re di Napoli, per gli anni 1451–1453*. Naples, 1965.

————, ed. *Regesto della cancelleria aragonese di Napoli*. Naples, 1951.

Mercati, Angelo, ed. *Raccolta di concordati su materie ecclesiastiche tra la Santa Sede e le autorità civili*. 2d ed. 2 vols. Vatican City, 1954.

Messer, A., ed. *Le codice aragonese*. Paris, 1912.

Migne, J. P., ed., *Patrologia graeca*. 161 vols. Paris, 1857–1904.

Mittarelli, G. B., ed. *Bibliotheca codicum manuscriptorum monasterii S. Michaelis Venetiarum prope Murianum*. Venice, 1779.

Monfasani, John, ed. *Collectanea Trapezuntiana: Texts, Documents, and Bibliographies of George of Trebizond*. Binghamton, N.Y., 1984.

Muratori, L. A., ed. *Rerum italicarum scriptores*. 25 vols. Milan, 1723–51.

———, ed. *Rerum italicarum scriptores*, 2d ed. 34 vols. Bologna, 1900–35.

Notar Giacomo. *Cronica di Napoli*, ed. P. Garzilli. Naples, 1845.

Onosander. *De optimo imperatore eiusque officio*, trans. N. Sagundino. Basel, 1541.

Panormita. *See* Beccadelli, Antonio.

Piccolomini, Enea Silvio. *Der Briefwechsel des Eneas Silvius Piccolomini*, ed. R. Wolkan. 3 vols. Vienna, 1909–18.

———. *In libros Antonii Panormitae poetae de dictis et factis Alphonsi regis memorabilibus commentarius*. Basel, 1538.

Plinius Secundus. *Historia naturale*, trans. C. Landino. Venice, 1535.

———. *Storia naturale*, trans. G. Brancati, ed. S. Gentile. 3 vols. Naples, 1974.

Plutarch. *De virtute morali*, ed. and trans. A. M. Acquaviva. Naples, 1526.

Pontano, Giovanni. *Carmina*, ed. J. Oeschger. Bari, 1948.

———. *I dialoghi*, ed. C. Previtera. Florence, 1943.

———. *De immanitate liber*, ed. L. Monti Sabia. Naples, 1970.

———. *Lettere inedite di Joviano Pontano in nome de' reali di Napoli*, ed. F. Gabotto. Bologna, 1893.

———. *De magnanimitate*, ed. F. Tateo. Florence, 1969.

———. *Opera omnia soluta oratione composita*. 3 vols. Venice, 1518–19.

———. *De sermone libri sex*, ed. S. Lupi and A. Risicato. Lugano, 1954.

———. *I trattati delle virtù sociali*, ed. F. Tateo. Rome, 1965.

Pope, Isabel, and Masakata Kanazawa, eds. *The Musical Manuscript Montecassino 871: A Neapolitan Repertory of Sacred and Secular Music of the Late Fifteenth Century*. Oxford, 1978.

Porzio, Camillo. *La congiura de' baroni*, ed. S. D'Aloe. Naples, 1859.

———. *La congiura de' baroni del regno di Napoli contra il re Ferdinando il primo*, ed. E. Pontieri. Naples, 1964.

Sagundino, Niccolò. *Rerum turcarum liber*. Louvain, 1553.

Sandeo, Felino. *De regibus Siciliae et Apuliae*. Hanau, 1611.

Tinctoris, Johannes. *Opera theoretica*, ed. A. Seay. 2 vols. Rome, 1975.

———. *Terminorum musicae diffinitorium (c. 1475)*, ed. and trans. A. Machabey. Paris, 1951.

Toppi, Nicola. *De origine omnium tribunalium*. 3 vols. Naples, 1655–66.

Trinchera, Francesco, ed. *Codice aragonese*. 3 vols. Naples, 1866–74.

Valla, Lorenzo. *Antidotum in Facium*, ed. M. Regoliosi. Padua, 1981.

———. *Antidotum primum*, ed. A. Wesseling. Assen, 1978.

———. *Collatio Novi Testamenti*, ed. A. Perosa. Florence, 1970.

———. "Dialogue on Free Will," trans. C. Trinkaus. In E. Cassirer et al., eds., *The Renaissance Philosophy of Man*, pp. 155–82. Chicago, 1948.

———. *Epistole*, ed. O. Besomi and M. Regoliosi. Padua, 1984.

———. *De falso credita et ementita Constantini donatione*, ed. W. Setz. Weimar, 1976.

———. *Gesta Ferdinandi regis Aragonum*, ed. O. Besomi. Padua, 1973.

———. *De libero arbitrio*, ed. M. Anfossi. Florence, 1934.

———. *Opera omnia*, ed. E. Garin. 2 vols. Turin, 1962.

Valla, Lorenzo. *The Profession of the Religious and the Principal Arguments from the Falsely-Believed and Forged Donation of Constantine*, trans. O. Z. Pugliese. Toronto, 1985.

———. *Repastinatio dialectice et philosophie*, ed. G. Zippel. 2 vols. Padua, 1982.

———. *The Treatise of Lorenzo Valla on the Donation of Constantine*, ed. and trans. C. B. Coleman. New Haven, 1922.

———. *De vero falsoque bono*, ed. M. de P. Lorch. Bari, 1970.

Vecce, Carlo, ed. *Gli umanisti e la musica: un'antologia di testi umanistici sulla musica*. Milan, 1985.

Vespasiano da Bisticci. *Commentario della vita di messer Giannozzo Manetti*, ed. P. Fanfani. Turin, 1862.

———. *Le vite*, ed. A. Greco. 2 vols. Florence, 1970–76.

Volpicella, Luigi, ed. *Regis Ferdinandi primi instructionum liber*. Naples, 1916.

Zurita, G. *Anales de la Corona de Aragón*. 7 vols. Saragossa, 1610–21.

SECONDARY WORKS

Altamura, Antonio. "La biblioteca aragonese e i manoscritti inediti di Giovan Marco Cinico." *Bibliofila*, 41 (1939), 418–26.

———. "La letteratura volgare." In *Storia di Napoli*, 7.293–361. 10 vols. Naples, 1975–81.

———. "Un opusculo inedito di Tristano Caracciolo." *Rinascita*, 2 (1939), 253–79.

———. *Studi di filologia medievale e umanistica*. Naples, 1954.

———. *Studi e ricerche di letteratura umanistica*. Naples, 1956.

———. *L'umanesimo del Mezzogiorno d'Italia*. Florence, 1941.

Amabile, Luigi. *Il Santo Officio della Inquisizione in Napoli*. 2 vols. Città di Castello, 1892.

Ametller y Vinyas, José. *Alfonso V de Aragón en Italia y la crisis religiosa del siglo XV*. 3 vols. Gerona, 1903–28.

Antonazzi, Giovanni. "Lorenzo Valla e la Donazione di Costantino nel secolo XV con un testo inedito di Antonio Cortesi." *Rivista di storia della chiesa in Italia*, 4 (1950), 186–234.

Atlas, Allan W. "Alexander Agricola and Ferrante I of Naples." *Journal of the American Musicological Society*, 30 (1977), 313–19.

———. *Music at the Aragonese Court of Naples*. Cambridge, 1985.

Atti del congresso internazionale di studi sull'età aragonese (Bari, 1972).

Babinger, Franz. *Johannes Darius (1444–1494)*. Munich, 1961.

———. "Maometto il Conquistatore e gli umanisti d'Italia." In *Venezia e l'Oriente tra tardo Medioevo e Rinascimento*, pp. 433–49. Florence, 1966.

———. "Maometto II, il conquistatore, e l'Italia." *Rivista storica italiana*, 63 (1951), 469–505.

———. *Mehmed the Conqueror and His Time*, trans. R. Manheim. Princeton, 1978.

———. "Nikolaos Sagoundinos, ein griechischer-venedischer Humanist des

BIBLIOGRAPHY

15. Jahrhunderts." Χαριστηρὶον εἰς 'Αναστάσιον Κ. 'Ορλανδὸν, pp. 198–212. Athens, 1964.

————. "Sechs unbekannte aragonische Sendschreiben im grossherrlichen Seraj zu Stambul." In *Studi in onore di Riccardo Filangieri*, 2.107–28. 3 vols. Naples, 1959.

Baron, Hans. *The Crisis of the Early Italian Renaissance*. 2d ed. Princeton, 1966.

————. "Leonardo Bruni: 'Professional Rhetorician' or 'Civic Humanist'?" *Past and Present*, 36 (1967), 21–37.

Barone, Nicola. "Notizia della scrittura umanistica nei manoscritti e nei documenti napoletani del XV secolo." *Atti della Reale Accademia di Archeologia, lettere e belle arte*, 20 (1899), pt. 2, no. 2, pp. 1–14.

————. *Nuovi studi sulla vita e sulle opere di Antonio Galateo*. Naples, 1892.

Barozzi, L., and R. Sabbadini. *Studi sul Panormita e sul Valla*. Florence, 1891.

Baxandall, Michael. "Bartholomaeus Facius on Painting: A Fifteenth-Century Manuscript of the *De viris illustribus*." *Journal of the Warburg and Courtauld Institutes*, 27 (1964), 90–107.

Belladona, Rita. "Pontanus, Machiavelli and a Case of Religious Dissimulation in Early Sixteenth-Century Siena." *Bibliothèque d'humanisme et Renaissance*, 37 (1975), 377–85.

Bentley, Jerry H. *Humanists and Holy Writ: New Testament Scholarship in the Renaissance*. Princeton, 1983.

————. "Il mecenatismo culturale di Ferrante I d'Aragona." *Esperienze letterarie*, 12 (1987).

Bertola, Ermenegildo. "Il *De prudentia* di Giovanni Pontano e la morale indipendente." *Sophia*, 10 (1942), 82–99.

Bianchini, Ludovico. *Storia delle finanze del Regno delle due Sicilie*, ed. L. de Rosa. Naples, 1971.

Billanovich, G. "Petrarch and the Textual Tradition of Livy." *Journal of the Warburg and Courtauld Institutes*, 14 (1951), 137–208.

Bindi, Vicenzo. *Gli Acquaviva letterati*. Naples, 1881.

Bonilla y San Martín, Adolfo. *Fernando de Córdoba (¿1425–1486?) y los orígenes del Renacimiento filosófico en España*. Madrid, 1911.

Braggio, Carlo. *Giacomo Bracelli e l'umanesimo dei liguri al suo tempo*. Genoa, 1890.

Branca, Vittore. "Un codice aragonese scritto dal Cinico." In *Studi di bibliografia e di storia in onore di Tammaro de Marinis*, 1.163–215. 4 vols. Verona, 1964.

————. "Ermolao Barbaro and Late Quattrocento Venetian Humanism." In J. R. Hale, ed., *Renaissance Venice*, pp. 218–43. London, 1973.

————. "L'umanesimo veneziano alla fine del Quattrocento: Ermolao Barbaro e il suo circolo." In *Storia della cultura veneta*, 3.1.123–75. Vicenza, 1976–.

Brucker, Gene A. *Renaissance Florence*. New York, 1969.

Burke, Peter. *Culture and Society in Renaissance Italy, 1420–1540*. New York, 1972.

Calmette, J. "La politique espagnole dans l'affaire des barons napolitains (1485–1492)." *Revue historique*, 110 (1912), 225–46.

Camporeale, Salvatore. *Lorenzo Valla: umanesimo e teologia*. Florence, 1972.

Cantarelli, G. B. *Monografia storica della città di Lecce*. Lecce, 1885.

Carlini, Antonio. "Appunti sulle traduzioni latine di Isocrate da Lapo da Castiglionchio." *Studi classici e orientali*, 19–20 (1970–71), 302–9.

Carratelli, Giovanni P. "Due epistole di Giovanni Brancati su la 'Naturalis historia' di Plinio e la versione di Cristoforo Landino." *AAP*, n.s. 3 (1949–50), 179–93.

———. "Un'epistola di Giovanni Brancati sull'arte retorica e lo scriver latino." *AAP*, n.s. 2 (1948–49), 109–23.

Caserta, Ernesto. "Il problema religioso nel *De voluptate* del Valla e nell'*Aegidius* del Pontano." *Italica*, 43 (1966), 240–63.

Castellano Lanzara, M. G. "Uno sguardo alla cultura napoletana al tempo dei re d'Aragona." *Amici della Spagna*, 34 (May, 1973), 8–14.

Catalano, Michele. *Storia della Università di Catania*. Catania, 1934.

———. *Storia documentata della R. Università di Catania*. Catania, 1913.

Cessi, Roberto. "La pace di Bagnolo dell'agosto 1484." *Annali triestini di diritto, economia e politica*, n.s. 3 (1941), 277–356.

———. "Per la storia della guerra di Ferrara (1482–83)." *Notizie degli archivi di stato*, 8 (1948), 63–72.

Cioffari, Vicenzo. "Fortune, Fate, and Chance." In Philip P. Wiener, ed., *Dictionary of the History of Ideas*, 2.225–36. 4 vols. New York, 1973.

Cochrane, Eric. *Historians and Historiography in the Italian Renaissance*. Chicago, 1981.

Colucci, Dina. *Antonio de Ferrariis detto il Galateo*. Lecce, 1939.

Compagna-Perrone Capano, A. M. "A proposito di *Alfonso il Magnanimo re di Napoli* e di *The Kingdom of Naples Under Alfonso the Magnanimous*." *ASPN*, 4th ser. 15 (1977), 375–82.

Corsano, Antonio. "Note sul pensiero religioso del Galateo." In *Atti del congresso internazionale di studi sull'età aragonese*, pp. 182–90. Bari, 1972.

Cortese, Nino. *Cultura e politica a Napoli dal Cinque al Settecento*. Naples, 1965.

———. "L'età spagnuola." In *Storia della Università di Napoli*, pp. 201–431. Naples, 1934.

Creighton, Mandell. "Some Literary Correspondence of Humphrey, Duke of Gloucester." *English Historical Review*, 10 (1895), 99–104.

Croce, Alda. "Contributa a un'edizione delle opere di Antonio Galateo." *ASPN*, n.s. 23 (1937), 366–93.

Croce, Benedetto. *Aneddoti di varia letteratura*. 4 vols. Bari, 1953–54.

———. "Antonio de Ferrariis detto il Galateo." *Humanisme et Renaissance*, 4 (1937), 366–82.

———. *History of the Kingdom of Naples*, trans. F. Frenaye. Chicago, 1970.

———. "Una lettera inedita di Alfonso d'Aragona." *Napoli nobilissima*, 1 (1982), 127–28.

———. *Nuove curiosità storiche*. Naples, 1922.

———. *Philosophy, Poetry, History*, trans. C. Sprigge. London, 1966.

———. *Politics and Morals*, trans. S. J. Castiglione. New York, 1945.

———. *La Spagna nella vita italiana durante la Rinascenza*. 2d ed. Bari, 1922.

Croce, Benedetto. *Storie e leggende napoletane.* 4th ed. Bari, 1948.

―――. "Il trattato *De educatione* di Antonio Galateo," *Giornale storico della letteratura italiana*, 23 (1894), 394–406.

d'Agostino, Guido. *La capitale ambigua: Napoli dal 1458 al 1580.* Naples, 1979.

d'Alos-Moner, Ramon. "Contribució a la biografia de Lorenzo Valla." In *Miscellanea Crexells*, pp. 1–7. Barcelona, 1929.

―――. "Documenti per la storia della biblioteca di Alfonso il Magnanimo." In *Miscellanea Francesco Ehrle*, 5.390–422. 5 vols. Rome, 1924.

D'Amico, John F. *Renaissance Humanism in Papal Rome: Humanists and Churchmen on the Eve of the Reformation.* Baltimore, 1983.

de Blasiis, G. "Tre scritture napoletane del secolo XV." *ASPN*, 4 (1879), 411–67.

de Fabrizio, Angelo. *Antonio de Ferrariis Galateo, pensatore e moralista del Rinascimento.* Trani, 1908.

de Frede, Carlo. "Alfonso II d'Aragona e la difesa del Regno di Napoli nel 1494." *ASPN*, 3d ser. 20 (1981), 193–219.

―――. "Biblioteche e cultura di signori napoletani del '400." *Bibliothèque d'humanisme et Renaissance*, 25 (1963), 187–97.

―――. "Il discorso di Re Ferrandino ai napoletani." *AAP*, n.s. 30 (1981), 207–22.

―――. "Le 'Epistole militari' di Ferrante I d'Aragona." *ASPN*, n.s. 31 (1947), 109–31.

―――. *I lettori di umanità nello Studio di Napoli.* Naples, 1960.

―――. "Un memoriale di Ferrante I d'Aragona a Luigi XI (1478)." *Rivista storica italiana*, 60 (1948), 403–19.

―――. *Studenti e uomini di leggi a Napoli nel Rinascimento.* Naples, 1957.

―――. "L'umanista Tristano Caracciolo e la sua 'Vita di Giovanna I.' " *Archivio storico italiano*, 105 (1947), 50–64.

de la Fage, Adrien. *Essais de diphthérographie musicale.* Paris, 1864.

de Lisio, P. A. *Studi sull'umanesimo meridionale.* Naples, 1974.

del Treppo, Mario. "The 'Crown of Aragon' and the Mediterranean." *Journal of European Economic History*, 2 (1973), 161–85.

de Marinis, Tammaro. *La biblioteca napoletana dei re d'Aragona.* 4 vols. Milan, 1947–52.

―――. *La biblioteca napoletana dei re d'Aragona: supplemento.* 2 vols. Verona, 1969.

―――. "La liberazione di Alfonso V d'Aragona prigioniero dei genovesi." *ASPN*, n.s. 34 (1953–54), 101–6.

de Mattei, Rodolfo. *Dal premachiavellismo all'antimachiavellismo.* Florence, 1969.

―――. "Politica e morale prima di Machiavelli." *Giornale critico della filosofia italiana*, 29 (1950), 56–67.

Denis, Anne. *Charles VIII et les italiens: histoire et mythe.* Geneva, 1979.

di Napoli, Giovanni. *Lorenzo Valla: filosofia e religione nell'umanesimo italiano.* Rome, 1971.

Dizionario biografico degli italiani. Rome, 1960–.

Dupré Theseider, Eugenio. *La politica italiana di Alfonso d'Aragona*. Bologna, 1956.

Faraglia, Nunzio F. *Storia della lotta tra Alfonso V d'Aragona e Renato d'Angiò*. Lanciano, 1908.

Fava, Mariano, and Giovanni Bresciano, eds. *La stampa a Napoli nel XV secolo*. 3 vols. Leipzig, 1911–13.

Fedele, P. "La pace del 1486 tra Ferdinando d'Aragona ed Innocenzo VIII." *ASPN*, 30 (1905), 481–503.

Feld, M. D. "A Theory of the Early Italian Printing Firm." *Harvard Library Bulletin*, 33 (1985), 341–77; 34 (1986), 294–332.

Filangieri, Riccardo. "L'età aragonese." In *Storia dell'Università di Napoli*, pp. 151–99. Naples, 1924.

————. "Report on the Destruction by the Germans, September 30, 1943, of the Depository of Priceless Historical Records of the Naples State Archives." *American Archivist*, 7 (1944), 252–55.

————. *Scritti di paleografia e diplomatica di archivistica e di erudizione*. Rome, 1972.

————. "Il tempietto di Giovanni Pontano a Napoli." In *In onore di Giovanni Gioviano Pontano nel V centenario della sua nascita*, pp. 11–49. Naples, 1926.

Fois, Mario. *Il pensiero cristiano di Lorenzo Valla nel quadro storico-culturale del suo ambiente*. Rome, 1969.

Foucard, C. "Descrizione della città di Napoli e statistica del Regno nel 1444." *ASPN*, 2 (1877), 725–57.

Frittelli, Ugo. *Gianantonio de' Pandoni, detto il "Porcellio."* Florence, 1900.

Fueter, Eduard. *Geschichte der neueren Historiographie*, 3d ed. Munich, 1936.

Fuiano, Michele. *Insegnamento e cultura a Napoli nel Rinascimento*. Naples, 1971.

Gabotto, F. *Un nuovo contributo alla storia dell'umanesimo ligure*. Genoa, 1892.

Gaeta, Franco. *Lorenzo Valla: filologia e storia nell'umanesimo italiano*. Naples, 1955.

————. "Una polemica quattrocentesca contro la *De falso credita et ementita Constantini donatione declamatio* di Lorenzo Valla." *Rivista storica italiana*, 64 (1952), 383–98.

Garin, Eugenio. "La cultura milanese nella prima metà del XV secolo." In *Storia di Milano*, 6.545–608. 16 vols. Milan, 1953–66.

————. "La cultura milanese nella seconda metà del XV secolo." In *Storia di Milano*, 7.539–97. 16 vols. Milan, 1953–66.

————. *Italian Humanism*, trans. P. Munz. Oxford, 1965.

————. *Portraits from the Quattrocento*, trans. V. Velen and E. Velen. New York, 1972.

Gattini, Giuseppe. *Saggio di biblioteca basilicatese*. Matera, 1903.

Geanakoplos, Deno J. "Theodore Gaza, a Byzantine Scholar of the Palaeologan 'Renaissance' in the Italian Renaissance." *Medievalia et humanistica*, n.s. 12 (1984), 61–81.

Gentile, Pietro. *La politica interna di Alfonso V d'Aragona nel Regno di Napoli dal 1443 al 1450*. Monte Cassino, 1909.

Gentile, Pietro. "Lo stato napoletano sotto Alfonso I d'Aragona." *ASPN*, n.s. 23 (1937), 1–56; n.s. 24 (1938), 1–56.

Gilbert, Allan H. *Machiavelli's "Prince" and Its Forerunners*. Durham, N.C., 1938.

Gilbert, Felix. *History: Choice and Commitment*. Cambridge, Mass., 1977.

———. *Machiavelli and Guicciardini: Politics and History in Sixteenth-Century Florence*. Princeton, 1965.

Gothein, Eberhard. *Die Culturentwicklung Süd-Italiens*. Breslau, 1886.

———. *Il Rinascimento nell'Italia meridionale*, ed. and trans. T. Persico. Florence, 1915.

Griggio, Claudio. "Tradizione e rinnovamento nella cultura del Galateo." *Lettere italiane*, 26 (1974), 415–33.

Gualdo Rosa, Lucia. *La fede nella "paideia": aspetti della fortuna europea di Isocrate nei secoli XV e XVI*. Rome, 1984.

Gundersheimer, Werner L. *Ferrara: The Style of a Renaissance Despotism*. Princeton, 1973.

Hersey, George L. *Alfonso II and the Artistic Renewal of Naples, 1485–1495*. New Haven, 1969.

———. *The Aragonese Arch at Naples, 1443–1475*. New Haven, 1973.

Hyde, J. K. "Medieval Descriptions of Cities." *Bulletin of the John Rylands Library*, 48 (1966), 308–40.

In onore di Giovanni Gioviano Pontano nel V centenario della sua nascita. Naples, 1926.

Iurilli, Antonio. "Coordinate cronologiche dell'*Esposizione del 'Pater noster'* di Antonio Galateo." *Giornale storico della letteratura italiana*, 159 (1982), 536–50.

Janik, Linda Gardiner. "Lorenzo Valla: The Primacy of Rhetoric and the Demoralization of History." *History and Theory*, 12 (1973), 389–404.

Kangle, R. P. *The Kautilya Arthasastra: A Study*. Bombay, 1965.

Kelley, Donald R. *Foundations of Modern Historical Scholarship*. New York, 1970.

Kennedy, George. *Classical Rhetoric and Its Christian and Secular Tradition from Ancient to Modern Times*. Chapel Hill, 1980.

King, Margaret L. *Venetian Humanism in an Age of Patrician Dominance*. Princeton, 1986.

Kristeller, Paul O. "The Humanist Bartolomeo Facio and His Unknown Correspondence." In C. H. Carter, ed., *From the Renaissance to the Counter-Reformation: Essays in Honor of Garrett Mattingly*, pp. 56–74. New York, 1965.

———. *Renaissance Thought: The Classic, Scholastic, and Humanist Strains*. New York, 1961.

———. *Renaissance Thought and Its Sources*, ed. M. Mooney. New York, 1979.

———. "An Unpublished Description of Naples by Francesco Bandini." In his *Studies in Renaissance Thought and Letters*, pp. 395–410. Rome, 1969.

Laurenza, Vicenzo. "Il Panormita a Napoli." *AAP*, 42 (1912), 1–92.

Lecoy de la Marche, A. *Le roi René*. 2 vols. Paris, 1875.

Logan, George M. "Substance and Form in Renaissance Humanism." *Journal of Medieval and Renaissance Studies*, 7 (1977), 1–34.

Lojacono, Diomede. "L'opera inedita *De maiestate* di Giuniano Majo." *Atti della reale accademia di scienze morali e politiche di Napoli*, 24 (1891), 329–76.

Lowinsky, Edward E. "The Goddess Fortuna in Music." *Musical Quarterly*, 29 (1943), 45–77.

Luiso, F. P. "Studi su l'epistolario e le traduzioni di Lapo da Castiglionchio junior." *Studi italiani di filologia classica*, 7 (1899), 205–99.

Lupi, Sergio. "Il *De sermone* di Giovanni Pontano." *Filologia romanza*, 2 (1955), 366–417.

Lytle, Guy Fitch, and Stephen Orgel, eds. *Patronage in the Renaissance*. Princeton, 1982.

Maioli, Bruno. "Una gloria di Caggiano rinverdita: l'umanista Gabriele Altilio (1436–1501)." *Humanistica lovaniensia*, 32 (1983), 358–66.

Mallett, Michael. *The Borgias*. New York, 1969.

———. "Diplomacy and War in Later Fifteenth-Century Italy." *Proceedings of the British Academy*, 67 (1981), 267–88.

———. *Mercenaries and Their Masters: Warfare in Renaissance Italy*. Totowa, N.J. 1974.

Mancini, Girolamo. *Vita di Lorenzo Valla*. Florence, 1891.

Manzi, Pietro. *La tipografia napoletana nel '500*. 6 vols. Florence, 1971–75.

Marchiori, Claudio. *Bartolomeo Facio tra letteratura e vita*. Milan, 1971.

Marinescu, Constantin. "Notes sur la vie culturelle sous le règne d'Alfonse *le magnanime*, roi de Naples." In *Miscel·lania Puig i Cadafalch*, 1.291–307. Barcelona, 1947–51.

———. "Le Pape Calixte III (1455–1458), Alfonse V d'Aragon, roi de Naples, et l'offensive contre les Turcs." *Bulletin de section historique de l'académie roumaine*, 19 (1935), 77–97.

Marletta, F. "Un uomo di stato del Quattrocento: Battista Platamone." *Archivio storico per la Sicilia*, 1 (1937), 29–68.

Marsh, David. "Lorenzo Valla in Naples: The Translation from Xenophon's *Cyropaedia*." *Bibliothèque d'humanisme et Renaissance*, 46 (1984), 407–20.

———. *The Quattrocento Dialogue*. Cambridge, Mass., 1980.

Martelli, Sebastiano. "La *vituperatio litterarum* di Antonio de Ferrariis (Galateo)." *Misure critiche*, 2 (1972), 43–65.

Martines, Lauro. *Power and Imagination: City-States in Renaissance Italy*. New York, 1979.

———. *The Social World of the Florentine Humanists, 1390–1460*. Princeton, 1963.

Mattingly, Garrett. *Renaissance Diplomacy*. Baltimore, 1964.

Mauro, Alfredo. *Francesco del Tuppo e il suo "Esopo."* Città di Castello, 1926.

Mayer, Elisabetta. *Un umanista italiano della corte di Mattia Corvino: Aurelio Brandolini Lippo*. Rome, 1938.

Maylender, Michele. *Storia delle accademie d'Italia*. 5 vols. Bologna, 1926–30.

Mazzatinti, Giuseppe. *La biblioteca dei re d'Aragona in Napoli*. Rocca S. Casciano, 1897.

Mazzini, Ubaldo. "Appunti e notizie per servire alla bio-bibliografia di Bartolomeo Facio." *Giornale storico e letterario della Liguria*, 4 (1903), 400–454.

Mazzoleni, Jole. *Le fonti documentarie e bibliografiche dal sec. X al sec. XX conservate presso l'Archivio di Stato di Napoli*. 2 vols. Naples, 1974–78.

McManamon, John M. "The Ideal Renaissance Pope: Funeral Oratory from the Papal Court." *Archivium historiae pontificiae*, 14 (1976), 9–70.

Mercati, Giovanni. *Per la cronologia della vita e degli scritti di Niccolò Perotti*. Rome 1925.

Miele, Lucia. *Saggi galateani*. Naples, 1982.

————. "Tradizione ed 'esperienza' nella precettistica politica di Diomede Carafa." *AAP*, n.s. 24 (1975), 141–51.

————. "Tradizione letteraria e realismo politico nel 'De principe' del Pontano." *AAP*, n.s. 32 (1983), 301–21.

Minieri Riccio, C. "Alcuni fatti di Alfonso I. di Aragona." *ASPN*, 6 (1881), 1–36, 231–58, 411–61.

————. *Biografie degli accademici alfonsini, detti poi pontaniani, dal 1442 al 1543*. Naples, 1881.

————. *Cenno storico della accademia alfonsina istituta nella città di Napoli nel 1442*. Naples, 1875.

————. *Cenno storico della accademia pontaniana*. Naples, 1876.

————. *Cenno storico delle accademie fiorite nella città di Napoli*. Naples, 1879.

————. *Notizia delle accademie istituite nelle provincie napoletane*. Naples, 1878.

Monfasani, John. *George of Trebizond: A Biography and a Study of His Rhetoric and Logic*. Leiden, 1976.

Monti Sabia, Liliana. "L'estremo autografo di Giovanni Pontano." *Italia medioevale e umanistica*, 23 (1980), 293–314.

————. "L'*humanitas* di Elisio Calenzio alla luce del suo epistolario." *Annali della facoltà di lettere e filosofia dell'Università di Napoli*, 11 (1964–68), 175–251.

Moores, J. D. "New Light on Diomede Carafa and His 'Perfect Loyalty' to Ferrante of Aragon." *Italian Studies*, 26 (1971), 1–23.

Morel-Fatio, M. A. "Maître Fernand de Cordoue et les humanistes italiens du XVe siècle." In *Mélanges Julien Havet*, pp. 521–33. Paris, 1895.

Moro, Donato. "Tre note per la biografia di Antonio Galateo." *Esperienze letterarie*, 4 (1979), 81–102.

————. "La vicenda otrantina del 1480–81 nella società italiana del tempo." *Rassegna salentina*, n.s. 5 (March–June 1980), 73–135.

Moscati, Ruggero. "Nella burocrazia centrale di Alfonso d'Aragona: le cariche generali." In *Miscellanea in onore di Roberto Cessi*, 1.365–77. 3 vols. Rome, 1958.

————. "Ricerche su gli atti superstiti della cancelleria napoletana di Alfonso d'Aragona." *Rivista storica italiana*, 65 (1953), 540–52.

————. "Lo stato 'napoletano' di Alfonso d'Aragona." *Clio*, 9 (1973), 165–82.

Murphy, James J., ed. *Renaissance Eloquence*. Berkeley, 1983.

Natale, Michele. *Antonio Beccadelli detto il Panormita*. Caltanisetta, 1902.

Natale, Michele. "Due codici inediti di Antonio Beccadelli." *Archivio storico siciliano*, n.s. 25 (1900), 396–400.

Nauert, Charles G., Jr. "C. Plinius Secundus (Naturalis historia)." In Paul O. Kristeller and F. Edward Cranz, eds., *Catalogus translationum et commentariorum*, 4.297–422. Washington, D.C., 1980.

——. "Renaissance Humanism: An Emergent Consensus and Its Critics." *Indiana Social Studies Quarterly*, 33 (1980), 5–20.

Nelson, Ernest W. "The Origins of Modern Balance-of-Power Politics." *Medievalia et Humanistica*, 1 (1943), 124–42.

O'Malley, John W. *Praise and Blame in Renaissance Rome*. Durham, N.C., 1979.

Palisca, Claude V. *Humanism in Italian Renaissance Musical Thought*. New Haven, 1985.

Palumbo, Pietro. *Storia di Lecce*. Lecce, 1977.

Paparelli, Gioacchino. *Feritas, humanitas, divinitas (l'essenza umanistica del Rinascimento)*. 2d ed. Naples, 1973.

——, ed. *La cultura umanistica nell'Italia meridionale*. Naples, 1980.

Paschini, Pio. *Lodovico Cardinal Camerlengo (d. 1465)*. Rome, 1939.

Pastor, Ludwig von. *History of the Popes*, trans. F. I. Antrobus. 40 vols. 2d ed. St. Louis, 1913–53.

Patch, Howard Rollins. "The Tradition of the Goddess Fortuna." *Smith College Studies in Modern Languages*, 3 (1922), 131–235.

Pedio, T. *Storia della storiografia lucana*. Bari, 1964.

Percopo, Erasmo. "Lettere di Giovanni Pontano a principi ed amici." *AAP*, 37 (1907), 1–86.

——. "Nuove lettere di Gioviano Pontano a principi ed amici." In *In onore di Giovanni Gioviano Pontano nel V centenario della sua nascita*, pp. 105–40. Naples, 1926.

——. "Nuovi documenti su gli scrittori e gli artisti dei tempi aragonesi." *ASPN*, 18 (1893), 527–37, 784–812; 19 (1894), 376–409, 561–91, 740–79; 20 (1895), 283–335.

——. "Pontaniana." *Studi di letteratura italiana*, 3 (1901), 193–207.

——. *Vita di Giovanni Pontano*, ed. M. Manfredi. Naples, 1938.

Perito, Enrico. *La congiura dei baroni e il conte di Policastro*. Bari, 1926.

Persico, Tommaso. *Diomede Carafa: uomo di stato e scrittore del secolo XV*. Naples, 1899.

——. *Gli scrittori politici napoletani dal '400 al '700*. Naples, 1912.

Petrucci, Franca. "Per un'edizione critica dei Memoriali di Diomede Carafa: problemi e metodo." *ASPN*, 4th ser. 15 (1977), 213–34.

Picker, Martin. "A Letter of Charles VIII of France Concerning Alexander Agricola." In Jan LaRue, ed., *Aspects of Medieval and Renaissance Music: A Birthday Offering to Gustave Reese*, pp. 665–72. New York, 1966.

Pieri, Piero. "L'arte militare italiana della seconda metà del secolo XV negli scritti di Diomede Carafa, Conte di Maddaloni." In *Ricordi e studi in memoria di Francesco Flamini*, pp. 87–103. Naples, 1931.

Pieri, Piero. "Il 'Governo et exercitio de la militia' di Orso degli Orsini e i 'Memoriali' di Diomede Carafa." *ASPN*, n.s. 19 (1933), 99–212.

————. *Il Rinascimento e la crisi militare italiana*. Turin, 1952.

Pirri, Pietro. *Le notizie e gli scritti di Tommaso Pontano e di Giovanni Gioviano Pontano giovane*. Perugia, 1913.

Piva, Edoardo. *La guerra di Ferrara*. 2 vols. Padua, 1893–94.

Pontieri, Ernesto. *Alfonso il Magnanimo re di Napoli (1435–1458)*. Naples, 1975.

————. *La Calabria a metà del secolo XV e le rivolte di Antonio Centelles*. Naples, 1963.

————. "La dinastia aragonese di Napoli e la casa de' Medici di Firenze (dal carteggio familiare)." *ASPN*, n.s. 26 (1940), 274–342; n.s. 27 (1941), 217–73.

————. *Divagazioni storiche e storiografiche*. Naples, 1960.

————. *Per la storia del regno di Ferrante I d'Aragona re di Napoli*. 2d ed. Naples, 1969.

————. "La Puglia nel quadro della monarchia degli aragonesi di Napoli." In *Atti del congresso internazionale di studi sull'età aragonese*, pp. 19–52. Bari, 1972.

Post, Gaines. *Studies in Medieval Legal Thought*. Princeton, 1964.

Prestipino, Vicenzo. *Motivi del pensiero umanistico e Giovanni Pontano*. Milan, 1963.

Radetti, Giorgio. "La politica di Lorenzo Valla." *Giornale critico della filosofia italiana*, 29 (1950), 326–34.

Rao, Ennio I. "Alfonso of Aragon and the Italian Humanists." *Esperienze letterarie*, 4 (1979), 43–57.

Ratti, A. "Quarantadue lettere originali di Pio II relative alla guerra per la successione nel Reame di Napoli (1460–63)." *Archivio storico lombardo*, 3d ser. 19 (1903), 263–93.

Regoliosi, Mariangela. "Lorenzo Valla, Antonio Panormita, Giacomo Curlo e le emendazioni a Livio." *Italia medioevale e umanistica*, 24 (1981), 287–316.

————. "Per la tradizione delle 'Invective in L. Vallam' di Bartolomeo Facio." *Italia medioevale e umanistica*, 23 (1980), 389–97.

Resta, Gianvito. *L'epistolario del Panormita*. Messina, 1954.

Ribuoli, Riccardo. "Polemiche umanistiche: a proposito di due recenti edizioni." *Respublica litterarum*, 4 (1981), 339–54.

Ricca Salerno, Giuseppe. *Storia delle dottrine finanziarie in Italia*. 2d ed. Palermo, 1896.

Ricciardi, Roberto. "Angelo Poliziano, Giuniano Maio, Antonio Calcillo." *Rinascimento*, n.s. 8 (1968), 277–309.

Richardson, Brian. "Pontano's *De prudentia* and Machiavelli's *Discorsi*." *Bibliothèque d'humanisme et Renaissance*, 33 (1971), 353–57.

Ridola, P. A. *Memoria genealogico-istorica della famiglia Gattini da Matera*. Naples, 1877.

Romano, G. "L'origine della denominazione 'Due Sicilie' e un'orazione inedita di L. Valla." *ASPN*, 22 (1897), 371–403.

Romano, Michele. *La trattatistica politica nel secolo XV ed il "De principe" di G. Pontano*. Potenza, 1901.

BIBLIOGRAPHY

Romano, Ruggiero. *Tra due crisi: l'Italia del Rinascimento*. Turin, 1971.

Rossi, Felice. *Elisio Calenzio*. Lauria, 1924.

Ruiz Calonja, Juan. "Valor literario de los preámbulos de la cancillería real catalano-aragonesa en el siglo XV." *Boletin de la real academia de buenas letras de Barcelona*, 25 (1954–56), 205–34.

Ryder, Alan. "Antonio Beccadelli: A Humanist in Government." In C. H. Clough, ed., *Cultural Aspects of the Italian Renaissance: Essays in Honour of Paul Oskar Kristeller*, pp. 123–40. Manchester, 1976.

———. "Cloth and Credit: Aragonese War Finance in the Mid Fifteenth Century." *War and Society*, 2 (1984), 1–21.

———. "The Eastern Policy of Alfonso the Magnanimous." *AAP*, n.s. 28 (1979), 7–25.

———. "The Evolution of Imperial Government in Naples under Alfonso V of Aragon." In J. R. Hale, J.R.L. Highfield, and B. Smalley, eds., *Europe in the Late Middle Ages*, pp. 332–57. London, 1965.

———. *The Kingdom of Naples Under Alfonso the Magnanimous*. Oxford, 1976.

———. "La politica italiana di Alfonso d'Aragona (1442–1458)." *ASPN*, n.s. 38 (1958), 43–106; n.s. 39 (1959), 235–94.

Sabatini, Francesco. *Napoli angioina: cultura e società*. Naples, 1975.

Sabbadini, Remigio. "Bartolomeo Facio, scolaro a Verona, maestro a Venezia." In *Scritti storici in memoria di Giovanni Monticolo*, pp. 27–36. Venice, 1922.

———. "Come il Panormita diventò poeta aulico." *Archivio storico lombardo*, 43 (1916), 5–28.

———. "L'orazione del Panormita al Re Alfonso." *Giornale storico della letteratura italiana*, 31 (1898), 246–50.

———. "La polemica fra Porcellio e il Panormita." *Rendiconti del reale istituto lombardo di scienze e lettere*, 50 (1917), 495–501.

———. *Storia documentata dell'Università di Catania*. Catania, 1898.

Santoro, Mario. "La cultura umanistica." In *Storia di Napoli*, 7.115–291. 10 vols. Naples, 1975–81.

———. "Il *De immanitate*: testamento spirituale del Pontano." *La Partenope: rivista di cultura napoletana*, 1 (1960), 5–16.

———. *Fortuna, ragione e prudenza nella civiltà letteraria del Cinquecento*. 2d ed. Naples, 1978.

———. "Il Panormita 'aragonese.'" *Esperienze letterarie*, 9 (1984), 3–24.

———. "Il Pontano e l'ideale rinascimentale del 'prudente.'" *Giornale italiano di filologia*, 17 (1964), 29–54.

———. "I primi decenni della stampa a Napoli e la cultura napoletana." In *Primo convegno dei bibliotecari dell'Italia meridionale*, pp. 13–28. Naples, 1956.

———. "Scienza e humanitas nell'opera del Galateo." *La zagaglia*, 2 (1960), no. 5, pp. 25–40; no. 6, pp. 50–63.

———. *Uno scolaro del Poliziano a Napoli: Francesco Pucci*. Naples, 1948.

———. *Tristano Caracciolo e la cultura napoletana della Rinascenza*. Naples, 1957.

Satullo, F. *La giovanezza di Antonio Beccadelli Bologna detto il Panormita*. Palermo, 1906.

Savino, Ezio. *Un curioso poligrafo del '400: Antonio de Ferrariis (Galateo)*. Bari, 1941.

Scalinci, Noe. "Asterischi galateani." *Iapigia*, 3d ser. 17 (1946), 16–50.

———. "L'opusculo *De podagra et de morbo gallico* di Antonio Galateo." *Bollettino dell'istituto storico italiano dell'arte sanitaria*, 7 (1927), 151–57.

Schwartz, Benjamin I. *The World of Thought in Ancient China*. Cambridge, Mass., 1985.

Schwoebel, Robert. *The Shadow of the Crescent: The Renaissance Image of the Turk (1453–1517)*. Nieuwkoop, 1967.

Seigel, Jerrold E. " 'Civic Humanism' or Ciceronian Rhetoric?" *Past and Present*, 34 (1966), 3–48.

Setton, Kenneth M. *The Papacy and the Levant (1204–1571)*. 4 vols. Philadelphia, 1976–84.

Setz, Wolfram. *Lorenzo Vallas Schrift gegen die konstantinische Schenkung*. Tübingen, 1975.

Shneidman, J. Lee. *The Rise of the Aragonese-Catalan Empire, 1200–1350*. 2 vols. New York, 1970.

Simeoni, Luigi. *Le signorie*. 2 vols. Milan, 1950.

Skinner, Quentin. *The Foundations of Modern Political Thought*. 2 vols. Cambridge, 1978.

———. *Machiavelli*. New York, 1981.

Soria, Andres. *Los humanistas de la corte de Alfonso el Magnanimo*. Granada, 1956.

Soria, Francescantonio. *Memorie storico-critiche degli storici napoletani*. 2 vols. Naples, 1781–82.

Sottili, Agostino. "Note biografiche sui petrarchisti Giacomo Publicio e Guiniforte Barzizza e sull'umanista valenziano Giovanni Serra." In Fritz Schalk, ed., *Petrarca, 1304–1374. Beiträge zu Werk und Wirkung*, pp. 270–86. Frankfurt, 1975.

Speyer, Wolfgang. "Die vollständige 'Vita Ioannis Ioviani Pontani auctore Fabio Pontano' im Codex Spoletinus 163." *Rinascimento*, n.s. 6 (1966), 233–57.

Stadter, Philip A. "Arrianus, Flavius." In Paul O. Kristeller and F. Edward Cranz, eds., *Catalogus translationum et commentariorum*, 3.1–20. Washington, D.C., 1976.

Starrabba, R. "Notizie concernenti Antonio Panormita." *Archivio storico siciliano*, n.s. 27 (1902), 119–33.

Storia di Napoli. 10 vols. Naples, 1975–81.

Struever, Nancy S. "Vico, Valla, and the Logic of Humanist Inquiry." In Giorgio Tagliacozzo and Donald P. Verene, eds., *Giambattista Vico's Science of Humanity*, pp. 173–85. Baltimore, 1976.

Studi su Antonio de Ferrariis Galateo. Galatone, 1970.

Tallarigo, Carlo Maria. *Giovanni Pontano e i suoi tempi*. 2 vols. Naples, 1874.

Tanteri, Vito. *Giovanni Pontano e i suoi dialoghi*. Ferrara, 1931.

Tateo, Francesco. *Astrologia e moralità in Giovanni Pontano*. Bari, 1960.

———. *Chierici e feudatari del Mezzogiorno*. Bari, 1984.

———. "La crisi dell'umanesimo nella coscienza degli scrittori del Regno aragonese." In *Atti del congresso internazionale di studi sull'età aragonese*, pp. 264–74. Bari, 1972.

Tateo, Francesco. "Per l'edizione critica dell'*Actius* di G. Pontano." *Studi mediolatini e volgari*, 12 (1964), 145–94.

———. "Riflessi della rinascita letteraria in Puglia." *Archivio storico pugliese*, 22 (1969), 111–23.

———. "Società e cultura umanistica nel Mezzogiorno." *Quaderni medievali*, 3 (1977), 74–85.

———. *Tradizione e realtà nell'umanesimo italiano*. Bari, 1967.

———. *L'umanesimo etico di Giovanni Pontano*. Lecce, 1972.

———. *L'umanesimo meridionale*. Bari, 1976.

———. "Le virtù sociali e l' 'immanità' nella trattatistica pontaniana." *Rinascimento*, n.s. 5 (1965), 119–54.

Toffanin, Giuseppe. *Giovanni Pontano fra l'uomo e la natura*. 2d ed. Bologna, 1938.

Trinkaus, Charles. "The Astrological Cosmos and Rhetorical Culture of Giovanni Gioviano Pontano." *Renaissance Quarterly*, 38 (1985), 446–72.

———. "Humanism, Religion, Society: Concepts and Motivations of Some Recent Studies." *Renaissance Quarterly*, 29 (1976), 676–713.

———. *In Our Image and Likeness: Humanity and Divinity in Italian Humanist Thought*. 2 vols. Chicago, 1970.

———. *The Scope of Renaissance Humanism*. Ann Arbor, 1983.

Vacca, Nicola. *Noterelle galateane*. Lecce, 1943.

Valeri, Nino. *L'Italia nell'età dei principati*. Verona, 1949.

Vinay, Gustavo. "Per una nuova interpretazione dell'*Asinus* pontaniano." *Giornale storico della letteratura italiana*, 105 (1935), 316–23.

Vitale, Giuliana. "L'umanista Tristano Caracciolo ed i principi di Melfi." *ASPN*, 3d ser. 2 (1962), 343–81.

Volpicella, Luigi. *Federico d'Aragona e la fine del regno di Napoli nel MDI*. Naples, 1908.

Weiss, Roberto. "The Greek Culture of South Italy in the Later Middle Ages." *Proceedings of the British Academy*, 37 (1951), 23–50.

———. "Jan van Eyck and the Italians." *Italian Studies*, 11 (1956), 1–15; 12 (1957), 7–21.

———. "The Translators from the Greek of the Angevin Court of Naples." *Rinascimento*, 1 (1950), 195–226.

Welti, Manfred E. "Il progetto fallito di un'edizione cinquecentesca delle opere complete di Antonio de Ferrariis, detto il Galateo." *ASPN*, 3d ser. 10 (1971), 179–91.

Witt, Ronald G. *Coluccio Salutati and His Public Letters*. Geneva, 1976.

Wittschier, Heinz Willi. *Giannozzo Manetti. Das Corpus der Orationes*. Cologne, 1968.

Woodley, Ronald. "Iohannes Tinctoris: A Review of the Documentary Biographical Evidence." *Journal of the American Musicological Society*, 34 (1981), 217–48.

BIBLIOGRAPHY

Zacchino, Vittorio E. "Il 'De educatione' di Antonio Galateo e i suoi sentimenti anti-spagnoli." In *Atti del congresso internazionale di studi sull'età aragonese*, pp. 620–33. Bari, 1972.

Zimolo, Giulio C. "Le relazioni tra Milano e Napoli e la politica italiana in due lettere del 1478." *Archivio storico lombardo*, 64 (1937), 403–34.

Zippel, G. "L'autodifesa di Lorenzo Valla per il processo dell'Inquisizione napoletana (1444)." *Italia medioevale e umanistica*, 13 (1970), 59–94.

―――. "La 'Defensio quaestionum in philosophia' di Lorenzo Valla, e un noto processo dell'Inquisizione napoletana." *Bollettino dell'istituto storico italiano per il Medio Evo e archivio muratoriano*, 69 (1957), 319–47.

―――. "Lorenzo Valla e le origini della storiografia umanistica a Venezia." *Rinascimento*, 7 (1956), 93–133.

Index

academy of Lecce, 269, 283
academy of Naples, 93–95, 133,
  136, 261, 269, 276, 283, 285–87
academy of Nardò, 261, 283
Acquaviva, Andrea Matteo, 254,
  260–65, 267–68, 276, 283, 287,
  293, 296
Acquaviva, Belisario, 254, 260–68,
  271, 276, 283, 287, 293, 296
Acquaviva, Giulio Antonio, 260, 263
Adamo di Montaldo, 57, 219
Adorno, Raffaele, doge of Genoa, 101
Aelian, 55, 93, 149
Agricola, Alexander, 75–76
Ahmed Pasha, 29
Albino, Giovanni, 68, 71, 81, 169,
  171–72, 177, 181–82, 238–39,
  240, 253, 254, 291, 293, 296,
  298
Alexander VI, pope, 33, 35–37,
  187–92, 246
Alfonso, duke of Bisceglie, 73
Alfonso I, king of Naples (Alfonso V
  of Aragon), 7, 9–24, 41, 47, 51–
  63, 67, 72, 73, 79, 80, 81, 86–
  97, 101–28, 141, 149–57, 162–
  68, 204, 209–12, 217, 219, 220,
  224–32, 234, 242–44, 253, 277–
  78, 280–81, 283, 284, 288–93,
  295, 296, 298
Alfonso II, duke of Calabria and king
  of Naples, 28–32, 35–36, 66, 68,
  80–83, 99, 129, 130, 169, 170,
  172, 179, 182, 186–88, 191–92,
  199, 206, 242, 247, 249, 255,
  260, 274, 277–78, 281, 292
Altamura, Antonio, 44

Altilio, Gabriele, 81, 192, 253, 291,
  293
Antonio da Bitonto, 116–17
Aquinas, Thomas, 198, 258
Aristeas, 71
Aristotle, 55, 126, 200, 247, 251,
  258
Arnold of Brussels, 78
Arrian, 56, 106–107
Aurelio, Marco, 106
Aurispa, Giovanni, 108
Avalos, Iñigo de, 54, 62–63

Bagnolo, peace of, 30, 129
Baldus, 175
Bandini, Francesco, 79, 89, 198
Barbaro, Ermolao, the Younger, 269
Barbaro, Francesco, 40, 104, 105,
  149, 231, 243, 298
Barga, Antonio da, 102
Baron, Hans, 42–43, 196–97
barons' revolt (1485–1486), 30–33,
  66, 78–79, 130, 142, 169, 172–
  81, 238, 242, 246, 260, 293, 298
Bartolus of Sassoferrato, 109, 175
Basel, Council of, 16, 113, 115
Bayezid I, Turkish sultan, 164
Beatrice of Aragon (daughter of Fer-
  rante I), 75
Beccadelli, Antonino, 88
Beccadelli, Antonio (Panormita), 51,
  52, 54, 57, 58, 60, 61, 63, 64,
  67, 68, 81, 101–102, 108, 109,
  112, 116, 118–20, 128, 131,
  133, 140, 188, 217, 218, 231,
  238, 242–48, 253, 265, 283,
  286, 290–94, 296–99; career of,

Beccadelli, Antonio (*cont.*)
84–100, 135–37, 147–61, 160–68
works of: De dictis et factis Alphonsi, 91, 204, 224–27; *Liber rerum gestarum Ferdinandi regis*, 99–100, 227–28
Belisarius, 13, 55, 211
Bessarion, cardinal, 55
Biondo, Flavio, 47, 54, 104, 164–65, 222, 291
Boccaccio, 40, 201
Bonincontri, Lorenzo, 79
Borgia, Cesare, 35, 38
Borgia, Jofrè, 35, 190
Borgia, Juan, 35
Botero, Giovanni, 299
Bracciolini, Poggio, 41, 59, 60, 104, 105, 108, 109, 118, 152, 162, 227, 276–77, 294, 298
Brancati, Giovanni, 65, 66–67, 69–71, 169–71, 181–82, 199, 201, 213, 214–15, 216, 253, 254, 291, 292, 293, 298
Brandolini, Aurelio, 73, 216–17, 253
Brandolini, Raffaele, 73, 74, 75, 76, 253
Bruni, Leonardo, 6, 40, 42, 55–56, 108, 152, 201, 291, 298
Budé, Guillaume, 295
Burke, Peter, 63

Caesar, Julius, 52, 222, 223, 229
Caiazzo, siege of, 52, 87
Calcillo, Antonio, 99, 294
Calenzio, Elisio (Luigi Galluccio), 81, 205, 217, 218, 220, 253, 291
Calixtus III, pope, 18–19, 23–24, 96, 123, 124, 149, 152–58, 162–68, 209, 219
Campofregoso, Pietro, doge of Genoa, 156
Capece, Scipione, 286
Caracciolo, Giovanni, 279

Caracciolo, Sergianni, 277
Caracciolo, Tristano, 254, 276–83, 287, 293, 296, 297
Carafa, Diomede, 71, 140–47, 182
Carafa, Oliviero, cardinal, 152
Carlos, prince of Viana, 24, 96, 158, 245
Caspe, compromise of, 11, 234
Castiglione, Baldassare, 146
Catholic kings of Spain. *See* Ferdinand the Catholic, king of Spain
Catone, Angelo, 198
Charles VII, king of France, 23
Charles VIII, king of France, 34, 35–37, 76, 82, 130, 184, 189, 191–93, 246, 250, 260, 284
Cinico, Joan Marco, 218, 220
Ciriaco d'Ancona, 109
Colonna, Crisostomo, 272–73
Commynes, Philippe de, 22
Constantinople, fall of, 18, 160, 162, 164, 166
Contrario, Andrea, 163
Coppola, Francesco, 31–33, 78, 142, 173, 281
Cornago, Juan, 72
Corvinus, Mathias, king of Hungary, 32, 33
Costantino de Tanti, 53
Croce, Benedetto, 10n, 51
crusade against the Turks, 18, 153–54, 161–68
Curlo, Giacomo, 56, 64–65, 93, 107, 119, 217, 294
Cyrus, king of Persia, 227

Dante, 201, 255
Decembrio, Pier Candido, 54, 118, 291
de Ferrariis, Antonio (Galateo), 254, 268–75, 276, 283, 293, 296, 297
de Frizis, Antonio, 261, 285
de Jennaro, Pietro Jacopo, 254, 255–59, 283, 293

de Lignamine, Giovanni Filippo,
232–33
della Casa, Giovanni, 146
del Tuppo, Francesco, 58–59, 78–79,
178, 217
de Marinis, Tammaro, 60, 65, 82,
220, 301
de Mattei, Rodolfo, 139
de Rosa, Loise, 3–6, 198
des Prez, Josquin, 76
Despuig, Luis, 88–89, 128, 151
Dionysius the Areopagite, 237
Donation of Constantine, 113–20,
122, 236–38, 295

Eleonora (daughter of Ferrante I), 66,
142, 213
Eleonora d'Aragona, 25
Enrico of Aragon (brother of Alfonso
I), 280
Erasmus of Rotterdam, 111, 121,
295
Este, Borso d', duke of Ferrara, 73,
96
Este, Ercole d', duke of Ferrara, 30,
142, 213
Eugenius IV, pope, 15–16, 18, 23,
62, 92, 109, 113, 114, 115, 120,
226, 229, 295

Facio, Bartolomeo, 56, 57, 59, 60,
61, 64, 67, 69, 112, 118–20,
125, 136, 162, 201, 212, 227,
234–35, 238, 242, 253, 290–92,
294–97; career of, 100–108
  works of: De rebus gestis ab Alphonso primo, 104–105, 228–32; De
  viris illustribus, 106
Federico, king of Naples, 31, 35, 37–
39, 78, 80–83, 186, 192, 205,
217, 218, 220, 255, 260, 269,
271, 272, 281
Felix V, antipope, 16
Ferdinand of Antequera, king of Aragon, 11, 113, 119, 122, 230,

233–36, 272, 291
Ferdinand the Catholic, king of
Spain, 37, 38, 175, 176, 180,
192, 256, 260, 261, 275, 278
Fernando de Córdoba, 116
Ferrandino, king of Naples, 36–37,
80–83, 130, 188, 192–93, 205,
246, 250, 255, 260, 281
Ferrante (son of Federico), duke of
Calabria, 39, 82, 272–73, 284
Ferrante I, king of Naples, 14, 17,
19, 21–35, 62–80, 81, 96–100,
102, 110, 124, 126, 128–37,
141, 144, 150, 152, 157–61,
166, 167, 169–91, 198, 199,
201, 204, 207, 210–15, 218–21,
227–28, 232–33, 238–47, 250,
253, 255, 260, 278, 281, 284,
292, 293, 296, 298
Ferrante II. See Ferrandino
Ferrara, War of, 30, 129, 169, 172,
182, 249
Ficino, Marsilio, 79–80
Fieschi, Giorgio, 102
Filelfo, Francesco, 54, 62–63, 291
Firmano, Domenico, cardinal, 162
fortune, 134, 210, 224, 231–32,
238, 241–52, 254, 264–65, 272,
274, 280–83, 296–97, 299
Foscari, Francesco, doge of Venice,
101
Francesco d'Aragona (son of Ferrante
I), 281
Frederick III, emperor, 89, 124, 211,
219
Fregoso, Tommaso, doge of Genoa,
101

Gaeta, siege of 12, 86, 150, 209,
229, 232. See also Ponza, battle of
Gaffurio, Franchino, 74
Galateo. See de Ferrariis, Antonio
Galluccio, Luigi. See Calenzio, Elisio
García, Juan, bishop of Lérida, 116
García, Juan, Dominican, 114

Gattini, Ciccolino, 232
Gaza, Theodore, 55, 61, 67, 93, 97,
    107, 149, 217, 291
Gennaro, San, 5
George of Trebizond, 54, 60, 61, 67,
    161–62, 291
Giannone, Pietro, 286
Gilbert, Allan H., 139
Gilbert, Felix, 139, 191
Giovanna II, queen of Naples, 9, 11,
    15, 62, 86, 113, 229, 232, 242,
    277
Giovanni d'Aragona, cardinal (son of
    Ferrante I), 80, 281
Giustiniani, Bernardo, 298
Gonsalvo de Córdoba, 38–39, 82,
    134, 255, 261
Gonzaga, Luigi, marquis of Mantua,
    226
Gothein, Eberhard, 43
Granada, Treaty of, 38
Guarino, Geronimo, 53
Guarino, Manuele, 103
Guarino da Verona, 40, 53, 101, 290
Guicciardini, Francesco, 130, 241,
    259

Han Feizi, 138
Hiero, 149
humanism, 40–46; civic humanism,
    42–43, 135–37, 196–202, 267–
    68; Christian humanism, 197,
    267–68; curial humanism, 197,
    267–68; feudal humanism, 261–
    68
Humphrey, duke of Gloucester, 62
Hunyadi, John, 165

Innocent III, pope, 15
Innocent IV, pope, 15
Innocent VIII, pope, 30–33, 130,
    172–87, 242, 299
Inquisition, 117; Spanish Inquisition,
    279, 285
Irnerius, 175

Isaac, Heinrich, 76
Isabella of Castille, queen of Spain,
    175, 180. See also Ferdinand the
    Catholic, king of Spain
Isabella di Chiaromonte, 23, 124
Ischia, battle of, 25
Isocrates, 69, 91–92, 102, 107

Jaime I, the Conqueror, king of Ara-
    gon, 8
Jean d'Anjou, 24–25, 31, 97, 98,
    100, 158, 159, 225, 240
Juan II, king of Aragon, 23, 24, 25,
    96, 158
Juana of Aragon, 213
Julius II, pope, 33, 177

Kautilya, 138
Kristeller, Paul O., 41–43

Landino, Cristoforo, 69–71
Lapo da Castiglionchio the Younger,
    91–92
Lascaris, Constantine, 67, 198
League of Italy, 18, 154, 156, 229
Legalists, 138
Leo X, pope, 73
Lerner, Max, 138
library of the Aragonese kings of Na-
    ples, 56–59, 64, 65–66, 78, 82,
    169, 284
Livy, 10, 52, 62, 71, 72, 89, 119–
    20, 131, 222, 223, 239, 294, 295
Lodi, Peace of, 7, 18, 129, 154, 156
Loise di Casalnuovo, 181
Loschi, Antonio, 108, 109, 297
Louis XI, king of France, 34, 170
Louis XII, king of France, 38, 134,
    260
Louis d'Anjou, 11
Ludovico d'Aragona, cardinal, 68

Macedonio, Lancellotto, 82
Machiavelli, Niccolò, 138, 143, 182,
    194, 204, 252, 259, 297, 299

Maio, Giuniano, 67–68, 77, 99,
199, 207–208, 219, 243, 253,
264, 283, 291, 293, 294
Malatesta, Sigismondo, 160
Malipiero, Pasquale, doge of Venice,
89, 96, 158
Manetti, Giannozzo, 10, 53, 60, 61,
67, 102, 136, 209–12, 217, 219,
253, 290, 292, 296; career of,
122–27
Martin the Elder, king of Aragon,
230, 236
Martorell, Francesc, 94
Marzano, Marino, prince of Rossano,
25, 26, 99, 159, 208
Mauritius, 149
Maximilian I, emperor, 37
Medici, Cosimo de', 17, 119, 123,
225
Medici, Giovanni de'. See Leo X, pope
Medici, Giuliano de', 28
Medici, Lorenzo de', 22, 28, 34, 73,
79, 187, 188
Medici, Piero de', 34, 189–90
Mehmed II, Turkish sultan, 163,
164, 221
merum mixtumque imperium, 9, 14
Milanese Succession, War of, 17, 23,
56, 123, 229, 242
Miralles, Melchiore, 58
Murad II, Turkish sultan, 164

napoletano misto, 71, 142, 201
New Testament, 111–12, 121, 126,
237–38, 294–95
Nicene Creed, 116–17
Nicholas II, pope, 15
Nicholas V, pope, 10, 17, 18, 23,
51, 102–103, 121, 123, 125,
160, 162, 163, 229
Nicholas of Lyra, 10

Olzina, Juan, 31, 128
Onosander, 149
Orca, Giovanni, 74

Orsini, Giovanni Antonio del Balzo,
prince of Taranto, 23, 24, 25,
150, 159, 240, 245
Orsini, Virginio, 177, 186, 188, 189
Otranto, Turkish occupation of, 29,
65, 168, 169, 172, 238, 242,
260, 269

Pandolfini, Battista, 66
Pandoni, Porcellio, 54, 60, 67, 92,
291
Panormita. See Beccadelli, Antonio
Paul II, pope, 28, 166, 232
Pazzi conspiracy, 28, 66, 169, 171,
238
peace of 1486, 32, 130, 172–81
peace of 1492, 183, 185–87
Pedro of Aragon (brother of Alfonso
I), 231
Pedro de Toledo, 286
Pellegrino, Gaspare, 53
Pendinelli, Stefano, archbishop of
Otranto, 29
Perotti, Niccolò, 163
Petrarch, 40, 119, 201, 237, 255,
288, 294, 296
Petrucci, Antonello, 31–33, 78, 97,
98, 130, 142, 173, 176, 220,
225, 281–82
Petrucci, Francesco, 173
Petrucci, Giovanni Antonio, 173
Philip II, king of Spain, 82
Piccinino, Jacopo, 18–19, 26, 153,
154–55, 156, 167
Piccolomini, Enea Silvio. See Pius II,
pope
Pius II, pope, 24, 25, 27, 55, 73,
96, 97, 107, 158–60, 166, 245
Plato, 258, 271
Pliny the Elder, 69–71, 169, 201
Plutarch, 71, 91–92, 261, 262, 267
Poliziano, Angelo, 68, 99, 294, 295
Pontano, Giovanni, 21–22, 58, 67,
68, 77, 79, 88–89, 94, 100, 140,
168, 169, 171, 199, 200, 202,

INDEX

Pontano, Giovanni (*cont.*)
205, 218, 227, 242–43, 246–52,
253, 254, 261, 262–63, 264,
265, 269, 275, 276, 283, 286,
290, 291, 292, 293, 297, 298–99;
career of, 127–37, 176–94
works of: De bello neapolitano,
239–41; *De fortitudine,* 249; *De fortuna,* 247–48; *De immanitate,* 220–
22; *De obedientia,* 249; *De principe,*
206–208; *De prudentia,* 251–52
Pontieri, Ernesto, 13n, 21n
Ponza, battle of, 12, 86, 110, 232,
243. *See also* Gaeta, siege of
pseudo-Dionysius, 237
Pucci, Francesco, 68, 77, 79, 253,
283

René, duke of Lorraine, 31, 173,
174, 177, 189–90
René d'Anjou, 11, 12, 16, 24, 31,
62, 113, 124
rhetoric, 203, 208–15, 216; epideictic rhetoric, 203, 210–15, 219
Riessinger, Sisto, 58, 77, 78
Robert the Wise, king of Naples, 40
Robert Guiscard, duke of Apulia and
Calabria, 15
Roger II, king of Naples and Sicily,
15
Romano, Egidio, 258
Romano, Orazio, 163
Roverella, Bartolomeo, 97–98, 99
Ryder, Alan, 14n, 20n, 165–66

Sagundino, Niccolò, 107, 163–64
Sallust, 238, 239
Salutati, Coluccio, 40, 152, 294,
296, 298
Sannazaro, Jacopo, 261, 286
Sanseverino, Roberto, 30, 31, 172,
173, 177, 249
Santoro, Mario, 44, 253, 270
Sanz, Luis, 256

Sarno, battle of, 25, 96, 131, 158,
159, 245
Scarampo. *See* Trevisan, Lodovico,
cardinal
Scrivani, Melchiorre, 108
Seigel, Jerrold, 196
Serra, Juan, 116
Setz, Wolfram, 113
Sforza, Francesco, duke of Milan, 16–
17, 18, 24, 25, 34, 88–89, 96,
101, 141, 158, 166, 169, 226,
229
Sforza, Galeazzo II, duke of Milan, 34
Sforza, Galeazzo Maria, duke of
Milan, 34, 129, 170
Sforza, Ippolita, 129, 182
Sforza, Ludovico il Moro, duke of
Milan, 34, 187, 189–92, 221, 246
Sigismund, emperor, 85, 107
Simonetta, Cicco, 170, 297
Sixtus IV, pope, 28–30, 169, 170,
232–33, 242
Skinner, Quentin, 139–40, 196–97
speculum principis, 202–208, 215,
219, 225–27, 264
Spinelli, Giovanni Battista, 277
Spinola, Francesco, 101
Spinola, Giangiacomo, 103
Spinola, Teodoro, 106
Studio of Naples, 57, 64, 67–68, 77,
199, 283, 285
Suetonius, 223, 227
Summonte, Pietro, 286

Tarentino, Pietro, 214–15
Tateo, Francesco, 44
Terracina, Treaty of, 16, 115, 120,
229
Thucydides, 138
Tinctoris, Iohannes, 75
Tomas de Aulesa, 119
Torres, Juan, 58
Trevisan, Lodovico, cardinal, 167–68
Troia, battle of, 25, 99, 245

University of Naples. *See* Studio of
  Naples

Valla, Lorenzo, 57, 61, 67, 100,
  103, 104, 136, 200, 215, 224,
  227, 230, 253, 286, 291, 294; career of, 108–122
    works of: Collatio Novi Testamenti,
  237–38, 294–95; *Declamation on
  the Donation of Constantine*, 113–14,
  236–38, 295; *Gesta Ferdinandi regis*, 230, 233–36
Vergerio, Pier Paolo, 107
Vespasiano da Bisticci, 10, 51, 52,

53, 60, 79, 105, 122, 125
Vettori, Francesco, 252
Vicentino, Pietro, bishop of Cesena,
  174, 180–81
Vico, Giambattista, 286
Viriatus, 52
Visconti, Bianca Maria, 17, 23
Visconti, Filippo Maria, duke of
  Milan, 12, 14, 16–17, 85, 86,
  151, 210, 226, 231, 232, 243
Vittorino da Feltre, 40

Xenophon, 59, 104, 110, 223, 224,
  227

Library of Congress Cataloging-in-Publication Data

Bentley, Jerry H., 1949–
Politics and culture in Renaissance Naples.

Bibliography: p.
Includes index.
1. Naples (Kingdom)—Civilization. 2. Renaissance—Italy—Naples
(Kingdom) 3. Humanism—Italy—Naples (Kingdom)—History. I. Title.

DG847.17.B46 1987   945'.7   87-945511
ISBN 0-691-05498-3

RANDALL LIBRARY-UNCW

3 0490 0361523 -